TRANSLATING THE MESSAGE

The American Society of Missiology Series, in collaboration with Orbis Books, seeks to publish scholarly works of high merit and wide interest on numerous aspects of missiology — the study of mission. Able presentations on new and creative approaches to the practice and understanding of mission will receive close attention.

Previously published in
The American Society of Missiology Series

American Society of Missiology Series, No. 13

TRANSLATING THE MESSAGE

The Missionary Impact on Culture

Lamin Sanneh

ORBIS BOOKS

Maryknoll, New York 10545

Fourth Printing, October 1992

The Catholic Foreign Mission Society of America (Maryknoll) recruits and trains people for overseas missionary service. Through Orbis Books, Maryknoll aims to foster the international dialogue that is essential to mission. The books published, however, reflect the opinions of their authors and are not meant to represent the official position of the society.

Manuscript editor: Lisa McGaw

ISBN 0-88344-361-9

To
Tom Beetham
and to
the memory of Eth

"Love is most nearly itself
when here and now cease to matter."
T. S. Eliot

The issue that frequently escapes the dragnet of the historian is the cumulative capital Christianity has derived from the common language of ordinary people. To the secular historian this fact has only political significance as a force for incitement; to the economic and social historian it is a fact that creates social mobility, and perhaps social tension. Yet to a Christian the confident adoption of vernacular speech as consecrated vessel places it squarely at the heart of religious change, and thus at the heart of historical consciousness. The central and enduring character of Christian history is the rendering of God's eternal counsels into terms of everyday speech. By that path believers have come to stand before their God.

Contents

List of Maps

Preface to the Series

The purpose of the ASM Series—now in existence since 1980—is to publish, without regard for disciplinary, national, or denominational boundaries, scholarly works of high quality and wide interest on missiological themes from the entire spectrum of scholarly pursuits, e.g., biblical studies, theology, history, history of religions, cultural anthropology, linguistics, art, education, political science, economics, and development, to name only the major components. Always the focus will be on Christian mission.

By "mission" in this context is meant a passage over the boundary between faith in Jesus Christ and its absence. In this understanding of mission, the basic functions of Christian proclamation, dialogue, witness, service, worship, and nurture are of special concern. How does the transition from one cultural context to another influence the shape and interaction between these dynamic functions? Cultural and religious plurality are recognized as fundamental characteristics of the six-continent missionary context in east and west, north and south.

Missiologists know that they need the other disciplines. And those in other disciplines need missiology, perhaps more than they sometimes realize. Neither the insider's nor the outsider's view is complete in itself. The world Christian mission has through two millenia amassed a rich and well-documented body of experience to share with other disciplines. The complementary relation between missiology and other learned disciplines is a key feature of this Series, and interaction will be its hallmark.

The promotion of scholarly dialogue among missiologists may, at times, involve the publication of views and positions that other missiologists cannot accept, and with which members of the Editorial Committee do not agree. Manuscripts published in this series reflect the opinions of their authors and are not meant to represent the position of the American Society of Missiology or of the Editorial Committee for the ASM Series. The Committee's selection of texts is guided by such criteria as intrinsic worth, readability, relative brevity, freedom from excessive scholarly apparatus, and accessibility to a broad range of interested persons and not merely to experts or specialists.

On behalf of the membership of the American Society of Missiology we express our deep thanks to the staff of Orbis Books, whose steadfast support over a decade for this joint publishing venture has enabled it to mature and bear scholarly fruit.

James A. Scherer, Chair
Sister Mary Motte, FMM
Charles R. Taber
ASM Series Editorial Committee

Acknowledgments

A short paper I read at a seminar at the Boston University School of Theology in 1982 on the nature of Christian mission began the path that led eventually to this book. I am grateful to the students at that seminar, and to Norman Thomas for the invitation. I spoke extensively with Masao Takanaka of Doshisha University, Kyoto, during his visit to Harvard, and profited much from our informal discussions. I am particularly indebted to Lloyd Patterson of the Episcopal Divinity School, Cambridge, for his expert advice which proved invaluable and which determined much of the shape of the book.

Several of my colleagues at Harvard have kept in step with various stages of the book. They thus helped to guide the book's development in many important ways. In this connection I wish to acknowledge the help of John Carman, whose numerous suggestions, comments, and questions imparted greater clarity to the material than would otherwise have been the case. Similarly Dieter Georgi, now of the University of Frankfurt, and Helmut Koester have both given useful advice on earlier drafts of the book. Ron Thiemann has also made many useful comments on the idea of the book, and I am grateful to him, as I am to his predecessor in the Office of the Dean, George Rupp, for his personal interest in the book. Portions of the draft manuscript were presented at the monthly faculty seminar at Harvard Divinity School, and I am grateful to colleagues there for their observations, criticism, and interest.

I am also grateful to friends in other institutions. George Peck, Max Stackhouse, and the late Orlando Costas, all of Andover Newton Theological School, Newton Center, have given much encouragement to the project by their keen interest and equally keen observations. In that connection mention should be made of Steve Peterson of Yale University Divinity School library and Gerald Anderson of the Overseas Ministries Study Center in New Haven, whose steady, unflagging interest spurred the book. To Lewis Rambo and Walter Davis at the San Francisco Theological Seminary I owe a debt of gratitude for the opportunity to present the material of the book in a summer school course at that institution. I am also immensely indebted to Patrick Ryan for his detailed comments and suggestions on a previous draft of the book.

I acknowledge gratefully the help and encouragement of my family. Eight-year-old Sia Manta kept an occasional but close eye on the book as it developed, and her penciled comments on stylistic peculiarities, done with the light touch of humor, alerted me to inadequacies that I cannot claim to have sufficiently overcome. Kelefa, eleven, encouraged me to carry the ideas of the book on much straighter, cleaner lines than one would find in the customary zigzags of academic writing. Sandra has insisted on immediate comprehensibility which lasts with deeper reading. I cannot claim to have met these and other exacting standards, though my trepidation would have been greater without awareness of them.

I attempt in this book to chart a fresh course in the study of the history of Christian mission by focusing on translation in its cultural dimension. As such the book is a methodological contribution toward imparting greater coherence to the disparate sources of Christian missionary activity. Much of the trail followed in the book exists in intermittent patterns in numerous accounts and writings. By reassembling many of these it is relatively easy to see the outlines of the broad path that points in the direction of this book. My central concern has been to sharpen those outlines, and to postpone for the most part developing the specific ramifications of the field. Consequently the specialist will have to forgo attention to detail on some issues, while the general reader is in parts encouraged to see what specialized investigations may contribute to the subject as a whole.

One person whose great shadow falls over much of the ground covered in this book is Tom Beetham. Of those most knowledgeable about Christianity in the new Africa, few can rival him in the depth and sympathy of his grasp or the scope of his view. During many years of friendship he has impressed me with his utter humility and sagacity. He embodies the exhortation "in love to prefer one another" (Rom. 12:10). In that regard I wish to call to mind the memory of Mrs. Ethel Green, during whose lifetime the idea of the book was conceived, and whose patient but incisive spirit infused purpose into the long, arduous task of assembling data. She never lived to see the finished task, having herself meanwhile completed the higher journey. In dedicating this book both to her memory and to Tom Beetham I acknowledge their influence, and for once defer to them.

TRANSLATING THE MESSAGE

Introduction

THESIS

The central thesis of this book is that Christianity, from its origins, identified itself with the need to translate out of Aramaic and Hebrew, and from that position came to exert a dual force in its historical development. One was the resolve to relativize its Judaic roots, with the consequence that it promoted significant aspects of those roots. The other was to destigmatize Gentile culture and adopt that culture as a natural extension of the life of the new religion. This action to destigmatize complemented the other action to relativize. Thus it was that the two subjects, the Judaic and the Gentile, became closely intertwined in the Christian dispensation, both crucial to the formative image of the new religion.

Chapter 1 analyses some of the consequences of this translation process, and the spirit of radical pluralism of culture involved in it. I treat in this respect language and culture as essential aspects of Christian transmission, especially where these interact with the themes of cross-cultural appropriation and pluralism. It seems to be part of the earliest records we possess that the disciples came to a clear and firm position regarding the translatability of the gospel, with a commitment to the pluralist merit of culture within God's universal purpose. On the fundamental issue of culture as a pluralist, nondivine enterprise, the apostles were not prepared to yield; yet such an attitude left them open to continued dealings with the Judaic heritage. The special contribution of Saint Paul in this development is considered in some detail.

The Gentile breakthrough, introduced as a theological matter in chapter 1, is investigated in chapter 2 in its historical and cultural ramifications. As we shall see in chapter 2, Christianity, having arrived at its rendezvous with the world of Greek learning and culture through translatability, found that its success in the adoption of Hellenic culture, in particular its metaphysical outlook, tempted it with the prize of cultural deification and the putting in place of a self-reinforced absolute system. However, the very translatability that allowed this transformation to take place also challenged it in the most radical way. The ninth-century Slavic missions brought that out clearly. By that stage the vernacular character of Christianity had been established in numerous parts of the empire and beyond, with Armenians, Copts, Goths,

1

and Ethiopians all following a version of the faith expressive of their national character.

Upon this theological and historical foundation this book builds in the subsequent chapters by examining the consequences of scriptural translatability, with modern Africa as the main focus. I try to show the deeper connections between Bible translating and related issues such as cultural self-understanding, vernacular pride, social awakening, religious renewal, cross-cultural dialogue, transmission and recipiency, reciprocity in mission, and, in a provisional way, what light the comparative Islamic example might throw on the subject. This list suggests the exploratory rather than exhaustive nature of the task I set myself.

Chapter 3 picks up and develops the missionary and colonial theme, showing parallels and divergences in the approach and consequences of the two forces. I consider specific historical contexts and explore the contributions of both Catholic and Protestant missionary pioneers.

Chapter 4 examines the connection between the vernacular Scriptures and indigenous nationalism in one area in Africa. Two main stages are described in this process: (1) the local reaction to mission on the basis of vernacular primacy and (2) the impact of vernacular translation on ethnic consciousness, with charismatic renewal as a subsidiary issue. In this way scriptural translation produced consequences for external transmission as well as for the internal appropriation of the message.

Chapter 5 focuses on the religious and theological dimensions of vernacular translation and explores the issue of indigenous agency and missionary leadership in the context of reciprocity. One major conclusion of the chapter is the significant overlap between indigenous revitalization and the translation enterprise of mission. I then go on to consider, in chapter 6, some of the philosophical assumptions of translation as these relate to the nature of culture. Specific linguistic and cultural examples are given in an attempt to indicate what the wider repercussions of scriptural translation might be.

The theme of comparative religious perspectives on translation is the subject of chapter 7, where the Islamic parallel is investigated for the light it throws on the Christian position. I include certain Islamic materials that I consider representative on the question of scriptural translation, and since the bulk of these materials specifically discusses either Christian attitudes or the duty of Muslims in mission, their inclusion needs no further justification.

The thought persisting through all this material is that particular Christian translation projects have helped to create an overarching series of cultural experiences, with hitherto obscure cultural systems being thrust into the general stream of universal history. Christian particularity has hinged on the particularity of culture and language, both essential components in translation. The autonomous cultural systems thus fostered had their genesis in, or because of, the message for which translation was deemed essential. The consequences for our understanding of the history of the modern world are clear, and therefore the theological suppositions on which the enterprise was launched need emphasizing, as I have tried to do in the opening chapter.

My decision to take translation beyond the narrow, technical bounds of textual work needs some explanation. It struck me as fairly obvious that missionary interest, say, in the vernaculars of Africa touched on the affected cultures in a very profound way. In most of these cultures, language is the intimate, articulate expression of culture, and so close are the two that language can be said to be synonymous with culture, which it suffuses and embodies. This is not difficult to imagine. Societies that have been less broken up by technological change have a more integrated, holistic view of life, and language as complete cultural experience fits naturally into this worldview. Missionary adoption of the vernacular, therefore, was tantamount to adopting indigenous cultural criteria for the message, a piece of radical indigenization far greater than the standard portrayal of mission as Western cultural imperialism. But this is to anticipate.

I need also to say a word about the differences between Protestants and Catholics concerning religious translation. In the manner I develop the material, it is enough to make my point even if Christians translated into nothing beyond Western languages, such as English, German, Spanish, French, Portuguese, and the Scandinavian languages, for holding the line there does not bring these languages any closer to the original tongue of Jesus than, say, Amharic, Bambara, Susu, Vai, or Zulu. To take the step of admitting English or French as a scriptural language is to commence a process of translatability that history can only reinforce as an irreversible pattern. Understood in this way, missionary translation has characterized the spread of Christianity in both its Catholic and its Protestant forms.

In another regard, Catholics and Protestants share an identical attitude toward translation. While it is true that Protestant missions have been preponderant in Bible translation work, this does not mean that Catholics were insignificant. If Protestants showed an eagerness to translate the Bible, that is because for them the Bible is a crucial standard of authority. A similar test may be applied to Catholics who showed an identical readiness to translate the catechism of the church because that represents for them their teaching authority. In any case, whatever the different standards of authority for Catholics and Protestants, in the work of translation both sides came to be engaged with indigenous cultures in enduring ways. In some striking cases, in fact, Catholics were more attuned to indigenous cultural nuances than their Protestant counterparts, with Catholic leaders committed to indigenous projects for the radical inculturation of Christianity. We may say, therefore, that Catholics and Protestants are much closer in outlook on translation than either is to Muslims for whom mission has proceeded on the standard of the nontranslatable Qur'ān, though the Catholic Latin Mass evokes similar Muslim sentiments toward the sacred Arabic.

OUTSTANDING ISSUES

One major consequence of the thesis of this book is to reopen the whole subject of mission and colonialism, with an indication of the fresh lines of inquiry now open to us. Modern historiography has established a tradition that mission was the surrogate of Western colonialism, and that—more germane to the thesis of this book—together these two movements combined to destroy indigenous cultures. In my years of formal training no serious scholar, to my knowledge, took issue with this viewpoint, and I myself conformed unquestioningly to its dictate. There was, of course, the classic work of Robinson, Gallagher, and Denny, *Africa and the Victorians* (New York: St. Martin's Press, 1961), which sought to shift the focus of attention from Britain to the colonial territories themselves by examining how the economic activity of those territories responded to internal forces: the book thus modified the idea of these territories as a clone of laissez-faire Anglo-Saxon liberalism. Such revisionism, however, left intact the standard connection between mission and colonialism, confirming the view of mission as destructive of indigenous originality. I wish in this book to present another point of view, which, however tentative, should help restore some objectivity to the subject and bring it forward once more as part of the active field of scholarly endeavor.

In its African manifestation, Christianity repeated the tensions of its Judaic and Hellenic phases, namely, a resolve on the part of African Christians to question, and sometimes to renounce, the Western presuppositions of the church. "Tension" rather than "schism" describes better what was involved, for the instrument that enabled local criticism to take root and flourish was the translation machinery that mission had itself put in place. We may see this tension in acts of local commitment to the new religion in spite of overt reaction, but, equally important, we may also find this tension working at the level of indigenous participation in Christianity where local converts engage in mutual criticism or in competition and debate what is appropriately indigenous and authentic. The flowering of Christian activity in modern Africa has taken place in ground suitably worked by vernacular translation.

The historian interested in change will find much to confirm that interest, and more besides, for the vernacular paradigm enabled local converts to acquire the new skill of vernacular literacy linked to the assurance of the familiar medium of mother tongues. This produced profound confidence in local converts to whom the Christian initiative passed, much in the way it did from Jerusalem to Antioch and thence to Athens and Rome. The historian is thus confronted with a signal fact about Christianity in the sense that its continuous translatability has left it as the only major world religion that is peripheral in the land of its origin; and yet what it lacks in the predominance of its birthplace it has more than made up for in the late fruits of its expansion.

The evidence for the adoption of the vernacular context as the final criterion in translation is so strong that it would not need pointing out were it not for the fact that scholars have maintained for far too long that Western motives and suppositions have guided not only the conception of mission but its practical operation in the field as well. The evidence suggests that this is not the case, or is not the case at the critical frontier of practice where missionaries themselves have been quick to see the limitations and even dangers of the imposition of Western notions. Specific examples are given in chapters 5 and 6. Attention is drawn to the deceptive power of seeking to translate in a straightforward manner, and then finding that more (or less) is being said by the translator than was intended. It does not take long before what is a calculated, simple, short step brings the translator into the quicksand of indigenous cultural nuances, and this helplessness may lead the translator to turn matters over to indigenous experts who, in any case, may feel called upon to challenge missionary leadership in a field where, by any yardstick, they have the advantage. I argue that all this material is relevant to the issue of mission and colonialism: with mission deliberately fashioning the vernacular instrument that Africans, who were in the middle, came to wield against their colonial overlords. Then, behind the backs of imperial masters, came the momentous outpouring of Christian conversion throughout the continent, suggesting that missionaries were effective in their conditioning of the vernacular environment rather than in their making of Christianity a photocopy of its Victorian version.

I would not deny that the nineteenth-century missionary movement was an outgrowth of social and economic currents then prevailing in the West, for such a view does not conflict with translatability. Nor would I deny that missionary expectations were determined to a large extent by home-bred ideas and personal experiences. That is as it should be. Yet on any balanced view, we would have to agree that field exposure sometimes wrought havoc with predetermined ways.

I can recall meeting in 1975 an elderly American missionary who had spent nearly a half century living among the Fulbe of Futa Jallon in Guinea. Forced out by the policies of the government of the late Sekou Touré, the missionary went to live in the village of Kabala in northeast Sierra Leone, not far from the Guinea border. His perennial concern was with the beauty of the Fulfulde language, with a certain romantic idealism leading him to aver some Semitic genius for the Fulbe people, a point he shares with numerous African scholars who also see the Semitic factor in Africa. Yet, in spite of his admirable accomplishments in the vernacular language, the elderly missionary viewed his work in the somber and unforgiving light of statistical failure: he had made relatively few converts, and that preyed on his mind. There were many missionaries like him who appraised their work in the light of Mission Board requirements and yet whose greatest contribution lay in the meticulous care they gave to the vernacular. The real issue is whether missionaries could successfully perpetuate Victorian values where they also successfully promoted vernacular translation and the literacy that went with it. That seems unlikely, suggesting a conflicting role for mission, which for the one part proceeded to impose the culture and industrial arts of the West, thus suppressing local cultures, while, for the other, it cultivated indigenous languages and literature to the neglect of education and technical skills. This schizoid approach has not advanced our understanding, merely repeating strictures we decided mission should carry, sometimes in spite of the evidence. A full-scale treatment of the subject of mission from this new perspective waits to be done, but where it touches on the colonial issue it can at least be examined in the light of the vernacular translation work.

The great paradigm shifts marking the course of Christian history are essentially five: the Judaic phase, the Gentile breakthrough in the Hellenic phase, the Reformation, nineteenth-century laissez-faire liberalism, and, in our age, the missionary movement in Africa and Asia when the vernacular paradigm came into its own. We stand today at the threshold of a new phenomenon in the history of the church when peoples and cultures are flocking to the cause, conscious as never before of the particular, unique contribution they can make. Christianity has become a pluralist dispensation of enormous complexity, and religious statesmanship requires the flexible approach of translatability to foster this pluralism rather than opposing it as a threat. How well Christians manage their great pluralist heritage in these twilight years of the twentieth century will have enormous implications for the kind of society people live in. Either believers accept the pluralist thrust of the gospel, and the particular social movements that appear to press hard on the assumed sanctity of national borders, as evidence of God's pilgrim purpose or they resist it with some arbitrary exclusivist cultural ideology. As the need and scale for asylum and sanctuary increase, so does the pressure to undertake a fresh translation of what it is, as the ancient prophet said, that God requires of the people and their leaders.

RATIONALE

I am concerned to demonstrate from the relevant historical sources evidence for the thesis of the book. Consequently I have resorted to extended quotations in order to present much of the available evidence on the view I wish to develop. My selection of sources is necessarily limited by the historiographical interest, and certainly not by confessional criteria. I evaluate the historiographical material by whether or not it supports the idea of cultural failure or fatigue as the reason for the spread of Christianity. Since I wish to demonstrate that Christianity had adopted translatability from a very early stage, I see culture as the natural extension of the new religion, and therefore view cultural failure as ultimately incompatible with Christian success. This helped me to understand why Christians developed such an eclectic cultural appetite without forgetting their own religious counsels. I consider historical opinions in this matter just as important as reports and other hard evidence. I depart from the concerns proper to a monograph and seek instead to mark out the broad outlines of the field. Much of the assumptions underlying the book are those of a historian of religion who has a deep fascination for how the religious phenomenon is formed by internal forces as well as by external circumstances, with "subjective" factors coalescing with "objective" factors to propel the religious momentum. One way of describing what I have done here is to say that I treat Christianity as a religious movement, or as a vernacular translation movement, in contradistinction to Christianity either as Scripture or as a dogmatic, creedal system, without, of course, denying the validity of those views.

It will be obvious that I combine the theological and the historical methods to describe translatability as a religious theme. I realize that this approach, although by no means new, is nevertheless unusual. I think the gains of that combined method far outweigh the liabilities. I have, in fact, tried to take my own medicine in this regard by using a "pluralist" model to develop the material, an approach that assumes the importance of multidisciplinary ways of examining the human enterprise. The "normative" issues with which theology concerns itself are important for illuminating the human factor in the shaping of values, while the "descriptive" preciseness of historical investigation gives solidity to the promptings of the Spirit.

Having said that, I need to point out that the historian of religion may properly engage in comparative analysis without making his or her own evaluative judgments the standard of interpretation. Assurances of open-mindedness by a Christian have a hollow ring in the deeply political world of today where ideological considerations of all sorts predispose us to impugn the motives of others. So we need to match our assurances with deeds, which in this book assumes the form of a final chapter but elsewhere took the form of a monograph. The Islamic comparison is intended in the final chapter to pull together the varied themes in the book and to shape them into a coherent but far from comprehensive statement. I compare, not primarily to judge but to elucidate. I suggest that by contrasting Christian mission with its Islamic counterpart, we gain a fuller appreciation for their distinctive attitudes to translatability. Whereas for Christians, mission has come preeminently to mean translation, for Muslims mission has stood stubbornly for the nontranslatability of its Scriptures in the ritual obligations. Yet, in their different ways, both religions have made tremendous gains as missionary faiths. The implications for cultural pluralism of such worldwide success by the two traditions are of abiding importance for everyone concerned. If we understand such contrasting themes in mission, it should prevent us from making facile or invidious comparisons. But more positively, it should enable interreligious exchange to take place on a more realistic basis, so that the issues raised in Islam's universal faith-order may instruct Christians caught in the vernacular consequences of translatability, and, conversely, the Christian insights of vernacular self-understanding within the divine providence may encourage Muslims to show more interest in cultures and languages other than that mandated by the sacred Arabic. Such mutual instruction can only enhance the cause of peace and human solidarity and be a telling common witness to religious open-mindedness in a broken world. We need such witness as a safety barrier against the forces of dogmatism and intolerance that threaten to de-escalate by a vicious spiral to the low points of the human spirit.

In the book as a whole I am mindful of the forces of pluralism released in the culture by the efforts of scriptural translation, and I am concerned to state, where the evidence warrants it, that Christians themselves were often not consistent in dealing with the pluralism of their own making. That implies, not just historical obtuseness, for we all carry our share of that, but powerlessness, which is even less discriminating. Thus a certain level of complexity is introduced in the material even at an early stage, with the apostles laboring mightily to proclaim the gospel but sometimes lagging behind in accepting some of the direct consequences of their proclamation. That original tension between cultural absolutization in the Jerusalem church and the Gentile breakthrough at Antioch has continued to characterize the church through the centuries. For often enough we also wish in our own special circumstances to deny the Gentile breakthrough and its pluralist consequences. Yet the peculiar history of the religion continues to insert the tension right at the heart of the enterprise itself. As long as we accept the need to translate, so long shall we continue to face the challenge to relativize worldly success and destigmatize taboo cultures.

1

The Birth of Mission: The Jewish-Gentile Frontier

The Gospel because it was the message of God to humanity, could daily reveal itself in the simplest of garments. . . . The complicated is immobile, the simple is mobile. . . . The New Testament, as is proved also by its language, was ordained for a destiny, the like of which no work which originated in the high literary culture has had, or could have had. . . . This simple book, with its carpenter's and tentmaker's language, was a book for all, and it could resound, unadulterated to humanity in all centuries, the message of the Gospel which had moved men in a small corner of the Mediterranean World. . . . The New Testament has become the Book of the Peoples because it began by being the Book of the People. [Deissmann, 1929, pp. 95, 106, 136]

The Jewish-Gentile frontier in the first century of Christian history, and how in the new Christian proclamation Jew and Gentile became interchangeable — a move that relativized the one as much as it destigmatized the other — must be our first subject of consideration. How Jew and Gentile stand under the radical pluralist dispensation demanded by God's absolute sovereignty is a fundamental issue. This radical pluralism is at bottom a theological issue, yet, because it generates acute tension at the level of culture, its historical implications are also obvious. For this reason we shall in this chapter try to combine history and theology in order to scrutinize the question upon which everything else in this book rests.

THE JEWISH FACTOR

The Jewish factor was an essential element in the rise and expansion of Christianity and constituted a significant influence in the development of mission. In the first place Christian mission was a stream that flowed into the low ground leveled by Jewish religious life. Christian mission was in its origin a movement conditioned by the atmosphere of the Diaspora, and the rewards it reaped were prepared in that soil. In the second place, the inner reality of Gentile Christianity had the special mark of the Jewish experience stamped upon it as a sign and a safeguard: as a sign because of its undeniable debt to its Jewish precursor, and as a safeguard because of the dangers in wishing to sever its links with its Jewish past. The tensions experienced on the Jewish-Gentile frontier stemmed in large measure from the nature of the special relationship existing between the early Christians and the Jews of the Diaspora.

When the apostles decided on mission as an inescapable obligation of the gospel, the first groups of people to whom they directed their message were Jews, Jewish proselytes, or Gentiles nurtured in the favorable atmosphere of Jewish presuppositions (e.g., Acts 10:22). In fact some scholars go so far as to argue that the idea of a worldwide mission was one not explicitly given by Jesus, who confined his preaching to his fellow countrymen and women. Yet all scholars are undivided about the vigorous course that the Gentile mission soon took, and the universal assumption of the apostles that such a development was fully consistent with the mind and intention of the now exalted Christ who was also the coming Messiah. Evidence of the Jewish background of the missionary movement can be found in the prominence given to the messiahship of Jesus, his certain return, and the equally certain establishment of the kingdom in the foreseeable future. The explicit words of Jesus confirm the Jewish intentions of his own work (Matt. 10:5–6, 23). Even the historical setting of the Great Commission (Matt. 28:16–18) makes it clear that Galilee and the immediate countryside were to be the center of preaching and witness. The arrival of the kingdom would occur on home territory, it was believed, and the apostles wished to be eyewitnesses to that event.

And yet, at a fairly early age, a turning point was reached in the direction of Christian preaching, so that the transition from the Jewish to the Gentile mission appears to have been a natural one for the early Christians. The pressure to expand the work beyond Jerusalem and the northern hill district of Galilee had been building since the momentous events of the passion week of Jesus, with the agonizing climax of the crucifixion as the concentrated point of no return. All concerned looked forward to the time when the long-awaited event would take place. Once their resolve was galvanized by the resurrection experience, the apostles and the sympathizers of Jesus went about their business of testifying to the Messiah in his glorified power, and they did this with unbounded confidence. In fact, the accounts portray their exploits with the facility of a deja vu: the events of conversion and progress into new fields were the fulfillment of promises made by Jesus Christ during his earthly ministry. In undertaking mission, therefore, the apostles were keeping the intimate company of their Lord and Master. Adolf von Harnack has observed rightly that mission issued from the overwhelming logic of the religion and spirit of Jesus, whatever the situation with regard to any explicit command. I quote his words:

> One might even argue that the universal mission was an inevitable issue of the religion and spirit of Jesus, and that its origin, not only apart from any direct word of Jesus, but in verbal contradiction to several of his sayings, is really a stronger testimony to the method, the strength, and the spirit of his preaching than if it were the outcome of a deliberate command. [Harnack, 1908, I:37.]

We might ask how, precisely, it came about that Christianity breached its Judaic walls and swept upon the Gentile world. To answer this question in detail, we should look at the internal conditions of the new religion and the external circumstances, and in both cases pay special attention to the Jewish factor.

INTERNAL CONDITIONS FOR MISSION

It is clear that even in the lifetime of Jesus, the disciples were gripped by a sense of the impending end of the age. Life, they believed, was a journey, and as they neared the time when the end was in view, they felt under increasing constraint to make necessary preparation to meet that deadline. The earliest message of this missionary vocation is enshrined in Matthew 10:7ff. It was believed as a matter of literal truth that the kingdom of heaven was at hand, and its heralds must strive to warn people of this fact. People were to be told to pay heed to the approaching cataclysm and to flee while there was time. Judgment was about to engulf the world just as the sickle is put to a field ready for the harvest. There was resolute, inner conviction that the path of mission was a costly, perilous one, and that those perils were in fact incontrovertible evidence of the ripeness of the age for the final judgment. Thus suffering and opposition became the sources of inner strength for the task of mission.

There was, in addition, an ethical reward for the costly enterprise of mission. Those who denied themselves worldly comforts in order to put their hand to the plow would be rewarded with the incorruptible trophy of membership in the kingdom of heaven. The notion of recompense was the lynchpin of the missionary endeavor, as indeed it was of the primitive church. The obligation to preach and spread the message, the call to renounce the world and create a messianic community, and the belief that people were living in a provisional age—all this cohered in the principle of recompense. The reward of the kingdom more than compensated for the cost of discipleship. Therefore, the inhabitants of this world, drawn into the nursery community of millennial expectancy, would qualify thereby to become the children of the kingdom, people whose citizenship was in heaven (Heb. 13:14). All worldly events conjoined to serve the single end of hastening the millennium. The religious principle of faith and devotion to one God was fixed on the idea of moral accountability. The sovereign rule of the moral law would be vindicated in the reign of God. In that reign all routes of escape from moral accountability would be blocked, and the rule of righteousness established. All would receive their just reward.

This vision of the kingdom infused a powerful sense of ethical serious-ness into earthly conduct. How people treated each other, how they acquired and disposed of their wealth, how they behaved in the world, what motives existed for their actions, and how they practiced restraint, forgive-ness, and charity toward others were all governed by the certainty that the kingdom of God (1 Thess. 4:16–18; 5:1–28) would appear in the foreseeable future. No one took the world as seriously as those who were called to make war upon it. God as Judge and Savior not only ensured the rule of justice and faith in redemptive steadfastness, but also called forth a strong sense of righteousness and trust in the salvific promise. Thus earthly existence had cast upon it this inexorable pressure to rise to the highest standards of ethical conduct.

Mission was understood as the urgent scramble to abandon the world and prepare for the inevitable confrontation. Psychologically, mission stressed the idea of individual responsibility, which heightened the sense of fear, isolation, and insecurity. It sought to meet this individual crisis by offering security, assurance, and the safety of a redeemed and supportive fellowship. The individual disposition of fear and anxiety was turned into an attitude of faith and trust, and the reliance on such inner resources in what would otherwise be a menacing world. Instead of being conformed to the world and thus exposed to its ways, Christians looked forward to the reign of God as the final security.

Mission, however, threw up a sense of genuine community. The idea of the kingdom was at bottom the idea of a fellowship, chastened, redeemed, and elected to exhibit the marks of love and forgiveness. The reality of God was thus intertwined with the ethical life of the fellowship of believers who were narrowly fenced off from the world.

Such a view of mission, though assuming a new point of departure, still presented the early disciples as a subapostolate of the wider Jewish religious activity. In the commissioning of the twelve apostles, for example, Jesus commands them to be scrupulous in restricting their mission to a branch of the Jewish tribes and to refrain from any missionary contact with Gentiles (Matt. 10:5–6). In the interlude between the ascension and the Pentecost, to take another example, Jesus commands the apostles to await the promise in Jerusalem (Acts 1:4), and leads them further to believe that the familiar world of Judaism would be the primary limits of their preaching (Acts 1:8).

In all this material, it seems that the followers of Jesus were just an offshoot of the Jewish dispensation. At this stage of development, the disciples assumed — or were led to assume — that the Gentile world was peripheral to the purposes of God. The ringing assertions of Jesus about the law, salvation, the kingdom, and the power of God left a deafening echo in the ears of his disciples, and only a few could hear the full cross-cultural implications of the Master's preaching. For many of them the teaching of Jesus remained in continuity with the Judaic heritage and the place of the synagogue in that. For instance, E. P. Sanders of Oxford University believes that Jesus was a prophet of restoration eschatology, preaching the imminent reassembling of the twelve tribes of Israel. Sanders interprets the work of John the Baptist, who called Israel to repentance, as forming a necessary background to the restoration hopes of Jesus, hopes that grew out of the general stream of Jewish religious life. Although Sanders courts criticism with his concentration on the acts of Jesus, particularly the temple incident with the money changers (Mk. 11:15-18), to the neglect of Jesus' words and teaching or of the cross, his attempt to place the work of Jesus within Judaism is a valid one (see Sanders, 1985).

Thus upon its inner resources the primitive missionary community carried the distinguishing sign of the Judaic identity. The apostles believed that God, having set up Abraham as the irrevocable standard of faith and obedience, had now defended that with the ultimate price of the cross, a price mysteriously prefigured in the act of Abraham himself toward Isaac.

However, the missionary preaching marked a significant shift when Jesus was presented as the Messiah and Son of God, glorified in the cross and exalted on God's right hand, from where he would come to judge the world as Messiah. In his earthly life Jesus was perceived as a rabbi, the Great Teacher who taught in parables and by extended disputations on the law. In that role he carried the distinguishing marks of a Jewish religious figure, and his actions were explicable only by reference to his Jewish heritage.

It is, of course, true that for a significant number of his compatriots Jesus was the healer and wonder-worker par excellence, a reputation that undoubtedly earned him the implacable enmity of the authorities. But to his close circle of disciples, such supernatural feats merely confirmed his rabbinic authority, and they continued to regard him as the superlative teacher, the one who opened people's eyes and ears to the wisdom enshrined in the Torah. It is obvious that in the postresurrection fellowship of the disciples, this rabbinic strand formed an unbroken knot in the missionary net that was spread to embrace a much wider audience. In the testimony of Stephen, for example, the significance of the life of Jesus is expounded as a consistent theme that reaches back to Abraham and the subsequent course of that peculiar history (Acts 7). All this implies the centrality of Jewish culture for the new religion, and hints at the radical revolution involved in the Gentile breakthrough.

The change that came upon the disciples may be understood in the light of the crucifixion and resurrection. The shift in understanding was not so much in the structure of religious belief (one God, Judge and Ruler; the judgment and the coming of the kingdom; and the special ethical code based on the Torah and nurtured in the synagogue) as in the terms of that structure. Jesus the rabbi had become Jesus the Messiah, both ideas firmly rooted in Jewish tradition. In the hands of the apostles, however, the earthly Jesus was the promised Messiah. Thus a familiar religious title came to bear a revolutionary meaning, which was ironically anticipated by the revolutionary expectations of political liberation. Once the step was taken, it was thought obvious in the minds of believers that the law and the prophets had pointed unerringly to where the apostles stood in relation to the glorified and risen Savior. Rudolf Bultmann, who is inclined to stress a gradual development in apostolic thought on this question, suggests enough to warrant the view that a definite change, if not already there, was certainly in the offing. He describes it thus:

> . . . the proclamation of Jesus as Messiah or Son of Man keeps quite within the frame of Jewish eschatological expectation. . . . however much his preaching in its radicality is directed against Jewish legalism, still its content is nothing else than true Old Testament — Jewish faith in God radicalized in the direction of the great prophets' preaching. And though it surpasses the latter in its individualization of man's relations to God, because it places not the People but first of all the individual into the immediate presence of God, and because it views not the people's future but God's Reign as the eschatological salvation, still even in that is only the consummation of tendencies that underlie the preaching of the great prophets. The concepts of God, world, and man, of law and grace, of repentance and forgiveness in the teaching of Jesus are not new in comparison with those of the Old Testament and Judaism, however radically they may be understood. And his critical interpretation of the Law, in spite of its radicality, likewise stands within the scribal discussion about it, just as his eschatological preaching does within Jewish apocalyptic. [Bultmann, 1951–55, I:33–34, 35.]

Harnack moves in the same direction when it comes to identifying the characteristics of the missionary preaching to the Gentiles. The list that he makes draws heavily on the contribution of law and synagogue, particularly the uncompromising worship of one God. Paul reminds and exhorts his audience in Corinth and Thessalonika that when they heard the message they turned from idols and images to serve the one, living God of apostolic preaching (1 Cor. 12:2; 1 Thess. 1:9–10). Harnack observes in this regard: "The 'living and true God' is the first and final thing; the second is Jesus, the Son of God, the judge, who secures us against the wrath to come, and who is therefore 'Jesus the Lord.' To the living God, now preached to all men, we owe faith and devoted service; to God's Son as Lord, our due is faith and hope" (Harnack, 1908, I:89).

The ethical seriousness of missionary preaching, then, as confirmed by the cataclysmic events of Passion Week (which coincided with the Jewish Passover Feast) and their unexpected outcome on Easter Sunday, turned on the assured coming of Jesus as Messiah to reign in the kingdom. Thus in retrospect even Easter, for all its unexpectedness, falls into a familiar pattern, affording historical veracity to the principle of Jewish messianic faith.

Thus the significant twist of perceiving Jesus as God's exalted became the gravitational force of the new world of faith and devotion. It gave an otherworldly direction to Christian life and devotion, with faith in the absolute righteousness of God finding its corollary in the provisional, relative character of this world. This opens the way for pluralism by stressing the nonabsolute character and coequality of all earthly arrangements. What one authority calls "the Easter faith" of the believers exerted a broadening pressure on the inherited boundaries of Jewish ritual fellowship to furnish the principle of inclusion by faith. Such a principle made the Gentile breakthrough a permanent mark of the gospel without, of course, excluding the Jews as such; and the elaborate, sophisticated footwork of Paul in the epistle to the Romans and to the Galatians in particular shows how he and others assumed the Judaic theme to be an integral part of the gospel proclamation.

We need not be dogmatic about whether apostolic preaching adopted or abandoned the Jewish conception of the divine commonwealth, but all would agree that the apostolic insight was developed in intimate closeness to that conception. In the final analysis, membership of the kingdom remained the divine plan of salvation, the radical difference now being that faith rather than a racially based ritual order was the qualification.[1] This "Easter faith" became the all-powerful force in energizing the body of believers. The inner dynamism of the new mission was fed from this explosive source, and Christians could not rest until all the terrain they had left behind was realigned accordingly. So stay in Jerusalem they did.

THE EXTERNAL CIRCUMSTANCES

The Jerusalem sojourn proved to be an essential preparation for the outreach to the wider Gentile world. The Christian movement was known among the Jews as the Nazarene sect, and the Christians as the Nazarenes. Now, however, imbued with an intense conviction in Jesus as Lord and Savior, the shadows of the Temple could afford only the congenial shelter of an incubation niche, and before long the Nazarenes were acquiring a new identity as "Christians," a Greek term first given to them in Antioch (Acts 11:26). It is, of course, true that the Jewish party in the church continued to enjoy some power and influence, and that eventually they seceded from the church to form a community of their own, known as the Ebionites. They upheld the Mosaic code and continued to hope for the Messiah to come. However, their rupture with the apostles indicates that the church understood itself as a separate community marked by faith in Christ as the vindicated Messiah (Eusebius, 1984, pp. 136ff., 256; Gibbon, n.d., I: 678; II: 806–7; "Ebionism," 1981). There was thus something corresponding to a spontaneous and almost abrupt force about the expansion of Christianity in the Greek-speaking world and beyond.

Yet, in spite of the growing divergence with Temple religious life, important factors of unity and continuity remained. Even when it ostensibly repudiated Judaism, primitive Christianity stood firmly within the Jewish orbit. As Gilbert Murray (1866–1957), the English classical scholar and statesman, once put it, "Christianity, apart from its positive doctrines, had inherited from Judaism the noble courage of its disbeliefs" (Ferguson, 1970, p. 224). Gibbon, for his part, expressed it thus:

> The primitive Christians were possessed with an unconquerable repugnance to the use and abuse of images; and this aversion may be ascribed to their descent from the Jews, and their enmity to the Greeks. The Mosaic law had severely proscribed all representations of the Deity; and that precept was firmly established in the principles and practice of the chosen people. [Gibbon, n.d., III:1.]

Thus the safeguard against losing the Jewish connection was retained through continuing Christian opposition to idolatry and the corresponding commitment to the oneness of God and to the towering sovereignty of the moral and ethical code. All three aspects of that commitment were raised on Jewish foundations. They marked the inner safeguard of the new religion on its precipitous course through the mainland of the Pax Romana.

In availing itself of the outward advantages afforded by the administration and climate of the empire, primitive Christianity gravitated toward the communities of the Diaspora ensconced in the empire. These communities were strategically located in areas of learning and prosperity, from the Tigris and Euphrates valleys to Spain and beyond. There was a powerful and prosperous community in Rome itself. The influence of that Roman Jewish community can be gauged from numerous converts made from the many religions that existed under imperial aegis. For example, the Roman authorities, including Seneca, complained bitterly about the inroads that Jewish worship was making into the citizenry, threatening the collapse of the state-sponsored cults.

In following the trails of the Jewish Diaspora, the Christians also learned to duplicate in the church the vigorous Hellenistic movement that had reached an advanced stage in the synagogue. Evidence of this can be seen in the creation of the Septuagint (LXX), the Greek translation of the five books of Moses, and in the use of Greek in synagogue life. Its most brilliant individual representative was Philo of Alexandria, a figure of immense importance for the Hellenization of Judaism (see Winston, 1981). Steeped in the best of Greek culture, Philo, who was active in the early part of the first century, achieved a brilliant synthesis of Greek learning and Jewish religious principles. For example, he adopted the Greek idea of *logos* (on which, more in chapter 2, below) and employed it to bridge the gulf between an uncompromising monotheism and a Platonism that excludes divine agency in the material sphere, finite and imperfect as that sphere is. The use of the *logos* concept was "a master-stroke. For here in one concept are fused the Jewish *memra,* the word of God ('God said Let there be light, and there was light'), the late Jewish Wisdom, as seen in *Proverbs, Job, Ecclesiasticus* and *Wisdom,* the Platonic doctrine of Forms, the Aristotelian doctrine of the Divine Intellect, and the Stoic Divine Reason; the ambiguity of meaning in Logos between word and reason made it an especially convenient term" (Ferguson, 1970, p. 224).

One particularly fruitful field for radical appropriation in Christianity was the gnostic factor. (For a full account of gnosticism, see the classic study by Hans Jonas, first published in 1958, with a second, enlarged edition in 1963.) The consensus of scholars today is that the Gospel of John was the most ambitious attempt in Scripture to assimilate the gnostic system — or at any rate, even if the internal evidence is less conclusive, gnostics and heterodox Christians found plenty in that Gospel to confirm their views. The Gospel may thus be seen as the leading document, along with the epistles of John and the book of Revelation, that testifies to the church's spiritual and intellectual encounter with gnosticism. It is possible that many believers who initially sympathized with the esoteric sentiments expressed in parts of John's Gospel and then subsequently identified themselves with mainstream Christianity, continued to think in terms of the gnostic paradigm with its emphasis on a preexistent being and on devotees sharing in that preexistent source. One writer who has developed this idea in terms of a special Johannine community is the Roman Catholic scholar Raymond E. Brown, who quotes a gnostic adept as having declared about this preexistent principle: "I derive being from Him who is preexistent and return to my own place from which I came forth" (cited by Brown, 1979, p. 151). The inclusion of the Johannine corpus, so different in tone and temper from the Synoptics, within the Christian canon shows the lengths to which the community of believers went in its practice of translatability.

Gnosticism is basically the philosophical system (or systems) which rests upon a metaphysical dualism between the spiritual and the material, between soul and body, between metaphysical truth and phenomenal representation, between light and darkness. The great Prologue of John's Gospel, for example, is steeped in gnostic ideas, with the theme of light and darkness emerging as a central issue in terms of which the life and work of Jesus is expounded. Basilides, a gnostic teacher of Alexandria who was active there round about A.D. 130, declared that while he and his followers "were no longer Jews, they were more than Christians" (Frend, 1984, pp. 205ff.). In expanding on his position, Basilides reveals the extent of his gnostic sympathies. According to him:

> In the beginning there were light and darkness . . . When each of these came to recognition of the other, and the darkness contemplated the light, the darkness, as if seized with desire of the better thing, pursued after it, and desired to be mingled with it and to participate in it. But while the darkness did this, the light by no means received anything of the darkness into itself, nor desired anything of it, albeit it too suffered the desire to behold. So it beheld the darkness as if in a mirror . . . Hence there is no perfect good in this world, and what there is of good at all is very little . . . Nevertheless by reason of this little bit of light, or rather of this sort of appearance of light, the creatures had power to generate a likeness tending towards that admixture which they had conceived from the light. [Dodd, 1953, pp. 103–4. Cf. Pagels, 1973.]

It would, however, be a mistake to pretend that John's Gospel was in any consistent fashion a gnostic book, for, as Dodd has pointed out, *"Gnosis is not in fact so much a knowledge of God,* in any profoundly religious sense, as knowledge *about* the structure of the higher world and the way to get there" (Dodd, 1953, p. 101). At the heart of John's Gospel, by contrast, lies a profoundly theological concern. The gnostic tension with Christianity arises from the attempt to turn Christianity into a religion of "secret discourses" entrusted to the specially instructed, a fact that conflicts with the public and community thrust of the gospel proclamation (Mk. 4:22; Lk. 8:17; 11:33; Jn. 7:4; 18:20; Pannenberg, 1969, pp. 149ff.). Whatever the case, as the Nag Hammadi documents indicate, gnosticism was a powerful movement that left an indelible mark on second-century Christianity (Frend, 1984, pp. 195ff.; Jonas, 1963, pp. 290–319; for a rigorous examination of the theme in the writings of the church fathers, and for an examination of the comparative Islamic tradition, the reader may wish to consult Smith, 1976).

So far as Paul's acquaintance with the whole Alexandrian school of gnosticism is concerned, the preponderant weight of scholarly opinion is against it, so that we cannot with any degree of confidence claim that Paul knew of Philo's work. On the other hand, when it comes to John the evangelist and his closeness to Alexandrian influences, a less hesitant assertion has been entered, as pointed out in Moffatt's brilliant synthesis of the evidence (Moffatt, 1981, pp. 522ff.). In any case, the advanced level of a Hellenized Judaism constituted a readily accessible precedent for the new religion of Christianity, and certainly Philo's philosophical achievement, with its intricate allegorical method, would be extremely attractive for Christians engaged in interpretation and exchange. The ground, appropriately elevated by the worshipers of a strict monotheism such as the Jews were, was suffused with the reconciling effects of gnostic ideas and learning, ready to receive the Christian input. Thus the impulse of mission had been significantly stirred by the stimulus of Jewish and gnostic elements, and the Christian wave would merge with these before its own tide swept it in a different direction. In this sense the Diaspora was important in facilitating the implantation of Christian communities throughout the empire, as the following observations point out:

> To the Jewish mission which preceded it, the Christian mission was indebted, in the first place, for a field tilled all over the empire; in the second place, for religious communities already formed everywhere in the towns; thirdly for what Axenfeld calls "the help of materials" furnished by the preliminary knowledge of the Old Testament, in addition to the catechetical and liturgical materials which could be employed without much alteration; fourthly, for the habit of regular worship and a control of private life; fifthly, for an impressive apologetic on behalf of monotheism, historical teleology, and ethics; and, finally, for the feeling that self-diffusion was a duty. The amount of this debt was so large, that one might venture to claim the Christian mission was a continuation of the Jewish propaganda. [Harnack, 1908, I:15.]

In following a parallel course with Judaism, Christian mission also came to make use of the arrangements that existed under the Roman civilization. In the first place, a Hellenizing movement had taken place in the length and breadth of the empire, and this produced a unity of language and ideas, which gave form and shape to the Christian expansion. In the second place, Roman administrative and political institutions, and the cosmopolitan atmosphere of the empire, encouraged social and intellectual exchange.

> The exceptional facilities, growth and security of international traffic: the admirable roads; the blending of different nationalities; the interchange of wares and ideas; the personal intercourse; the ubiquitous merchant and soldier — one may add, the ubiquitous professor, who was to be encountered from Antioch to Cadiz, from Alexandria to Bordeaux. The church thus found the way paved for expansion: the means were prepared; and the population of the large towns was as heterogeneous and devoid of a past as could be desired. [Harnack, 1908, I:20–21.]

There was, in addition, a significant deposit of Roman ideas of jurisprudence, human rights and duties, court procedures, administrative impartiality, and a liberal philosophical outlook, which all helped to acclimatize Christianity in the empire. "On all essential questions the church had no reason to oppose, but rather to assent to, Roman law, that grandest and most durable product of the empire" (Harnack, 1908, I:21).

The religious policy of the empire redounded to the benefit of the church. The toleration shown toward all religions, including Christianity, removed costly obstacles in the path of initial introduction, and although Christian preaching was required to observe the rule of no offense to the state religion, no disabilities were incurred at this stage for being a Christian. The ground was being laid for the inward transformation that was to give Christianity a fresh language and culture.

This allowed a confident outlook to form among Christians and enabled them to uphold the tradition of worship of one God. Indeed, Gibbon writes about the comparative freedom of Christians in the first hundred years since the death of Christ when "the disciples of the Messiah were indulged in a freer latitude both of faith and practice than has ever been allowed in succeeding ages" (Gibbon, n.d., I:393). Like the Jews before them, Christians were able to gain a recognition for themselves, although they stuck to the line of refusing idol worship and making offerings to the emperor. Even the tragic events of the Neronic persecution, in which both Peter and Paul were reported to have perished, failed to destroy Christian confidence, for the outrages could be attributed to the excesses of one man (Gibbon, n.d., I:460). Persecution did continue in Rome and elsewhere, but the younger Pliny, for example, reporting to the emperor Trajan (about A.D. 110), said he was careful to observe standard safeguards in extracting confessions. As the provincial governor of Bithynia, where he was appointed ca. A.D. 85, he sent to Rome for trial the cases of those Christians possessing the privileges of Roman citizenship.

Polytheism was a source of friction, and Christians suffered for refusing to worship other gods (Gibbon, n.d., I:396-98), but, as Tacitus reported of Nero's bitter persecution, the fate of Christians "aroused compassion" among the general populace. Commenting on persecutions in the primitive church, Helmut Koester, in a personal communication (1985) to the author, has observed that only in the middle of the third century, with the measures of Decius in 251, was what he called "Christianity as a whole" affected. As will be argued in chapter 2, below, the organizational power of Christian religious and social life in time came to provoke intervention from political authorities. If such organizational power was achieved no earlier than the third century, it would explain why official persecution was delayed to the same extent.

Christian preaching received great encouragement from the steadfastness of believers, and the general conditions of life more than offset the setbacks implied in withdrawal from state ceremonies. This was certainly the case with regard to the organizational life of Christians. There were in existence numerous official and voluntary associations on both the municipal and provincial levels, and when the need arose to organize believers, such organizations furnished the necessary models and parallels. The enormous likely burden of first having to design new forms of church life and then attempting to secure general acceptance for them was averted even before it was confronted (Gibbon, n.d., I:420).

The general democratic leveling of society provided its own particular stimulus. In many respects the old order had changed under the equalizing pressure of the *cives Romani,* which embraced provincials, Greeks, and barbarians. The upshot was a cosmopolitan atmosphere highly conducive to individual development and choice. The Christian preaching did not hinder this. On the contrary, it encouraged and intensified it.

There was, furthermore, an expectant mood among the citizenry, which took a deeply religious turn just as Christianity was appearing on the scene. Exposure to the ritual ceremonies of the state fed the appetite for religious innovation. Participation in the state religion aroused feelings of devotion and curiosity, which spread beyond the limits of state sponsorship. As cogently demonstrated by Franz Cumont in his *Oriental Religions in Roman Paganism,* there was an irruption of Syrian and Persian religious elements into the empire, and this oriental stream met and elevated the desultory outpourings of state ceremonials. The empire itself, its appetite awakened, fed on a titillating combination of familiar and strange notions, as documented so carefully by John Ferguson in *The Religions of the Roman Empire.*

The combined and cumulative effect was to introduce a keen personal note into religious inquiry, and although not all of this was conducive to sound morals, it undoubtedly sharpened the awareness of numerous thoughtful people, some of whom might be high state officials. The proliferation of religious cults, especially of the healing variety, and the continuing attempt to rank idols in a hierarchy dictated by the formal preeminence of Jupiter, pointed people toward the monotheist ideal and the hope for a savior who could satisfy common cravings. All this was propitious ground for Christian preaching. Harnack sums up these factors thus:

> By the blending of states and nations, which coalesced to form a universal empire, cosmopolitanism had become a reality. But there was always a reverse side to cosmopolitanism, viz., individualism. . . . There was a real demand for *purity, consolation,* and *healing,* and as these could not be found elsewhere, they began to be sought in religion. [Harnack, 1908, I:105.]

First wrapping itself round its Judaic roots and then taking shelter under the liberal climate of Roman imperial administration, the Christian missionary movement thrived from a double advantage. The energy of the missionary movement, with its source in membership of the eschatological congregation, flowed naturally into the dynamism of Roman imperial power. The successful assimilation of Christianity in the Constantinian era (from A.D. 312), overlapping with the ebb of eschatological excitement, altered the missionary momentum, and a period of swift consolidation followed, reaching a high point during the pontificate of Gregory the Great (from A.D. 591). Although the disparity between church and mission became for the most part irreversible (the appearance of Saint Francis of Assisi in the thirteenth century was a signal of renewed interest in the subject of mission), it was obvious that mission conveyed the materials that were worked into the structure of the church. Mission subsisted on the signs of vitality in ancient life, and reconstructed from these an achievement that simultaneously advanced the Christian cause and retained the best in the old. Mission was thus both an advance and a completion in the perspective of the older dispensation of Roman paganism. Ulhorn, writing in 1882, puts the case succinctly, although he remained mesmerized by the idea of Christianity encountering a less than equal resistance. He urges us to see that

> From the time of the emperors onwards a new influence made itself felt, and unless we notice this influence, we cannot understand the first centuries of the early Christian church, we cannot understand its rapid extension and its relatively rapid triumph. . . . Had the stream of new life issuing from Christ encountered ancient life when the latter was still unbroken, it would have recoiled impotent from the shock. But ancient life had by this time begun to break up; its solid foundations had begun to weaken; and, besides, the Christian stream fell in with a previous and cognate current of Jewish opinion. In the Roman empire there had already appeared a universalism foreign to the ancient world. Nationalities had been effaced. The idea of universal humanity had disengaged itself from that of nationality. [cited by Harnack, 1908, I:22n.]

Although this passage tends to discount the powerful internal pressures that propelled Christian mission forward, and does so by the hypothesis of an insuperable external barrier, it nevertheless highlights the remarkable conjunction of events that favored the expansion of Christian mission. It is now time to turn to the single most important individual in spearheading the Gentile mission in Rome and elsewhere, and, in so doing, reexamine an aspect of the internal pressure.

THE PAULINE FACTOR IN CROSS-CULTURAL MISSION

The martyrdom of Stephen (Acts 7:54–60) proved a turning point for the mission to the Gentiles. Although the apostle Peter and other leading figures of the Jerusalem church had not declared themselves as a body on the side of Stephen, there were enough sympathizers of the martyr to carry on where he left off. It was this group who eventually arrived in Antioch after fleeing the persecution in Jerusalem, and began in earnest a mission to the Gentiles. There was in fact a split in the ranks of the party of Stephen. There were those who continued to make the Jews the primary target of their preaching, and they studiously avoided straying into non-Jewish territory. They would have originated from Jerusalem. There was a second party who, after leaving Jerusalem, sought out Gentiles, and Greeks in particular, in Antioch and elsewhere and cultivated a committed following among them. Although these missionaries had been present in Jerusalem, they were natives of Cyprus and Cyrenia. Their initiative in Antioch set in motion a current of strong response, which, from the subsequent decisive intervention of Paul and Barnabas, swept forward to flood the Mediterranean world. The relevant passage from the Acts of the Apostles reads as follows:

> Now those who were scattered because of the persecution that arose over Stephen travelled as far as Phoenicia and Cyprus and Antioch, speaking the word to none except Jews. But there were some of them, men of Cyprus and Cyrene, who on coming to Antioch spoke to the Greeks also, preaching the Lord Jesus. And the hand of the Lord was with them, and a great number that believed turned to the Lord. News of this came to the ear of the church in Jerusalem, and they sent Barnabas to Antioch. When he came and saw the grace of God, he was glad; and he exhorted them all to remain faithful to the Lord with steadfast purpose. . . . So Barnabas went to Tarsus to look for Saul; and when he had found him, he brought him to Antioch. For a whole year they met with the church, and taught a large company of people. [Acts 11:19ff.]

In a later passage in the same source, Barnabas and Saul (Paul) were commissioned as emissaries to the Gentile world (Acts 13:1–3), although in their own minds the Jewish connection in this effort was retained (Acts 13:5). This phase of the development of the missionary movement was important in identifying not only God-fearing people (Acts 10:23) but also uncircumcised Greeks as a worthy target of Christian preaching. That was to leave a permanent mark on the religion, as the terms "Christ" and "Christian" testify.

As a result of the exploits of Paul and Barnabas, churches sprang into existence in Syria and elsewhere where the people, unlike the Jews, had little experience of faithfulness to the law. Yet, even without that background, the new Greek and Syrian converts felt in every sense of the word to be the people of God and anxious to remain in fellowship with the Jerusalem church (Acts 11:29f.; 12:25). Their confidence in this matter was founded on the reality of the Gentile breakthrough, and it helped to reinforce the pluralist impetus of the gospel. The pattern of the creation of these Gentile churches falls outside the present scope, as does the issue of the personalities and experiences of the chief architects. But the preeminent role of Paul in this process should be assessed, not only with regard to the revolutionary impact of the Gentile mission but in respect of the new cross-cultural perspective created by that breakthrough.

PAUL AND THE PLURALIST FERMENT

The emergence of the Gentile church produced profound theological repercussions, which it fell to Paul to try to enunciate and systematize. He did so in relation to what lay at hand, namely, the Jewish religious heritage of which he was a part. He came to be in radical tension with his own cultural roots, not because those roots were unsound but because the Gentile breakthrough had cast a shadow over any claims for cultural absolutism, Jewish or other. The anti-Semitic connotations that we have read into Paul are ideas thrust upon the text in disregard of the apostle's intentions.

Through the eyes of the Gentile church Paul encountered an unsettling reality about the seriousness of God's irrevocable design to draw all people to the divine. The death and resurrection of Jesus had inaugurated the new age in which Paul, like Peter, discovered on a Gentile frontier that "God is no respecter of persons but that in every nation any one who fears him and does what is right is acceptable to him" (Acts 10:34–35). Just as that recognition breached the walls of separation between Jew and Gentile, so Paul's experience shattered his confidence in the notion of cultural exclusiveness that might be embodied in a stern Judaic creed. This is how Harnack sketches the broad intellectual outlines of Paul's Gentile experience:

The new religious level was the level of the Spirit and regeneration, of grace and faith, of peace and liberty; below and behind it lay *everything old,* including all the earlier revelations of God, since these were religions pertaining to the state of sin. This it was which enabled Paul, Jew and Pharisee as he was, to venture upon the great conception with which he laid the basis of any sound philosophy of religion and of the whole science of comparative religion, viz., the collocation of the "natural" knowledge of God possessed by man (i.e., all that had developed in man under the sway of conscience) with the law of the chosen people (Rom. lf.). Both, Paul held, were revelations of God, though in different ways and of different values; both represented what had been hitherto the supreme possession of mankind. Yet both had proved inadequate; they had aggravated sin, and had ended in death. Now *a new religion was in force.* This meant that the Gentile mission was not a possibility but a duty, whilst freedom from the law was not a concession but the distinctive and blissful form which the gospel assumed for men. [Harnack, 1908, I:55.]

Paul's ambiguous and often very critical relationship to Judaism cannot be isolated from his participation in the Gentile mission, and with good reason. As missionaries of the modern era were to find, encountering the reality of God beyond the inherited terms of one's culture reduces reliance on that culture as a universal normative pattern. A fresh standard of discernment is introduced by which the essence of the gospel is unscrambled from one cultural yoke in order to take firm hold in a different culture. Contrary to much of the prevailing wisdom in this field of study, mission implies not so much a judgment on the cultural heritage of the convert (although in time the gospel will bring that judgment) as on that of the missionary. Most of the great missionary pioneers of the nineteenth and twentieth centuries became uncompromising advocates of the cross-cultural acclimatization of Christianity, a step that required them to concede the centrality of indigenous sources and materials. Men and women who were never distinguished as explicit champions of their own culture found the attractions of another irresistible, and as a consequence became promoters of the lore and wisdom of other people. Examples abound in our own age of missionaries who by dint of sheer application acquired the necessary equipment for penetrating and exploring the veins of truth and beauty to be found in other cultures. Whatever their motive, such missionaries were laying the foundations of indigenous revitalization to which the Christian cause would be tied.

The anti-Western strictures of modern missionaries would compare with Paul's self-critical stance toward his own culture, for in both cases the culture of the message-bearer necessarily acquired a peripheral status once the step was taken to engage another culture seriously. It is, therefore, a profound misunderstanding of Paul's words to construe them as a fixed, permanent repudiation of Judaism. That would narrow Christianity into a single, unconnected beam of light that illuminates nothing that went before it or that came after it. Thus Paul's acute soul-searching with regard to the heart of his religious tradition must be seen as the troubled shadow of the experience of being covered in the intense light that revealed the Gentiles as standing at the center of God's salvific action. Such a prospect filled him with awe and with remorse that he had ever excluded such a possibility by an inflexible subservience to culture as divine embodiment. God's redemptive power had broken through to the Gentile world, thus radically shifting the stage of God's continuous dealings with the nations. The center of Christianity, Paul perceived, was in the heart and life of the believer without the presumption of conformity to one cultural ideal. The temple, we might say, was not the exclusive building centered in Jerusalem but the believers themselves whose body is the temple of God (1 Cor. 3:16; 6:19).

This insight is eloquently expressed in the epistle to the church at Ephesus. "Therefore remember," it counseled the new believers,

> that at one time you Gentiles in the flesh, called the uncircumcision by what is called the circumcision, which is made in the flesh by hands — remember that you were at that time separated from Christ, alienated from the commonwealth of Israel, and strangers to the covenants of promise, having no hope and without God in the world. . . . So then you are no longer strangers and sojourners, but you are fellow citizens with the saints and members of the household of God, built upon the foundation of the apostles and prophets, Christ Jesus himself being the cornerstone, in whom the whole structure is joined together and grows into a holy temple in the Lord; in whom you also are built into it for a dwelling place of God in the Spirit. [Ephesians 2:11–12, 19–22.]

Clearly the idea of Gentiles as also coming within the full boundary of salvation was understood for the revolutionary breakthrough it was.

C. H. Dodd, the eminent New Testament scholar, wrote of Paul in this connection:

> He had not suspected that God was like that. His theological studies had told him that God was loving and merciful; but he had thought this love and mercy were expressed once and for all in the arrangements He had made for Israel's blessedness — "the plan of salvation." It was a new thing to be assured by an inward experience admitting of no further question that God loved him, and that the eternal mercy was a Father's free forgiveness of His erring child. [Dodd, 1964, p. 80.]

Yet that assurance calls up a troubling fact, for trust in the channels through which the law was movingly enshrined must now be so massively drained of the element of exclusivity as to create a permanent breach. Through that breach Paul was confronted with the evidence of his eyes concerning God's gracious dealings with the Gentiles. The pagans, too, had a place in "the plan of salvation."

> For himself, no doubt, whether as Jew or as Christian, the so-called Law of Moses was absolute law. Within the sphere of law there was nothing higher or more perfect. Yet the identical principle appeared also among the pagans. The pagan sense of right and wrong was God's law written on the heart — the same law as that delivered on Sinai, Paul would have said. . . . He had sympathy enough to perceive that the Stoic too must fall upon this problem. There are passages in Stoic writers tinged with a melancholy which recalls the moving transcript

from Paul's experience. . . . It is at bottom a human problem, and not a specifically Jewish one, that he is facing, but his own bitter experience in Pharisaic Judaism lent a cutting edge to his analysis. [Dodd, 1964, pp. 73–74.]

Any modern-day missionary worth the name can testify to this insight and concur with the observation that it comes initially as an unsettling experience. Those who, like Paul, felt the raw sharpness of the break with the past were constrained to interpret it as having occurred by the action of a God whose power exceeded one cultural expression of it. Hence Paul talks of the unfathomable mystery of God (Rom. 11:33–36), the unsearchable wisdom and the inexhaustible goodness of One whom he had once presumed to know exhaustively by inherited cultural measures. As Dodd rightly observed, "Behind all the scholastic arguments of the Epistles to the Romans and the Galatians lies the crucial question whether religion is a matter of national inheritance and external tradition, or a matter of ever-fresh personal response to the gracious dealing of God" (Dodd, 1964, pp. 39–40).

But no one is beyond this error of assuming a built-in advantage for culture, especially when culture is underpinned by economic and political power. Even the Gentiles, without centuries of instruction in the habit, were not above this piece of cultural pretentiousness (Rom. 11:18, 19, 25). For most of us it is difficult enough to respect those with whom we might disagree, to say nothing of those who might be different from us in culture, language, and tradition. For all of us pluralism can be a rock of stumbling, but for God it is the cornerstone of the universal design.

Reflecting on the historical consequences of this question, Gibbon draws attention to the enormous diversity and pluralism of primitive Christianity, which a later age abandoned. He writes:

The government of the church has often been the subject, as well as the prize, of religious contention. The hostile disputants of Rome, of Paris, of Oxford, and of Geneva, have alike struggled to reduce the primitive and apostolic model to the respective standards of their own policy. [By contrast,] the apostles declined the office of legislation, and rather chose to endure some partial scandals and divisions, than to exclude the Christians of a later age from the liberty of varying their forms of ecclesiastical government according to the changes of times and circumstances. The scheme of policy which, under their appro-bation, was adopted for use of the first century, may be discovered from the practice of Jerusalem, of Ephesus, or of Corinth. The societies which were instituted in the cities of the Roman empire were united only by the ties of faith and charity. Independence and equality formed the basis of their internal constitution. The want of discipline and human learning was supplied by the occasional assistance of the prophets, who were called to that function without distinction of age, of sex, or of natural abilities, and who, as often as they felt the divine impulse, poured forth the effusions of the Spirit in the assembly of the faithful. [Gibbon, n.d., I:418.]

This is not to say that cultural anarchy has a place in the divine scheme. Each cultural embodiment of God's redemptive purpose should be viewed as authentic on its own terms, and inadequate only insofar as it falls lamentably short of the Lord's utter brokenness. It should not be viewed in terms of how it fits neatly into the jigsaw of an earthly empire. Paul's profound unease with a certain narrow interpretation of Israel's covenant with God stems from an awakened mistrust of human achievement as a substitute for the truth, and that unease is not moderated when directed to his Gentile listeners. Thus he warns them about the grave consequences of reliance on their own merits, a warning that was painfully grounded in his own experience. "Note then the kindness and the severity of God," he writes to the Gentile church, "severity towards those who have fallen, but God's kindness to you, provided you continue in his kindness; otherwise you too will be cut off" (Rom. 11:22). And cut off precisely at the point where they might become most confident—even conceited—in their cultural self-sufficiency.

The challenge for the Gentile church, then as now, was to be centered in the "kindness of God," not in the self-estimation that they constituted a normative rule for other people. There is, of course, a normative lesson to be learned in all this, but that has to do with the higher logic of the divine providence by which we may be chosen as God's instruments without that in any way divinizing us or setting aside our accountability. That remorseless consistency drives a sword through the heart of our cultural complacency, and by its thrust we are healed.

It was the experience of the Gentile church that brought Paul to the radical edges of his own tradition. His religious sentiments were progressively molded by the exposure to the Gentile movement. Dodd wrote (1964, p. 47) that "Paul the Jew had to suffer the shattering of his deepest beliefs before he came through to a new conception of a missionary's work. He had to learn that there was no distinction of Jew and Gentile. It needs some effort of imagination to realize what this surrender cost him." Paul understood henceforth that the conscience of the "heathen" performed a kerygmatic value not too dissimilar from the tablets of revelation, a line of reasoning he was prepared to develop thus because he followed it through Israel to the frontiers of Roman civilization and Greek culture.

ETHNIC AND LINGUISTIC FACTORS IN MISSION

These factors raise an issue that can be framed in terms of a problematic. How might the church, Gentile or other, rise to its missionary obligation unless it believed that its experience, which is necessarily culturally defined, was in some fashion normative of the divine truth? Mission is essentially praxis, and that entails involvement and communication. Whatever the criteria for the essence of the message, the specific and the concrete foundations for mission emanate from cultural and historical specificity. At this point we are brought face to face with the presuppositions of Christian engagement.

There are two basic ways to proceed. One is to make the missionary culture the inseparable carrier of the message. This we might call mission by *diffusion*. By it religion expands from its initial cultural base and is implanted in other societies primarily as a matter of cultural identity. Islam, with which Christianity shares a strong missionary tradition, exemplifies this mode of mission. It carries with it certain inalienable cultural assumptions, such as the indispensability of its Arabic heritage in Scripture, law, and religion.

The other way is to make the recipient culture the true and final locus of the proclamation, so that the religion arrives without the presumption of cultural rejection. This we might call mission by *translation*. It carries with it a deep theological vocation, which arises as an inevitable stage in the process of reception and adaptation. Conversion that takes place in mission as diffusion is not primarily a theological inquiry. It is, rather, assimilation into a predetermined positivist environment. On the other hand, conversion that takes place in mission as translation rests on the conviction that might be produced in people after conscious critical reflection. What is distinctive about this critical reflection is that it assumes, either implicitly or explicitly, a relativized status for the culture of the message-bearer. Christian missionaries, from Peter and Paul down to our own day, have spent a good deal of their time denouncing false conversions, and urging believers to adopt a code of critical self-examination lest they presume too much on the worth of any person, whether as transmitter or as recipient.

We are not here pretending that these two ways are always separate or, for that matter, easy to disentangle. For example, in the Jerusalem church it is obvious that most of the apostles thought at first primarily in terms of cultural diffusion, and in any case it would be hard to separate the genuine from the false in every specific case of conversion even (and especially) in those heady days. Similarly, it is clear that important Muslim missionary agents insisted on sincere intention as a desideratum of true religion. As one classical Muslim scholar put it, "Assuredly the worth of an act is by its intention." Furthermore, any religion may settle into becoming a cultural complex and spread by diffusion. Nevertheless, the preponderant balance of emphasis fell to one or the other side. Mission as diffusion is unquestionably the stronger strand in Islam, whereas mission as translation is the vintage mark of Christianity.

We may draw the following conclusion about the problematic. In Paul's mind mission was the solvent of cultural xenophobia, essentially his own. He was thus prepared, indeed compelled, to subject the Gentile church to the same analysis, namely, that the same provisional destiny awaits their cultural expression of the gospel. To help instill this lesson, confidence in Christ's millennial reign is affirmed and held before them. Christianity is first and foremost a pluralist religion. The gospel demands a plural frontier for its diffusion, looking with alarm at the notion of a hermetically sealed culture as the exclusive conveyance of God's truth. As Paul affirmed, there is no respect of persons with God (Rom. 2:11), and nothing in itself is unclean (Rom. 14:14). The positive sides of these statements are equally valid: all persons are precious in God's sight (1 Pet. 2:4), and all things indeed are pure (Rom. 14:20). In the same fashion, no one is the exclusive or normative pattern for anyone else, and no one culture can be God's favorite. The result is pluralism on a radical scale, one that even institutional Christianity finds difficult to accept or promote. But if translatability is the taproot of Christian expansion, then resistance to it by ecclesiastical institutions is like the rebellion of the branches against the tree.

Thus cross-cultural boundaries are accorded an intrinsic status in the proclamation of the gospel, and Christians who stood at such frontiers acquired a critical comparative perspective on their own cultural identity. They were encouraged, as Paul was, to shed the restrictions of their own particular culture in order to face with unencumbered eyes the magnitude of God's salvific work in another cultural milieu. Any cultural tradition that turns in on itself will necessarily harden into a defensive complex, with little relevance for the spontaneous improvement of others. Mission helps to burst the old wineskins with the pressure of cross-cultural interpretation, dissolving the barriers of cultural exclusiveness.

Mission as translation, then, encouraged faith and obedience in the God whose humility and humanity were appropriately expressed in multiple cultural systems without those systems turning into exclusive norms of truth. This might suggest an arid and Spartan view of culture, but in fact it ennobled culture by interposing the safeguard of nondeification. God is not an interchangeable cultural concept, a pious embodiment of cultural self-regard. But neither is God an abstract force who is encountered outside the limits of cultural self-understanding. To the Jew, God must speak as a Jew, with a repetition of that particularity in respect to the Gentiles. The result is a profound stimulation of the inner life of the hinterland, for the light of truth will connect up with the glimmers of genuine ethical quest. For example, the expansion of primitive Christianity in its Judaic and classical phases led to renewed interest in the pre-Christian materials of the age, and it is doubtful whether many of what would now be regarded as vital philosophical ideas and cultural forms would have seen the light of day without the ventilating breath of Christianity. Harnack is emphatic on the point when he writes: "Christianity possessed in a more unsullied form the contents of what is meant by 'the Greek philosophy of religion' " (1908, I:315). The present-day analogy is the immense currents of cultural revitalization going on in the third world, where the overlap with the Christian impact is significant.

The Gentile church, understood as the "New Israel," is relevant to an understanding of the nature of Christian mission. The righteous servants of the Hebrew dispensation have their counterparts in "the saints" of the "New Israel." The Gentile era was therefore the expectant ferment latent in the earlier promise. Chosen to be the people of God for their age and time, Gentile Christians also entered into a covenant of faithfulness and witness before the world, pressing and being pressed to cross new frontiers. This point was appreciated with increasing clarity through the unsettling experience of translation, interpretation, and other efforts of Christian apologetics. The preponderance of Greek-speaking Christians in certain parts of the primitive church forced the apostles to embark on translation, interpretation, and exegesis.

However, translation is a highly problematic enterprise. The original is assumed to be inadequate, or defective, or inappropriate, but at any rate ineffective for the task at hand. Thus a peripheral role comes to be assigned to the original mode. In addition, translation forces a distinction between the essence of the message, and its cultural presuppositions, with the assumption that such a separation enables us to affirm the primacy of the message over its cultural underpinnings. Thus translation involves some degree of cultural alienation on the part of the translator, though the recipient culture may eventually compensate him or her with the consolation of an adopted member. This resolves the question of final accountability, for the translator must henceforth shift the ground of comprehension to the new medium. Thus it was that ancient Greek, without any claim to being the native or working language of Jesus and the close circle of apostles, became the preponderant medium of religious discourse. The original Aramaic and Hebraic languages, which formed the basis of Jesus' preaching, became a minor undercarriage, making a halting intrusion in the generally smooth progress of the new discourse. (Much later, the issue of linguistic accountability rose with some urgency in the nineteenth-century revival of Slavic mission. In that case the British and Foreign Bible Society decided to make use of the best south Slavonic linguists available, thinking it "more important to be expert in the recipient language and culture than in the original languages." [Bundy, 1985, p. 393])[2]

Thus mission as translation makes the bold, fundamental assertion that the recipient culture is the authentic destination of God's salvific promise and, as a consequence, has an honored place under "the kindness of God," with the attendant safeguards against cultural absolutism. By drawing a distinction between the message and its surrogate, mission as translation affirms the *missio Dei* as the hidden force for its work. It is the *missio Dei* that allowed translation to enlarge the boundaries of the proclamation. The kerygmatic preaching of the apostles, and certainly of Jesus, at first took the Hebrew Scriptures as the limit of salvific promise, though the fulfillment of that promise might breach that limit. But by understanding afresh the scope of that promise, the apostles felt confident about pursuing the promises of God deep in the heartland of Greek culture and Roman power.

Ultimately this gives the gospel a pluralist character without imposing on it a uniformizing destiny. Access to Jesus as Savior, Redeemer, and Judge was to be through the specificity of cultural self-understanding, and that cultural specificity is the ground of divine self-disclosure, with Jesus as the divine outpouring on the human scale. Through the locus of cultural identity the Savior and Redeemer would emerge as recognizably one of us, though that would also bring the sword of discernment into our affairs. The fullness of life that the Savior brings will place in a redeeming light the sin of human self-sufficiency.

Mission is also a catalyst for change. The specific cultural medium of access to God becomes itself the stage for serious and sustained self-examination. The enlarged scope of the "kindness of God" must always stand in stark contrast to the restrictive claims of human pretensions. The springs of Christian renewal are located in the fact that there is a gap between God's universal purpose and the sin of human self-sufficiency, and this realization leads in the biblical perspective to the conviction of ethical answerability.

Thus, although access to God is through the specificity of cultural self-understanding, that can also be escape unless a disjunction is perceived between cultural embodiment and the divine initiative. God needs to be close and specific enough to be recognizably real to us, and yet be untrammeled enough by our cultural presuppositions to be searchingly true to the divine self. God has to be righteously against us provided also God is first rightly for us. In this light mission is the safeguard against cultural immobility, for it feeds renewal by placing the specificity of cultural self-understanding in the searching presence of God. Where it is successful, mission is the vehicle for bringing about a decisive conjunction between human particularity and its normative tendencies, for the one part, and God's breakthrough in justice and mercy, for the other.

The critical function of mission is extended through explicit missionary criticism—a criticism, we must understand, that takes place always in the context of translation and interpretation. When we have rightly and properly distinguished between the desire to do mission in other cultures and the designs of cultural imperialism, we are still left with a substantial body of material in the Gospels that justifies adopting a profoundly critical stance toward culture by putting the interests of God above those of the culture. This has been true of Christianity in periods of struggle and minority existence as well as in times of favor and political respectability. There is, as eloquently stated by H. Richard Niebuhr, an inherent tension between Christ and culture. Paul tells a section of his Christian audience that through Christ they are more than conquerors (Rom. 8:37). Yet, almost in the same breath, he catalogues the ceaseless contention that he as a Christian must continually experience in his relations with worldly authorities (1 Cor. 4:9–13; 2 Cor. 4:7–12). Christians are in the world, but not of it (1 Cor. 7:29–31). The claims of God, however successfully mediated and embodied in earthly structures, must ultimately be seen to be in radical tension with them, for obedience to God overthrows other rival sovereignties that make their home in culture. Missionaries are under obligation to signal loyalty to God as fundamentally indivisible, although in practice they cannot coerce people into compliance.

It is this profound unwillingness to merge Christ and culture that stiffened the apostolic resolve, and Paul was consequently prepared to risk sounding authoritarian in order to drive the vital point home. In one place he admonishes the Gentile church about being mindful lest they share the fate of those who may have excluded themselves from the hope of the gospel. There is a touching protectiveness about such concerns, in Paul as in modern missionaries. It is a legitimate warning, and the missionary would feel its force even before new converts entertained its possibility. It is the insight of cross-cultural mission that those who embrace the new religion might be particularly vulnerable to idealistic extremism, and however missionaries may be mistrusted as spiritual overlords, they serve a living lesson. Although it is their choice to frame the caution in a language that causes no offense, they have no such choice about the essential disparity between Christ and culture. Any absolutizing force is an offense to the gospel, and a cultural tradition that arrogates to itself a deifying prerogative can expect nothing but implacable opposition from Christians. No amount of effortless acculturation can absolve the Christian from this fundamental obligation, and this gauntlet the apostles appear to have taken up.

In addressing this issue the apostle Paul brings his Jewish heritage to bear. His impatience with the Galatian Christians stems from his firsthand knowledge of the agony of those who exploited their new-found freedom in Christ to bring themselves under cultural determinism. Compelled to observe the inconsistencies of the new Greek converts of Galatia, Paul does so in the painful context of disagreements within the church about whether the Gentile barrier ought in the first place to have been breached. So he recounts with obvious regret his major differences with the Jerusalem church and the open rift with Peter and Barnabas at Antioch, a strong Gentile center (Gal. 2:1–15). In the dispute with Peter, Paul adduced for his defense arguments from his own Jewish background, developing a principle that he wished to apply to the Gentile issue. The standard by which Gentiles are judged, he contends, does not differ in kind or in scale from that applied to the natural descendants of Abraham (Gal: 3:6–9). Eventually, in fact, even the Christ-principle of redemption by faith is itself expoundable by reference to the Abrahamic ideal, thus giving the Jewish heritage an extended application beyond its constituted borders. Thus the Jewish religious culture is not repudiated as such. What was resisted was an interpretation that would exaggerate certain elements in it to the exclusion of others.

For example, certain sections of the Pharisaic party upheld the view that the law was the preexistent plan according to which the world was made, and that God was preoccupied with studying it. This led to a feeling of superiority and the belief that other nations existed on Israel's behalf. (4 Ezra 6:55–56, dated to A.D. 100, speaks of other nations as spittle. In an earlier passage [3:36], an allowance is made for individuals who may have kept the divine precepts, although that is distinguished from other nations being called.) Paul was no stranger to such claims of superiority, but he found them detrimental in discerning God's mind and purpose. Some might react to this by repudiating all forms of national identity, or at least conceiving a fundamental contradiction between culture and faith. But that was not the apostle's way. Instead Paul propounds cultural pluralism without reducing Christ to a cultural ideology: "There is neither Jew nor Greek, there is neither slave nor free, there is neither male nor female; for you are all one in Christ Jesus. And if you are Christ's, then you are Abraham's offspring, heirs according to promise" (Gal. 3:28–29).

It was Paul's achievement that while he disentangled the gospel from any exclusive cultural definition, he retained the particularity of culture as the necessary saddle for launching Christianity in the world. For instance, he faced the combined demands of Jewish particularity in seeking messianic consolation and the Greek expectation of philosophical emancipation by affirming the cross as the promise and the gift. He writes to the church at Corinth: "For the Jews demand signs and Greeks seek wisdom, but we preach Christ crucified, a stumbling block to Jews and folly to Gentiles, but to those who are called, both Jews and Greeks, Christ the power of God and the wisdom of God" (1 Cor. 1:22–24). The gospel is thus recognized by both "Jew" and "Greek" as a confirmation of their respective particularity. In Paul's mind Christ came into the world, risky as that was, not to make a composite montage of our differences but to bring our true stature into God's own picture. As we share in that divine fellowship we rise to the fullness of life whose source is God. The community of Christians is thus more than the lifeless graveyard of identical bodies. It is the richness of individual talents crossed with the empowerment of divine love. The following summary of his achievement pinpoints Paul's contribution to mission as a dynamic, cross-cultural movement out of which churches grew as a natural consequence.

> Recognizing the supreme fruits of the Spirit in faith, love, hope, and all the allied virtues, bringing out the outbursts of enthusiasm into the service of edification, subordinating the individual to the larger organism, claiming the natural conditions of social life, for all its defects and worldliness, as divine arrangements, he overcame the dangers of fanaticism and created churches which would live in the world without being of the world. But organization never became for Paul an end in itself or a means to worldly aggrandizement. "The aims of his ecclesiastical labours were unity in brotherly love and the reign of God in the heart of man, not the rule of savants or priests over laity." [Harnack, 1908, I:78.]

THE DICHOTOMY OF CHURCH AND MISSION

Two impulses, running on concurrent lines, developed quickly as a result of the impact of the preaching and ministry of Jesus and by virtue of apostolic faithfulness. One was the urge to spread the message with every available facility. The other was the desire to regulate the emerging community of believers whose religious life was lived first in the shadows of the synagogue and then in spontaneous cells of devotion scattered along the trails of the Diaspora. In the first ardor of faith, believers committed their resources to the dissemination of the message, concerned to remove any impediments in its way. The notion, to be modified later, of what Bultmann (1951–55, I:33) calls the imminent *coming* of Jesus as Messiah (as opposed to Jesus' *return* as such) created a vigilant spirit among the first Christians, and they became identified as the eschatological congregation. (It is fair to add that many scholars disagree with Bultmann on this point, arguing that, for the first disciples, "the Jesus who was to come was the Jesus who had come (Acts 1:11)" [Blunt, 1929, p. 18]). A spirit of otherworldliness gripped their imagination, and a corresponding ascetic ethic guided their earthly conduct. However, the instinct for "self-diffusion," as defined by Harnack, was stimulated by faith in the anticipated end of the age and succeeded in producing a burgeoning movement spread over many areas, bound together by ties of mutual succor and a common devotion to Jesus as Lord. The concern then grew for a rule of faith and practice in the light of the diversity of church polity, much of it in response to specific needs and experiences. A broad consensus emerged on the standard by which apostolic authority would be recognized, and this would help hold together the plural congregations thrown up by successful missionary activity.

These two impulses of the urge to mission and to regulate, though distinct, sometimes fused into a single motivation of seeking to use the rule of discipline and support in order to maintain the missionary momentum. Whatever their worldly circumstance, the first Christians felt themselves on trial for their faith and interpreted their travails as urgent proof of the approaching end. As Tertullian expressed it in his characteristically flamboyant style, Christians saw their persecution as the energizer of mission and the seal of their heavenly hope: "The oftener we are mowed down by you, the larger grow our numbers. The blood of Christians is a seed. . . . That very obstinacy which you reprobate is our instructress" (cited in Harnack, 1908, I:366).

In time, however, instruction took less dramatic form and a routine pattern came to settle on religious experience, at which point the impulse to mission, for so long the predominant urge of faith and practice, resolved itself into an organizational striving. The task was to develop the instruments of unity in the faith without inhibiting local initiative. So the children of the Spirit would be held together with the heirs to the Pax Romana.

The impulse to mission did not expire, but it took an inward turn as

Christianity settled to digest the copious extraneous materials it had imbibed from Hellenic, Roman, and Oriental sources. Indeed, this "syncretic" process conferred a concrete universal character on the religion even though a profound antipathy toward "syncretistic" compromise remained at the core of the message. The upshot was to make the church the center and focus of the message, with a decided subordinating of mission as a department of the church. This shift also had fundamental implications for the basis of Christian ethics, for the authoritative principle that had once hinged on eschatological fear now resided in the church as the divinely sanctioned order. The church became the repository of apostolic and missionary teaching, and catechetical schools were founded to inculcate its authority. Tertullian's virtue of obstinacy had now acquired a highly dogmatic though supple meaning.

In this situation the idea of mission could easily be revived to promote the capture of the culture for the church, and much of the evidence suggests that this was done. On one level of our analysis, this situation was inevitable, for cultural self-understanding is a necessary medium for the transplanting of the message. But, on another level, this stage is open to a host of difficulties.

It is easy for the momentum of successful transplanting to generate a counterpressure by thrusting up a strong institutional church, which consequently becomes more concerned with its inner life than with external outreach. Even if such a church were alert to wider opportunities, it would be inhibited by the pressure to claim the specific cultural milieu of its self-understanding as normative for faith and practice. This would not prevent the church from spreading, but the diffusionist path would now guide its expansion. Since the gospel comes alive from translation, the slowing down of this process involves a certain fossilization of the message, although in brief moments of prophetic wakefulness the reform impulse might nudge an inured church forward. In the main, however, mission would exist as diffusion.

MISSION AND THE ISSUE OF SYNCRETISM

The Jewish factor in the expansion of Christianity was important for safeguarding the monotheist core of the gospel. Christianity carried with it an irreconcilable attitude to polytheism, and owed this temper to its Judaic heritage. There is only one God, or one source of true divinity, and other deities cannot be autonomous centers of divinity without encroaching on this sacred territory. However it is approached, polytheism in the Judeo-Christian view is an unsustainable fragmentation of divine power, and when it weakens faith and trust in that power, then it deserves to be opposed. Both religions share this heritage with Islam. There is a stark, unremitting accent on the monotheist faith as the duty and demand of the religious life, the test that ultimately repudiates all other forms of dependence. Christian preaching expanded on this and, still keeping close to its Judaic kin, it held up the Christ-event as the predicate of the living God who is the subject of faith and worship.

In its development, however, Christianity parted ways with both its Judaic heritage and the Islamic application of it. For one thing, Judaism remained preeminently the concern of the people called Jews, and conversion was perceived as both a religious step and an incorporation into a racial community. For another, although Islam made submission to one God the towering call of mission, it placed this alongside the revelation of the Arabic Qur'ān, so that when the "sword of truth" was unsheathed against polytheists and unbelievers, its double blade gleamed with the pointedness of God's oneness and the inflexibility of the Arabic revelation. It was consequently always difficult to judge which blade cut the deeper, the conviction of the one God or the power of the Arab cause. However, once a conjunction was made between the conviction and the Arab cause, it was correspondingly easier to blunt the edge of any potential difficulty. To be an Arab, pure and proud, is to be a Muslim, sound and staunch. In the Arab heartland and beyond, "Arabization" came to stand for "Islamization," and cultural identity for religious status. That was the strength of Islam. As described in a rather sketchy way in chapter 7, below, the contrast with Christianity is, in this matter, quite stark.

Like Judaism and Islam, Christianity was committed to monotheism but, unlike both of them, it found translation to be the method best suited to spreading the gospel. However, translation made Christianity vulnerable to secular influences and to the threat of polytheism. The degree to which Christianity became integrated into a particular culture was a useful means of assessing the success of Christian preaching. But it was also a means of determining the level of compromise. Once an entire culture opened itself to the Christian presence it was possible for the missionary to influence and mold that culture without fear of total rejection.

This way Christianity was in turn likely to be influenced by the culture itself. Yet this risk appears to be no greater than that incurred in the Judaic or Islamic tradition. On the contrary, if, as early Christians believed, God is the universal source of life and truth, then they were obliged to pursue that conviction across cultures. This conviction also implies that no culture would be fundamentally alien to the source of life and truth, and therefore mission was an assurance of continuity with that source. But mission also represented the challenge and promise of a new beginning in faith and obedience. The apostolic proclamation actively sought a serious ethical and religious commitment, but it did this on a double front. First, it announced the completion of tendencies introduced in earlier ages. Second, it signaled a fresh point of departure in the religious and ethical life. Mission thus encouraged self-affirmation while requiring self-transformation at the same time. That was the risk and the hope, the "com-promise" and the promise.

Historians make a great deal of the view that a certain level of cultural unity was essential to the success of primitive Christianity, taking the position that had the church encountered stiff external barriers its faith would have been negatively different. I have tried to modify this argument by calling attention to the internal factors for Christian expansion. This does not deny that historical factors played a role, but it does resist the conclusion that historical circumstances also determined the content of Christian preaching.

A more serious issue, however, is whether it can really be maintained that the apostles did not come up against any major obstacles in their path. The external forces militating against Christians are obvious, including the cruel tortures of Roman authorities. Then there was the obstacle of religious and philosophical challenge, which sought to undermine the gospel from within. Christians had to be wary of the facile tolerance that placed them on the same footing as the other numerous cults in the empire. But they also had to be careful not to create too great a distance between themselves and society lest they forfeit their credibility. In the end they were gravely misunderstood and misinterpreted, and had to endure cruel loyalty tests. The Roman authorities, such as Pliny the Younger, were moved as a consequence to intervene on behalf of the harassed Christians with an appeal to due process and the fundamental rights of the individual. On the formal level, that gave Christians a much needed breathing space. But at the informal level, there was no let up to the pressure from other religious groups and the cosmopolitan citizenry with their critical philosophical outlook. To meet that challenge, Christians were forced to enter into sustained discussion and encounter. There is no doubt that in the ongoing tussle with their detractors, Christians emerged better furnished with materials and more amply endowed with new resources of expansion. But in the initial stages, much hesitation and even reluctance marked the community of believers as they stood on the frontier of the Greco-Roman world, conscious of the receding shadows of Palestine behind them and the threatening vistas of radical indigenization ahead.

At this critical juncture, the Judaic heritage again proved invaluable, and it was the apostle Paul who drew from that source ideas and rules that a later generation of Christians could use as guidance even though they might not be as conscious of the source of those materials. One important idea, drawn from rabbinic sources, was that mission was a risk in which the advocate committed his or her resources without the assurance of commensurate recompense, though one could believe that a higher reward awaited in the kingdom to be established (1 Cor. 9:20–22). It was like the sower of the parable scattering the precious seeds of the kingdom with the knowledge that some will be lost on inhospitable soil but that the chance of success elsewhere warrants taking such liberties (Matt. 13:3–8). An overcautious evangelist, anxious to preserve the purity of the message, would deem such risk-taking foolhardy in the extreme, though in that case the message might shrivel from lack of exposure. In the end, in fact, there is no reasonable alternative to such risk-taking and, for authority, Christians could go back to their Lord and Master.

MISSION, REFORM, AND CULTURAL RELATIVISM

Christians came to be familiar with three basic models of religious organization, if we may paraphrase ideas developed in another connection by Humphrey Fisher, a historian of Islam. These models were not necessarily phases that succeeded each other in a clear, differentiated fashion. Rather, they offered styles of religious organization. It may happen that one historical period may be more conducive to a particular style of religious organization than another, but it may also as often be the case that all three styles occur in one given period, with one group of believers distinguished by one type of religious organization and another group distinguished by a different kind.

The first style may be characterized as quarantine, when, from timidity, anxiety, expectation, or eschatological fear, the believers maintain a close vigilance over their life and conduct in relative seclusion from the world. All contact with outsiders is reduced to a minimum, and the disciples devote themselves to prayer, the breaking of bread, exhortation, and mutual aid. In quarantine the highest standards are maintained, new members admitted, and a common life developed in which resources and responsibilities are equally shared. There is an intensity of religious life such as could not survive intact outside the secure walls of quarantine. Believers partake of the pure message without the mediating device of interpretation or second-hand assurance. Under the security of quarantine, people adhere to a literal understanding of the Scriptures, gripped by fear and a fervent conviction that their community represented the decisive virtuous break with an unrighteous world destined to be destroyed in the imminent end (Acts 2:43–47; 1 Pet. 4:7–13; 1 Thess. 4:16–18). This style of religious organization occurs right across Christian history, from New Testament times to modern forms of Christian utopianism. If quarantine becomes permanent, then it creates extreme marginalization. In this respect, although there were elements of quarantine in the primitive church, those elements did not become predominant or permanent.

The second type is syncretist in nature, although in the transition to that stage the primitive church held onto the forms of certain teachings while substantially modifying their contents. Leaving the secure walls of quarantine behind them, the believers encountered the world of other beliefs and ideas, which insinuated themselves into the main body of Christian teaching. For example, the practice of circumcision, upheld in quarantine, is considerably modified outside quarantine until it is dropped altogether as a prerequisite of faith (Gal. 5:2–6, 11; 6:12–15). It is retained only as a metaphorical concept (Rom. 2:29; Phil. 3:2-3). Another is sacrifice. In quarantine, Christians keep themselves clear from any contact with meat offered in sacrifice. However, this rule changes drastically to allow individual freedom to determine what is best in the circumstances (1 Cor. 8; 10:23). Marriage is another. The apostles, some of whom were married, nevertheless felt compelled to promote sentiments of celibacy. However, the exigencies of life in the world force a rethinking of this position, and the ground is surrendered with the most grudging gesture (1 Cor. 7: 1-2, 7-9 revives the theme of celibacy). Slowly but unrelentingly the thick walls of quarantine begin to fall away until believers find themselves standing shoulder to shoulder with people who do not share their faith but who share the world with them. Observances that had been maintained as rituals of separation and transition gradually change to become rites of initiation and confirmation. The idea of holiness as keeping oneself separate from the world yields to that of conducting oneself responsibly in the world (Romans 12). With so many forces working to wear down the insulation of quarantine, any retreat from the world is considered inappropriate for this style of religious organization. Yet believers, if they have anything distinctive about their vocation, would also feel that the pressure to conform to the world should not be allowed to overwhelm the message either. This brings us to the third type of religious organization.

This is reform and prophetic witness. Christians are in the world but not of it. It is a delicate line, which only the most gifted, and almost certainly only the minority, might hope to draw. The majority of believers would continue to occupy the broad area of overlap with the world to pursue life mindful of bread-and-butter issues. It is toward such instances of likely compromise within the household itself that the prophetic word is directed initially. The lapses of those who ought to know better are more scandalous than those of outsiders and, furthermore, partial fulfillment of the religious obligation is more reprehensible than total ignorance. This situation would lead to increasing impatience and growing intolerance of the status quo, and those taking an adamant position are able to draw upon the ideal sources that sustain quarantine. The battle lines are then redrawn: the idea of charismatic purity that quarantine embodies is recast to produce the vision of a religious community standing in need of judgment and salvation. The destiny of the world is consequently made to depend on the witness of the redeemed community of believers. Reform in itself does not reject the world, nor does it reject human instrumentality in setting the world aright. It distinguishes between the earthly kingdom and its heavenly counterpart and carries this distinction further into the matter of human means and the divine end for which they might be employed but not exchanged.

The manner in which the reform impulse arises is extremely important for understanding its function in the religious community. Rather than being an abstract code imposed from a predetermined vantage point, reform grows out of the experience of a worshiping community with a profound stake in the world. The weaknesses and inadequacies of this community, now sharpened and enlarged under the scrutiny of God's "plan of salvation," represent the world in microcosm. Thus it is that when Paul reflects on the life and conduct of the believers at Corinth, with excesses at worship, retaliatory suits in the law courts, intolerance in doctrine and extremism in morals, he challenges the church to say what distinguishes it from the world. In bringing the prophetic word to bear on the church, the apostle has also diagnosed the ills of the world, suggesting that Christian faithfulness is a prescription for the health of the wider society. An acute source of weakness in the church was rivalry among the believers themselves, the kind of competitiveness that perpetuates worldly inadequacies, failing completely to uphold the standard of God's *qualitative* action toward us and among us (1 Cor. 1:10–16; 3:4–7, 21–22; 4:6–7, 15–16). This situation, although inevitable from the spontaneous and at times haphazard nature of Christian expansion, should not, in the apostle's view, be allowed to harden itself into an "empirical imperative": that what *is,* is what *ought* to be.

The reform impulse was strengthened, in the first place, by the assertion of apostolic authority, chiefly that of Paul, and second, by the availability of preaching and teaching materials, which were subsequently gathered into a scriptural canon. The apostles began to call the believers back to the faith, with detailed instructions on how to receive sinners and backsliders back into fellowship. Sanctions were announced and threatened against persistent offenders. The apostles warned against persevering in sin, holding up the fellowship as the place where offenders found rehabilitation, reassurance, and renewal. In contrast, the world was held up as the source of false absolutes and false pretenses. Christians were encouraged to signal their abhorrence of it by following a lifestyle of self-control, moderation, endurance, forgiveness, and all the other virtues of the gospel.

Essentially the reforms and the prophetic challenge turned to the spiritual side of faith. Christians were to set examples of civic duty and political obligation, but political or military instruments were not the means for achieving Christian renewal. The means, however exalted, could not substitute for the end; nor could the magistrate, especially if that person upholds righteousness, legislate for the Creator. The church militant is the church vigilant, and is as such the sign of the triumphant promise of God's reign. Prophetic action in history is the active participation of believers in the sign and promise of God rather than surrender to the world as the ultimate destiny. Religious jihad has no role in the gospel in either the positive sense of pressing forward or the negative sense of undoing the harm done through uncritical syncretism. The apostles used combative language, but always in the terms of spiritual warfare and athletic readiness. The "sword of truth" for them was carried in spiritual combat, and was as often drawn against themselves as against unbelievers.

It is, of course, true that Christians endured terrible physical privations, which someone like Tertullian took great delight in reporting. Yet, however eagerly Christians might have sought martyrdom and however much they might have believed that violence had divine purpose, they have refrained from taking up arms themselves to assist God to achieve the divine purpose. All that was to change later, but in the fundamental sources of Christian faith and conviction, there is not a scrap of evidence to support armed militancy as the basis of faithfulness to the glorified and risen Lord.

In the end the reform impulse became a permanent feature of the Christian enterprise. Once the believers turned their backs on quarantine as an irretrievable stage that might recur in the millennial age but not until then, they widened their repertoire to take in other forms of apologetics. A flexible scale was devised to allow Christians to act meaningfully in the world without losing their identity. The missionary expansion of the faith had brought believers to the permanent threshold of plural encounter, and anyone who was seriously committed would now have to face up to the task of translating the gospel across cultures. Mission embodied this prophetic spirit and as such became the end and burden of the church.

In one sense the issue of cross-cultural interpretation had arisen with the very career of Jesus, for the word Jesus brought was the familiar message of the prophets (Lk. 4:17–21) with which he expounded his work. He assured his listeners that he had not come to abolish but to complete the law and the prophets, as a later tradition, recorded in Matthew 5:17, makes explicit. His work was not a work of building from scratch but of reinterpreting old and familiar teachings. Consequently the Judaic heritage was an essential force in the rise of Christianity. David Daube has documented with a wealth of detail the close parallel between the New Testament and rabbinic Judaism, in his influential book of that title (Daube, 1956). Christianity was born in a cross-cultural milieu, with translation as its birthmark.

In commenting on the multiple cultural forms that Christianity rapidly took in the course of its progress, Harnack returned to the Judaic theme, and, although he conceives a "defective" break at the Christian turning with Judaism, he admits enough of a debt to indicate a strong element of continuity:

> Christianity may be just as truly called a Hellenic religion as an Oriental, a native religion as a foreign. From the very outset it had been syncretistic upon pagan soil; it made its appearance, not as a gospel pure and simple, but equipped with all that Judaism had already acquired during the course of its long history, and entering forthwith upon nearly every task in which Judaism was defective. [Harnack, 1908, I:314.]

The syncretist motif persisted through the extraordinary range of Christian appeal. In the first place, diverse nationalities were touched by

Christian preaching: Parthians, Medes, Elamites, Greeks, and barbarians could all be found in the community of believers and sympathizers. In the second place, Christian religious practice showed an enormous appetite for absorbing materials from other religious traditions, and although this indicated success in penetrating the wider society, it nevertheless posed a threat of uncritical syncretism. Eventually the threat was met with a return to the central place that Jesus Christ occupied in apostolic teaching. But the unreformed picture of Christian religious practice was bewildering in the extreme. The following is Harnack's assessment:

> Powerful and vigorous, assured of her own distinctive character, and secure from any risk of being dissolved into contemporary religions, [the church] believed herself able now to deal more generously and complaisantly with men. . . . Saints and intercessors, who were thus semi-gods, poured into the church. Local cults and holy places were instituted. The different provinces of life were distributed afresh among guardian spirits. The old gods returned; only their masks were new. Annual festivals were noisily celebrated. Amulets and charms, relics and bones of the saints, were cherished eagerly. And the very religion which erstwhile in its strictly scriptural temper had prohibited and resisted any tendency towards materialism, now took material shape in every one of its relationships. It had mortified the world and nature. But now it proceeded to revive them, not of course in their entirety, but still in certain sections and details, and . . . in phases that were dead and repulsive. Miracles in the churches became more numerous, more external, and more coarse. Whatever fables the apocryphal Acts of the Apostles had narrated, were dragged into contemporary life and predicated of the living present. [Harnack, 1908, I:315–17.]

This situation is the logical opposite of quarantine, which the middle term of reform seeks to bridge. Although Christianity was syncretistic in finding multiple cultural systems congenial to its message, it was not a parody of any one system. Harnack sums up the risk and the hope of the new universal world of syncretism to which the missionary proclamation had brought the church. Christianity, he says, showed itself to be syncretistic. But, he continues:

> . . . it revealed to the world a special kind of syncretism, namely the syncretism of a universal religion. . . . unconsciously, it had learned and borrowed from many quarters; indeed it would be impossible to imagine it existing amid all the wealth and vigor of these religions, had it not drawn pith and flavour even from them. These religions fertilized the ground for it, and the new grain and seed which fell upon that soil sent down its roots and grew to be a mighty tree. Here is a

religion which embraces everything. And yet it can always be expressed with absolute simplicity: one name, the name of Jesus Christ, still sums up everything. [Harnack, 1908, I:312.]

Christianity entered the multiple world of cross-cultural encounter with an open mind and a firm faith. The risk that it took with the first step it exploited with the second. As a consequence the Greco-Roman world, which left its mark on the faith, was itself profoundly molded from within. The central pillars of the Aristotelian and Platonic systems concerning the demonstrability of knowledge were absorbed and reconstituted. In that world, too, the reform impulse, charged with faith in one God, welled up to exceed the meager syllogistic trickle of the elite. R. G. Collingwood, a modern philosopher, comes to grips with this issue when he writes:

And all the best Greco-Roman thought devoted its powers to elaborating and manipulating this beautiful instrument of precision, the Aristotelian syllogism. Into a world so occupied, Christianity, however truly foreshadowed and prepared by many tendencies of the Greco-Roman mind, came as a destructive and revolutionary force. Instead of a syllogistic logic, it preached faith as the organ of knowledge; instead of a natural world, it set up, as the sole object of that knowledge, God. Human thought, hitherto dissipated in a syllogistic network over the infinite field of natural fact, was now to be focussed upon a single point, and in that concentration to substitute immediate conviction for reasoned argument. Thus the Platonic position was reversed. Plato had considered faith an inferior kind of knowledge, because it could not, when challenged, argue in its own defense. Christianity saw in the same fact a ground of its superiority. . . . It was because the object of faith is God; and God, being infinite, has no relation to anything outside himself by which he can be indirectly known. . . . There is no resemblance between God and a Euclidean axiom; and the intellectual intuition that grasps the axiom cannot grasp God. Yet the whole of Christianity depends for its value on the assurance that God is revealed in us; and that implies on our part some faculty capable of accepting the revelation. That is the primitive Christian conception of faith.

Christianity, more Aristotelian than Aristotle, recognized that two faculties whose objects were so widely different must themselves widely differ: the faith by which we apprehend the infinite and wholly spiritual nature of God must be utterly unlike the perception by which we apprehend the particular finite things in the world of sense. . . . In exalting faith above reason, therefore, Christianity was not in any sense undoing the work of Greek thought, but rather building upon it. . . . What Christianity added to Greek thought was the idea of a yet higher kind of knowledge, a knowledge in which we apprehend not the finite but the infinite, not nature but spirit, not the world but God. [Collingwood, 1927–28, pp. 4–5.]

In the earlier stage of expounding the message against the specifically Judaic background of Palestine, the apostles achieved a breakthrough by upholding faith in one God. Moved by the life and ministry of Jesus, they came to reason that radical faith in one God implied a corresponding radical break from cultural exclusivism and as a consequence the mission of the church was established to pursue the Spirit's promptings across all inherited barriers. This had a purifying impact on culture by stripping it of any absolutizing tendency, and by encouraging a pluralist response. The reform impulse acted to relativize culture under the scheme of God's own absolute dispensation and to free God as the universal object — and subject — of faith. The Jewish-Gentile frontier became a paradigm not only of God's universal reality, though that was crucial, but also of the reform impulse, which cleansed syncretism without allowing it to lapse into the predestined utopia of quarantine. There was now not one cultural center but a multiple frontier across which God was the center of gravity. No one culture was any longer the exclusive standard of the truth of God, a position that challenged the Greco-Roman world as relentlessly as it had done the Judaic world. In his observations on the birth of a new historiography, R. G. Collingwood in a different work alludes to this issue of culture as divine norm:

For the Christian, all men are equal in the sight of God: there is no chosen people, no privileged race or class, no one community whose fortunes are more important than those of another. All persons and all people are involved in the working out of God's purpose, and therefore the historical process is everywhere and always of the same kind, and every part of it is a part of the same whole. The Christian cannot be content with Roman history or Jewish history or any other partial and particularistic history: he demands a history of the world, a universal history whose theme shall be the general development of God's purpose for human life. The infusion of Christian ideas overcomes not only the characteristic humanism and the substantialism of Greco-Roman history, but also its particularism . . . Greco-Roman ecumenical history is not universal history in this sense, because it has a particularistic centre of gravity. Greece or Rome is the centre round which it revolves. Christian universal history has undergone a Copernican revolution, whereby the very idea of such a centre of gravity is destroyed. [Collingwood, 1946, pp. 49–50.]

Particularism, or the ideology of cultural idealism, is a serious matter, which the spirit of reform must inescapably confront. Particularism makes a prescriptive ideal of syncretistic achievement, erecting it as the permanent and absolute standard of the truth. Thus particularism lays false claims to the values that even the state of quarantine had failed to secure. Consequently, it promotes the spirit of false absolutism, which Christians are called upon to reject.

Quarantine, syncretism, and reform must not be understood in terms of rigid separation, for there is an inevitable overlap between them. It would, in fact, be better to think of them not as stages but, as has been stressed here, as types and styles of religious organization and understanding, all existing — sometimes — together, though in varying degrees of sharpness. They might be a function of place and circumstance rather than of the lapse of time. It would be too artificial to set up a watertight compartment between them, for it is possible to move back and forth among all three types. However, as a schematic representation the model is designed to depict major rhythms in the process of the expansion and assimilation of Christianity. In spite of obvious overlaps and subtle variations, the tripartite model is a useful one in enabling us to distinguish among forms of religious life and action among the early Christians. Furthermore, the model enables us to place the impulse of reform in some meaningful context as a bridge between cultural *particularity* — not particularism — and the primacy of the reign of God. Both quarantine and accommodation in fact threaten religious integrity: the one by cutting us off from the world, and the other by surrendering to it. Reform, on the other hand, points to God's action at the stage where the message intersects the world of culture, and mission is the promise and engagement with that action.

SUMMARY AND CONCLUSION

Several points may be made concerning the theme of this chapter. First, primitive Christians inherited in Judaism the law and the synagogue as the exclusive standards of religious truth. Second, from their understanding of the life and work of Jesus Christ, they came to a fresh view about God's impartial action in all cultures. The "many tongues" of Pentecost affirmed God's acceptance of all cultures within the scheme of salvation, reinforcing the position that Jews and Gentiles were equal before God. Third, the Gentile breakthrough became the paradigm for the church's missionary expansion. So far as their view of Jesus is concerned, the disciples went on to see him as the resurrected Lord and Savior, surrendering the titles "Rabbi" and "Messiah" to the terms of the Easter experience. Fourth, from that position the believers turned to the world to "make disciples of all nations," beginning in Jerusalem and going on to Antioch, Ephesus, Corinth, Smyrna, Athens, Rome, and beyond.

The encounter of the first Christians with Judaism was a positive force. That encounter made Jewish particularity a safeguard against monotheist unfaithfulness, with the Jewish Diaspora acting as a pathfinder for the young church. However, Christians were vulnerable to foreign religious influences, resulting in their absorbing (and being absorbed in) powerful prevailing intellectual and cultural elements. Such was the case with gnosticism. The primitive Christians found themselves at risk in embracing so wholeheartedly the dominant cultural modes of the age. Mission appears to have been proceeding as cultural diffusion rather than as prophetic proclamation. The irony is plain. If new converts were required to pass the cultural test of Hellenic achievement, then what distinguished that from the test that the Jerusalem church, for its part, applied to Gentile converts?

Paul entered the scene to answer decisively that question. His presence in the church marked a turning point. Paul formulated pluralism as the necessary outworking of the religion he believed Jesus preached. That pluralism was rooted for Paul in the Gentile breakthrough, which in turn justified cross-cultural tolerance in Christian mission. One idea in Paul's thought is that God does not absolutize any one culture, whatever the esteem in which God holds culture. The second is that all cultures have cast upon them the breath of God's favor, thus cleansing them of all stigma of inferiority and untouchability. These two ideas constitute what we may regard as the incipient radical pluralism of Pauline thought. When he stressed faith over against works, Paul was intending to enunciate the inclusive principle of God's right and freedom to choose us without regard to our cultural trophies. Faith, as the absolute gift of a loving, gracious God, is the relativizing leaven in culture. Western psychology and its theological variants have unjustifiably subjectivized the issue, pitting inward assurance against social engagement. In fact, Paul desired above all to safeguard the cultural particularity of Jew as Jew and Gentile as Gentile, though challenging both Jews and Gentiles to find in Jesus Christ their true affirmation.

Paul's legacy to the church includes this exacting vigilance over the true nature of culture. Christian life is indelibly marked with the stamp of culture, and faithful stewardship includes uttering the prophetic word in culture, and sometimes even against it. Paul was a cultural iconoclast in his defiance of the absolutist tendencies in culture, but he was not a cultural cynic, for in his view God's purposes are mediated through particular cultural streams.

The mission of the church applied this insight by recognizing all cultures, and the languages in which they are embodied, as lawful in God's eyes, making it possible to render God's word into other languages. Even if in practice Christians wished to stop the translation process, claiming their form of it as final and exclusive, they have not been able to suppress it for all time. It is this phenomenon that the concept of translatability tries to represent. In acknowledging that Christianity has fostered "ethnic identity" in its spread across the world, we also recognize the critical judgment that Christians may exercise on matters of ethnic exclusiveness. The death of many Christian communities can be traced to that exclusiveness.

Christian cultural attitudes may be defined in three broad categories.

First is quarantine, which is the self-sufficient attitude nurtured in isolation, sometimes even in defiance of the world. Second is accommodation, wherein attitudes of compromise predominate over those of defiance. Third is prophetic reform, in which a critical selectiveness determines the attitude toward the world. Translatability ensures that the challenge at the heart of the Christian enterprise is, even in setback, kept alive in all cultural contexts, though prophetic reform may exploit it best. It is for this reason that the triumphant Hellenized church itself came to face an irresistible challenge.

NOTES

1. I owe these and other thoughts on this theme to Helmut Koester of Harvard University and to Dieter Georgi of the University of Frankfurt, in personal communications.

2. See chapter 2, below, for discussion of the Slavonic mission.

SELECT BIBLIOGRAPHY

Barclay, William. 1958. *The Mind of St. Paul.* New York: Harper and Brothers.

Barraclough, Geoffrey. 1968. *The Medieval Papacy.* New York: W. W. Norton; repr. 1979.

Beker, J. Christian. 1982. *Paul the Apostle: The Triumph of God in Life and Thought.* Philadelphia: Fortress.

Black, Matthew. 1970. "The Biblical Languages." P. R. Ackroyd and C. F. Evans, eds., *The Cambridge History of the Bible,* 3 vols; vol. 1, repr. 1988.

Blunt, A. W. F. 1929. *The Gospel according to St. Mark.* Clarendon Bible Commentaries series. Oxford: Clarendon Press; repr. 1957.

Brown, Raymond E. 1979. *The Community of the Beloved Disciple: The Life, Loves and Hates of an Individual Church in New Testament Times.* New York: Paulist Press.

Bultmann, Rudolf. 1951–55. *The Theology of the New Testament.* 2 vols. New York: Charles Scribner's Sons.

Bundy, David D. 1985. "Bible Translation in Cross-cultural Mission." Review of Peter Kuzmic, *Analecta Croatica Christiana,* 17, Zagreb, 1983, in *International Review of Mission* 74, no. 295, pp. 392–94.

Cadoux, C. J. 1916. "St. Paul's Conception of the State." *The Expositor* 12.

Cerfaux, L. 1959. *Christ in the Theology of St. Paul,* 2nd ed. New York: Herder and Herder. Eng. trans. of 1951 Fr. ed.

Collingwood, R. G. 1927–28. "Reason Is Faith Cultivating Itself." *Hibbert Journal* 26, no. 1.

_____. 1946. *The Idea of History.* London: Oxford University Press; repr. 1961.

_____. 1972. *An Essay on Metaphysics.* Lanham, Md.: University Press of America; repr. 1984.

Cumont, Franz. 1956. *Oriental Religions in Roman Paganism.* New York: Dover Books; first published 1911.

Daube, David. 1956. *The New Testament and Rabbinic Judaism.* London: Athlone Press.

Deissmann, Adolf. 1929. *The New Testament in the Light of Modern Research: The Haskell Lectures, 1929.* New York: Doubleday.

Dodd, C. H. 1953. *The Interpretation of the Fourth Gospel.* Cambridge, England: Cambridge University Press; repr. 1965.

———. 1958. *The Epistle of Paul to the Romans.* London: Hodder & Stoughton.

———. 1964. *The Meaning of Paul for Today.* London: Fontana Books.

"Ebionism." 1981. In James Hastings, ed., *Encyclopaedia of Religion and Ethics,* vol. 5. New York: Charles Scribner's Sons.

Eusebius. 1984. *The History of the Church.* Harmondsworth, England: Penguin.

Ferguson, John. 1970. *The Religions of the Roman Empire.* London: Thames and Hudson; repr. 1982.

Frend, W. H. C. 1984. *The Rise of Christianity.* Philadelphia: Fortress Press.

Georgi, Dieter. 1986. *The Opponents of Paul in Second Corinthians.* Philadelphia: Fortress Press.

Gibbon, Edward. n.d. *The Decline and Fall of the Roman Empire,* 3 vols. New York: Modern Library.

Harnack, Adolf von. 1908. *The Mission and Expansion of Christianity in the First Three Centuries,* 2 vols. New York: Putnam.

Jonas, Hans. 1963. *The Gnostic Religion: The Message of the Alien God and the Beginnings of Christianity.* 2nd ed. Boston: Beacon Press.

Koester, Helmut. 1982. *Introduction to the New Testament,* 2 vols. Philadelphia: Fortress Press.

Kuzmic, Peter. 1983. *Analecta Croatica Christiana,* 17, Zagreb.

Meier, John P. 1986, "Jesus among the Historians." *New York Times Book Review.* December 21.

Moffatt, James. 1918. *Introduction to the Literature of the New Testament.* 3rd ed. Edinburgh: T. & T. Clark: repr. 1981.

Pagels, Elaine H. 1973. *The Johannine Gospel in Gnostic Exegesis: Heracleon's Commentary on John.* Nashville: Abingdon Press.

Pannenberg, W., ed. 1969. *Revelation as History.* New York: Macmillan.

Pelikan, Jaroslav. 1971. *The Emergence of the Catholic Church (100–600).* Chicago: University of Chicago Press.

Philo. See Winston, David.

Robinson, Ronald; John Gallagher; and Alice Denny. 1961. *Africa and the Victorians.* New York: St. Martin's Press.

Sanders, E. P. 1985. *Jesus and Judaism.* Philadelphia: Fortress Press.

Smith, Margaret. 1976. *The Way of the Mystics.* London: Sheldon Press.

Winston, David, trans, and ed. 1981. *Philo of Alexandria.* Classics of Western Spirituality series. New York: Paulist Press.

2

Mission and the Cultural Assimilation of Christianity: The Hellenistic Factor

Orthodoxy was not yet clearly marked off from heresy: it was easy to slide from one to the other, as Tatian passed from orthodoxy to Valentinianism, and Tertullian to Montanism. If Celsus sometimes confused Christianity with Gnosticism, as Origen alleges, it is probable that his confusion was shared by a good many contemporary Christians. . . . For the people of the Empire it was a time of increasing insecurity and misery; for the Church it was a time of relative freedom from persecution, of steady numerical growth, and above all of swift intellectual advance. Clement of Alexandria perceived that if Christianity was to be more than a religion for the uneducated it must come to terms with Greek philosophy and Greek science; simple-minded Christians must no longer "fear philosophy as children fear a scarecrow." [Dodds, 1970, pp. 104, 106.]

Christianity is remarkable for the relative ease with which it enters living cultures. In becoming translatable it renders itself compatible with all cultures. It may be welcomed or resisted in its Western garb, but it is not itself uncongenial in other garb. Christianity broke free from its absolutized Judaic frame and, through a radical pluralism, adopted the Hellenic culture to the point of near absolutization. By looking at the expansion of mission beyond Rome and Byzantium, we can see how this risk of absolutization was confronted.

The case made in the previous chapter is here elaborated, to wit, that the safeguard to cultural idolatry is the radical pluralism that translatability fosters, thus pressing the relevant cultures toward pluralism and ethical accountability. A subsidiary issue is the status, whether explicit or implied, that translatability confers on pluralism. It needs to be observed that

Christians were not altogether agreed on the merits of pluralism, but our concern now is to point to it as the direct and inevitable offshoot of translatability. That it was an issue within the church at all suggests it belonged with the overall enterprise of Christianity, part of that legacy that Judaization, Hellenization, Westernization, and other transformations represent.

THE FUNCTION OF TRANSLATION

Translatability is the source of the success of Christianity across cultures. The religion is the willing adoption of any culture that would receive it, equally at home in all languages and cultures, and among all races and conditions of people. But translatability is also the source of much else that is less assuring. The enormous variety of the religion is bewildering enough, and a source of acute dismay for the rule-makers. Equally serious is the possible cultural emasculation of the religion into a captive faith, professed by cultural zealots and refused only at the peril of being declared a traitor. The dilemma seems inescapable, but it is not crippling. The very pluralism that the religion fosters is also the safeguard against monolithic tyranny.

In its most creative phases, Christianity has been a transcultural phenomenon, and indeed its doctrinal system remained plausible at all because of the rich variety of cultures that sustained the church. Yet this is not the same as saying that pluralism received positive support by the promoters of doctrine who were in fact inclined to wage war against vernacular cultures. What can be said with confidence, even if it has not been said with consistency, is that the expansion of Christianity had a direct effect on the emergence of renewal movements at the local level. That historical theme, not its hostile treatment, is what we shall explore in some detail.

Such an approach has two immediate consequences for our understanding of mission. First, Christian expansion was not at the expense of the authentic values of culture. Those cultural features that were already weakening, either because of a lack of necessary stimulus or from natural exhaustion, received the coup de grace. Other elements capable of combining with the tide of Christian advance acquired a renewed strength. Second, cross-cultural experience helped to check the tendency toward the divinization of one cultural stream by promoting all cultures as essentially equal in the scale of divine providence. That is what Harnack referred to as the new "philosophy of religion." No people, whatever their proximity or lack thereof to the sources of scriptural knowledge, can be denied a place in the life of God through Jesus Christ, for the conscience was capable of reflecting the light of God (Rom. 2:14–15). It was an insight emanating from faith in Christ and was at once optimistic and challenging, evocative of both "the kindness of God" and God's severity.

A religion that translates so naturally into the terms of culture would accordingly be at risk when faced with a powerful current, and Christianity in the Roman empire was susceptible precisely to that fate. At an advanced stage of the assimilation, the religion was defended more as a "Roman" phenomenon than as the Way of Jesus. In much of the early missionary literature the reader will be struck by the lack of local detail and color and by an excessive interest in dogmatic questions. This was particularly the case in places that had come under Roman imperial influence. In such places Christianity came into the ascendancy, fostering the corresponding ascendancy of Latin in the West and Greek in the East. As has been rightly remarked, "The effect of the church's use of the official languages of the empire was to ensure the survival of these long after the empire itself was only a memory" (Frend, 1984, p. 560).

The church thus provided the impetus behind the standardization of ecclesiastical structure and the use of a common liturgy, and together these acted to suppress the vernacular in many places. Yet the comparative thinness of local details was not because the lives of believers were untouched by their culture, but because the upholders of doctrine chose to ignore or deprecate it. By contrast, modern missionaries were more forthcoming, though not necessarily more enlightened, on the subject.

Yet, in spite of the centralizing vortex of Latin Christendom, some significant vernacular gains could be attributed to the stimulus of Christian contact and activity. Christopher Dawson, for example, in his widely acclaimed book *Religion and the Rise of Western Culture,* calls attention to the vernacular impact of the religion, an impact that was profound even though we are likely to overlook it, carried as we are by the imposing claims for the normative standard of Latin Christianity. He writes:

> With the fall of Anglo-Saxon culture [following the Norman invasion of 1066], the Scandinavian world became the great representative of vernacular culture in Northern Europe. And it was, above all, in Iceland that the scholars of the twelfth and thirteenth centuries took up the tradition of King Alfred and founded the great school of vernacular historiography and archeology to which we owe so much of our knowledge of the past. We are apt to regard medieval culture as intolerant of everything that lay outside the tradition of Latin Christendom. But we must not forget that the Northern Sagas are as much the creation of medieval Christendom as the *chansons de geste* and that it is to the priests and schools of Christian Iceland that we are indebted for the preservation of the rich tradition of Northern mythology and poetry and saga. [Dawson, 1950, p. 115.]

Christianity appears to stimulate the vernacular. It would also appear that in its formal, organized character, the religion encourages uniformity that conflicts with the vernacular. It is a safe prediction that the success of Christianity will ultimately come to depend securely on its vernacular roots, and that bureaucratic centralization will come to require some form of cultural absolutization. It may be this phenomenon that T. S. Eliot has in mind when he refers to religious specialization having its foundation in the tension between sacred and secular, between church and state, and ultimately in the issue of conflict and alienation (Eliot, 1968, pp. 141ff.).

I see translation as a fundamental concession to the vernacular, and an inevitable weakening of the forces of uniformity and centralization. Furthermore, I see translation as introducing a dynamic and pluralist factor into questions of the essence of the religion. Thus if we ask the question about the essence of Christianity, whatever the final answer, we would be forced to reckon with what the fresh medium reveals to us in feedback. It may thus happen that our own earlier understanding of the message will be challenged and even overturned by the force of the new experience. Translation would consequently help to bring us to new ways of viewing the world, commencing a process of revitalization that reaches into both the personal and the cultural spheres. This locates the message in the specific and particular encounter with cultural self-understanding, although it is important to stress that the encounter still leaves culture subject to God's law. The essential condition of faith, then, becomes the need for God's revelation in Jesus Christ to be grounded in the life and experience of the believer, wherever that happens to be. As the book of Proverbs puts it, "The spirit of man is the candle of the Lord" (20:27), illuminating the place of habitation as God's own.

The problematic relation of Christianity to culture hinges on the necessity for the message to assume the specific terms of its context and the equal necessity for it to be opposed to the normative idealization that leads to particularism. Christianity is parallel to culture, but it is not completely proportionate to it. The religion is not culture, but it is not other than culture.

Viewed in this way, the gospel is potentially capable of transcending the cultural inhibitions of the translator and taking root in fresh soil, a piece of transplanting that will in time come to challenge the presuppositions of the translator. This is a critical position, which Christians reached by being plunged willy-nilly into the world of translation. Any sensitive translator will be awakened to the realization that a certain judgment is being reserved for what had until then been taken for granted. New paradigms and vastly different presuppositions must now replace earlier symbols and the certainties they enshrined. That can be unsettling in the extreme, and only a supremely saintly person would not invoke economic or political sanctions where this was possible to try to offset the loss of power entailed in the shift.

Yet however strongly one might wish to resist the consequences of translation, little can be done to stop those repercussions from spreading. When one translates, it is like pulling the trigger of a loaded gun: the translator cannot recall the hurtling bullet. Translation thus activates a process that might supersede the original intention of the translator. Mainly for this reason we distinguish between the motive of mission and the consequences, between the "trigger," so to speak, and the "bullet." We should distinguish between missionary *intentions,* and their complex combination of cultural, political, and economic considerations, on the one hand, and, on the other, missionary *methods* in the development and employment of the vernacular. It would be wrong to set up too rigid a division between these two factors, yet a distinction, however contiguous, there must be in order to make for greater clarity in the material.

When we consider the transformation that took place in the world of Hellenism, we shall see that, as Christianity penetrated into the culture, it succeeded in establishing Hellenistic cultural paradigms into a condition of its own identity. We need to explore in some detail the philosophical and religious basis of this transformation, and suggest how it contributed to the revitalization of the Hellenistic world while extending the range and influence of Christians.

THE STAGE OF TRANSITION

The great turning point for Christians in the period under review was undoubtedly the edict of toleration extended to the religion in the fourth century by Constantine, a step that changed the church from being a hard-pressed and disadvantaged society to becoming a privileged part of the empire. Yet scholars are agreed that had Constantine not come on the scene, someone else, like him, would have come along to do just that. A simple view of the matter might lead us to bemoan the Constantinian era of the church, convinced that Christianity then lost its innocence and sinned forever thereafter, like Israel after the establishment of the monarchy. Yet the enlightened children of the empire perceived the religion as the pole of the new vitality that eluded them elsewhere. The faith and endurance of the believers testified to a spirit of loyalty that was the envy of secular powers. And yet when those secular powers looked to the church they saw a community of disparate social classes, who, in spite of the differences in their outward circumstances, were welded together by an enviable bond of trust, caring, and firmness of purpose. As one writer remarked, Christianity

> made no social distinctions; it accepted the manual worker, the slave, the outcast, the ex-criminal. . . . above all, it did not, like Neoplatonism, demand education. . . . Its members were bound together not only by common rites but by a common way of life and . . . by common danger. . . . The Church provided the essentials of social security: it cared for widows and orphans, the old, the unemployed, and the disabled; it provided a burial fund for the poor and a nursing service in time of plague. . . . Christians were in a more than formal sense "members one of another." [Dodds, 1970, pp. 134, 136, 137–38.]

There has been discussion about the general thesis of Dodds, some critical questions being raised about whether the third century was in dark crisis with its ominous shadow cast over the civilized world. Although this debate is relevant to the issue, considered in this chapter, of whether or not Christianity succeeds only in situations of cultural collapse, it does not concern the accuracy of the facts of this book.[1]

Something of extraordinary significance was happening right on the authorities' own doorstep. For example, Galen (ca. 130–200), the great Greek physician, observed that Christians possessed three of the four cardinal virtues: they demonstrated courage, self-control, and justice, lacking only the virtue of intellectual capacity (Dodds, 1970, p. 121). The dramatic circumstances in which Constantine, following a startling vision, turned to the church suggests that the new religion had acquired resilience and was a force to be reckoned with. The emperor's "conversion," if it was that, was thus the climax of the growing impact of Christian presence. We may note, however, that it is still an intriguing question whether the emperor had or had not transposed the Christian cross into a symbol of the pagan world he wished to combat.[2]

At any rate, conscientious rulers, after they had done with the ineffectual persecution of the church, relented and pursued the path of conciliation and reason. In the end a conscience-striken empire was brought to its knees, and the detractors became the consecrators. The faith that was once despised now gave heart and solace to the world. The church was transformed from a community wracked by fear and suspicion into a body destined for the world. Christian endurance had paid off, but the sequel might not galvanize to the same extent as the struggle for survival. Was there any rousing virtue in official privilege?

The transition to political respectability was indeed fraught with innumerable temptations. Having come upon power and influence, the church might succumb and face a different kind of struggle, less dramatic and less rousing, perhaps, but no less important. The challenge was how not to allow itself to be turned into the instrumental ends of politics. While embracing the empire, would the church be sufficiently free to pursue its own interests?

From a metropolitan center like Rome or Constantinople, the spectacle of the religion affording justification for state and society might be appealing, but it contained the seeds of conflict between church and state. Richly endowed prelates, receiving the protection of the state, might be required to sanction action that could conflict with the teachings of the church. Christian unease with such an arrangement would be understandable. By the same token the organized state, faced with the analogous organized strength of the church, could not afford to ignore it, and from this dilemma arises the tension. Political intervention was one side of the same coin, of which the other was the successful spread and appeal of the church (see Tierney, 1980).

In the account that now follows, we shall develop the specific nature of this spread by first pinpointing the intellectual basis of Christian expansion before turning to the language issue. The overriding consideration will be the close interplay between the successful planting of the church and the revitalization of culture, with some hints at later developments.

THE ROMAN AND HELLENISTIC PHASE: A SYNOPSIS

From a world so impoverished intellectually, so insecure materially, so filled with fear and hatred as the world of the third century, any path that promised escape must have attracted serious minds. Many besides Plotinus must have given a new meaning to the words of Agamemnon in Homer, "Let us flee to our own country." That advice might stand as a motto for the whole period. The entire culture, pagan as well as Christian, was moving into a phase in which religion was to be co-extensive with life, and the quest for God was to cast its shadow over all other human activities. [Dodds, 1970, pp. 100–101.]

Christianity expanded with extraordinary success in the post-Apostolic period, a time coinciding with the epoch following the death of Emperor Marcus Aurelius. The numerical expansion continued, with important demographic shifts in the ranks of believers. Yet in terms of the earlier mode of Christian expansion, there was no major new initiative. The religion continued to move along the ground made ready and accessible by the forces of Hellenistic influence. Christians continued to call to repentance and faith, concerned with maintaining observances and other acts of devotion that distinguished them from their origin. They were encouraged when God added to their number, but they were unperturbed by the view of themselves as a minority. In the realm where it mattered most, they were conquerors and the victory was theirs. The statistical measures applied to compute the worth of faith were introduced at a much later age, to be erected into an all-consuming issue in our own time. But at that time, whether one person turned to the Way of Jesus or whether whole multitudes were convicted, the message of repentance, faith, and forgiveness remained the same: compelling, urgent, decisive, and without the coercive threat implicit in statistical rivalry. In the centuries following the Apostolic age, an important shift occurred, a shift that, though in apparent continuity with the past, nevertheless marked a new beginning for the faith insofar as its internal life was concerned.

In the Apostolic age and the decades of the immediate era following that, Christians were an afflicted group who survived through dogged heroism rather than by accommodation or surrender. When they thought about it in the private chamber of their hearts, the leading detractors were moved by the courage of Christians in face of death and torture (Dodds, 1970, p. 132). Persecution had turned the faith into a *religio pressa* and Christians into conspicuous heroes. However, as the religion spread and Christianity became a familiar presence as a *religio licita,* with certain guarantees and privileges, persecution abated and toleration soi-disant ensued. That also changed the character of mission. Proclamation continued, but it occurred alongside the process of assimilation that inaugurated the quietist phase of Christian growth.

One early Christian source reveals the extent to which believers had taken their place in society alongside others, being willing to engage in peaceful apologetics as occasion demanded. This source, the anonymous Epistle to Diognetus, believed now to have been written not in A.D. 124, as generally claimed, but sometime in the third century, preserves a sentiment that has earlier echoes. It states:

> The difference between Christians and the rest of mankind is not a matter of nationality, or language, or customs. Christians do not live apart in separate cities of their own, speak any special dialect, nor practice any eccentric way of life. . . . They pass their lives in whatever township—Greek or foreign—each man's lot has determined; and conform to ordinary local usage in their clothing, diet, and other habits. . . . they are residents at home in their own countries. . . . they take their full part as citizens. . . . For them, any foreign country is a motherland, and any motherland is a foreign country. [Staniforth, 1968, pp. 176–77.]

Harnack, convinced of the instructive value of hardship, is inclined to perceive in assimilation a retreat from innocence. In other words, he recognizes the change that had come over the Christians, but reckons it with pessimism. He describes the change as follows:

> From the standpoint of morals, the position of living under a sword which fell but rarely, constituted a serious peril. Christians could go on feeling themselves a persecuted flock. Yet as a rule they were nothing of the kind. Theoretically they could credit themselves with all the virtues of heroism, and yet these were seldom put to the proof. They could represent themselves as raised above the world, and yet they were constantly bending before it. [Harnack, 1908, II:121.]

In order to take account of the growth that occurred in this quietist phase, we need to revise the notion, advanced here by Harnack and elsewhere by Bultmann and others, that the disciples were galvanized primarily by their faith in Jesus as the coming Messiah, a faith that was appropriately reinforced by the experience of persecution. At whatever point it occurred, it is certain that Christians acquired an unshakable conviction that Jesus was the present Savior, the Savior-come rather than the Savior-coming, and that the victory was already won. This conviction, without excluding eschatological expectations, existed as an aspect of resurrection faith of the disciples. It was the Easter experience unrefined by the lapse of time. The fellowship of faith centered not so much on Christ "who suffered under Pontius Pilate . . . and would come again to judge the quick and the dead" as on "Christ in you, the hope of glory" (Col. 1:27). It was this internal assimilation of the faith on the personal level that found a parallel in the assimilation taking place in public life. Thus in the places where Christians congregated and worked, a process of quiet adaptation was started. Christians learned to integrate themselves into society, establishing by their example the transforming capacity of the faith upon the mass of their fellow citizens.

The seeds of the transformation were sown in the areas of overlap with Hellenistic culture. As Harnack has observed, "Where Hellenistic education was unknown the new faith seems to have made little or no progress" (Harnack, 1976, II:88). On the other hand, peoples who remained untouched by the religion, even though they might have come within the empire, sank into relative oblivion, to be lifted into the light of history as fossils by scholars, such as occurred with the book by N. H. H. Sitwell, *The World the Romans Knew*. This is not to deny that the new religion spread in places unaffected by Hellenistic learning, but only that its progress was not necessarily impeded by Hellenistic influence. On the contrary, its simultaneous spread within and without the empire suggests for primitive Christianity an independent momentum.

Yet the coincidence between Christianity and Hellenism was not the facile promotion of the religion, for Hellenistic learning questioned in a fundamental way the claims of Christianity (see Dodds, 1970, pp. 105–6, 116ff.). It is true that the numerical strength and social depth of the church rendered it immune to the quibbles of the philosophers, but it is also true that the religion emerged from that challenge with a substantial deposit of Hellenistic culture, which gave it a new language and outlook. For instance, Origen and the other apologists responded to the philosophical challenge by treating Jesus as less a historical figure than a doctrinal concept as the Second Person of the Trinity, a major concession that invited emulation in other spheres, too. As had been remarked, "The human qualities and human sufferings of Jesus play singularly little part in the propaganda of this period; they were felt as an embarrassment in the face of pagan criticism" (Dodds, 1970, p. 119).

In its vigorous encounter with Hellenism, Christianity faced the challenge of adopting the specific cultural framework of the empire while holding to the principle of "the Gentile breakthrough," which denies to any one culture a normative, absolute status. It is important for us to appreciate the profound level at which Christians identified themselves with Hellenistic culture, what Frend refers to as the process of "acute Hellenization," and to understand the method by which this was done as well as its outcome. In their attempt to deny the charge that the religion was no better than crass superstition and childish fable, as Pliny the Younger was at pains to assure the emperor, Christians were forced to assume the terms of discourse of their traducers, as both Origen and Clement of Alexandria prove. In coming forward to preach a doctrine of hell and the hope of salvation, Christianity "wielded a bigger stick and a juicier carrot" than the pagan world with which it was in contest (Dodds, 1970, p. 135).

Yet, for their part, the critics had proved by their earnestness that the new religion possessed great power. People who considered themselves safe and secure in their insights and accomplishments were being roused to bring the best they possessed to the encounter with Christianity (Dodds, 1970, pp. 107, 110). The critics found that it was not enough to ridicule the believers as infantile and unbalanced, or vilify their rituals as moral outrage. They felt driven to appeal to the charge of political subversion as a way of rousing feelings against Christians (Dodds, 1970, pp. 103, 105). The intellectual line of attack was clearly not enough. Ultimately sanctions might have to be applied: "In the foreground of their calumnies stood two charges of Oedipodean incest and Thyestean banquets, together with that of foreign, outlandish customs, and also of high treason" (Harnack, 1908, II:128).

The aim of educated critics was to move against Christianity on two fronts at once: *(a)* to demonstrate by rational criteria the absurdity of Christian claims, and *(b)* to hold up to popular ridicule the pretensions of half-baked adepts. Or, to put it somewhat differently, the challenge was mounted from two fronts: at the popular level, which resorted to invective; and at the intellectual level, which utilized argumentation. Not surprisingly, the evidence for the second of these fronts is more impressive and consistent than the first. Aristides, the orator, for example, wrote with contempt of Christianity, scandalized that the religion had the temerity to promote itself as a philosophy and take on the best in Hellenism. He protested: "They [the Christians] take no thought for style, but creep into a corner and talk stupidly. They are venturing already on the cream of Greece and calling themselves 'philosophers'! As if changing the name meant anything. As if that could of itself turn a Thersites into a Hyacinthus or a Narcissus!" (Harnack, 1908: II:129n.).

The same issue of the new religion promoting itself as a philosophy is discussed by Helmut Koester. He affirms:

The apologists were not primarily interested in the defense of Christianity against accusations that had been raised by the pagan world and by the Roman state — although this motive plays a considerable role. The primary model of apologetic works was instead the Greek *protrepticus,* that is, a literary genre designed as an invitation to a philosophical way of life, directed to all those who were willing to engage in the search for the true philosophy and make it the rule for their life and conduct. The *Protrepticus* of Aristotle was most influential for the formation of this genre; although it is now lost, its influence extended as far as Augustine's *City of God*. . . . the motif of invitation to the true philosophy was still determinative for Christian apologetics. [Koester, 1982: II:338-40.]

In promoting itself as a philosophy, Christianity provoked a reaction among the cultured elite. Julian the Apostate evoked the spirit of Aristides when he declared:

You yourselves must realize the difference to the intelligence which results from a study of our writings as compared with yours. From yours no one could hope to attain to excellence, or even to ordinary goodness; from ours any person could improve himself, even if he were largely devoid of natural endowment. . . . Consider, therefore, whether we are not your superiors in every respect: knowledge of the arts, wisdom and intelligence. [Cochrane, 1940, p. 267; cf. pp. 269-90.]

One of the most sustained attacks was that launched by Porphyry, a native of Tyre, whose real name was Malchos (234-305), in whose work "Hellenism wrote its testament with regard to Christianity" (Harnack, 1908; II:139). Porphyry's criticisms represent what highly cultured Greek thought found obnoxious and objectionable in Pauline Christianity, which was regarded as "a foe to all noble and liberal culture" (Harnack, 1908, II:137; see also Ferguson, 1982, pp. 206, 235). Yet Porphyry's determination to expose Christianity as philosophically unsound brought him within striking range of Christian preaching, as Augustine was quick to demonstrate. Augustine identifies Porphyry's dilemma accurately. In *City of God* (X.9. 383-84) he writes of it thus:

Porphyry goes so far as to promise some sort of purification of the soul by means of theurgy, though to be sure he is reluctant to commit himself, and seems to blush with embarrassment in his argument. On the other hand, he denies that this art offers to anyone a way of return to God; and so one can observe him maintaining two contradictory positions, and wavering between a superstition which amounts to the sin of blasphemy and a philosophical standpoint. For at one moment he is warning us to beware of such practices as fraudulent and fraught with danger in their performance . . ., and the next minute he seems to be surrendering to the supporters of magic, saying that the art is useful for the purification of one part of the soul.

Yet Augustine, in differing from Porphyry, drew near to him, revealing thereby the strengths and advantages of the man who might otherwise have remained an enigmatic figure in the history of philosophy. A modern intellectual biography of Augustine confirmed that he

> re-read the treatises of Porphyry and Plotinus. He evoked the dilemma of these men in so masterly a fashion, that modern interpretations of . . . Porphyry still gravitate around the tenth book of the *City of God.* . . . In the hands of Augustine, he achieves heroic stature; Augustine's final formulations are made to grow, majestically, from a detailed critique of Porphyry's abortive quest for a "universal way to set free the soul"; and so the demolition of paganism, in the first ten books of the *City of God,* can close with the generous evocation of a magnificent failure. [Brown, 1969, p. 307.]

From its encounter with Greek philosophy, the religion obtained invaluable insights into that world, which added greatly to its pluralist heritage. Similarly, Christians received a tremendous bonus from the Greek religious tradition, a bonus they were successful in turning to their own good. This was the case with the *logos* concept. The *logos* stood for the divine reason, the controlling principle of the universe and which was manifested in speech. As such it retained a strong religious element. That element was stiffened with the cult of Jupiter and the tradition of ruler-worship among the Romans, but among the Greeks it existed as a powerful intellectual and religious movement whose greatest insight was developed and centered on the person of Zeus. Here is a hymn that gathers in itself the intense spirit of philosophical speculation and religious devotion, laying stress on the two gnostic ideals of salvation of the reasoning *logos* and salvation as a system of knowledge:

> O God most gracious, called by many a name, Nature's great King,
> through endless years the same;
> Omnipotence, who by thy just decree
> Controlest all, hail, Zeus, for unto thee
> Behoves all thy creatures in all lands to call.
> We are thy children, we alone, of all
> On earth's broad ways that wander to and fro,
> Bearing thine image wheresoe'er we go.
> Wherefore with songs of praise thy power
> I will forth shew.
> Lo! yonder heaven, that round the earth is wheeled,
> Follows thy guidance, still to thee doth yield
> Glad homage; thine unconquerable hand
> Such flaming minister, the levin-brand,
> Wieldeth, a sword two-edged, whose deathless might
> Pulsates through all that Nature brings to light;
> Vehicle of the universal Word, that flows
> Through all, and in the light celestial glows

Of stars both great and small. O King of Kings
Through ceaseless ages, God, whose purpose brings
To birth, whate'er on land or sea
Is wrought, or in high heaven's immensity;
Save what the sinner works infatuate.
Nay, but thou knowest to make crooked straight:
Chaos to thee is order: in thine eyes
The unloved is lovely, who did'st harmonise
Things evil with things good, that there should be
One Word through all things everlastingly.
One Word—whose voice alas! the wicked spurn;
Insatiate for the good their spirits yearn:
Yet seeing see not, neither hearing hear
God's universal law, which those revere,
By reason guided, happiness to win.
The rest, unreasoning, diverse shapes of sin
Self-prompted follow: for an idle name
Vainly they wrestle in the lists of fame:
Others inordinately Riches woo,
Or dissolute, the joys of flesh pursue.
Now here, now there they wander, fruitless still,
For ever seeking good and finding ill.
Zeus the all-bountiful, whom darkness shrouds,
Whose lightning lightens in the thunder clouds;
Thy children save from error's deadly sway:
Vouchsafe that unto knowledge they attain;
For thou by knowledge art made strong to reign
O'er all, and all things rulest righteously.
So by thee honoured, we will honour thee,
Praising thy works continually with songs,
As mortals should; nor higher meed belongs
E'en to the gods, than justly to adore
The universal law for evermore.
　　　　[Cited in Ferguson, 1973, pp. 143–44.]

How sweet indeed the name of *logos* sounds in a believer's ear! That hymn was by Cleanthes, born in 331 B.C., dying nearly a hundred years later. He built on the work of Zeno (d. 264 B.C.), the founder of Stoic philosophy. For Zeno the universe is an active principle that is interchangeable with reason, the *logos,* and eternal law. Alexander Pope (1688–1744) ("Better to err with Pope, than shine with Pye") expressed the insight of Zeno and his school in the following well-known lines:

All are but parts of one stupendous whole,
Whose body, Nature is, and God the soul.

With that kind of heritage behind them, Porphyry and men of his ilk felt an obligation to answer the new religion that paraded under philosophic plumes. So the formidable resources of Hellenistic learning were put in place to demolish Christian claims. But the advantage lay with those who used cooperation as the best form of conquest, and these were Christians.

It was the plural character of Christian life and witness that created an enduring difficulty for the critics. In a wrestling match, to borrow a figure from Cleanthes, the champion could retire from the field of contest assured that the challenge had been decisively met. But in the different combat of the Christian dispensation, the challenge was more elusive and as difficult to contain. The post-Apostolic age brought into being groups of Christians as the agents of mission, thus signaling a double shift in the nature of Christian mission. First, no one individual dominated the work of the church, and Christian witness became the combined effort of communities of believers who were themselves grappling with Christian teaching. This shift may be described in the following words. Toward the close of the Apostolic age,

> there was probably hardly one regular missionary at work. The scene was occupied by a powerful church with an impressive cultus of its own, with priests, and with sacraments, embracing a system of doctrine and a philosophy of religion which were capable of competing on successful terms with any of their rivals. This church exerted a missionary influence by virtue of her very existence, inasmuch as she came forward to represent the consummation of all previous movements in the history of religion. And to this church the human race round the basin of the Mediterranean belonged without exception, about the year 300, in so far as the religion, morals and higher attainments of these nations were concerned. [Harnack, 1976, II: 143.]

The second shift may be signaled by the move from individual responsibility to the diverse and collective witness of the believers, corresponding also to a shift from verbal proclamation to cultural innovation. Porphyry had been preoccupied with the first stage of Christian witness where the methods of conventional debate were best suited. But he was outflanked by the "wing'd chariot" of the Christian movement. As such the religion could afford to sit lightly to the scruples of the leading philosophers and move forward like an oriental caravanserai with its complex baggage of doctrinal teachings, paradoxical claims, baffling mysteries, social diversity and an eclectic ethical code.

It should not, however, be understood that these shifts in missionary strategy occurred by rigid succession. The apostle Paul was already commending the believers in Thessalonika and Philippi for their collective missionary "example" to the world (1 Thess. 1:8; 4:9-10; Phil. 2:14ff.; 4: 14ff.). Similarly, even when the mission of the church rested on the shoulders of brilliant leaders like Paul and Barnabas, it still drew upon the influence and example of collective witness, so that both proclamation and diffusion existed side by side. Nevertheless, the two approaches, however historically intertwined, required different emphases and styles of witness. Proclamation, aimed at individual conversion, was eminently suited to the temperament of a pioneer, while diffusion, coming after a degree of acculturation, depended largely on mutual interaction.

We have remarked upon the advantage Christians enjoyed by virtue of cooperating with the world. The negative sides of this fact are easy enough to set forth, and may be summarized by the charge that toleration spoiled Christians by withdrawing from them the purifying sword of persecution. On the more positive side, however, we encounter what I have termed the "translatability" of the religion. By it the religion expressed its universal ethos, its capacity to enter into each cultural idiom fully and seriously enough to commence a challenging and enduring dialogue. By this mutual attraction and intelligibility the "word of God" formed a congenial shelter for the heritage described so eloquently by Cleanthes. Thus the mission of God assumed the terms of its milieu. All roads of authentic mission led to this one bridge.

While the message was abridged to provide meaningful access for self-realization and cultural fulfillment, it nevertheless demanded personal conviction from those it encountered. Thus faith and culture became closely identified, however much believers might feel called upon to engage in radical acts of criticism and protest. This identity between the gospel and the world it transformed provided one of the finest illustrations of the work of consummation wrought by Christianity, and so genuine was this transformation that it appeared as a natural extension of the life of the church. We must again turn to Harnack for a summary of the implications of this process. Although he does not employ the term "translatability," he hints sufficiently at its characteristics to suggest that its precise formulation would be an advantage to his material:

> From the very outset Christianity came forward with a spirit of *universalism,* by dint of which it laid hold of *the entire life of man* in all its functions, thoughts, and actions. This guaranteed its triumph. In and with its universalism, it also declared that Jesus whom it preached was the *Logos.* . . . From the very first it embraced humanity and the world, despite the small number of the elect whom it contemplated. Hence it was that those very powers of attraction, by means of which it was enabled at once to absorb and subordinate the whole of Hellenism, had a new light thrown upon them. They appeared almost in the light of a necessary feature in that age. . . . [Christianity] was . . . something which could blend with coefficients of the most diverse nature, something which, in fact, sought out all such coefficients. [Harnack, 1908, II:145.]

Such an attitude to cultural assimilation, conceding a little along the lines of tactical advance without deviating from the course of the main thrust, implies a principled commitment to contextual engagement. The outcome was contextual revitalization as a precondition of Christian advance. What the church received in surrender it handed back as transforming reward. For example, the *logos* concept now shines with the light cast upon it by the gospel, and most of us know it at all from that sublime elevation. In that fresh context it lost nothing of its original force and yet it acquired an enlarged capacity as it came to bear the image of the Christian proclamation. Christianity thus came to make better copy of the portraits of other cultures.

This suggests that the religion has a special affinity with multiple cultural forms, with the message interacting with "coefficients of the most diverse nature." All cultural forms by which human beings represented themselves were thus in principle worthy of bearing the truth of Christianity, from which their true value was revealed. The other way to put this is to say that no one cultural expression of the religion was the exclusive representation of the gospel, and that any attempt to press culture into a normative ideology introduced a time-fuse to be set off by an inevitable vernacular reaction. Christians first crossed this pluralist threshold with the Judaic heritage of Jesus. Henceforth Christians felt themselves free to operate with multiple cultural forms as the natural mode of God's salvific activity in the world, encountering only the obstacle of organizational or institutional objections, but never that of the opposition of Jesus and the apostles.

In the Roman world this issue of pluralism preoccupied the Christians. In the first place the church became the arena of the most diverse social concentration of people. In his oft-quoted missive to the emperor Trajan, Pliny the Younger remarked with bitter sarcasm on how the spread of Christianity had coincided with (in his mind, caused) a remarkable revival of the old pagan religions, affecting both cities and villages, and he was in no doubt that Christians were to blame for this state of affairs. He contended:

> People of every age and rank and of both sexes are and will continue to be gravely imperilled. The contagion of that superstition has infected not only cities *(civitates)* but villages *(agros)* and hamlets; but it seems possible to check and correct it. It is clear, at least, that the temples which had been deserted are again frequented, and the sacred festivals long intermitted are revived. Sacrificial victims for which purchasers have been rare are again in demand. [Cited in Hadas, 1956, p. 131.]

After discounting possible exaggeration by Pliny, it is clear that his description confirms that Christianity had spread widely in the empire, penetrating villages and small towns. Thus apart from the prospects of major towns and cities coming under Christian influence, officials were confronted with the impossible task of containing the fast-growing religion, which had spread throughout the empire and beyond. For example, Justin

Martyr (ca. 100–165), himself a Palestinian born of settlers in Flavia Neapolis (Nablus), remarked: "For there is not a single race of human being, barbarians, Greeks, or whatever name you please to call them, nomads or vagrants or herdsmen living in tents, where prayers through the name of Jesus the Crucified are not offered up to the Father and Maker of the universe" (Trimingham, 1979, p. 94).

Some leading Christian thinkers of the time, faced with the increasing social diversity of the church and feeling instinctively that Roman administrative institutions might not be adequate to the specific requirements of catechetical unity, began to voice their concerns. They wanted to establish a principle of uniformity that would rise above the diversity upon which the church seems to come so naturally. Their arguments are eloquent, and students of the subject have tended to adopt their criteria in evaluating the worth of indigenous assimilation. The result has been the perpetuation of antivernacular prejudice. The vernacular assimilation that seems to come so easily and naturally for the church is treated as inferior, and even as a danger, to the uniformity of the rule books. Pluralism became opposed to doctrinal rectitude as darkness was to light. In the words of Irenaeus, the second-century church father of Lyons, we catch the first glimmers of the disquiet caused by the social and geographical diversity of the church. He wrote:

> For although the languages of the world are varied, yet the meaning of the Christian tradition is one and the same. There is no whit of difference in what is believed or handed down by the churches planted in Germany or in Iberia or in Gaul or in the East or in Egypt or in Libya or in the central region of the world. Nay, as the sun remains the same all over the world . . . so also the preaching of the church shines everywhere. [Harnack, 1908, II:152.]

Yet if the church followed the sun in its vicissitudinous course through the world, it should not abandon the pursuit if it led through complex strata of terrain, vegetation, and habitation. In fact formal doctrine, as Irenaeus hints, is inclined to oppose the adaptive power of the environment against the rule of uniformity. So the sun and the community, as respective symbols of doctrine and culture, are made to be mutually exclusive or at least to be in permanent tension.

However, the forces that promoted the successful implantation of Christianity on a great variety of soils could scarcely be contained within the bounds of a neat formula, so diverse and apparently conflicting are the channels God uses to establish the kingdom. Any prejudged cultural formula forced upon this material was bound to put historical experience under unbearable strain, and thus lead to explosive tension at the vernacular level.

Confronting the same issue of pluralism, Tertullian, by contrast, swung predictably to the other extreme and embellished the theme with facile or even fanciful conversions of exotic races. He challenged his opponents:

On whom else have all the nations of the world believed, but on Christ who has already come? . . . with others as well, as different races of the Gaetuli, many tribes of the Mauri, all the confines of Spain, and various tribes of Gaul, with places in Britain, which, though inaccessible to Rome, have yielded to Christ. Add the Sarmatae, the Daci, the Germans, the Scythians, and many remote peoples, provinces, and islands unknown to us, which we are unable to go over. [Harnack, 1908, II:176.]

THE LANGUAGE FACTOR IN RELIGIOUS ASSIMILATION

We shall see later that those who promoted Christianity as cultural pluralism made timely use of Scripture, including the experience of those who were present at Pentecost (Acts 2:7-12). But for the moment we should restrict our remarks to the second aspect of the Christian pluralism, namely, the language factor, which underlies much of mission, but is especially prominent in the process of cultural assimilation.

To return to Irenaeus, he reported that while in residence in Lyons he had to preach in Celtic and that "there were Christians among the Celts who possessed the orthodox faith 'without ink or paper'" (Harnack, 1908, II: 400). However, Greek was predominant there, with some use of Latin. Thus Lyons was a multilingual city in which Christianity took root.

In Egypt, Christianity spread among the Copts, the native population, in the middle of the third century. Coptic villages along the Nile embraced the new faith, and a period of great ferment followed in which Coptic versions of the Bible began to appear. The first person who published his biblical studies in the language was Hieracas. Several Coptic dialects were employed to render the Scriptures into the indigenous language.

A major breakthrough came also with the conversion of Armenia Major by at least the beginning of the fourth century. Armenians practiced both Greek and Syrian Christianity and possessed the literature of these peoples. In some parts of Armenia, Syriac became the ecclesiastical language.

The man who led the mass of Armenians into the church was Gregory the Illuminator, hailed in the sources as the founder of Armenian Christianity, although, as Eusebius indicates, Christianity had been present in the country much earlier than Gregory. The new religion was immensely important in helping to preserve a sense of Armenian identity. For example, it helped to "safeguard the Armenians against the Persians" (Harnack, 1908, II:346), who had been pressing hard on their heels.

The chief church of Armenia was erected on the site of the most sacred sanctuary of the nation, and it was there that Gregory was consecrated

Catholicus of Armenia. He encouraged the cult of martyrs as a deliberate parallel to the earlier pagan festivals, and through its practice the Armenians arrived at a powerful sense of their national identity. One of his lineal descendants, with the help of an educated monk, devised a fresh alphabet for the Armenian language, which was then employed to translate from the Greek and Syriac a number of religious works. As Kenneth Scott Latourette suggests, the introduction of Christianity helped foment a sense of Armenian nationalism: "A people for whom religion was a matter of state had, under their natural leaders, transferred their allegiance from one cult to another. . . . The majority identified the Armenian church and its Christianity with Armenian nationalism" (Latourette, 1937, I:106).

To step a little out of chronological order, we may develop the theme of nationalism by recalling how what one authority calls "the Magyar robber state" of Hungary was transformed "into the Apostolic Kingdom that was to be the eastern bulwark of Christendom" (Dawson, 1950, p. 136). A remark attributed to Saint Stephen, the founder of the Apostolic Kingdom, imputes the greatness of Rome to its encouragement of cultural pluralism, which the new Christian order in Hungary was admonished to emulate, "for weak and fragile is a kingdom with one language and custom" (*nam unius linguae, uniusque moris regnum imbecille et fragilum*) (Dawson, 1950, p. 137). Enlightened minds at that time perceived cultural pluralism as the antidote to political inertia and social parochialism, whereas in our day it is viewed with suspicion by leaders of thought and society for being a threat to truth.

In North Africa the language issue commanded lively interest. As is well known, Latin was to eclipse Greek in certain circles, and the evidence is that this occurred first in Roman Africa, where, for example, Augustine describes his own preference for it over Greek (*Confessions,* I. 13), although Novatian is credited with its introduction in Rome. Nevertheless other languages were employed in the religious life there. The use of Coptic has been described. The influential and Hellenized Jewish community in Alexandria developed the use of Greek in translation and synagogue life. Similarly Latin was prominent, with Tertullian employing it in theological argumentation. He is consequently regarded as the father of ecclesiastical Latin. The resident population of Carthage, severely weakened from Roman military action, also had their own language, Punic, whose

> strength is patent; both bishops and priests had to know Punic in those days. . . . On the other hand, no Punic version of the Bible, so far as we know, was ever essayed—implying that the Christianization of the Punic population meant at the same time their Romanizing. . . . For the benefit of Christians who knew nothing but Punic the Bible was translated during worship, and there was also preaching in Punic. [Harnack, 1908, II:413, 415n.]

The failure to produce a Punic version of the Bible was an ill omen for the church in North Africa, for it left indigenous populations excluded from any meaningful role in Christianity, a point I have made elsewhere.[3] Without the native Scriptures the local populations construed the church as an instrument of foreign domination and became as a result alienated from the Romanized Christians. When Islam spread in the region in the seventh century, it encountered only the ghost of a long-spent force, which it proceeded accordingly to lay.

The language question lay at the very heart of the mission of Christianity and served to underpin the world of pluralism that came into being in the church. The spread of the religion thus turned on the revitalization of the immediate cultural setting. This gave Christianity an eclectic appearance, with its elaborate and varied adoption of disparate sources. It would bring consistency into the discussion if we were to substitute "translatability" for this eclectism. In pondering the spread of Christianity against the rich and diverse culture of the contemporary world, Harnack considers that the reasons

> were native to the very essence of the religion (as monotheism and as evangel). On the other hand they lay in its versatility and amazing power of adaptation. But it baffles us to determine the relative amount of impetus exerted by each of the forces which characterized Christianity: to ascertain, for example, how much was due to its spiritual monotheism, to its preaching of Jesus Christ, to its hope of immortality, to its active charity and system of social aid, to its discipline and organization, to its syncretistic capacity and contour, or to the skill with which it developed in the third century for surpassing the fascinations of any superstition whatsoever. Born of the spirit, it (i.e., Christianity) soon learnt to consecrate the earthly. . . . It was a universal religion in the sense that it enjoined precepts binding upon all men, and also in the sense that it brought men what each individual specially craved. Christianity became a church, a church for the world. [Harnack, 1908, II:467–68.]

The qualities identified in that passage as versatility, adaptation, tolerance of syncretism, and the genius for being to each person what the individual craved can all be subsumed under the rubric of translatability. By that rule the center of the religion shifted to the particular culture that was being addressed. That, I suggest, was the genius of the religion, the ability to adopt each culture as its natural destination and as a necessity of its life. When the church, furnished with dogmatic justification, committed the message to only one cultural formulation, it adopted a collision course with the consequences of translation. Consequently, in the struggle between a Judaic, Hellenistic, Latin, or Victorian Christianity and its "Gentile" or ethnic variants, we see a repetition of that classic tension between dogma and experience, between cultural ideology and its pluralist expression.

CHRISTIANITY AND THE CONFLUENCE OF CULTURES

As we have seen, Christianity sought indigenous coefficients, and, finding them, flourished by them, so that both borrower and borrowed were transformed in a common direction. This stands in stark contrast to the view that Christianity profited from cultural decay and political confusion. This is not to deny that cultural fatigue and political exhaustion might allow the religion to play a renovative function, in which case the central resources of the religion have to be translated into indigenous terms. This process begins with recapitulating older themes and ideas and then reconstituting these as the basis for renewal. Translation thus came to invest Christianity with indigenous solidity. The vernacular became a necessity for the life of the religion, the soil that nurtured the plant until its eminence acquired doctrinal heights.

Not all writers have identified this question with the confidence it deserves. Latourette, for example, pursuing the guileless path of a de-culturized Christianity, puts forward the familiar view in the form of a hypothesis: "Had Christianity been born in a vigorous young culture whose adherents were confident of its virtues, it might have met a different fate" (Latourette, 1937, I:163–64). Yet the historical evidence, which Latourette has within his magisterial scope, conflicts with this view, and he was too scrupulous a scholar not to notice it, although the premise of the religion encountering an unequal force was too deeply ingrained not to qualify his handling of the evidence. He continues: "Yet it must be remembered that Christianity was only one of the many competing cults in the decaying Roman Empire. Some of these, notably Neoplatonism, had the endorsement of a much larger proportion of the upper classes than did the eventual victor" (Latourette, 1937, I:164).

Thus the evidence previously used to uphold the view of early Christianity as living off the weakened relics of a dying culture may also be used to advance a contrary position. Latourette himself speaks confidently of the encounter of Christianity with vigorous forms of pagan worship (Latourette, 1937, I:193), including the transformation of a popular huge Carthaginian temple into a Christian church (ibid., 196), and the contribution of famous Christian converts to the cultural life of the wider society (ibid., 198). One of these converts was Victorinus, who translated into Latin some of the works of the Neoplatonists and of whom Augustine spoke in highest terms (*Confessions,* VIII. 2, 4, 5). Gibbon, who also felt the need to modify the notion of Christianity as a religion of failure, that is, a religion that made success of others' failure, documents the instances of people converting from what he termed the advantages of natural endowment or fortune (Gibbon, n.d., I:440–41).

Christianity continued to expand in the strongholds of pagan cults all over Italy. Although Turin was a strong Christian center, it also boasted a vigorous pagan cult espoused by the educated classes. In Ravenna, the seat of the imperial residence, a large proportion of the population was still attached to the traditional deities. At the end of the sixth century, paganism was still thriving: in Monte Casino where there was a statue to Apollo and an altar; in Sicily, Sardinia, and Corsica; and in Milan and Genoa where, as late as the middle of the seventh century, Christian mission was still progressing.

In Gaul and outlying regions the entry of Christianity was again in the context of a lively admixture of cultures. After the conversion of Martin of Tours in the fourth century, Christianity became dominant in the towns, although its power was manifested in belief in miracles and demonic powers. A cult grew around Martin himself. The peasant population, however, came under a Romanizing influence with the adoption of Latin and the corresponding abandonment of the Celtic tongue. But in the Rhineland the population stuck firmly to German, with a tenacious defense of older religions and customs.

In the valley of the Vistula, the Goths were converted, bringing to the cause their own national contribution. Some of the Goths were allied to the colorful and highly individual Bishop Audius, who came from Syria. With an ascetic cast of mind, he stressed purity of life, although his views were most unconventional. Eventually it was left to Ulfilas (311–381), a Goth himself and consecrated a bishop, to carry forward the momentum of Christianity among his people.

What may have been his most noteworthy achievement was his translation of a large part of the Bible into the Gothic tongue. For this purpose he is said to have been careful to give nearly as possible a word-for-word rendering from the Greek, probably with some reference to the Latin versions. Yet he also sought to observe the Gothic idiom and, as is inevitable in translations, introduced something of his own interpretation. [Latourette, 1937, I:213–14.][4]

MISSION IN THE UPPER DANUBE

It is time to turn our attention to the Upper Danube region. There is no doubt that in its Slavonic career, the new religion discovered a compatibility with the indigenous cultures. Although the power of Rome had been in decline by the time Christianity arrived on the scene, the region was not a cultural vacuum or a political wasteland. However, the efforts of political centralization mounted by two competing powers, Rome and Byzantium, conflicted with the vernacular pressures that Christianity bolstered.

The interests of empire, whether Roman, Byzantine, or nineteenth-century Western colonialism, were often at odds with the indigenizing force of Christianity. It is doubtful, indeed, that modern nationalism would have taken the form it did without the substantial legacy of vernacular revitalization spawned by Christian mission. So among the Slavonic peoples cultural nationalism eventually found explicit political channels in the Balkans, and in Africa and elsewhere a similar formula worked to identical ends.

Among the Slavic people the church took root in the vernacular soil stimulated by the translation enterprise. Eventually mission was curbed (in official jargon "reformed") in order to weaken its vernacular impact and bring local churches under firmer central control. But the sluicegates were open. A determined opposition against the centralizing moves was mounted, forcing the authorities to resort to intimidation to arrest the vernacular momentum, a strong hint of the rocky times ahead. Here again the issue was the tension between the concentrated bulk and its sundry parts, between dogmatized religion and its dynamic historical expression. Church formularies became instruments of coercion, and thus amenable to political manipulation. Faith in God was given a political meaning.

Yet it cannot be overstressed that this tension is inevitable in Christianity: the vernacular strength of the religion would pull away from the force of the center. Yet the "center," whether defined as scriptural or as ecclesiastical, may serve a necessary prophetic role by preventing absolutization and idolatry of culture, so that one vernacular frontier does not presume to be the normative pattern for all others. But it is hardly a useful safeguard to arrogate to itself what it repudiates in others, and the "center" must itself guard against usurping the place of the God to whom it bears witness. Christianity is embroiled in this profound tension, confidently affirming God in the channels of living experience and just as confidently rejecting these as identical with God. God is within us, and yet God is beyond us. God is among us, but God is also against us. The center seems irrevocably fixed in "Jesus Christ and him crucified," only to appear in the kingdom about whose precise coming we remain in foreordained ignorance.

In the struggle of the Slavonic people for a truly vernacular church, then, we are brought to the center of Christianity as a vernacular movement. In spite of centralizing pressures on the Slavic Christians, the church took on a vernacular aspect, which translation invigorated. Even the agents of centralization felt their cause could best be served by cooperating with the forces working at the indigenous level. So the leading voices of the church strove for a Slavonic hierarchy constructed out of indigenous materials, which might eventually conform to the unity of faith and practice promoted in the formularies.

The mission to the Slavs was mounted from Byzantium, although the earliest forays were from the direction of Rome and Italy, reaching into Slavic Dalmatia. But it was in Moravia, lying on the eastern flank of the East Frankish empire in the Upper Danube, that the stage was set for a profound indigenization movement that sent ripples through the whole Slavonic world.

Moravia had lain in the sphere of Frankish influence, but the ruler, Ratislav, broke with the Franks and sought help from the direction of

Byzantium, openly encouraging the introduction of the Byzantine liturgy, which was adapted from the Greek to the language of his people. In fact the Slavic language formed the basis of missionary work and became its chief instrument.

> The first object of the mission was instruction in the Slavic language, the translation of liturgical books into Slavic, and the education of a native clergy in the reading and understanding of the translated liturgical texts. . . . Specialists in Slavonic liturgy point out that in reality there exist Slavonic translations of almost all the liturgical books used at that time in Byzantium. Many of the manuscripts containing the translations are from the tenth century, which shows us that the translators were anxious to give to the Slavs the whole body of Byzantine liturgical texts in their own language. [Dvornik, 1970, pp. 106–7.]

The two pioneer missionaries, invited thither by Ratislav, were the brothers Constantine-Cyril, who died young at forty-two (February 869), and Methodius (d. April 885). The evidence is strong that the two were knowledgeable in the southern dialect of the Slavic language then widespread in the Balkan peninsula. Both were committed promoters of Slavonic translations, and both came under pressure to abjure the vernacular and impose a centrally directed Latin rite. Both suffered for their work, only later to be rewarded with canonization for their inspired labors. Christianity does arrive at its goal of unity, but only by claiming its vernacular rewards. Constantine, who had a deep appreciation for the richness of the Slavic language, translated the most important part of the Roman Mass into Slavonic. In order to do so it was necessary to create an alphabet, which came to be known after its creator as the Cyrillic alphabet, the standard usage in the Eastern Orthodox Church, including Russia. To the Frankish priests who opposed his liturgical innovations, Constantine replied with a forthright defense of his work. The Franks had contended that the liturgy could be performed only in the three ancient languages of Hebrew, Greek, and Latin, on the grounds that Pilate had used these to compose the inscription placed on the cross of Christ (Lk. 23:38). Pilate could scarcely have suspected the use he would be to the champions of the Way of Jesus.

Yet the vernacular issue was by no means settled in the Frankish church itself, and it would need more than the authority of Pilate to silence the advocates. For example, the Synod of Frankfurt, convened in 794, handed down a decision in Canon 52 protesting against the exclusive use of the three ancient languages. The bishops declared: "Ut nullus credat quod nonnisi in tribus linguis Deus adorandus sit. Quia in omni lingua Deus adoratur et homo exauditur si justa patierit." ("It is not to be believed that God is only to be worshipped in the three languages. Because God is worshipped in all languages man is heard if he strives in pursuing the right." (Latin in Dvornik, 1970, p. 367; trans. by author.) When the time came, similar words in the mouth of Martin Luther would have a revolutionary ring, and the Frankish church would be rocked to its very foundations.

Even if we interpret the declaration of the synod by the most conservative rule to mean that the bishops had in mind only the use of the vernacular in private devotions, it is still an important point that such great store should be set by the vernacular. In that enterprise the example of Moravia proved contagious, as we shall shortly see.

The interest in the vernacular came from very high quarters, indeed from Charlemagne himself. He began a grammar of the vernacular, believed to be of the Rhenish-Franconian that he spoke himself. Yet the major impetus behind the development of the vernacular was the missionary movement.

> The impetus to write vernacular still came from the mission-field and to it the emperor had something to say. There can be no doubt that to him, as to all his contemporaries, the language of Christianity in the liturgical sense remained Latin, one of the three sacred languages. . . . But the Anglo-Saxons and the Goths had shown that the language of religious exposition could be vernacular; and this was to be encouraged. . . . Most significant . . . are the very large number of vernacular glosses, sermons, hymns and confessions that survive . . . . This wide-ranging reach of the written vernacular for religious and educational purposes throughout the Carolingian world is of first significance. . . . That people should understand underlies a large part of all surviving vernacular translation of the period. [Wallace-Hadrill, 1983, pp. 378, 380, 381.]

To resume with Constantine and Methodius, they made wide use of prayers and formularies translated into the Slavonic by Frankish missionaries, materials which were in popular use in Moravia. Constantine enlarged on this work, thereby giving the vernacular a fresh impetus.

> His translation is in many ways an adaptation of the peculiar genius of the Slavic idiom elevated to a literary language and to the needs of the young Moravian church. . . . Constantine was well acquainted with the translations of the Gospels into other eastern languages. . . . He stressed his intention of translating the Gospels as accurately as possible, respecting, however, the difference in expression and in meaning of certain words of both languages. In such cases he thought himself entitled to a more independent rendering of some of the passages in order to be able to explain the true meaning of the original.
>
> In his translation Constantine followed the principles expounded in

his treatise. Slavic philologists recognize the excellent qualities of his translation, which reveals a very deep knowledge of the Greek and Slavic languages and of their character. The translation is sometimes not verbal, as Constantine tried to make Greek expressions more understandable to the Slavic Christians. . . . Constantine introduced his translations of the four Gospels in a special poetic composition. . . . *We read there a passionate appeal to the Slavs to cherish books written in their own language* . . . this was the first translation of the Gospels into a vernacular language to appear in the West. [Dvornik, 1970, pp. 117–18, italics added.]

His example inspired similar movements elsewhere, such as among the Franks. There a translation effort was carried out in the South Rhine-Frankish idiom. Otfrid von Weissenburg composed a versified epical harmony of the Gospels, and in his introduction he appended a kind of manifesto to the vernacular. He wrote, probably with the work of Constantine in mind, "In our time many are trying to do so, writing in their own language, endeavouring to glorify their own nation. Why should the Franks neglect such things and not start to chant God's glory in the language of the Franks?" (Dvornik, 1970, p. 370).

Dedicating himself to the development of the vernacular, Otfrid helped to revive interest not only in religious matters but in secular subjects as well. He directed his attention to his learned contemporaries "who knew how to think and who can be encouraged through the vernacular to read more for themselves. Moreover, he combines learning with piety with great technical skill; something which no one had hitherto attempted in German on such a scale. Like the *Heliand* poet, Otfrid moved within the Germanic thought-world of warrior-ethos, loyalty and obedience, the lord-man relationship" (Wallace-Hadrill, 1983, p. 386). Otfrid worked between 863 and 871.

The translation work of the brothers Constantine and Methodius came under strong attack from Rome, and an ecclesiastical inquiry was ordered. The trilingual case for the Roman rite again reared its head, and Constantine was required to pass muster before it. At the center of the attack was what was perceived as the bold innovation of creating an alphabet for the Slavs. The convocation was held in Venice where the brothers arrived for the purpose. Constantine pointed out in self-defense how there were other peoples besides Hebrews, Greeks, and Latins, nations that had their own alphabet. He listed in this connection Armenians, Persians, Basques, Iberians, Suzdalians, Goths, Avars, Turks, Khazars, Arabs, Egyptians, and Syrians among others. The sun, more than Irenaeus suspected, did shine on all these, too.

Next Constantine turned to Scripture to support his contention that every people had the right to glorify God in its own language. The longest excerpt was from chapter 14 of 1 Corinthians. His biographer reproduced it from the old Slavonic translation made by the two brothers. In all, Constantine used fourteen scriptural quotations in defense of his innovations.

The inquiry, and the strong attack on the vernacular that preceded it, were straws in the wind, and at the end of the eleventh century and during the twelfth the stormclouds broke over the Moravian church. But in the meantime, Constantine's work was spared. In the papal bulls promulgated by Hadrian II and John VIII, the Slavonic liturgy was approved, and Constantine would have been suitably assuaged that the papal dispensations imitated the style of his own defense.

Shortly after Constantine's death, his brother and successor, Methodius, was hauled before Pope John VIII to answer charges connected with continuing to celebrate the Mass in Slavonic, a "barbaric language," it was alleged. This was in 879. But again the attack came to nothing. The pope confirmed Methodius in his rank of archbishop of Moravia, and allowed the vernacular to stand. "He also approved very solemnly the liturgical innovation of celebrating the Mass and holy offices in the Slavic language. . . . Against the assertion that the liturgy should be celebrated only in Latin, Greek and Hebrew, he quoted several passages of Holy Writ (Ps. 116:1; Acts 2:11; Phil. 2:11; 1 Cor. 14:4)" (Dvornik, 1970, p. 165).

But Methodius could not have missed the clear import of attempts to undo his work. Perhaps sensing that a tumultuous future lay ahead for the work in Moravia, he became an indefatigable sponsor of religious translation work into the Slavonic. That time of testing, when it arrived finally, brought devastation in its wake, a heavy toll being exacted for the decades of dogged heroism and creative enterprise.

Methodius's biographer rose to his defense, wrong perhaps in the detailed recounting of the saintly man's achievements, but correct in standing by the cause for which his subject struggled. Methodius was expelled from Moravia, and his disciples were persecuted. It is believed that much valuable language work was irretrievably lost in the turmoil. In his chosen successor, however, a Moravian nobleman by the name of Gorazd and a champion of the cause, he continued to hold out against his detractors.

Contemporary witnesses of the work in Moravia are united in the view that the success of the Christian expansion was inseparably intertwined with the development of the vernacular. As an epitaph to the achievement of Constantine and those like him, the testimony of a contemporary historian must suffice: "Besides that he ordered that the Mass and other canonical hours should be sung in churches in vernacular language, as it is done till today often in Slavic lands, especially in Bulgaria, and many souls are gained for Christ in this way" (Dvornik, 1970, p. 208).

Although the two brothers had succeeded in resisting the opposition, they had not completely overcome it, and their opponents in Rome continued to grow in confidence. Finally in the pontificate of Gregory VII (1073-85), a strong order was handed down to suppress the Slavic liturgy.

The Czech king Vratislav II (1061–92), an ardent promoter of the cause, treated it as bluster and ignored it, allowing the continued use of the native liturgy. But the order was not withdrawn, and his successor, Bretislav II, less sure of his ground, yielded to pressure, and in 1096 the persecution of the Slavonic Christians commenced. It dealt a mortal blow to Slavonic liturgy and letters in Bohemia, although the traces etched in the fabric of the culture were too deep to be permanently buried.

It is not necessary, for our purposes, to delve into the intricacies of this debacle. (Numerous details are given in Dvornik, 1970, who is the acknowledged authority in the field, and Christopher Dawson, 1950, who considers especially the forces of confusion following the assassination of Pope John VIII and the cynical policies of the Carolingian bishops of Germany and an unscrupulous Byzantine power; see Dawson, p. 127.) The springtime of Slavic emancipation, had it been allowed to come about, could only have done so on soil faithfully cultivated by Constantine and his allies. But at the whiff of that first promise, a deadly frost descended on the fields.

However, not all the ground was lost, although some painful readjustment was necessary. The names of the great vernacular pioneers among the Slavs acquired a negative meaning in the atmosphere induced by the persecution, and they were dropped by the partisans. Yet their achievement was not repudiated. It was merely reassigned to a more acceptable figure, a putative device to save the heritage. Thus Saint Jerome was invoked as the father of the Slavonic liturgy, and in that fraudulent combination the two marched forward to receive a rescript from Pope Innocent IV in 1247. The Croatian church, a legatee of the renewal movement in Moravia, was able to continue the use of the Slavonic liturgy as a consequence of this cumbersome contrivance.

Political developments also came to the rescue. Rome lost control of Serbia in 1219, and the Byzantine patriarch moved swiftly to consecrate the first archbishop of Serbia, creating thereby an autonomous Serbian church. The transmission to the Serbians of the Slavonic liturgy and letters strengthened the forces of vernacular renewal and autonomy. "On this basis the Serbs were able to create in the thirteenth and fourteenth centuries a flourishing national literature inaugurated by St. Sava" (Dvornik, 1970, p. 258).

At a certain point of its development, the vernacular revival might turn into a force favoring political nationalism, and perhaps even leading to cultural self-righteousness. In that extreme form, cultural heroes are amalgamated into suitable messianic figures who are looked up to as world conquerors, and with that the stage of cultural absolutization is reached. Yet the distortions of such fanaticism cannot be blamed solely on the vernacular cause, for cultural grievances may stem from oppressive foreign domination and explode into messianic fervor. And in any case it is much too facile to construe the excesses of vernacular agitation as the inevitable consequence of cultural pluralism in order simply to justify a return to dogmatism, and thus to a source of the agitation. Ultimately, the vernacular forces could not be entirely suppressed, and in Moravia and outlying regions the memory of Saint Methodius was invoked to give them potency. First in 1204, then in 1268, and again in 1346 the figure of Methodius was appealed to by the stalwarts in petitions to Rome. The pope acceded to their demands, and in 1346 permission was granted for the reinstatement of the Slavonic liturgy in a Benedictine abbey in Prague.

Prague was to remain a center of religious and intellectual ferment for several centuries, and a good deal of that could be attributed to the awakening impact of the vernacular renewal commenced by Constantine and Methodius. John Hus (ca. 1369–1415) and his followers launched their movement of protest and reform from there. Jerome of Prague (1380–1460), a friend and collaborator of John Hus, was also a native of the city and was instrumental in bringing the teachings of John Wyclif to his native country after a period of study at Oxford from where he returned in about 1402. He also shared the harsh fate of John Hus, who was condemned to be burned at the stake as a heretic by the Council of Constance in 1415. Another equally significant figure was Luke of Prague (ca. 1460–1528), regarded by many as a forerunner of the Protestant movement. He was a founder of the Brethren church (the "Moravian church"), which he eventually guided into mainstream Protestantism. His hymnal, written in 1501, is considered the first Protestant hymnal. Various of his writings were translated into the dialect of the Cottian Alps.

Prague continued to feed the general religious and intellectual stir well into the seventeenth century when the Palatinate Wars sent Bohemia and much of Western Europe into upheaval. An important strand of that tangled web of events was concern for the tradition of cultural autonomy made familiar by earlier vernacular movements. (For a detailed account of the role of Prague in the intellectual ferment of seventeenth-century Europe, see Yates, 1972.)

On the occasion of the 1,100th anniversary of the Moravian Mission, His Beatitude Dorotheos, the metropolitan of Prague and All Czechoslovakia, testified to the continuing significance of the sainted brothers for the sense of Slavic national identity:

> The testament of Orthodox Moravia, left to us by St. Methodius, has been the keynote throughout the history of our nation; it has become the guide of the Slavic idea. . . . Methodius and Cyril helped to develop the culture of Great Moravia, especially the language, . . . thus uniting [the] separate Slavic tribes into well-organized states. In so doing, they [awakened] in the nation a sense of national self-awareness. [Dorotheos, 1985, pp. 225, 219.]

In the nineteenth century the British and Foreign Bible Society played a similar role in awakening the Slavonic national impulse, especially in the effects it had on the development of South Slavonic languages and literature. The emergence of modern Serbian and Crotian literature is due largely to the impetus of such missionary translation (Bundy, 1985, p. 394).

To return to the earlier period of the effects of religious translation on the indigenous culture, it is important to emphasize that the attempts to suppress vernacular renewal merely succeeded in inciting it. Finally, Martin Luther arrived on the stage from which earlier national figures had been so dramatically removed. By the time he was threatened with the same extreme fate, the vernacular cause was unstoppable and his triumph correspondingly assured. His story, better known, need not be repeated here in all its detail. A modern secular historian gives the following summary, which must suffice:

> Secluded in the Wartburg, disguised in secular clothing and passing by the name of Sir George, Luther needed work. The sudden leisure after such crowded years was bad for a temperament always given to brooding; for him temptation (Luther's word for it was *Anfechtung,* the devil's attacks) took the form of spiritual languor and physical discontent. . . . The work he found could not have been better chosen for his purpose: he set himself to translate scripture into German. As he had always said, the Word would do it all. If there is a single thread running through the whole story of the Reformation, it is the explosive and renovative and often disintegrating effect of the bible, put into the hands of the commonality and interpreted no longer by the well-conditioned learned, but by the faith and delusion, the common sense and uncommon nonsense, of all sorts of men. One country after another was to receive its vernacular bible in this century, and with it a new standard of its language; in 1521–2 Luther, who had for so many people already done so much to bring the gospel to life after its long sleep in the scholastic night-cap, began the work for his Germans. [Elton, 1964, p. 52.][5]

Not all the reformers of the sixteenth century were committed with equal or consistent clarity to the deeper implications of the vernacular Scripture. It seems almost inevitable, given the circumstances, that a triumphant national church would arrogate to itself the norms of absolutism it had so noisily rejected in the Mother Church, and certainly in many parts of Europe the German Reformation was resisted by local populations. In Bohemia, Poland, and other places the Reformation movement excited strong local feelings in spite of sympathy for its reformist principles. It is instructive to ponder the fact that where the vernacular renewal had been most successful there also the opposition to the German reformers was staunchest. The seeds of that resistance were sown in an earlier age. From the early tenth century onward, the Wends and other Slavonic peoples opposed the invasion of their lands by the *deus theutonicus,* the German

"Teutonic deity." As Friedrich Heer writes: "Rome, and Roman Christianity, were detested in Eastern Europe in so far as they were German importations. When the Polish, Czech and Hungarian Churches . . . set themselves to break the spell of Rome they became the champions of their peoples' resistance to German overlordship" (Heer, 1962, p. 359).

The Reformation, having adopted the principle of the German vernacular, surrendered it when it required compliance from non-Germanic peoples of Europe. This is the view held by the Czech scholar, M. Weingart, who wrote: "This Czech-Slavic type of culture was of paramount importance for the preservation, or at least, for the strengthening of the national character. If the ancient Czechs did not succumb to germanization as quickly and to such an extent as the Wends, this is indeed due to the growth of the Czech Old Church Slavonic letters . . ." (Dorotheos, 1985, p. 224).

Yet the Protestant impulse did stir deep in the heart of the Slovenian people. It was the Protestant Baron Ungnad, prefect of Styria in the southeastern Alps, who gave help and encouragement to Slavic translators. From a press he set up in his home in Württemberg, he sent out in the mid-sixteenth century editions of translations in both Slovenian and Serbo-Croatian, with the aid of the Grand Duke of Württemberg. These early translations were also known as *Windish,* not to be confused with the *Wend* dialects, the language of Slavs in eastern Germany. It was Katherine von Gerlach, the grandmother of the Moravian mystic Count Zinzendorf, who gave money for the publication of many of the Wend Scriptures.

The person who carried the translation enterprise among the Slavic peoples into its modern phase was a man called Vuk. Born in 1787 in Serbia, when that land was under Turkish occupation, he became a keen reviver of his people's literary tradition and an energetic advocate of reform of the orthography and other linguistic matters. His labors bore fruit before his death in 1862, and the unification and standardization of the Slovak was accomplished. It did much to increase the sense of Slovak national identity (North, 1938, p. 300).

Yet there was a regression from this dynamic understanding of the issue of translatability, with Protestant churches acquiring the "Establishment" complex of authority, privilege, and power. In a candid and astringent examination of what happened to Lutheranism in the second half of the sixteenth century, Harnack argues that only words rather than reality separated it from the Catholicism it repudiated. The Lutheran church, he charges, had by then "threatened to become a miserable doublette of the Catholic Church" (Harnack, 1976, VII:265).

Perhaps the general conditions of social and political life in the emerging Europe conflicted with the idea of pluralism as a condition of religious renewal and social harmony and, when faced with the phenomenon, the church retreated into a dogged defense of doctrinal rectitude and the sanctity of social institutions. In very few of the sources do we get any appreciation for cultural pluralism as existing in the divine providence and in turn making translation necessary and plausible. Instead we have the same pressure for transforming the church into a unitary instrument to mirror in the religious sphere what existed in the secular realm as the sovereign state. Thus the political values of social cohesion, territorial integrity, and linguistic uniformity conjured their religious counterparts in confessional unity, ecclesiastical uniformity, and liturgical harmonization.

It is generally recognized that sixteenth-century Christianity paired with the forces of territorial politics to give concrete expression to cultural nationalism. Lord Acton (1834–1902), for example, in his writings, bemoans the fact that Christian thinkers failed to strike a creative course by reflecting critically on the secular forces of the time, contending that the tradition of separation of powers, so painfully maintained by the medieval world of learning, was largely overthrown by the sixteenth-century reformers (Acton, 1952).[6]

Protestantism merely carried this process further, but shared with Catholicism an equal interest in the ascendant cultural values of the day. An eleventh-century source, to take one instance, describes the powers of the Papacy, which resembled a feudal monarchy with an absolute authority rivaling that of kings. The "divine right of kings" idea was the secular elaboration of this doctrine. Whatever the truth in Acton's contention that medieval political thought had allowed for the separation of powers, by the time the Reformation arrived both the church and the state conceived of authority as stemming from one source, a split-level structure having one foundation. When that foundation was challenged the entire edifice felt the shock.[7] Paul's warning to the Gentile church about not assimilating too uncritically to the world and thus thinking to save themselves by their own achievement, with the idea that Gentiles are not exempt from the unrelenting test applied to the Jews, is appropriate here as well. The temporal order cannot substitute for the kingdom of God, although it might be a witness for it.

THE PROBLEM OF HELLENISM AND THE CHRISTIAN VISION

By the time of the Slavic mission, Christianity had been effectively translated into Hellenistic terms, and those it encountered subsequently were judged by the rules of Greek rational thought. The question no longer was whether or not the church should pursue the path of translation and repeat the Hellenistic experience in other cultural terms, but whether or not the process of translation itself had stopped with the Hellenistic transformation. That dogmatic cultural attitude came into serious conflict with the Slavonic mission, demanding that Slavic Christians legitimize their status by repudiating their national culture and receive the intellectual and spiritual "circumcision" of the chosen Greek.

As a historian of religion, Arnold Toynbee, for one, is convinced that when the church translated the gospel into Greek terms it sacrificed the prophetic vision for scientific truth. Consequently attention was diverted from the essence of the vision to the forms of rational proof, and Christians came to defend the forms as ultimately possessed of the essence itself.

The first step of translating the gospel into Greek terms was made necessary by the very nature of Christianity itself. The second step of absolutizing the Hellenistic medium was made a necessity of cultural harmonization. The one step left Christians free to make the Christian vision true for their age and place, and the other tied Christians to forms imposed from outside, and with the assumption that they are not historical beings. Thus translation facilitates not only the fresh articulation of the vision in indigenous terms; it also opens the way for the absolutization of the powerful cultural current that the religion had captured for itself. Only by continuing to express its vision in continuingly fresh ways can Christianity avoid the idolatry of form. Mission as translation seeks to do precisely that.

Although the Hellenistic transformation of the gospel represents a singular achievement, we must also realize the hazards entailed in that. (It is important to remember that in spite of its proximity to sources of Greek thought, the Greek Orthodox Church, for example, has contended over the centuries against the rational claims of the Enlightenment. Even today, strong voices are being raised against the division of reason and revelation, of science and religion.[8]) The rational refinement of the gospel reduced it to a cognitive system to such an extent that only a small minority of the elite excelled in juggling its obtuse parts. (One of the most articulate statements on the Christian religious phenomenon as nonrational is Rudolf Otto's classic work, *The Idea of the Holy*.) Anyone reflecting on this can see how this Hellenistic legacy became an increasingly heavy liability as the church entered into new fields of human experience saddled with a metaphysical system out of keeping with changing circumstances. The new conditions then made the earlier achievement appear as a failure, demanding fresh ways of holding on to the vision. Toynbee argues forcefully for precisely such a recasting of Hellenistic terms. The Hellenistic metaphysics, he asserts, in which the church has rendered the gospel

> is there merely because of the historical accident that, during the first four or five centuries of the Christian era, the Christian Church had to try to talk to a philosophically educated Hellenic public in that public's own metaphysical terms. This past episode of history is surely no reason why, in a twentieth century Western and Westernizing World, this forced translation into the language of a now superseded metaphysics — a translation made in another time and place to meet a local and temporary requirement — should be taken as a shibboleth. It

would be no remedy, however, to replace this old translation into the metaphysics of the Hellenic World of the fourth and fifth centuries of the Christian Era by a new translation into the metaphysics of the Western World of the twentieth century; for this more recent blueprint is likewise bound to be superseded in its turn by the continuance of the cumulative construction of the scientific chart of the Universe. [Toynbee, 1956, pp. 129–30.]

But Toynbee's diagnosis is self-defeating without an acceptance that both the Hellenic and the modern Western transformation of Christianity are valid and necessary. The church does not err in confidently appropriating the requisite cultural materials to express the gospel, and the triumph of the religion in the modern West attests to the success with which it can be done. (In a rigorous appraisal of Toynbee's views, the Oxford scholar Albert Hourani finds fault with Toynbee's failure to take seriously the particularity of Christian claims. That failure, Hourani argues, vitiates Toynbee's analytic procedure. [Hourani, 1980, pp. 135–60]. The error lies in making the religion one's exclusive cultural inheritance, something that Toynbee defines as "the worst sin of idolization" (Toynbee, 1956, p. 131). In this regard, Toynbee's strictures echo those of Islamic critics for whom, however, the idea of translatability is considered an abandonment of true religion, as one specific example, considered in chapter 7, below, illustrates. However, because Christianity was identified with translatability, Christians, when confronted with schemes of cultural absolutization, have found in translation the requisite antidote, which is to reinvest the vision of the gospel with the robes of transcultural expression, something in fact akin to that original incarnation by which "the word became flesh and dwelt among us" (Jn. 1:14).

Christianity in time expanded from Europe into Asia and Africa, among other places. In other words, it was able to break out of its Western cultural confinement, repeating the process by which the church's missionary center shifted from Jerusalem to Antioch. In some important respects, however, the modern shift was unprecedented, for it was the extraordinary multiplicity of the vernacular boundaries that became the subject of Christian mission rather than the cosmopolitan values of the empire. Yet some continuity with the past was retained. In examining the modern missionary phase, however, we are also describing important permutations in the indigenous culture, with missionaries emerging as the enterprising agents of vernacular renewal, and thus as implicit critics of the alienating impact of Western colonialism. The contention of the primitive church that the affairs of empire pale into insignificance when contemplated in the splendor of God's kingdom (Rom. 8:18–25, 31, 35–39; Phil. 3:20; Gal. 4:26) found a historical parallel in the tension between mission and colonialism of our own day.

SUMMARY AND CONCLUSION

Four stages are set out as characterizing the translatability of Christianity in Hellenic culture and beyond. First, we have the impact of the empire on the church. In the effort to interpret themselves to the world of Greek learning and culture, Christians adopted many of the terms of their detractors. That fact was combined with the experience of leading converts who brought into the church old ways of thought, and the result was the inner transformation of Christianity. This brought the church into line with the Greek philosophical heritage. Nevertheless, Christian community life continued to be marked by an extraordinary degree of social complexity, with provincials and different social classes making up the membership of the church and playing an active role in it. In spite of that, the trend still was to fix on the church a Hellenic character.

Second, the Hellenized church itself came under challenge from vernacular forces in the Slavic mission. In their conflict with Rome on this matter, Slavic missionaries defended the employment of Slavonic languages for translation and the observance of the liturgy, appealing to the principle of the Gentile breakthrough to justify their position that Latin was not the exclusive language of Christianity, being itself only an adopted medium. Repression followed. However, the Slavic translation movement had by then fostered vernacular renewal in many parts, spawning the sentiment for the Slavic national ideal.

Third, the exposition places the Reformation in the wider context of translatability and its vernacular consequences. The theme persists into the Catholic renewal in the Counter-Reformation, with Catholic missionaries making the study of indigenous languages and cultures the basis for missionary practice. Similarly, the Slavic national ideal has continued to find contemporary advocates who find in the ninth-century missions the genesis of the notion.

Fourth, we find a reflection on the implications for the Western church of the vernacular appropriation of Christianity by non-Western societies, showing how the Gentile ferment, which first erupted at Antioch, continues to characterize the mission of the church. Consequently non-Western populations found in Christian mission legitimacy for their own "Gentile" heritage.

NOTES

1. Readers wishing to evaluate Dodds' overall scheme should see Robert C. Smith and John Lounibos, eds., *Pagan and Christian Anxiety: A Response to E. R. Dodds* (Lanham, Md.: University Press of America, 1984).

2. For a masterly outline of the controversy, see Jacob Burckhardt, *The Age of Constantine the Great,* trans. Moses Hadas (New York: Pantheon Books, 1949), pp.

292–335. The University of California Press (Berkeley) reprinted this work in 1983.

3. See L. Sanneh, *West African Christianity* (Maryknoll, N.Y.: Orbis Books, 1983), pp. 10–11 and the accompanying bibliography.

4. See also G. W. S. Friedrichsen, *The Gothic Version of the Gospels* (London: Oxford University Press, 1926), and Charles A. Anderson Scott, *Ulfilas, Apostle of the Goths* (Cambridge, England: Macmillan and Bowers, 1885).

5. Martin Luther's completed translation of the Bible was not published until 1534.

6. For an appraisal of Acton, see Irene Coltman Brown, "The Historian as Philosopher," *History Today* 31 (October 1981): 49–53.

7. For some revisionist thoughts on the Reformation, see A. F. Pollard, "Social Revolution and Catholic Reaction in Germany," *The Cambridge Modern History* (Cambridge, England: Cambridge University Press, 1903). See also, in a different connection, *The Dictatus Papae* (March 1075); and, for a treatment of the evolution of the papal institution, see Thomas F. X. Noble, *The Republic of St. Peter: The Birth of the Papal State, 680–825* (Philadelphia: University of Pennsylvania Press, 1984).

8. See in this connection, the short, unpublished manuscript of Dimitri Kitsikis of the University of Ottawa: "The Opposition of Greek Synthetic Thought to Western Divisive Thought of the Renaissance," paper submitted at the World Congress for the Synthesis of Science and Religion, Bombay, India, January 9–12, 1986. The proceedings of that Congress are to be published.

SELECT BIBLIOGRAPHY

Acton, Lord. 1952. *Lectures on Modern History.* London: Macmillan and Co.

Augustine. 1961. *Confessions.* New York: Dorset Press; repr. 1986.

_____ 1972. *City of God.* Harmondsworth, England: Penguin Books.

Bainton, Roland H. 1969. "The Bible in the Reformation." In G. W. H. Lampe, ed., *The Cambridge History of the Bible,* 3 vols., vol 2. Cambridge, England: Cambridge University Press; repr. 1988.

Boniface. See Emerton, Ephraim.

Brown, Irene Coltman. 1981. "The Historian as Philosopher: Acton, Conscience and the Modern Nation." *History Today* 31 (October).

Brown, Peter. 1969. *Augustine of Hippo.* Berkeley: University of California Press.

Bundy, David. 1985. "Bible Translation in Cross-cultural Mission." *International Review of Mission* 74, no. 295 (July).

Burkchardt, Jacob. 1880. *The Age of Constantine the Great.* Berkeley: University of California Press; repr. 1983.

Cochrane, Charles Norris. 1940. *Christianity and Classical Culture.* New York: Oxford University Press; repr. 1977.

Crehan, F. J. 1969. "The Bible in the Roman Catholic Church from Trent to the Present Day." In G. W. H. Lampe, ed., *The Cambridge History of the Bible,* vol. 2. Cambridge, England: Cambridge University Press; repr. 1988.

Dawson, Christopher. 1950. *Religion and the Rise of Western Culture.* London: Sheed and Ward.

Dodds, E. R. 1970. *Pagan and Christian in an Age of Anxiety.* New York: W. W. Norton.

Dorotheos, Metropolitan. 1985. "Influence of the Moravian Mission on the

Orthodox Church in Czechoslovakia." *International Review of Mission* 74, no. 294 (April).

Dvornik, Francis. 1970. *Byzantine Missions among the Slavs: SS. Constantine-Cyril and Methodius.* New Brunswick, N.J.: Rutgers University Press.

Eliot, T. S. 1968. *Christianity and Culture.* New York: Harcourt, Brace Jovanovich.

Elton, G. R. 1964. *Reformation Europe: 1517–1559.* Cleveland: Meridian Histories of Europe series.

Emerton, Ephraim, trans. 1940. *The Letters of Saint Boniface.* New York: W. W. Norton; repr. 1976.

Ferguson, John. 1973. *The Heritage of Hellenism.* London and New York: Thames and Hudson.

_____ 1982. *The Religions of the Roman Empire.* London: Thames and Hudson.

Friedrichsen, G. W. S. 1926. *The Gothic Version of the Gospels: A History of the Style and Textual History.* London: Oxford University Press.

Frend, W. H. C. 1984. *The Rise of Christianity.* Philadelphia: Fortress.

Georgi, Dieter. 1986. "Who Is the True Prohpet?" *Harvard Theological Review* 79, nos. 1–3.

Gibbon, Edward, n.d. *The Decline and Fall of the Roman Empire.* New York: Modern Library.

Gregory, Bishop of Tours. 1969. *History of the Franks.* trans. and ed. Ernest Brehaut. New York: W. W. Norton.

Hadas, Moses, trans. and ed. 1956. *A History of Rome: From Its Origins to 529 A.D. as Told by the Roman Historians.* New York: Doubleday Anchor Books.

Harnack, Adolf von. 1908. *The Mission and Expansion of Christianity in the First Three Centuries,* 2 vols. New York: Putnam.

_____ . 1976. *History of Dogma,* 7 vols. Gloucester, Mass.: Peter Smith.

Heer, Friedrich. 1962. *The Medieval World: Europe: 1100–1350.* New York: Mentor Books.

Hourani, Albert. 1980. *Europe and the Middle East.* Berkeley: University of California Press.

Kerenyi, C. 1962. *The Religion of the Greeks and Romans.* New York: E. P. Dutton; London: Thames and Hudson.

Koester, Helmut. 1982. *Introduction to the New Testament,* 2 vols. Philadelphia: Fortress Press.

Latourette, Kenneth Scott. 1937–45. *A History of the Expansion of Christianity,* 7 vols. New York: Harper and Brothers.

Loewe, Raphael. 1969. "The Medieval History of the Latin Vulgate." In G. W. H. Lampe, ed., *The Cambridge History of the Bible,* vol. 2. Cambridge, England: Cambridge University Press; repr. 1988.

el-Masri, Iris Habib. 1987. *The Story of the Copts,* 2 vols. Cairo: The Coptic Bishopric for African Affairs; Los Angeles: Saint Fam Coptic Association.

Milburn, R. L. P. 1969. "The 'People's Bible': Artists and Commentators." In G. W. H. Lampe, ed., *The Cambridge History of the Bible,* vol. 2. Cambridge, England: Cambridge University Press; repr. 1988.

Noble, Thomas, F. X. 1984. *The Republic of St. Peter: The Birth of the Papal State: 680–825.* Philadelphia: University of Pennsylvania Press.

North, E. M. 1938. *The Book of a Thousand Tongues.* New York: Harper and Brothers.

Otto, Rudolf, 1980. *The Idea of the Holy*. New York: Oxford University Press.

Pollard, A. F. 1903. "Social Revolution and the Catholic Reaction in Germany." In *The Cambridge Modern History*. London: Cambridge University Press.

Radice, Betty, trans. and ed. 1969. *The Letters of the Younger Pliny*. London: Penguin Books: repr. 1985.

Scott, A. Anderson. 1885. *Ulfilas, Apostle of the Goths, together with an Account of the Gothic Churches and Their Decline*. Cambridge: Macmillan and Bowers.

Sitwell, N. H. H. 1984. *The World the Romans Knew*. London: Hamish Hamilton.

Smalley, Beryl. 1969. "The Bible in the Medieval Schools." In G. W. H. Lampe, ed., *The Cambridge History of the Bible,* vol. 2. Cambridge, England: Cambridge University Press; repr. 1988.

Smith, Robert C., and John Lounibos. 1984. *Pagan and Christian Anxiety: A Response to E. R. Dodds*. Lanham, Md.: University Press of America.

Sparks, H. F. D. 1970. "Jerome as Bibical Scholar." In P. R. Ackroyd and C. F. Evans, eds., *The Cambridge History of the Bible,* vol. 1. Cambridge, England: Cambridge University Press; repr. 1988.

Staniforth, Maxwell, trans. and ed. 1968. *Early Christian Writings: The Apostolic Fathers*. Harmondsworth, England: Penguin Books; repr. 1982.

Tierney, Brian. 1980. *The Crisis of Church and State: 1050–1300*. Englewood Cliffs, N.J.: Prentice Hall.

Toynbee, Arnold J. 1956. *An Historian's Approach to Religion*. London and New York: Oxford University Press.

Trimingham, J. Spencer. 1979. *Christianity among the Arabs in Pre-Islamic Times*. London: Longman; Beirut: Librairie du Liban.

Wallace-Hadrill, John Michael. 1983. *The Frankish Church*. Oxford: Clarendon Press.

———. 1988. *Bede's Ecclesiastical History of the English People: A Historical Commentary,* London: Oxford University Press.

Weingart, M. 1956. *Pravoslavnyaya Mysl.,* no. 4.

Yates, Frances A. 1972. *The Rosicrucian Enlightenment*. London: Routledge and Kegan Paul; repr. St. Albans: Paladin Books, 1975.

3

Mission and Colonialism:
Vernacularization and Westernization

At its most self-conscious stage, mission coincided with Western colonialism, and with that juncture students of the subject have gone on to make all kinds of judgments about the intrinsic bond between the two forces. Historians who are instinctively critical of received tradition in other spheres are more credulous in perpetuating the notion of mission as "imperialism at prayer." In the nineteenth century this idea persisted under the slogan of "Christianity and 6 per cent" (Cochrane, 1957, p. 211), by which it was understood that mundane interests prospered under a religious guise. Thus mission came to acquire the unsavory odor of collusion with the colonial powers. Modern political nationalism has capitalized on this by strengthening the prejudice against mission as a discredited relic of colonialism.

The forces pitted against a fair understanding of mission in the late twentieth century are formidable. To start with, many people are committed to the ideological position that mission is oppressive, and anachronistic to boot, and Christians have been afflicted by the consequences. For the other part, many third-world writers have added their voice of criticism, encouraged in part by the vogue enjoyed by liberation theology. Most mainline Western Christian bodies have, as a consequence, retreated from the subject, afflicted by a heavy sense of guilt. It is not, therefore, easy to inveigh against such strong and deep obstruction.

Yet the subject deserves at the minimum an impartial hearing. As we noted in chapter 2, the historian Arnold Toynbee wrestled gallantly with the issue, juggling the unreconciled idea of mission as translation with that of mission as cultural imperialism, an ambidexterous feat that takes him no further than the contradictory step of trying to turn in two directions at once. Yet the identifying of those two directions is itself an advance even if his evaluation missed the mark.

Africa: Scripture Language Profile

Countries not listed below are treated more fully in the original source (*Scriptures of the World*, United Bible Societies, 1984).

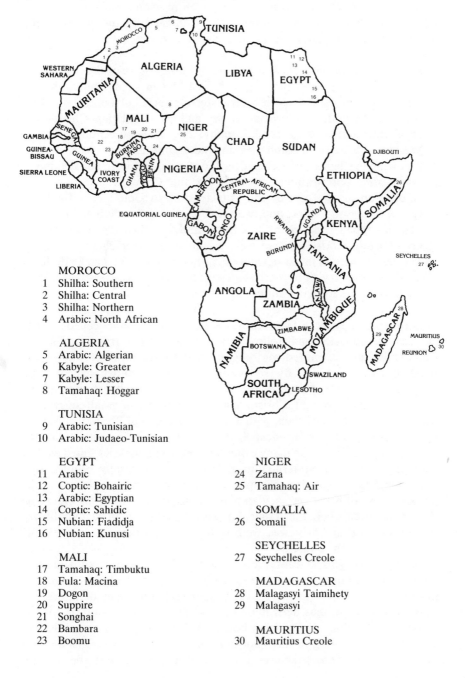

MOROCCO
1 Shilha: Southern
2 Shilha: Central
3 Shilha: Northern
4 Arabic: North African

ALGERIA
5 Arabic: Algerian
6 Kabyle: Greater
7 Kabyle: Lesser
8 Tamahaq: Hoggar

TUNISIA
9 Arabic: Tunisian
10 Arabic: Judaeo-Tunisian

EGYPT
11 Arabic
12 Coptic: Bohairic
13 Arabic: Egyptian
14 Coptic: Sahidic
15 Nubian: Fiadidja
16 Nubian: Kunusi

MALI
17 Tamahaq: Timbuktu
18 Fula: Macina
19 Dogon
20 Suppire
21 Songhai
22 Bambara
23 Boomu

NIGER
24 Zarna
25 Tamahaq: Air

SOMALIA
26 Somali

SEYCHELLES
27 Seychelles Creole

MADAGASCAR
28 Malagasyi Taimihety
29 Malagasyi

MAURITIUS
30 Mauritius Creole

SPANISH MISSIONS IN THE NEW WORLD

Toynbee recognized that modern missions were a continuation of the early church, with the important difference that ecclesiastical politics and intra-religious rivalry cast a political light on missionary efforts. In other words, Christian mission continued to be dogged by the contradiction between translation and cultural diffusion. He wrote:

> In converting the Graeco-Roman Society in the course of the first five centuries of the Christian Era, the Early Christian Church had smoothed the convert's path by transferring local cults and festivals from pagan gods to Christian saints and by translating Christian beliefs into terms of Greek philosophy. The sixteenth century Jesuit Western Christian missionaries in India and Eastern Asia were following in Clement of Alexandria's footsteps, and were not striking out a new line without precedent in the Church's history. . . . Opposition on the part of the Franciscans and Dominicans finally ruined the Jesuits' work, and, with it, Christian (amended) prospects, first in Japan, and then in China; and, in their dealings with non-Western Christians who were members of other churches. . . . The Jesuits were as intransigent as any of their fellow Roman Catholic missionaries in trying to coerce independent heterodox Christians into union with the Roman Church. [Toynbee, 1956, p. 160.]

Before the shipwreck of a promising endeavor, as Toynbee called it, early modern missionaries had followed the logic of the translatability of Christianity and submitted the religion in the most intimate way to the terms of local culture. By so doing, such missionaries had become indigenizers in the best sense of the term, rather than cultural imperialists. Translation thus brought Christian mission into an original congruence with the vernacular paradigm, with a tacit repudiation of Western culture as the universal norm of the gospel. The most convincing vindication of indigenizing mission is the many examples where missionaries failed as they attempted to impose Western cultural forms on non-Western peoples. In a more enlightened age, for example, the Roman church might assure its influence by allowing vernacular expressions of the faith to enter the church, but even where the vernacular was resisted it remained a vital force in the life of local Christians, waiting for an opportune time to take its rightful place in the church.

Toynbee recognizes translation as a factor in the rise of Christian mission, but he misappropriates it as representing only the liberal temper of the missionary movement. We know, of course, that in the modern phase of mission, translation has been the dominant mode of operation of conservative as well as liberal Christian bodies. When Roman Catholic missionaries started operating in the Spanish dominions in the Americas and the Philippines, they found themselves on a collision course with the Spanish secular authorities. These authorities passed an injunction to impose the Castilian language on the Indians as the medium of religious instruction, requiring the missionaries to work under that restriction. The missionaries refused to cooperate.

In their single-minded concern to preach the Gospel, the missionaries refused to be diverted by *raison d'état* from taking the shortest way to reach the Indians' hearts. Even in the Philippines, where there was no pre-Castilian *lingua franca,* they learnt, and preached in, the local languages; and they went much further in the Viceroyalty of Peru, where a native *lingua franca* had already been put into currency by the Spanish conquerors' Inca predecessors. The missionaries in Peru reduced this Quichua lingua franca to writing in the Latin alphabet; in A.D. 1576 a chair of Quichua was founded at the University of Lima, where it was maintained until A.D. 1770; and in 1680 a knowledge of Quichua was made an obligatory qualification for any candidate for ordination in Peru to the Roman Catholic Christian priesthood. [Toynbee, 1956, p. 161.]

In reflecting on the phenomenon of vernacular renewal in the *comunidades de base,* or Christian base communities, in Latin America, Penny Lernoux writes in her prize-winning book, *Cry of the People,* about how the present process of local revitalization had its historical antecedents in the sixteenth century.

Though paternalistic, the earliest missionaries were anything but intellectual snobs; from the beginning of the conquest they tried to build on existing Indian structures. Most of the first churches were adaptations of Indian temples, and pre-Columbian rites were often included in the ceremonies. In 1558 Pope Paul IV ordered "that the days dictated (by the Indians) to the sun and their idols should be selected for special celebrations to Christ, the Blessed Mother, and the saints." The first Masses were recited, sung, and, especially, danced. One of the early missionaries in Guatemala told all new missionaries that the first thing they had to do was to teach the Indians to dance the Gospel.
    Despite its superficiality and cruelty, this forceful evangelization of Indians and African slaves produced a syncretic religion, one of the Latin America's few genuinely indigenous creations. [Lernoux, 1984, p. 381; cf. pp. 382–86, 404–5, 412.]

From the point of view of this book, even the insistence on Castilian as the language of religious life in the Spanish dominions represents itself a further translation of the heritage of the apostles, to be justified only on the basis of the gospel having to assume culturally specific terms in its progress through history, of which Castilian was only one stage rather than the final destination.[1] That rule of cultural specificity would, of course, be violated in the context of non-Spanish cultures where political pretensions might encourage the authorities to claim a normative, universal value for Castilian. All forms of authentic Christian mission would come into contention with such a course of action.

The sixteenth- and seventeenth-century Catholic missionaries found that vernacular translation had a deeper implication for other aspects of the local culture. Thus the conceptual representation of the gospel had its counterpart in the aesthetic sphere where Christian iconography went in search of its contextual equivalents. In some cases, the procedure to establish local parallelisms acted as a stimulus, and aesthetic forms and styles that had been in danger of extinction were resuscitated and endowed with greater range, thus repeating the process of the Christian transformation of Hellenistic culture. This aesthetic transformation took the form of a characteristic blend in Mexico, for example. There

> the spirit of a benignant vein in Meso-American visual art that had always been subordinate and had latterly been almost entirely submerged under the savagery of an Aztec ascendancy was reproduced, and given predominance, in a cheerfully extravagant version of the Early Modern Western baroque style. In the ultra-Baroque village churches of the Puebla district the writer found himself in the presence of the aesthetic and emotional equivalent of a pre-Columbian fresco, depicting the merry paradise of the usually grim Mexican rain-god Tlaloc, which he had seen a few days before at Teotihuacan; and the sixteenth-century missionaries' success in divining and meeting their Indian peasant converts' spiritual needs was attested in A.D. 1953 by the loving care that the converts' descendants were still lavishing on these magnificent works of an exotic architecture and art that had been bequeathed to them by the Spanish friars who had arrived in the wake of the *conquistadores*. [Toynbee, 1956, pp. 161–162.]

We should not, however, allow the art historian's value of aesthetic appreciation to divert attention from the religious factor in cross-cultural assimilation. Whatever the surface attractiveness of form, religious art is a channel of disclosure, and in the Mexican case the rituals of rain-making have helped to sustain and shape new artistic expressions that came with the missionaries.

The distinctive forms of religious adaptation in Mexico are the result of the specific encounter of Catholicism with the culture. Nevertheless, it is right to argue that such a pattern of adaptation follows closely the delineations of translatability, of the prominence that the vernacular acquires in the Christian setting. The special Catholic character of this indigenous convergence gives prominence to saints, virgins, martyrs, the dead, demons, and evil spirits — all of this infused with a popular local ethos. Consequently, Mexican accommodation to Christianity is essentially a creation of the people. It isn't the result of the theories of a handful of theologians; it is the spontaneous expression of a people who, in order to face their misfortunes, *had* to believe. For centuries religion has not been the opium but the balm of the Mexicans. With the same freedom and confidence in the supernatural with which they converted the ancient gods into saints and Christian demons, the Mexicans have adopted and transformed Western art forms. [Paz, 1987.]

The introduction of Western art in the mission field took place in the context of translation, and that produced a new situation altogether. Missionaries accepted the indigenous culture as the final destination of the message, and they were prepared to go to similar lengths in renouncing Western culture as the normative pattern for all peoples. Mission had brought the missionaries to the point of radical tension with their own culture. They gave evidence of that

in translating Christianity into terms of their prospective converts' art, philosophy, and ethos. They recognized that, in coming on to these prospective converts' ground, they would be improving the chances of success for their own mission, and, in this cause they showed themselves ready to waive their natural human prejudice in favour of their ancestral Western manners and customs and to discard anything in Western Christianity that, as they saw it, was merely one of Christianity's accidental Western trappings and was not of the essence of Christianity itself. [Toynbee, 1956, p. 160.]

THE EXAMPLE OF JAPAN

The issue of the Western cultural trappings of Christianity and the obligation to seek indigenous equivalents for the gospel was to rise with particular sharpness in the early years of the Jesuits in Japan. Thanks to rich documentation on what took place in Japan, we are now able to represent the issue in exceptionally clear terms, often with the words of the missionaries or the Japanese themselves. It proves that Christianity is unable to escape the cultural framework of the people it addresses.

Two phases may be described of the introduction of Christianity to Japan. The first phase saw a dogged attempt to impose European culture on the Japanese as the price for membership in the church, and the second was an equally determined effort to repudiate European culture as incompatible with Japan's amour propre whose encouragement was essential to the successful planting of the church. There was a third phase of extreme Japanese reaction against Christianity, but that is at least twice removed from the issue of mission as translation.

The first phase may be said to coincide with the career of the Portuguese Jesuit, Francisco Cabral, who was the mission superior in Japan between 1570 and 1581. Cabral was an uncompromising advocate of the cultural mission of Europe, convinced that the only safeguard to authentic Christianity was European cultural and political hegemony. It led him to painful contradictions. The Jesuits were present in Japan to make converts, first to the church but also to the ranks of the order. Yet Cabral saw no future in a Japanese church led by the Japanese themselves, and he viewed with grave alarm the admission of Japanese to the Society of Jesus. " 'If one does not cease and desist admitting Japanese into the Society,' he warned after he had left Japan and was Jesuit Provincial of Goa in 1596, 'that will be the reason for the collapse of the Society, nay! of Christianity in Japan, and it will later hardly prove possible to find a remedy' " (Elison, 1973, p. 16).

Cabral was struck by the cultural wealth of Japan, the energy and intelligence of the people, but in his version of cultural Pharisaism such evidence proved the contrary. The Japanese, he said, were too inclined to learning and to novelties to be trustworthy, and the missionary could never take them at face value, so full of cunning and insincerity were they. Those Japanese who had entered the Society of Jesus were consequently subject to ridicule, treated badly, and pushed to low positions. If all that was designed to strike at the self-esteem of Japanese Christians it could not have succeeded more. As for the question of learning the Japanese language, Cabral held this in contempt. The language, he felt, was unworthy of study, although circumstances later forced him to change his tune and permit instruction in the language. This was in 1576 when at a conference at Kuchinotsu he underlined the importance of knowledge in Japanese, calling for a college to be established for this purpose. Yet he remained adamant that Japanese custom should not be allowed to enter the church.

The second phase was an abrupt departure from the regime of Cabral, and it was ushered in by the arrival of the Italian Jesuit, Alexandro Valignano, who agreed with his Portuguese predecessor that Japanese culture was startlingly different from that of Europe, but he differed from Cabral's conclusion in equally startling ways. Japan's cultural difference from Europe, he insisted, was an argument for adopting Japanese culture rather than attempting single-mindedly to suppress it and impose Europe's cultural hegemony. "Valignano ordered a complete reversal of approach. Everywhere in every possible way everything was to be done in the Japanese fashion and with Japanese ceremony; and this was a matter of principle. The measures ordained by the Visitator constituted a remarkable surrender of Europe to Japan" (Elison, 1973, p. 56).

Valignano himself wrote that "the Japanese manner of life is so strange . . . that those who live among them, if they wish to accomplish anything, must accommodate themselves to their ways" (Elison, 1973, p. 56). The consequences for flouting Japanese custom, he warned, would produce the most serious of setbacks for the cause: "thus is lost the reputation of our law jointly with its fruit" (ibid.). He proceeded to untangle the braided contradictions of Cabral. Christian mission, he felt instinctively, was vernacular in essence, and was thus inherently tolerant of all cultures. Our very difference from others is reason for respecting them as unique bearers of God's universal aim for the human race, not grounds for elevating our own cultural accomplishments as normative for them. "Valignano started from the proposition that the cultures of Europe and Japan differed in essence. Hence it followed that men who came from Europe to work in Japan had not merely to adapt themselves to local circumstances and custom but 'like children begin to learn again' all the essentials of behavior" (Elison, 1973, p. 18).

Valignano pressed his insights for practical details. Accommodation of the mission to Japanese culture, he urged, was an absolute necessity, *es del todo necesario que nos acomodemos*. He required "that there be made by the Japanese themselves a compendium and sure manual of the customs and good breeding which we have to observe, among ourselves as also toward outsiders, of the manner which the *bonzes* use, so that we all should keep one mode of behavior and not wander, as until now, sometimes ignorant of what we are doing or what we should do" (Elison, 1973, p. 57).

On his second visit to Japan, in 1590, Valignano, it is claimed, introduced movable type in Japan. It was used by the mission to print translated works in Japanese. Elison writes: "The literature eventually produced by the mission press included not only devotional tracts and the rather quaint intrusion of Aesop into Japan but also works of monumental importance for the study of contemporary Japanese linguistics. . . . The translation of European works such as the *Imitatio Christi* can only be called superb, and prove that language at least formed no barrier to spiritual transmission" (Elison, 1973, p. 20).

Valignano also produced a catechism in Japanese, the earliest translation work of any importance undertaken in that language. The catechism is a tour de force on the importance of cultural accommodation, and Valignano spared no effort to press the case for the vernacular. Here he turned the tables on the cultural Pharisaism of Europe. Japan, he argued, was in many important respects a model for Europe, and he suggested that culture contact between the two might help to reform the uncouth European (Elison, 1973, p. 57). Jesuit missionaries were to live in Japanese-style houses, and every detail of their residence should be patterned after Japanese style, including special tea pavilions and cubicles for storing implements pertaining to wine. The Japanese eating customs were also to be observed, including the use of low tables. He forbade the keeping of pigs or goats, or the slaughter of cattle or trade in their skin, all of which constituted an offense to the Japanese. Japanese usage was to be observed in details of diet and table manners. The Christian community was to identify itself with Japanese society and adhere to the eating of rice and soup, with fruit for dessert. It was of utmost importance, he concluded, that "Europeans, when they cross over to Japan, abandon their original habits and customs and learn Japanese habits and customs" (Elison, 1973, p. 61).

This is not to imply that Valignano's motive was totally free of a sense of moral superiority vis-à-vis Japanese society. Indeed, as a recent study indicates, Valignano had at one stage been very negative about Japan and its people (Spence, 1985, pp. 42, 176–77). However, as field experience mellowed him, Valignano adopted a different course, still critical, but this time toward the Western cultural assumptions of Christian mission (Spence, 1985, p. 225). He was adamant that Christian mission was not the cultural diffusion of Europe. Similarly, it is not necessary to prove the soundness of his method by the successful planting of the church in Japan. As it was, the church was rejected. What is important for our purposes is that Valignano believed, and rightly so, that Christianity should be at home in all cultures, and that cross-cultural exposure would help to mitigate Europe's cultural arrogance. Such an eventuality would be a positive gain for the march of God's kingdom. Thus, in his case too we see a missionary in radical tension with his own culture, receiving from the feedback of mission a deepened sense of mistrust in the normative application of Western cultural patterns in the rest of the world. The Gentile mission, even among the Japanese, had created repercussions for a Jerusalemite view of the church, and in the bitter dispute between Valignano and Cabral we catch more than a few echoes of Saint Paul's struggles with Saint Peter. The very difference of Japan from Europe, Valignano argued, is the basis for abandoning the idea that Japan had to conform to Europe. On the contrary, Europe through the church has to shed its superiority complex if it wants to reach the soul of Japan.

Cabral's position, we have pointed out, was full of contradictions whereas Valignano seems to be in tune with the vernacular proclivity of Christianity. It is interesting that the two of them would be at one concerning the teachings of the church and would presumably have nothing to argue about if they had remained in Europe. But the missionary enterprise introduced a new standard for evaluating the message of Christianity with reference to its immediate cultural context, a standard by which both men were required to discharge their obligation. Cabral came woefully short of it, with grave implications for the future of the cause in Japan.

This vernacular standard was the magnetic field in which the attempt to transmit Christianity from Europe was primed for indigenous assimilation. Missionaries themselves began to respond from the hidden stimulus of field exposure. Those who, like Cabral, remained resolute about fidelity to the European cultural hardware found themselves involved in all sorts of contradictions, and it was a matter of time before missionaries realized that the signals on the ground were an essential part of the message.

The hidden stimulus of field exposure was clearly operative right from the very beginning of the mission to Japan even if Cabral came into collision with it. We need only consider one example to show how mission as translation helped to mine the field. Francis Xavier was the first Jesuit missionary to come to Japan, in August 1549. To prepare himself for that mission he had earlier, in December 1547, encountered a Japanese, named Yajirō, at Malacca, who was subsequently baptized at Goa in May 1548.

Yajirō became, in the language of anthropological protocol, Xavier's native informant. Yajirō gave early promise of his usefulness to the Jesuits, whom he impressed with his aptitude as a Christian convert. He was quick at his lessons and abounding in his zeal. He mastered the Portuguese language and added to that knowledge of the Scriptures, with the Jesuits struck by the speed with which he learned the Gospel of Matthew. Consequently the Jesuits came to repose much trust in Yajirō for the Christianization of Japan.

However, it was not long before Xavier began to question the usefulness of Yajirō for the mission to Japan. While still in China, Xavier discovered that an important connection existed between China and Buddhism in Japan, and that knowledge of the religion at its roots as well as in its Japanese manifestation was essential for Christian mission. And so it was that he came to apply to Yajirō the test of vernacular competence, which showed the convert's grave shortcomings. Xavier wrote in February 1549: "The religions of the Japanese are handed down in certain recondite letters unknown to the vulgar, such as among us are [sic] the Latin. On which account [Yajirō], an uneducated man and quite plainly unschooled in such manner of books, states that he is not equipped to give evidence on the religions of his native land" (Elison, 1973, p. 32).

Xavier continued to rely on Yajirō as a *faute de mieux,* but the vulnerability of the Jesuit missionary was plain. After he arrived in Japan, Xavier discovered that the inaccurate information on Japanese religion and vernacular concepts on which he based his preaching had landed him in an untenable situation. He began to make a painful retreat after he learned about the true Japanese conception of religion. By that stage, of course, he had demonstrated the limited usefulness of foreign notions or the misguided remedy of reliance on secondhand authority. Xavier was, however, correct in seeking to enter Japan by the vernacular door, although he may have held back from facing squarely some of the consequences of vernacularization, a point that a much later missionary figure like Henry Venn isolated for stringent criticism, as we shall see in chapter 4.

An equally important consequence of mission as translation was the final status of Yajirō. The Jesuits came to value him less as a brilliant trophy of missionary success than as a potential agent for the vernacularization of the church in Japan. So his Christian credentials were judged inadequate for his status as a genuine Japanese convert. Indeed, his exposure to foreign ideas and customs was seen as a serious obstacle for Christian pioneering. From this view it turns out that Christian mission is itself inadequate until it acquires a vernacular credibility.[2]

Thus the insistence, or even suspicion, that Christ and Western culture are one and the same without the possibility of distinction, as claimed by someone like Ernst Troeltsch, is answered by the radical process of vernacularization, a process that reduces Western culture to a peripheral status from the point of view of the new context. Mission may therefore be viewed as a force for cultural relativism, although in proclaiming the saving acts of God it brings culture under the judgment of God rather than allowing it to absolutize itself.

THE EXAMPLE OF INDIA

The Roman Catholic Initiative: Robert de Nobili

Catholic missions to India were seen as an extension of the Portuguese seaborne empire. At Goa, the capital of Portuguese Asia, the missionaries were controlled, and their work on the mainland incorporated under the ancient prerogative of the *Padroado* by which the pope invested the Portuguese Crown with rights and privileges over all Catholic missions in Africa, Asia, and Brazil, a concession to Portugal's maritime predominance. Goa was Portugal abroad, and access to it was strictly controlled. A huge cultural gap separated it from the India of the mainland. It functioned like a cruise liner berthed in Indian waters, with missionaries and their converts being extended links of the firm Portuguese anchor.

Portugal's control of the Catholic mission introduced complications into relations with the church, and when Lisbon's grasp on the seaborne trade began to be seriously challenged by other European powers, a nervous Portuguese Crown proceeded to impose restrictions on missionaries not from Portugal and to monitor closely work on the ground. Francis Xavier, for example, lost his patience with the Portuguese in India, threatening to "flee" to Japan because he could not stand the corruption of the Portuguese officials, claiming it was a "martyrdom" to see the good work of missionaries being destroyed by official greed and immorality. "Everywhere and at all times," he lamented, "it is rapine, hoarding and robbery. . . . I never cease wondering at the number of new inflections which, in addition to all the usual forms, have been added in this language to the avarice of conjugation of that ill-omened verb 'to rob' " (Cronin, 1959, p. 29). Even the Vatican found the *Padroado* arrangement irksome, replacing it in the 1620s with the Propaganda Fide.

The first Jesuit missionary to India was Thomas Stephens, an Englishman, who at thirty arrived in Goa in 1579. He was known under the Portuguese form of his name, Padre Estevão. However, the missionary whose work really rocked the boat was Robert de Nobili (1577–1656), an Italian nobleman born in Rome and who at the age of seventeen received the call to enter the Society of Jesus, much to the distress of his well-endowed family. De Nobili embarked on a radical transposition of Christianity into Hindu terms, thereby obtaining the honorifique "the Sannyāsi," the title of that form of ascetic and wild holiness that respectable religion everywhere tries to shun. Immersing himself in the study of Tamil and Sanskrit, de Nobili strove hard to observe Hindu customs in language, food, dress, and house. He adopted a Tamil name, Tattuva Bodhakar (from the Sanskrit *tatva,* "reality," hence "teacher of reality"), and abandoned the Portuguese language. At Madurai in south India, where he was now based, he turned his home into a *madam,* an Indian mud hut. No longer living in exile, de Nobili saw India as his native home.

Barely a month in India, de Nobili's inner resolve to put on India like a natural hue, rather than as a temporary cloak, was severely tested. He had witnessed the rite of *suttee,* the practice in which the wives of deceased men showed their *sati* (faithfulness) by voluntarily throwing themselves into the funeral flames. Although *suttee* is of dubious origin, not being mentioned in the oldest of the Vedas or in the *Ramayana,* it became a deeply entrenched part of Hindu custom. De Nobili hung back from self-righteous condemnation and instead tried to understand the custom from the Hindu point of view. His attitude was that Hindu India has something to teach him and all missionaries. After ascertaining the precise way in which religious and social relationships are structured, de Nobili assimilated into the Saivite Brahmin caste of Raja, and his first converts accorded him the religious term "guru," the "one who imparts knowledge" and whose life is a model. The paradigm is from the Saivite Vedanta Sāra, not the Gospels, an indication that de Nobili's own European priestly habits would have to be changed accordingly, the black cassock and leather shoes of the Jesuit for the red-ochre cloth and rough wooden sandals of the sannyāsi. This description of his personal "translation" completes his cultural journey from West to East:

> The consultors' approval reached Nobili in November 1607, a year after his arrival in Madurai. At once he discarded his black cassock and leather shoes. He had his hair shaved close to the skull and, since Indians considered a bare brow naked and indecent, he made a rectangular mark on his forehead with sandal. . . . His body he draped in three pieces of red-ochre cloth, two round his shoulders, the third round his loins extending below the knees. . . . On his feet he clamped high wooden sandals. Though the light red-ochre cloths proved more comfortable in hot weather than his black cassock, the sandals were meant to be awkward and penitential. He obtained a water-gourd to carry in his left hand when he went out, and a bamboo stick with seven knots to carry in his right hand. In Indian eyes Nobili was now what he claimed to be, an ascetic, his life devoted to serving God: a beggar clothed in the sunrise. [Cronin, 1959, pp. 70–71.]

For de Nobili, as for the early Christians, Christianity had not come to uproot but to build upon, not to reject but to renew. He saw Christianity as the flowering of all that was best in India, not the pretext for imposing a Western culture on Indians. With his knowledge of Sanskrit and Tamil, de Nobili was able to respond to the searching critique to which Brahmin scholars submitted Christianity.[3] Thus *avatars* ("incarnate beings"), Yoga, *bhakti* ("devotion," Christianity being referred to as *Bhakti-marga,* "the great devotion"), *maya* ("illusion"), *brahma, samsara* (the affliction of metempsychosis), *Trimurti* (the "triune" deity of Saivite doctrine), *vedam* ("knowledge," the term for Christianity), and *puja* ("sacrifice") all left their mark on the Christianity of de Nobili. The refinements he subsequently made to his theology reflected the depth of Indian impact on his thinking. In one matter he continued to defy the India he had learned so wholeheartedly to embrace, and that was the observance of the Mass where he made the Latin formula of consecration over unleavened bread and wine imported from Europe instead of using locally produced rice-cakes and wine made from raisins soaked in water as had been the wont until the practice was discontinued in 1599 (Cronin, 1959, pp. 146–47).

Nevertheless, de Nobili was acutely conscious of the fatal mistake of linking Christianity to the Portuguese cause in India, for the inevitable decline of Portuguese power would leave the church helplessly exposed. The lessons of history were plain for all to read: a strong Christian community must be reared on its own roots, and India must for that reason have its own clergy rooted in its traditions. The alternative was at best foreign stigma and at worst oblivion. The model for creating a trained Indian clergy existed in Madurai University, an ancient foundation of learning where Tiruvalluvar, rated as the greatest of Tamil poets, worked sometime between A.D. 800 and 1000. In the new Christian institution de Nobili would seek to establish on firm foundations the teaching of Indian languages and philosophy, giving pride of place to the mother tongue. He found sanction for this in Catholic tradition:

> No less an authority than St Thomas Aquinas had pointed out the great advantage that accrued to the Fathers and early apologists from the fact that they had been pagans. Nobili, despite his mastery of Sanskrit, Tamil and Telegu, despite the fact that he could quote at ease from the Vedas, Puaranas and most famous Indian poems, was aware that no amount of learning could replace the deepest springs within the soul, fed by blood, tradition and climate, and crystallized in a mother tongue. [Cronin, 1959, p. 173.]

De Nobili had set an example himself, and not only his theological discourse but his cosmology took on the strong ornate colors of Tamil and Sanskrit culture. Tamil poetry was exuberant with its ornate details and its exultant multilayered clauses, with Brahmin writers adding a contrived and refined flourish to all this. De Nobili learned this style and utilized it in his writings. And so in the jeweled tongue of Tamil poets, de Nobili set to lyrical style a Christian vision of nature as God's exquisite creation, with the form of discourse serving to encourage the belief in creation that Hindu philosophy has found a major stumbling block. As the first European to have discovered the Vedas, de Nobili had taken a keen interest in Indian astronomy, helping to spread knowledge of what India had to teach the world in this matter. As a partial return, he introduced India to the latest astronomical discoveries of Galileo who had built the first astronomical telescope in 1609, as well as to Kepler's law of elliptical orbits discovered in

1609, a hypothesis with which it was now possible to compute exact measurements, volume, and distance of planets and the numerous stars of the Milky Way and the Pleiades. To India's understanding of crystals de Nobili added the knowledge of optics. But de Nobili's chief works were religious and philosophical, and his five-volume *Spiritual Teaching,* composed in Tamil as the *Gnanopadesam,* capped his lifelong interest. His *Defence of Religion,* written in Tamil and Telegu, showed his mastery of the popular genre. In all this work de Nobili was preaching Christianity from Indian classical sources, quite willing, anxious even, to drift free of the colonial tide that would continue to sweep over India. He had repeated for Christians in India the transformation that Hellenization had done for the Western church.

The Protestant Initiative: William Carey

With the Protestants we find a similar emphasis on the importance of the mother tongue and a devotion to translatability, if not at the level of cultural assimilation, then certainly at that of scriptural translation where the consequences were no less momentous.

The coming of William Carey (1761–1834) to India in 1793 was to constitute a remarkable episode in the history of Christian mission. From a humble English Nonconformist background, Carey came to occupy an important place in the missionary initiative toward Asia and Africa: the founding of the Baptist Missionary Society in 1792, the London Missionary Society in 1795, and, more than a century after he had first mooted the idea, the International Missionary Council were results of his exertions. Carey was clear that the expansion of Christianity abroad should not be the perpetuation of denominationalism or the imposition of Western ecclesiastical forms. By implication, Carey allowed for the indigenous expression of Christianity, trusting that the gospel, faithfully proclaimed, would stimulate the arrangements proper to it. His unbounded confidence in the worldwide range of the gospel challenged Christians to think seriously of societies beside their own, and certainly beyond the formal limits of British overseas jurisdiction.

Carey had originally intended to serve in Tahiti, but was eventually diverted to India where he arrived at Calcutta. Through various trials and hardship Carey went on to pursue studies in Sanskrit and Bengali, both of which he mastered. He was able to translate most of the Bible into Bengali and to devote time to acquiring knowledge of Indian plants. In order to support his work Carey had taken employment with the English East India Company but found the company unsympathetic to religious work. As a consequence he moved to Serampore under the shadow of the more amenable Danish authorities.

At Serampore, Carey and his colleagues set up a printing press, and at their suggestion he took up employment again with the East India Company teaching Bengali. His developed linguistic research contributed to the renaissance of Bengali prose literature. With his missionary companions at

Serampore, Carey took a leading part in establishing Serampore as a major language center. By 1832 the press there had produced religious material in forty-four languages and dialects. Furthermore, Carey continued with his interest in Sanskrit, and together with a colleague, Joshua Marshman, a self-educated man, he produced a translation of the Indian epic poem, the *Ramayana,* in an attempt to introduce Western readers to the Indian classics.

This impressive linguistic enterprise was mounted on a solid foundation of dictionaries and grammars and the establishment of a college where Indians could be trained. The curriculum at the college included not only the Christian Scriptures and theology but also the philosophies and religions of India.

As is well known, Carey and his colleagues made few numerical inroads into India. The importance of their work lies less in statistical gains than in their brilliant development of the vernacular, and that notwithstanding their self-avowedly evangelical motives. On the contrary, it was his evangelical zeal that led Carey to explore the world of India in its religious, linguistic, botanical, and social diversity. No barrier of unfamiliarity, no obstacle of ignorance or suspicion was great enough to restrict what he considered the universal range of the gospel. Consequently, he expended himself in fields far removed from statistical gains, though still true to his religious ideals. He thus came to initiate a variety of schemes, including "modern education, new conceptions of agriculture, new industries, the first steam engine, the first Indian newspaper, great movements of social reform, and had a major part in the translating of the Bible into four languages" (North, 1938, p. 3). If the fruits of his labor obscure by their unintendedness the lofty conviction from which they sprang, they are still the legitimate consequences of a religious initiative.

It is relevant also to consider the problematic relationship with British colonial authorities. Carey had earlier experienced difficulties with the East India Company authorities in Calcutta. After he moved to Serampore, these difficulties did not abate. There, between 1806 and 1812, attempts were made to restrict the work and to halt all missionary endeavor in India. The authorities argued that mission was a threat to British rule by inciting a spirit of religious animosity, which, by some inexplicable chemistry, undermined the basis of colonial rule. The diagnosis was correct, but in an oblique way: Christian mission, by furnishing a systematic account of the indigenous heritage, tacitly encouraged pride and confidence in the people, and in time this must prevail against the unstated logic of colonial overlordship. So far so right. But the authorities erred seriously in imputing to mission the sinister motive of inciting interreligious violence as a precursor to general sedition. The methodical and sensitive manner in which Carey and others set about studying Indian languages and religions is scarcely the recipe for communal and political chaos. By taking the best that India had to offer and putting it in a form that preserved it while exposing it to wider interest, Carey and the others might have been plausibly accused of elitism, but hardly of popular inflammation. The instinct of the authorities was right where their logic was flawed.

One brief example must suffice on a large subject. In the eighteenth century the Danish missionary Schwarz, operating at Tanjore, met the ruler Raja Hyder Ali, who desired some negotiations with the English government and had said, "Do not send me to any of your agents, for I trust neither their words nor their treaties. But send me to the missionary of whose character I hear so much from every one; him will I receive and trust" (Müller, 1874, p. 16). Colonial high-handedness rather than missionary Jacobinism proved a far more fertile source of popular disaffection.

In the event, Carey's work laid the basis for a profound philosophical and philological inquiry into India, and a long line of distinguished scholars came into their own by pushing along the frontiers that he, with such distinction, had penetrated, and that at a time when most Western scholars had little inkling of the treasures Carey had learned to take in his giant stride.

One of these distinguished scholars was Max Müller, one of the great minds of the nineteenth century, a man who made accessible to the West a vast wealth of Indian classical literature. Though a German by birth, Max Müller emigrated to England where he eventually became professor of comparative philology at Oxford. He was one of the earliest proponents of the academic study of religion that we know today as "history of religion."

Max Müller's view on mission we would today regard as sentimental: the sunny assumption that the statistical advance of the church worldwide would be proof of the genius of the religion. But he followed closely enough the work of Christian missions in India to deepen his appreciation of India's heritage. For example, when he looked at Buddhism he was able to appreciate its missionary dimension, illuminating aspects of the history of Buddhism by a comparison with Christian mission. He thus underlined the importance of the Great Council of Pataliputra in 246 B.C. at which a Buddhist missionary movement was launched in and beyond India, comparing the role of the king and his edicts with that of Constantine.

It may be observed here that Max Müller's ideas were picked up in West Africa where Edward Blyden analyzed his views in the context of the missionary heritage of the Western church (Blyden, 1967, pp. 241–42). Blyden was to make further use of Max Müller's work in another connection, to be explained subsequently.

In particular, when he contemplated the deeper implications of Christian mission in India, Müller saw that its statistical range bore no relationship to the effects it had produced on Indian culture. A tangible evidence of this came in the shape of Ram Mohun Roy (1772–1833), the founder of the Brahma-Samaj, a Neo-Hindu movement that helped to revitalize and strengthen Hinduism with reference to its classical heritage. Thus was born the movement to rehabilitate the Vedas, including the oldest of the sacred books, the Rig-Veda.

The Hindu revival in the modern period of Indian history owed no small part of its beginnings to the wider repercussions of Christian mission. In many places in India, missionary establishments had brought in the teaching of Indian religions and their inclusion in Christian devotional life. One missionary prelate, Bishop Cotton, for example, advised students at a missionary institution in Calcutta to use a hymn from the Rig-Veda in their daily prayers (Müller, 1874, p. 57). Even if one took an exceptionally hard line on the polytheist ethos of Hinduism, Max Müller was convinced that Christians would emerge refreshed and enhanced from their contact with the religion.

All the evidence adduced here is not proof that the Indian church (or churches, since there are many Christian traditions in India) became only a minor satellite of the Hindu religious orbit. On the contrary, historically there has been resistance to the prospect of being swallowed up in the *advaita* world of Hinduism, and Christians have occasionally clung tenaciously to Western cultural forms as insurance for their separate identity. What should be stressed here is that the pressure to articulate Christian insights with reference to the Hindu environment will escalate for the church if it in turn takes seriously its missionary obligation. Mission will be the crucible in which Indian Christians will become enmeshed in the world of vernacular self-understanding, with equally inevitable implications for the vernacular itself.

Already in his reflections on the place of Christianity among the religions of the world, Max Müller was led to contemplate a pluralist comparative framework that accords an equal place to the other religions. More than that, he argued strongly for bringing together all these religions, not in a facile merger, but in such a way that one tradition can illuminate the insights of the other and in so doing reveal processes that clarify the history of the religious phenomenon. This is why he believed that the history of religion is "more deeply interesting than the history of language, of literature, of art, or politics" (Müller, 1874, p. 34).

One account describes how missionaries were drawn closer to the ordinary people in an attempt to provide a responsible translation. (It took over twenty-nine years to translate the entire Bible.) The scene was China in 1913. We should notice the tutorial status of the missionaries vis-à-vis their Chinese instructors.

> Now we sit down to our task, ten men including our Chinese teachers. . . . We are trying to settle the text of the Book of the Acts. How simple it looks in English, but almost every verse means a battle. . . . A verse is read and the debate begins: "The style is too low, just what the coolies on the street use." "But we want a style that even the coolies can understand. The trouble with our Bibles is that they have been translated for the learned and not for the common people." "This phrase is quite impossible in our section; it is a classical phrase with us and will never be understood." "But it isn't what the Greek says. . . ." "I hold that if Luke had been writing in Chinese, he

would have used just this phrase. . . ." So the debate goes on and the result for a morning's work is a few verses. . . . Three months of such work and the first draft of Acts is ready to be printed and sent to the printer later to undergo two long and careful revisions. [North, 1938, p. 8, citing *China Year Book,* 1913.]

It is not necessary to carry further this line of reasoning to appreciate how Christian mission laid the basis for comparative studies in general, and excited a profound revitalization process within the vernacular itself. It is the logical opposite of colonialism, for the means and methods of mission, though perhaps not the motives, conspired together with the consequences to determine a vernacular destiny for the cause. That this took place while India or Japan or wherever was at the same time being drawn into a world system suggests that indigenous renewal is a condition for effective and meaningful participation in the family of nations.

THE AFRICAN FACTOR IN MISSION

When we consider the African situation, we encounter a similar problem of mission in dialectical tension with colonialism. The position in sixteenth- and seventeenth-century West Africa has already been described in detail in the present writer's book *West African Christianity,* and we may therefore move rapidly to a consideration of the modern epoch of mission to Africa.

David Livingstone and His Legacy: A Reassessment

One of the most famous missionaries to Africa of all time was David Livingstone, the Scottish physician and traveler who fired the imagination of the Western world in the nineteenth century. He gave popular expression to the notion that commerce, civilization, and Christianity must go hand in hand, particularly in the so-called Dark Continent where, as he saw it, the scourge of the slave had to be lifted.

Many writers have seized on Livingstone's ideas as a catalyst for the onset of colonialism, believing that the call for the "Three Cs," as it came to be known, was an implicit demand for legitimate government and Western tutelage. In his masterly account of the colonial consequences of mission, Roland Oliver has described in detail what possible links there were between the different Christian missions and Western colonial intrusion and rivalry in East Africa (Oliver, 1970). Yet Oliver is careful to note that the overwhelming tendency of mission was to open the way for African leadership in the church, and in some significant cases for an Africanization process, which conflicted with Western cultural notions. Oliver writes:

It is therefore against the background of ecclesiastical organizations already largely African in personnel and increasingly self-supporting in finance that the specific contribution of the European missionary factor . . . has to be examined and assessed. . . . As the indigenous institutions took shape, the pastoral missionary became less an initiator than a caretaker, holding an already well-defined position until a native of the country should be ready to occupy it. [Oliver, 1970, p. 245.]

In one place Oliver is able to recognize that mission in the end came to diverge sharply from the methods and goals of empire.

During the modern period, . . . the missionary world was conscious of being engaged, with only stationary or diminishing forces, against a steadily growing body of Western influences, whose operation was by no means necessarily favourable to the growth of African Christianity. . . . As at that time when their position has appeared to be threatened by the violent inroads of the Arabs, so now, missionaries felt compelled to enter the political arena and to protect by wider than spiritual methods what they believed to be the interests of the African Church. [Oliver, 1970, p. 247.]

Thus Oliver hints at the internal contradictions between mission and colonialism, and between "the interests of the African Church" and the methods and consequences of empire. A perceptive scholar, Oliver would be the first to agree that such contradictions stem from a profound disparity between the forces of indigenization activated by the translation enterprise of mission and considerations of alien suzerainty. An African church, rooted in the vernacular, must inevitably come into conflict with a political system based on the superiority of foreign institutions. As the American Christian leader John Raleigh Mott put it, that form of Christianity that was perpetuated under the protection of Western colonialism would be overthrown, along with its political ally, in the wake of indigenous nationalism (Mott, 1910, pp. 29–31).

An important difference, however, is that mission furnished nationalism with the resources necessary to its rise and success, whereas colonialism came upon it as a conspiracy. At the heart of the nationalist awakening was the cultural pride that missionary translations and the attendant linguistic research stimulated. We might say with justice that mission begot cultural nationalism, as the Slavic mission so clearly demonstrated. And in this respect, to return to the celebrated Scot, Livingstone was both witness and agent of that phenomenon.

In the early 1850s Dr. Livingstone, more than a decade after he had first come into contact with Africa, gave an account of his reflections on the wider implications of scriptural translation. He took as his example the work of his protégé, Robert Moffat, who began work in Botswana, then Bechuanaland, in the 1820s. He called Moffat's translation enterprise a work of immense labor, drawing attention to the fact that Moffat was the first to reduce the speech of the Bechuanas, called Sichuana, to a written form. Livingstone himself knew the language, which made a deep and indelible impression on him. He spoke of its richness, its copiousness, and its subtlety. Some European students of the language, he said, may imagine that there would be few obstacles in mastering the tongue of a primitive people. However, his own experience was different.

> In my own case, though I have had as much intercourse with the purest idiom as most Englishmen, and have studied the language carefully, yet I can never utter an important statement without doing so very slowly, and repeating it too, lest the foreign accent . . . should render the sense unintelligible. . . . The capabilities of this language may be inferred from the fact that the Pentateuch is fully expressed in Mr. Moffat's translation in fewer words than in the Greek Septuagint, and in a very considerably smaller number than in our own English version. [Livingstone, 1857, p. 114.]

Livingstone then went on to consider the wider cultural effects of translation. The orderliness and simplicity of the language of the Bechuanas should not, he cautioned, lead to the wrong conclusion that the people had fallen from a former state of civilization. Instead it should challenge us to consider the universal human characteristics of language. He says:

> The language is however so simple in its construction, that its copiousness by no means requires the explanation that the people have fallen from a former state of civilisation and culture. Language seems to be an attribute of the human mind and thought, and the inflections, various as they are in the most barbarous tongues, as that of the Bushmen, are probably only proofs of the race being human, and endowed with the power of thinking; the fuller development of language taking place as the improvement of our other faculties goes on. [Livingstone, 1857, p. 114.]

From such philosophical reflections Livingstone was driven to defending the purity of native speech, being anxious to preserve it from corrupting contact with Western civilization:

> It is fortunate that the translation of the Bible has been effected before the language became adulterated with half-uttered foreign words, and while those who have heard the eloquence of the native assemblies are still living; for the young, who are brought up in our schools, know less of the language than the missionaries; and Europeans born in the country, while possessed of the idiom perfectly, if not otherwise educated, cannot be referred to for explanation of any uncommon word. [Livingstone, 1857, p. 114.]

This suggests a conflict between the need for mission schools and the demands for scriptural translation. The veteran missionary Edwin Smith, who translated the Ila New Testament of Zambia, spoke to this question, and clarified it in the following words:

> Men need two kinds of language, in fact; a language of the home, of emotion, of unexpressed associations; and a language of knowledge, exact argument, scientific truth, one in which words are world-current and steadfast in their meanings. Where the mother tongue does not answer both needs, the people must inevitably become bilingual; but however fluent they may succeed in being in the foreign speech, its words can never feel to them as their native words. To express the dear and intimate things which are the very breath and substance of life a man will fall back on the tongue he learnt not at school, but in the house — how, he remembers not. He may bargain in the other, or pass examinations in it, but he will pray in his home speech. If you wish to reach his heart you will address him in that language. [Smith, 1930, p. 8.][4]

Livingstone's clear articulation of mission as translation is thus reinforced by his equally direct exposition of the wider cultural effects of such an enterprise. We can see the apparent irony of the missionary upholding the dignity of indigenous speech and concepts while local populations drift in the tide of Westernization. Two roles are thus defined of the missionary: that of safeguarding the indigenous heritage and that of providing modern schools, roles which, at least according to Livingstone himself, appear contradictory. Yet Livingstone would have realized that Africans would be able to participate meaningfully in the changing world of colonialism with the confidence gained from deeper cultural self-understanding. That spirit inspired an earlier missionary, the English Quaker Hannah Kilham (d. 1832), with her work on the role of African languages in primary education (see Sanneh, 1983*a*, pp. 66, 140–41).

There is a further paradox concerning the role of Livingstone himself. This classic representative of the modern missionary was busy with a stalwart defense of the virtues of primitive tribes while, according to a school of history, he justified colonial rule on the grounds of native inadequacy. Yet primitive virtue is hardly compatible with the decadence of Western colonial contact. It is of course true that Livingstone did encourage the spread of what he called "civilization," and that many people, perhaps including himself, understood the term as an extension of the instrument of empire, believing that by that instrument a Christian society might come into being in Africa and elsewhere.[5] So the mission outpost on the so-called Dark Continent would, according to this understanding, be the signal of both the distress and the promise of unconquered peoples.

Yet someone like Livingstone was prepared to trust the vernacular Bible to usher in the kingdom of God, and so thorough was his faith in that agency that he wished to relinquish it into the hands of native Africans without European superintendency. He states:

> When converts are made from heathenism by modern missionaries, it becomes an interesting question whether their faith possesses the elements of permanence, or is only an exotic too tender for self-propagation when the fostering care of the foreign cultivator is withdrawn. If neither habits of self-reliance are cultivated, nor opportunities given for the exercise of that virtue, the most promising converts are apt to become like spoiled children. In Madagascar a few Christians were left with nothing but the Bible in their hands; and though exposed to persecution, and even death itself, as the penalty of adherence to their profession, they increased tenfold in numbers, and are, if possible, more decided believers now than they were when, by an edict of the queen of that island, missionaries ceased their teaching. [Livingstone, 1857, p. 115.]

Such trust in the inherent capabilities of the vernacular environment to nurture the gospel seed and rear its own version of the tree of salvation brought Livingstone into radical tension with his own European cultural roots. He began to see his own Christian heritage in a critical comparative light, convinced that Europe had no monopoly of truth, that even the simplest primitive person could stand right at the heart of God's favor, and that all cultures performed an equally necessary, though inadequate, function in mediating the mystery of God. Europe's advantage vis-à-vis Africa lay in its responsibility to proclaim the gospel with the help of those material resources with which Africa was poorly furnished, but it was not an advantage of intrinsic moral superiority. As the riches, so the accountability.

Livingstone's field labors impelled him to carry his criticism right back to the sources of Western Christianity itself. He waxed eloquent on the theme, and in full tilt toward a recitation of Europe's own shortcomings, he recovered early enough to avoid an erroneous idealization of the Christian cause in Africa. His experience in Africa, he contended, led him to view the so-called Golden Age of Christianity in a radically new light.

> The popular notion, however, of the primitive church is perhaps not very accurate. Those societies especially which consisted of converted Gentiles . . . were certainly anything but pure. In spite of their conversion, some of them carried the stains and vestiges of their former state with them when they passed from the temple to the church. If the instructed and civilized Greek did not all at once rise out of his former self, and understand and realise the high ideal of his new faith, we should be careful, in judging of the work of missionaries among savage tribes, not to apply to their converts tests and standards of too great severity. If the scoffing Lucian's account of the impostor

Peregrinus may be believed, we find a church probably planted by the Apostles manifesting less intelligence even than modern missionary churches. [Livingstone, 1857, p. 107n.]

That passage throws an intriguing light on what may have been Dr. Livingstone's understanding of "civilization." He seems to imply that civilization as such was of little advantage to the Greek regarding what Paul had called "the kindness and severity of God." It is hard to believe that Livingstone would have made such civilization a necessity for salvation with the African. We may surmise that he regarded civilization, however he meant it, as a remedy for sin rather than the substitute for grace, and would therefore have differed radically from the conclusions of someone like Troeltsch. He is indeed conscious not only that the African is fully possessed of humanity but also that the tribesman, untrammeled with cultural conceit, has a disposition of potential faithfulness to the gospel. Altogether, then, mission had brought Livingstone to the very edges of his own culture, and what he needed was assurance that he was not in rebellion. He testified in superlatives of the character of the Bechuana people, convinced from his intimate knowledge of them that, once the seed was planted, he had few qualms about its future, for the people "possess that imperishability which forms so remarkable a feature in the entire African race" (Livingstone, 1857, p. 115). He assured his compatriots: "I would not give any one to understand by this that [Africans] are model Christians — we cannot claim to be model Christians ourselves — or even in any degree superior to the members of our own country churches" (ibid., p. 109).

Nevertheless, the great man cannot be let off so lightly. He is embroiled in a growing tension and appears to have lost his footing. There is, for instance, the mission school set upon the task of "civilizing" native Africans, on the one hand, and, on the other, the vernacular Bible to be driven like a plowshare in virgin fields; there is, too, the demand for colonial rule with which to contend with the evils of the Muslim slave trade, yet a recognition that Western contact of that kind is detrimental to precolonial originality; furthermore, missionaries must assume custody of that precolonial originality lest it diminish in importance at the hands of *deraciné* modern Africans; then, to make the ground even more slippery, missionaries should cooperate with history in promoting the machinery of colonial expansion while simultaneously working for a future of African Christian ascendancy, which would call into question foreign rule. Not many people could emerge from that tension without a fundamental surrender, but Livingstone was marked by it without being crippled. He continued to emphasize and promote the native African theme, conscious that its consequences would be incompatible with foreign suzerainty. He spoke thus: "Protestant missionaries of every denomination in South Africa all agree on one point, that no mere profession of Christianity is sufficient to entitle the converts to the Christian name. They are all anxious to place the Bible in the hands of the natives, and with the ability to read that, there can be little doubt as to the future." (Livingstone, 1857, pp. 117-18).

That theme recurs in numerous parts of the missionary endeavor, suggesting not just a reluctance to make easy or superficial converts, but a commitment to the principle that conversion shall be mounted on indigenous foundations. That theme is the mighty drum roll of Christian expansion in Africa and elsewhere, and it is amplified and embellished by countless repetitions and variations in the literature.

Such insistence on the primacy of the vernacular need not be coupled with explicit missionary support of its consequences for it to have the necessary impact on local populations. For example, missionaries might justify to themselves or to Home Committees that a successful translation would bring in converts in ensembles, an assurance that would be music to the statistical ear. Some might even argue that they were building for a future in which indigenous churches, cloned on the Western pattern, would emerge, with missionaries as the instruments by which providence chose to raise primitive people to the standard of the West. These justifications, whether defensible or not, do not affect the issue at stake. Whatever their motives, all the major missions, as well as their potential converts, were agreed on the necessity and importance of translation. The narrow view that translation was only an efficient method for quantitative superiority has not, in fact, been borne out by the history of translation. Instead, much wider responses in the cultures affected were set off by it.

In this respect Livingstone was not only a representative figure of his age, he was in many ways its guiding light. He had delineated in broad outline the possible scope of colonial hegemony, but he also placed himself at the high frontier of Christian mission by anticipating the vernacular consequences of translation and their implications for Western cultural presuppositions.

In the ensuing atmosphere of colonial hegemony, which followed hard on Livingstone's heels, some missionaries found it impossible to give way to the radical consequences of vernacularization, still holding to remnants of the "civilizing" theory of Western expansion. However, the religious historian need not put too much weight on such sound and fury, for it might be nothing more than protestation at a lost cause. Yet the volume and accessibility of missionary criticism under such circumstances have provided the standard metier for popular accounts, partly because of the volume and accessibility, and partly also because, in its religious stereotype, it offers a safe outlet for the modern Western guilt. It is, however, important in this subject to avoid the twin traps of missionary self-documentation and epistolary success in order to explore the deeper connections and continuities between mission and the vernacular. The inexorable march of time favored the emergence of the African church, a fact to which Roland Oliver has so eloquently called our attention.

The seeds of the divergence between mission and colonialism were sown with the translation enterprise. The idea of the church rooted in African soil, self-propagating, self-reliant and, furthermore, reared on the vernacular Scriptures, must sharply diverge from the notion of a local Christian society that is set to receive in drips Western cultural transfusion. In other words, Western colonialism cannot be altogether auspicious for the African church, and certainly the explosive growth of new churches since independence in the twentieth century is enough of a hint that colonialism had inhibited the gospel in many parts.

We may, therefore, wish to take back something from the confidence with which Harnack, following Origen, developed the argument that the unifying power of the empire helped launch the primitive church in the world. It is, of course, true that the role of the West in the planting of young churches across the world is without parallel, and in that sense the West had a uniform impact. Yet we cannot claim with the same confidence that the success of the missionary enterprise was everywhere bound up with the interests of the empire. The sheer diversity of indigenous churches marks a dramatic turn from the normative ideals of colonial rule. Pluralism of the modern variety came of age in the missionary era, indicating how Christianity will flourish in a variety of climates, and how the imperial connection actually obscures the basic pattern of growth.

Whatever the actual details of the relationship between mission and colonialism, with the London Missionary Society at one extreme of the spectrum and the Pietist Lutherans at the other, the whole atmosphere of reaction to colonialism is an unfavorable climate in which to try to expound the subject of mission. Yet even for those who would find mission guilty of all the sins of the West toward the third world, it should help their case to know precisely the nature of this guilt. A long-standing grievance is that the third world, including Africa, is the victim of Western cultural imperialism, and Western missions have been faulted for this. The sweeping nature of the charge makes it difficult to tackle it head on.

For this reason it seems important to try to identify the consistent element at the ground level of Christian mission, namely, translation, and to try to relate this to the modern encounter with colonialism. From that approach we are able to determine where mission is logically consistent with itself, such as when it adopts the vernacular, and where it deviates from its own inner dynamism, such as when it makes Western culture the basis of its proclamation. We may put this position in terms of a formula: the church proclaims the gospel only because it is true; it is not true only because the church proclaims it. The gospel justifies the proclamation, but the proclamation does not justify the gospel, whatever the appearance to the contrary. Consequently, what Christians say and do may on the ground level be distinguished from each other with reference to the appropriation of the message. Thus the assumed logical connection between mission and colonialism begins to dissolve when we apply this test.

We may, in this vein, regard Livingstone as a radical spirit whose real stature has been concealed by the sweeping nature of the nationalist grievance. Indeed, Livingstone's ideological opposite was Cecil Rhodes, "the empire-builder in the hard political sphere." If for Livingstone the slogan was "Commerce and Christianity," for Cecil Rhodes it was "philanthropy plus five percent." Both dominated Central Africa: Rhodes left a legacy of white domination, Livingstone of rising African aspirations. For example, in the bitter conflict over the abortive Central African Federation of the 1950s, a federation aimed at uniting under white minority rule the territories of Southern Rhodesia, Northern Rhodesia, and Nyasaland, and in the violent sequel of the Rhodesian civil war, we witness the clash between "the Exploiter tradition of Rhodes, with the settler-politicians as its guardians, and the Tutor tradition of Livingstone" whose guardians were the Kenneth Kaundas, the Joshua Nkomos, the Kamuzu Bandas, and the missionaries of the St. Faith's Mission in Southern Rhodesia and the Church of Scotland Mission in Nyasaland (see Keatley, 1963, pp. 124, 467). To take Nyasaland, the African Caledonia that reminded Livingstone so much of his beautiful native Scotland, the missionaries were instrumental in bringing about a national awakening. They helped bring peace to the country when in 1887 they successfully negotiated a peace treaty between the invading Angoni people and the native Atonga. The missionaries followed up by adopting the language of the Manganja, Chi-Nyanja, and employed it as the lingua franca of the country. By this action the missionaries were creating "a sense of Nyasa nationalism. . . . the missionaries gave to the Nyasas a heritage of national unity and of deep regard for learning that was to serve them well in the political battles of the 1950s and 1960s" (Keatley, 1963, p. 129).

The Victorians painted Livingstone in colors of garish flattery and displayed him in stained glass, where he became a convenient target for rock-throwing patriots. It is not there but on the ground in Africa that Livingstone's spirit exerted its profoundest influence. After journeying through territories Livingstone in his own time had traversed, Patrick Keatley testified, "The best way to make contact today with David Livingstone is simply to talk to Africans. You could do this anywhere, but perhaps best in Nyasaland (Malawi), his beloved land by the lake, where his influence remains most profound. . . . He gave himself no airs, was never pompous, and never underrated the ability of his African students to make excellent missionaries themselves. 'I have no hesitation in saying one or two pious native agents are equal if not superior to Europeans' " (Keatley, 1963, pp. 124–25). In summing up the respective influence of Livingstone and Rhodes, Keatley comments that the forces menacing the political dream of Rhodes were the Africans who "were the spiritual heirs of the other empire-builder, David Livingstone. . . . And it is not particularly difficult to predict which of the two empires will last the longer, for Livingstone chose much the sounder foundation" (Keatley, 1963, p. 121). After Livingstone died, his African companions, Susi and Chuma, removed his heart and buried it deep in the earth before carrying the body 1,500 miles by foot to the coast whence it was taken to England for burial at Westminster Abbey. The Africans believed that Livingstone's heart remained in Africa.

In an address before the Royal Geographical Society in 1913, its president, Lord Curzon, decided to stress a different aspect of Livingstone's heritage. In particular he paid tribute to Livingstone's triple contribution to mission, science and the humanitarian cause (see Curzon, 1913, pp. 422–23; Simmons, 1955, pp. 172–73). We may attempt a different kind of summary as follows: first, Livingstone identified the vernacular Bible as the real engine of mission; numerical gains are now subordinate to the main task of missions. Second, missionaries are the real indigenizers, and the worth of their labors is to be assessed in the light of their capacity to preserve the older African heritage. Third, educated Africans are singularly unsuited to this indigenizing task for which they would have to be specifically fitted through a fundamental appreciation of their own culture. Fourth, "civilization" is not a necessary qualification for salvation though it might be a remedy for sin. Fifth, primitive Africa as Livingstone saw it was at no special disadvantage vis-à-vis the West with regard to God's "plan of salvation"; on the contrary, those parts of Africa untouched by Europe constituted, in his view, a more auspicious bridge for the gospel than the Europeanized parts. Sixth, time was against the perpetuation of European dependencies in Africa, whether political or ecclesiastical.

Thus in the strict sense of mission as statistical conquest, Livingstone had little encouragement to offer his missionary colleagues, for he was convinced that native African instruments were more effective than foreign agency. There was, of course, a role for missionaries, but that was more like the toil and hazards of the sower than the teeming labor of the reaper.

> If we call the actual amount of conversions the direct result of Missions, and the wide diffusion of better principles the indirect, I have no hesitation in asserting that the latter are of infinitely more importance than the former. I do not undervalue the importance of the conversion of the most abject creature that breathes: it is of overwhelming worth to him personally, but viewing our work of wide sowing of the good seed relatively to the harvest which will be reaped when all our heads are low, there can, I think, be no comparison. . . . Time is more important than concentration. [Livingstone, cited in Oliver, 1970, p. 10.]

Dr. Livingstone was far from being a romantic idealist about Africa. On the contrary, he saw its weaknesses and was unendurably moved by its plight, to alleviate which human effort alone, though necessary, was inadequate. With a Christian conscience, Livingstone also knew that the true kingdom was established on a dual foundation of personal salvation and social rehabilitation, and that it was a mean compliment to Africans to extend to them bread with one hand while with the other to withhold the leaven of the Bread of Life. The one leaves them under our obligation and the other empowers them as God's children.

Livingstone, as a Christian realist, did not neglect earthly concerns, although he also reckoned with the religious interests of the Christian cause wherein all who are touched by the Spirit, whosoever they may be and however pitiable their material circumstances, may claim equal citizenship. Livingstone's commitment to that truth allowed mission to press ahead in uncharted territory, undeterred by barriers of overwhelming ignorance and incredible stubbornness. Missionaries who followed his example were encouraged to sow even where it was clear others would reap. Livingstone's prophetic words would act as the unspoken charter for the missionary enterprise at its most authentic. As he himself described it, all enlightened endeavor on behalf of Africa was in a cause for the promotion of the "means by which God in His Providence is working, and bringing all His dealings with man to a glorious consummation" (Livingstone, 1857, p. 673).

Livingstone and Valignano thus share more in common than either their ecclesiastical background or their chronological identity would indicate, and that common ground was their readiness to be molded by field exposure in mission. Livingstone consequently came to look upon the expansion of Europe in Africa in a critical light, evoking Valignano's own much earlier position regarding "the surrender of Europe to Japan."

This is in no way a defense of Livingstone against the view that he helped open the way for colonialism in Africa, bringing Africa into the world economic and political system. In fact he did do that, and perhaps worse. His wish to see the Zambesi region develop into a successful commercial field — cultivating and exporting cotton, fostering intertribal harmony, and rechanneling energies previously expended on the slave trade — had in it the seeds of imperial rivalry and expansion. (It is important to remember that the first Christian missions in the Zambesi area were the Dominicans and the Jesuits, whose evangelistic efforts among the Africans failed. But they had ideas of developing the region into a viable commercial field. [See Rea, 1976.] In a letter to Moffat (April 20, 1860), Livingstone described his nervousness at increasing Portuguese and French intrusion in the region, with the alarming prospects of restarting the defunct missions of the seventeenth and eighteenth centuries. He concluded:

It is therefore high time for the church to move, and I think that the field opened by the Shire is a glorious one. It opens a cotton country of unlimited extent, and presents features different from any you passed through in the south. It is very beautiful; but the missionaries have a hard task in the reduction of the language, and the people know nothing of their motives. It is, too, the slave market. . . . There is no large confederation of natives to hinder [the missionaries], and the introduction of lawful commerce and the gospel will eat the unlawful traffic out. [Wallis, 1945, p. 91.]

In a candid expression of his secret strategy, Livingstone wrote in a confidential letter to Professor Sedgwick of Cambridge that he had a design in mind that he would not divulge in public.

That you may have a clear idea of my objects, I may state that they have more in them than meets the eye. They are not merely exploratory, for I go with the intention of benefiting both the African and my own countrymen. I take a practical mining geologist to tell us of the mineral resources of the country, an economic botanist to give a full report of the vegetable productions, an artist to give the scenery, a naval officer to tell of the capacity of river communications, and a moral agent to lay a Christian foundation for anything that may follow. All this machinery has for its ostensible object the development of African trade and the promotion of civilisation; but what I can tell to none but such as you, in whom I have confidence, is this. I hope it may result in an English colony in the healthy high lands of Central Africa. [Kirk, 1965, I:309.]

In spite of such views by Livingstone, his commitment to Christian mission on the ground sowed seeds of an equally revolutionary future. Furthermore, imperial expansion as permanent conquest and mission as translation proceeded from radically divergent assumptions, or at the least produced radically different consequences, however close in national spirit mission and the imperial enterprise may be. Mission aimed at the establishment of national churches and envisaged a future without itself, whereas colonialism saw only the perpetuation of dependency. As Habib Bourguiba, the founder of modern Tunisia, put it, "the mistake which lies at the root of all the others" was that the colonialists never foresaw the day when they would have to leave (Bourguiba, 1961). It is not necessary to deny a link between colonialism and mission in order to appreciate the tensions between them at ground level. Hence the significance, in their different ways, of Livingstone and Cecil Rhodes to our subject.

All this is not to imply that strong indigenous institutions were the goal of mission everywhere, or even that successful mission necessarily strengthened those institutions. This is a complex issue, for religion and politics have much to do with each other. Yet political structures, especially where they outlive their life and usefulness, may have deleterious effects on cultural renewal, and in that case mission may have to contend against those structures. Where the process of structural change or decay is already advanced, mission will hasten it toward a natural conclusion. Some such idea may have been present in the minds of missionaries who spoke of overcoming indigenous resistance, although we misrepresent the case to say that Christianity cannot prevail against a strong cultural tradition, or that the religion profits only from cultural failure. It is instructive to remember that Marx conceived a dialectical role for imperialism (as antithesis) in toppling the deities of traditional society in Asia and thus laying the foundations of Western society. Marx accused Asian religions of trans-forming "a self-developing social state into never changing natural destiny, and thus brought about a brutalizing worship of nature, exhibiting its degradation in the fact that man, the sovereign of nature, fell down on his knees in adoration of Hanuman, the monkey, and Sabbal, the cow" (Schlesinger, 1974, p. 340).

In a letter of 1859, Moffat, for example, asserts some such view in the following words:

> It is where the political organization is most perfect, and the social system still in its aboriginal vigour, that the missionary has the least success in making an impression. Where things have undergone a change and the old feudal usages have lost their power, where there is a measure of disorganization, the new ideas which the gospel brings with it do not come into collision with any powerful political prejudice. The habits and modes of thinking have been broken up, and there is a preparation for the seed of the word. [cited in Wallis, 1945, pp. 70–71.]

But Moffat is aware that he is describing theory and that there is very little basis in fact to such assertions. "I am not," he admits, "sanguine on this point in regard to the Matabele" (Wallis, 1945, pp. 70–71). Indeed the work of Bengt Sundkler in Swaziland suggests how Christian religious materials may have the opposite effect, bolstering indigenous political structures when these are under enormous external and internal pressures (see Sundkler, 1976). J. Lewis Krapf, a contemporary of Moffat, is even more emphatic on this point, warning his fellow missionaries not to repose too much faith in the idea of European suzerainty over Africa. His prophetic words bear citing in full:

> Expect nothing, or very little from political changes in Eastern Africa. Do not think that because East Africans are "profitable in nothing to God and the world" they ought to be brought under the domination of some European power, in the hope that they may bestir themselves more actively and eagerly for what is worldly and, in consequence, become eventually more awake to what is spiritual and eternal. On the contrary, banish the thought that Europe must spread her protecting wings over Eastern Africa, if missionary work is to prosper in that land. . . . Europe would, no doubt, remove much that is mischievous and obstructive out of the way of missionary work, but she would probably set in its way as many and, perhaps, still greater checks. [Krapf, 1860, pp. 416, 417.]

Walter Miller (1872–1952) of North Nigeria

In one example Christian mission saw a specific connection between itself and colonialism. This was in north Nigeria where the English pioneer missionary Walter Miller, serving with the (Anglican) Church Missionary Society, preceded the colonial occupation forces. Confronted by the resistance of Muslims to Christian religious activity, Miller beckoned the advancing British to hasten their occupation of the country, convinced, like Moffat in Matabeleland, that in the crisis of confidence that would follow in the wake of colonial subjugation, Muslim resistance would be overcome and the people would be more amenable to persuasion. Eventually, in 1902, Lord Lugard, the proponent of the Dual Mandate doctrine, which qualified the Western economic exploitation of Africa's natural resources with the obligation to advance Africans, completed the takeover of north Nigeria, although, in spite of being the son of a missionary, Lugard was resolute against allowing missions in the Muslim north.[6] Miller was left to prospect for converts in fringe communities. In his book *Reflections of a Pioneer,* Miller became preoccupied with the unrequited love of a missionary, his heart heavy with work still unconsummated among Muslims. It did not take long for his illusions to be shattered by the reality of colonial rule insofar as the fortunes of mission are concerned.

The example of Miller is also an object lesson in the missionary "affair" with the north. Miller came to tie the Christian cause in north Nigeria to the cultural and political awakening of the population. He was directly responsible for encouraging the founding of a political organization, the Northern People's Congress, to advance African political aims against the British authorities. In a provocative piece, Miller drew up a balance sheet on the British colonial administration in the north, and came out on the unfavorable side. As a consequence, he fired the imagination of Muslim leaders, who used his ideas to mobilize Muslim opinion against the colonial power.

A foremost Nigerian nationalist, Aminu Kano, for example, appealed to Miller's ideas in a campaign against the colonial administration. Miller had written a work, published in 1947, with the titillating title, *Have We Failed in Nigeria?* Aminu Kano turned his review of the work into an extended comment on the disadvantages of British rule. He wrote thus:

> Dr. Miller lays great stress on the administrative failure and the social decay in the country. To criticize [Dr. Miller's] book sitting comfortably on [sic] an armchair is one thing; to go into the nooks and corners to see the real life of the Northern people is another. Dr. Miller has shown how inefficient is the administrative system, how lacking in initiative, how dilatory, how corrupt and how aimless and unimaginative. . . . When dealing with this administrative failure . . . common in this Anglo-Fulani feudal . . . bureaucracy Dr. Miller reveals . . . that an administrator in this Nigeria told him, "If you keep the country quiet and stir up no dust, write a good annual report of the condition of the province which you administer, however bad it may have been, and conclude with the formulas—the relationship between the Government and the Native Administration has been all

that could be desired — then you are sure to get a promotion, probably acceleration". . . .

I believe, as thousands of my fellow Northerners do believe, that Dr. Miller's book describes much of the real state of affairs in this oppressed land. All of us who find time should read it. [In Paden, 1973, pp. 285–87.]

Clearly Miller's significance lay in his stimulation of local forces, particularly in his appeal to a sense of Hausa identity. This is the clue to Aminu Kano's pejorative reference to what he called "the Anglo-Fulani feudal . . . bureaucracy." For Miller, then, the flirtation with colonial sponsorshop was short-lived. In the end he settled down to what suited Christian mission best, to discover in the exposure of field experience the grounds for repudiating the logic of empire. He was promptly claimed by Aminu Kano and his band of protagonists, showing that missionary influence need not lead to formal membership in the church to be real.

I am aware that elsewhere in Nigeria a different story could be told. When Hope Waddell of the United Presbyterian Mission was about to set out for Old Calabar in 1845, he insisted that he and his party should receive the guarantee of protection from the Royal Navy, which was given. The missionaries were immediately involved in deep political struggles with King Eyo Honesty II, the ruler of Creek Town in Old Calabar. Eventually the missionaries gained control of Creek Town, reducing King Eyo to a puppet role, his court being converted to an open-air church for Sunday services. When local feelings were inflamed by missionary insensitivity with the desecration of local shrines and other acts of high-handedness, the British consul was appealed to by the missionaries to take military action against the Efik population. The Admiralty responded with the dispatch of H.M.S. *Antelope,* whose naval gunners razed the town. When a similar military intervention took place at Lagos, the missionary in charge, Rev. C. A. Gollmer, wrote triumphantly that "I look upon it as God's interposition for the good of Africa and may we not hope that now the word of God will gain free course among the Ijebus, too?" (Moorhouse, 1973, p. 93). Missionaries continued to operate under the protective shadow of the naval gunners, convinced that military control of the West African coastline would advance the Christian cause. In Old Calabar itself missionaries pressed demands on the local people and invoked military reprisals if their demands were unmet. When the people reacted to this situation by a decision of noncooperation, the missionary response was robust.

Before long HMS *Scourge* steamed up the coast and put a landing party ashore, which summoned the local chiefs to a conference on board. There they were told that by inviting the missionaries to their country they had entered into a perpetual obligation to help them, that they must never again take any measures against the missionaries, that if they molested the missionaries and the Africans who were being educated by the missionaries, they would incur the extreme displeasure of the Queen of England. [Moorhouse, 1973, p. 94.]

Within a short period of time Creek Town and the adjacent districts had been completely subdued by the missionaries. Missionary ladies took the local girls and put them in Victorian clothes, thus imposing on the culture through its women the decorum and modesty deemed appropriate to Christianity. Africans understood the momentous changes afoot. One old man lamented bitterly in Krio language: " 'Fine ting dis be, white woman come and make law for we' ('this is a fine thing which has come to pass, that the white woman has come and made a new law for us')" (Moorhouse, 1973, p. 94).

Such examples of missionary high-handedness can be multiplied, from collusion with the fifteenth-century conquistadores in Ecuador to alliance with Portuguese colonialism in Africa and elsewhere. The issue for us, however, is how historically translatability has brought the church into line with vernacular aspirations. There is little doubt about vernacular sentiments stiffening the anticolonial resolve while at the same time deepening the roots of the church. (It is instructive to reflect on how certain American Protestant missionary bodies found themselves consistently on a collision course with colonial authorities, and, instead of flinching, pressed the case for an improvement in the conditions of native Africans. The American Presbyterians in the Congo (now Zaire) found themselves in this position. (See *Reform in Leopold's Congo* by Stanley Shaloff.)

Be that as it may, it was only a matter of time before the emergence of the African Church, and nothing fueled it so effectively as such instances of missionary high-handedness. In the Niger Delta, where the gunboats had pounded away so relentlessly at African resistance, the movement for repudiating missionary control was to achieve some of its most noteworthy gains, as we shall see in the next chapter. The vernacular instrument would in course of time topple the stratagem that the cannons had so doggedly defended. Mission fashioned that instrument, and was in turn fashioned by it.

Although Crowther, the African bishop in charge of the Niger mission, adopted English as the language of Christianity, insisting on its exclusive use in the schools of the Niger Mission (Moorhouse, 1973, p. 109), he was in fact one of the foremost and most effective pioneers of the Yoruba language (see chapter 4, below). By the time Crowther was an old man, a groundswell of vernacular reaction built up to press the case for an African reconceptualization of Christianity (Sanneh, 1983a, pp. 168–209). The African church movement of the nineteenth century was the result of vernacular forces mobilized by the juggernaut of translation.

Adam Mischlich, Islam, and Colonialism

In one story of missionary involvement with colonialism, Islam emerges as the favored party. This was when the Germans moved into Togoland (now Togo) in West Africa. The Hausa Muslim inhabitants of the town of Kete-Krachi, an immigrant settlement, had been involved in a long-running feud with local "pagans," that is, the followers of African traditional religion, who appeared better organized and more numerous than the immigrant Hausas. The Muslims had tried several times to invite European intervention on their side without much success. Then in 1894 the Germans were prevailed upon. The administrator, Gruner, arrived in the town late at night after a long, forced march, but was not allowed by the Muslims to have his well-earned rest until he helped put down the chief shrine of the "pagans," including the arrest and execution of the chief priest, the Dente Bosomfo.

The Muslim cause was bolstered by the installation of a leading Hausa scholar, al-Ḥajj ʿUmar of Keta-Krachi, with the Germans shielding him from the hostility of the local chiefs. And then in 1902 a remarkable partnership developed between al-Ḥajj ʿUmar and the Germans. The new administrator was Adam Mischlich, a former Basle missionary turned colonial functionary. (Mischlich had had his mission station burned down in retaliatory moves by liquor merchants who were incensed by his attack on the alcohol trade.) It was Mischlich who masterminded al-Ḥajj ʿUmar's installation in Kete-Krachi as chief imam. But Mischlich's chief interest in al-Ḥajj ʿUmar was in getting the Muslim scholar to work on the vernacular traditions of his people before the advent of the West destroyed the culture. As a former missionary, Mischlich was knowledgeable in several African languages, including Hausa and Twi. He tried to infect al-Ḥajj ʿUmar with his enthusiasm for linguistic and anthropological studies. Mischlich was self-conscious about the relationship, and said that it was as a result of several personal entreaties that al-Ḥajj ʿUmar was persuaded to write in Hausa an account of the history, culture, and handicrafts of Hausa society in precolonial times. "Without my suggestions," Mischlich insists, "the essay would never have been written down" (Maier, n.d.; see also Maier, 1983; Mischlich and Lippert, 1903).

That story is one of the most remarkable examples of the disinheritance of the old Africa by the twin forces of Islam and Western colonialism, and only the missionary habits of Mischlich helped to mitigate the wholesale overthrow of precolonial Africa. The old missionary was able to interpose the careful documentation of African customs and traditions before the so-called civilizing power of the new masters held complete sway. From the accounts, al-Ḥajj ʿUmar seems to have been a reluctant collaborator with Mischlich, a reluctance probably akin to the spirit that stiffened the opposition of local Muslims to the "pagan" shrine. If that is the case, it provides an important clue to the attitude of representative Muslims toward indigenous African traditions. Muslim religious scholars like al-Ḥajj ʿUmar would much sooner stake their fortunes on the Arabic cultural heritage of Islam than cultivate the vernacular as the basis of missionary success. Thus Africa's ancient heritage would come to languish in proportion to the completeness of Islam's triumph. Mischlich's error was in ascribing to

Muslim scholars a fundamental readiness to accept what Christian missionaries understood as indigenous necessity.

On this matter, Blyden, who was extremely critical of colonialism and the
conspiratorial shadow it had cast over Christianity in Africa, was nevertheless at pains to call attention to the old religious heritage. As ally, he chose
not Muslim authorities with whom he was equally familiar and of whom he
was more approving, but Max Müller, indicating the usefulness of Christian
interest and commitment for his project. In his Hibbert Lectures of 1878,
Müller had felt it incumbent on him to defend the religious phenomenon
whatever the level of simplicity. He was cited by Blyden as affirming that

> fetishism was a corruption of religion, in Africa as elsewhere, that the
> Negro is capable of higher religious ideas than the worship of Stocks
> and Stones, and that many tribes who believe in fetishes cherish at the
> same time very pure, very exalted, very true sentiments of the Deity.
> Only we must have eyes to see, eyes that can see what is perfect
> without dwelling too much on what is imperfect. The more I study
> heathen religions, the more I feel convinced, that, if we want to form
> a true judgment of their purpose, we must measure them, as we
> measure the Alps, by the highest point which they have reached.
> Religion is everywhere an aspiration rather than a fulfilment; and I
> claim no more for the Religion of the Negro than for our own, when
> I say that it should be judged not by what it appears to be, but by what
> it is—nay, not only by what it is but by what it can be and by what it
> has been in its most gifted votaries. [Blyden, 1908, p. 62.]

In fact Christian interest, even in a colonial guise, encouraged fraternity
with Muslim groups in Africa even if this meant siding with them against
the old religions. It is a matter for genuine speculation whether in such cases
the Islamic stigma on traditional religions had also formed or only colored
the colonial view. In any case, examples can be multiplied of colonial
authorities making common cause with Muslims in the drive to dispossess
traditional rulers and their local religious counterparts, from the French in
Senegal (Klein, 1968) to the British in Tanzania (then called Tanganyika)
(Ranger, 1971) and, of course, in north Nigeria. Both Miller and Mischlich,
therefore, represent a common phenomenon of mission as inherently
anticolonial, with Miller acting out of that logic at the close of colonial rule
while Mischlich demonstrated it at the outset. Such, then, is the consistency
of the vernacular thrust of Christianity, and the tangible efforts of these
two individuals give it historical cogency.

While still on the subject of colonialism, we should recall the case of
Ghana (formerly Gold Coast) where, as early as 1871, a group of people, all
African Christians educated in mission schools operated for the most part
with local funds, produced a constitutional document designed to prepare
Africans for self-government. It was called the Fante Confederation
(Hayford, 1903, pp. 327ff.). The confederation was in fact the upshot of

earlier attempts at organizing African opinion when, in the governorship of Sir Benjamin C. Pine (1857–58) leading local Christians formed a body of opinion and earned the unsavory name "the opposition men." The leaders of the Fante Confederation were later arrested on charges of political agitation. An inquiry subsequently established their innocence and showed that they genuinely represented informed African opinion. Furthermore, their Christian character was vindicated, with their leaders "certainly not the inferior of any European on the Gold Coast in character, ability, or mercantile position" (Bartels, 1965, p. 88).

The Vernacular Issue

The Fante Confederation was succeeded by the Reference Group, a body of educated Fante Christians who made the issue of the vernacular their guiding principle. In 1887 they adopted a series of measures in support of giving the people the gospel in their own vernacular. The members of the group committed themselves to translating portions of the Scriptures into the vernacular, and this was done. The group also campaigned for the use of the vernacular in church services.

One of the most spectacular effects of the development of the vernacular was the work of the Rev. Carl Christian Reindorf, an African Christian leader. Reindorf published a book, *The History of the Gold Coast and Asante,* which he wrote originally in the Ga language. He subsequently translated it into English and had it published in Switzerland in 1889. In addition to employing the vernacular, Reindorf pioneered a fresh historical method in the gathering and use of evidence. He drew not only on documentary sources but made systematic and critical use of oral tradition, which he gathered from a wide selection of people, augmenting this with published material. It would be well into the 1960s before historians discovered the comparable importance of oral sources.

Missionary translation was instrumental in the emergence of indigenous resistance to colonialism. Local Christians acquired from the vernacular translations confidence in the indigenous cause. While the colonial system represented a worldwide economic and military order, mission represented vindication for the vernacular. Local Christians apprehended the significance of world events, and as such the purposes of God, through the familiar medium of mother tongues, with subject peoples able to respond to colonial events in light of vernacular self-understanding.

The example of Ghana may be cited once more. News had reached the colony of the defeat of Russia at the hands of Japan in the Russo-Japanese War of 1905. Local reaction was to perceive an important moral lesson in the overcoming of mighty imperial Russia by the little-regarded Japan. *The Gold Coast Aborigines* newspaper carried an editorial to that effect, inviting its readers to ponder the words of Jeremiah 9:23 in this connection, which said, among other things, "neither let the mighty *man* glory in his might," a piece of bold political prophecy that raised the fortunes of the national cause. In a similar way, local people had reacted to the defeat of the Italians at the hands of the Ethiopians on March 1, 1896, showing that Christian activity and national sentiment had a close affinity. The steady progress of Christianity in Africa after the withdrawal of the colonial powers—between 1964 and 1984 Christian numbers increased from about 60 million to roughly 240 million—indicates that mission and colonialism had been in profound dialectical tension, if not conflict. The end of colonial rule has seen the acceleration of the real Christianization of Africa, with the vernacular force able to shift the residue of colonial antagonism. The real gains of mission have to be measured in the positive disposition toward the West in spite of colonialism, as well as in the great vernacular movements that have revitalized the traditional heritage.

SUMMARY AND CONCLUSION

Several points are made in this chapter. First, Roman Catholic missions in the early modern era came to defend indigenous languages against the colonial requirement that Spanish be established in the church. The Vatican acted to recognize vernacular languages and institute them in the liturgy and in the discipline of the church. Second, in Mexico the Catholic accommodation extended to the incorporation into the church of indigenous art forms. Third, the Catholic initiative in this matter persisted into Japan and India, with fluctuations in the pattern of relationship with indigenous themes. Beginning with resistance, Catholic missionary practice changed later to one of accommodation, one effect of which was the tendency for missionaries to see local converts largely in terms of indigenous agency rather than as willing pupils of the West. Fourth, in Japan the Catholic mission developed the vernacular for the purposes of educating missionaries in the ways of the culture, insisting on familiarity and respect for Japanese religious and cultural materials as a condition for mission. In India the situation was marked by the example of individual Catholic pioneers who assimilated into the Hindu religious worldview. There was a recognition in this assimilation of the irreplaceable value of mother tongues for the Christian cause.

Fifth, in coming to Protestant missions we find that their translation work made mother tongues the centerpiece of mission. This involved a shift from Western languages and the commercial monopolies of rising colonial powers, to the indigenous societies, resulting in a bifurcated encroachment of the West in its secular and religious thrust. Coastal areas, with their port cities, formed the golden rim of the Western colonial advance, while hinterland areas, with their seats of traditional learning and culture, became the saddle of Christian influence. Thus were sown the seeds of vernacular renewal, with the recasting of classical idioms into mother tongues encouraging popular movements in areas of missionary outreach.

Sixth, the translation factor wrought a similar effect in Africa. Commercial exploration of Africa's coastline mapped the path for European colonial advance, with Christian missions overlapping to a considerable extent with Western ventures. However, such historical intertwining in fact masked a real divergence between the logic of colonial overlordship and the interest of the emerging African church where vernacular translation often converged with steps to encourage indigenous ascendancy. In some places missionaries aided and abetted indigenous sentiments by encouraging the founding of political organizations. Here, too, the Western presence was felt along the divergent lines of its political and religious involvement. In their vernacular work, Christian missions helped nurse the sentiments for the national cause, which mother tongues crystallized and incited. The dramatic effects of vernacular translation thus prejudiced the colonial cause as much by historical coincidence as by ideological justification. For that reason, vernacular translation outdistanced and outlasted the fortunes of colonialism.

NOTES

1. On the assimilation of Christianity into Castilian culture, see the book of collected essays edited by Bernard F. Reilly: *Santiago, Saint-Denis, and Saint Peter: The Reception of the Roman Liturgy in Leon-Castile in 1080* (New York: Fordham University Press, 1985).

2. It is intriguing to reflect in this connection that no straight line seems to have developed from Francis Xavier to later generations of Jesuits, the zigzags in policy accounting for periodic returns to mission as European hegemony. See John Lockman, *The Travels of the Jesuits,* 2 vols., 2nd ed. (1762). On the life of Xavier there is the exhaustive work by Georg Schurhammer, *Francis Xavier: His Life, His Times,* 4 vols. (Rome: Jesuit Historical Institute, 1973–82). Vols. 2 to 4 cover India, Indonesia, Japan, and China.

3. For a sympathetic, even idealistic account of de Nobili's activity in this sphere, see André Rocaries, S. J., *Robert de Nobili, S. J.: ou le "Sannyāsi" Chrétien* (Toulouse: Editions Prière et Vie, 1967).

4. Oliver Wendell Holmes pithily expressed it thus in *Autocrat of the Breakfast Table:* "Language is a solemn thing; it grows out of life, out of its agonies and its ecstacies, its wants and its weariness. Every language is a temple in which the soul of those who speak it is enshrined."

5. See, in this connection, the views of the missionary T. J. Bowen, who, writing in 1857, argued forcefully for "civilization" as a concomitant of the gospel (Bowen, 1857, pp. 321f.).

6. On Lord Lugard's views, see his book, *The Dual Mandate in Tropical Africa* (Edinburgh: Blackwood & Sons, 1922) and his chapter, "The White Man's Task in Tropical Africa," in Philip W. Quigg, ed., *Africa: A Foreign Affairs Reader* (New York: Frederick A. Praeger, 1964), pp. 5–16. See also Fr. Emefie Ikenga-Metuh, "Muslim Resistance to Missionary Penetration of Northern Nigeria, 1857-1960," *Mission Focus* 3, no. 2 (1986): 28–40.

SELECT BIBLIOGRAPHY

Ajayi, Jacob F. A. 1965. *Christian Missions in Nigeria: 1841–1891: The Making of an Elite.* London: Longman; repr., Evanston: Northwestern University Press, 1969.

Anderson, Rufus. See Beaver, R. Pierce.

Ayandele, Emmanuel A. 1966a. "The Missionary Factor in Northern Nigeria: 1870–1918." *Journal of the Historical Society of Nigeria* 3, no. 3 (December).

———. 1966b. *The Impact of Christian Missions on Modern Nigeria.* London: Longman.

Bartels, Frederick L. 1965. *The Roots of Ghana Methodism.* Accra: Methodist Book Depot; Cambridge, England: Cambridge University Press.

Beaver, R. Pierce, ed. 1967. *To Advance the Gospel: Selections from the Writings of Rufus Anderson.* Grand Rapids, Mich.: Wm. B. Eerdmans.

Bennett, Adrian B., and Kwang-Ching Liu. 1974. "Christianity in the Chinese Idiom: Young T. Allen and the Early Chiao-huihsin-pao 1868–1870." In John K. Fairbank, ed., *The Missionary Enterprise in China and America.* Cambridge: Harvard University Press.

Besier, Gerhard, 1984. "Mission and Colonialism in Friedrich Fabri's (1824–1891) Thinking." In *Missionary Ideologies* (see Christensen; below).

Blyden, Edward W. (1908). *African Life and Customs.* New York.

———. 1967. *Christianity, Islam and the Negro Race.* Edinburgh: Edinburgh University Press; first published 1887.

Bourguiba, Habib. 1961. "The New Outlook for Africa." *International Affairs* 37, no. 4 (October).

Bowen, T. J. 1857. *Missionary Labours and Adventures in Central Africa.* Charleston, S.C.

Casely-Hayford, J. 1903. *Gold Coast Native Institutions.* London.

Christensen, Torben. 1984. "Danish Missions in India." In Torben Christensen and William R. Hutchison, eds., *Missionary Ideologies in the Imperialist Era: 1880–1920.* Aarhus, Denmark: Forlaget Aros. Distributed in North America by *Harvard Theological Review.*

Cochrane, Charles Norris. 1977. *Christianity and Classical Culture.* New York: Oxford University Press; first published 1940.

Cronin, Vincent. 1959. *A Pearl to India: The Life of Robert de Nobili.* London: Rupert Hart Davis.

Curtin, Philip D. 1964. *The Image of Africa: British Ideas and Action 1780–1850.* Madison: University of Wisconsin Press.

Curzon, The Rt. Hon. Earl. 1913. "David Livingstone: Centenary of His Birth." *The Geographical Journal* 41, no. 5, (May), pp. 421–23.

Dah, Jonas N. 1984. "The Basel Missions in Cameroun." In *Missionary Ideologies* (see Christensen, above).

Delavignette, Robert. 1964. *Christianity and Colonialism.* New York: Hawthorn Books.

Eggert, Johanna. 1984. "The School Policy of the German Protestant Missions in Tanzania before the First World War." In *Missionary Ideologies* (see Christensen, above).

Elison, George. 1973. *Deus Destroyed: The Image of Christianity in Early Modern Japan.* Cambridge: Harvard University Press.

Etherington, Norman. 1984. "South African Missionary Ideologies 1880–1920: Retrospect and Prospect." In *Missionary Ideologies* (see Christensen, above).

Fletcher, Irene M. 1962–63. "The Fundamental Principle of the London Missionary Society." *Transactions of the Congregational Historical Society* 19.

Gallagher, J. 1950. "Fowell Buxton and the New African Policy, 1838–1842." *The Cambridge Historical Journal* 10.

Garrett, Shirley Stone. 1974. "Why They Stayed: American Church Politics and Chinese Politics in the Twenties." In John K. Fairbank, ed., *The Missionary Enterprise in China and America*. Cambridge: Harvard University Press.

Gensichen, Hans-Werner. 1984. "German Protestant Missions." In *Missionary Ideologies* (see Christensen, above).

Glüer, Winfried. 1984. "German Protestant Missions in China." In *Missionary Ideologies* (see Christensen, above).

The Gold Coast Aborigines (2 January, 1905).

Hansen, Holger Bernt. 1984. "Mission and Colonialism in Uganda: A Case Study of Forced Labour." In *Missionary Ideologies* (see Christensen, above).

Hayford, C. 1903. *Gold Coast Native Institutions*. London.

Heer, Friedrich. 1962. *The Medieval World: Europe 1100–1350*. New York: Mentor Books.

Ikenga-Metuh, Emefie. 1986. "Muslim Resistance to Missionary Penetration of Northern Nigeria, 1857–1960." *Mission Focus* 3, no. 2, pp. 28–40.

Johnston, Harry H. 1913. "Livingstone as an Explorer." *The Geographical Journal* 41, no. 5 (May), pp. 423–48.

Keatley, Patrick. 1963. *The Politics of Partnership*. Harmondsworth, England: Penguin Books.

Kirk, John. 1965. Reginald Foskett, ed., *Zambezi Journals and Letters,* 2 vols. London.

Klein, Martin. 1968. *Islam and Imperialism in Senegal: Sine-Saloum 1847–1914*. Stanford: Stanford University Press; Edinburgh: Edinburgh University Press.

Krapf, J. Lewis. 1860. *Travels, Researches*. Boston: Ticknor and Fields.

Lernoux, Penny. 1984. *Cry of the People*. New York: Penguin Books.

Livingstone, David. 1857. *Missionary Researches and Travels in South Africa*. London: John Murray.

Lockman, John. 1762. *The Travels of the Jesuits,* 2 vols. London: T. Piety; 2nd ed.

Long, James. 1850. *Vernacular Christian Literature for Bengal*. Calcutta.

Lugard, Lord. 1922. *The Dual Mandate in Tropical Africa*. Edinburgh: Blackwood & Sons.

———. 1964. "The White Man's Task in Tropical Africa." Phillip W. Quigg, ed., *Africa: A Foreign Affairs Reader*. New York: Praeger.

Maier, D. J. E. n.d. "The Changing Political Views of al-Ḥājj 'Umar of Kete-Krachi." Unpublished paper, Department of History, University of Northern Iowa.

———. 1983. *Priests and Power: The Case of the Dente Shrine*. Bloomington: Indiana University Press.

Miller, Stuart Creighton. 1974. "Ends and Means: The Missionary Justification of Force in Nineteenth Century China." In John K. Fairbank, ed., *The Missionary Enterprise in China and America*. Cambridge: Harvard University Press.

Miller, Walter. 1936. *Reflections of a Pioneer,* London: Church Missionary Society.
———. 1947. *Have We Failed in Nigeria?* London.
Mischlich, A., and J. Lippert. 1903. *Beiträge zur Gesichte der Haussastaaten.* Berlin. Contains Hausa chronicle.
Moorhouse, Geoffrey. 1973. *The Missionaries.* Philadelphia: J. P. Lippincott Co.
Mott, John R. 1910. *The Decisive Hour of Christian Missions.* Edinburgh.
Müller, Max. 1874. *On Christian Missions.* New York: Scribner, Armstrong, and Co.
North, Eric M. 1938. *The Book of a Thousand Tongues.* New York: Harper and Brothers.
Oliver, Roland. 1970. *The Missionary Factor in East Africa.* London: Longman; originally published 1952.
Österlin, Lars. 1984. "The Crusade of the West and the Church in China." In *Missionary Ideologies* (see Christensen, above).
Paden, John. 1973. *Religion and Political Culture in Kano.* Berkeley and Los Angeles: University of California Press.
Paz, Octavio. 1987. "Here People Talk to God." *New York Times Book Review,* December 20.
Pirouet, M. Louise. 1978. *Black Evangelists: The Spread of Christianity in Uganda: 1891–1914.* London: Rex Collings.
———. 1984. "Women Missionaries of the Church Missionary Society in Uganda, 1896–1920." In *Missionary Ideologies* (see Christensen, above).
Ranger, Terence. 1971. "Christian Independency in Tanzania." In David B. Barrett, ed., *African Initiatives in Religion.* Nairobi: East African Publishing House.
Rea, Francis William. 1976. *The Economics of the Zambezi Mission (1580–1759).* Rome: Jesuit Historical Institute.
Reilly, Bernard F. 1985. *Santiago, Saint-Denis, and Saint Peter: The Reception of the Roman Liturgy in Leon-Castille in 1080.* New York: Fordham University Press.
Reindorf, Carl Christian. 1966. *The History of the Gold Coast.* Accra: Universities of Ghana Press.
Rennstich, Karl. 1984. "The Understanding of Mission, Civilization and Colonialism in the Basel Mission." In *Missionary Ideologies* (see Christensen, above).
Rocaries, André. 1967. *Robert de Nobili, S. J.: ou le "Sannyāsi" Chrétien.* Toulouse: Editions Prière et Vie.
Sanneh, Lamin. 1983a. *West African Christianity.* Maryknoll, N.Y.: Orbis Books.
———. 1983b. "The Horizontal and Vertical in Mission: An African Perspective." *International Bulletin of Missionary Research* 7, no. 4 (October).
———. 1984. "Prelude to African Independency: The Afro-American Factor in African Christianity." *Harvard Theological Review* 77, no. 1.
———. 1985a. "Researching Mission History." *International Review of Mission* 74, no. 294 (April).
———. 1985b. "Christian Mission in the Pluralist Milieu: The African Experience." *International Review of Mission* 74, no. 294 (April).
———. 1987a. "Christian Missions and the Western Guilt Complex." *The Christian Century* (8 April).
———. 1987b. "The Future of Missions in Africa." *New World Outlook* (April).
———. 1988. "Pluralism and Christian Commitment: Conflict or Convergence?" *Theology Today* (April).

Schlesinger, Arthur, Jr. 1974. "The Missionary Enterprise and Theories of Imperialism." In John K. Fairbank, ed., *The Missionary Enterprise in China and America,* Cambridge: Harvard University Press, pp. 339–73.

Schurhammer, Georg. 1973–82. *Francis Xavier: His Life, His Times,* 4 vols. Rome: Jesuit Historical Institute.

Schütte, Josef Franz. 1980. *Valigano's Mission Principles for Japan.* Trans. John J. Coyne. Vol 1: *From His Appointment as Visitor until His First Departure from Japan (1573–1582).* St. Louis: Institute of Jesuit Sources.

Shaloff, Stanley. 1970. *Reform in Leopold's Congo.* Richmond, Va.: John Knox Press.

Simmons, Jack. 1955. *Livingstone and Africa.* London: English Universities Press; repr. 1956.

Smith, Edwin. 1930. *In the Mother Tongue.* London: British & Foreign Bible Society.

Spence, Jonathan D. 1985. *The Memory Palace of Matteo Ricci.* London and New York: Penguin Books.

Storry, Richard. 1963. *A History of Modern Japan.* Harmondsworth, England: Penguin Books.

Sundkler, Bengt. 1976. *Zulu Zion and Some Swazi Zionists.* Oxford: Clarendon Press.

Thornton, A. P. 1965. *Doctrines of Imperialism.* New York: John Wiley and Sons.

Toynbee, Arnold J. 1956. *An Historian's Approach to Religion.* New York and London: Oxford University Press.

Tuma, Tom, and P. Mutibwa, eds. 1978. *A Century of Christianity in Uganda.* Nairobi: Uzima Press.

Varg, Paul A. 1974. "The Missionary to the Nationalist Revolution." In John K. Fairbank, ed., *The Missionary Enterprise in China and America.* Cambridge: Harvard University Press.

Waldenfels, Hans. 1984. "The Interaction of European Politics and Roman Catholic Missionary Enterprise in the Chinese Mission." In *Missionary Ideologies* (see Christensen, above).

Wallis, J. P. R. ed. 1945. *The Matabele Mission.* London: Chatto and Windus.

Walls, Andrew F. 1984. "British Missions." In *Missionary Ideologies* (see Christensen, above).

———. 1987. "The Legacy of David Livingstone." *International Bulletin of Missionary Research* 11, no. 3 (July).

Widmer, Eric. 1976. *The Russian Ecclesiastical Mission in Peking during the 18th Century.* Cambridge: Harvard University Press.

Wilson. H. S., ed. 1969. *Origins of West African Nationalism.* London: Macmillan and Co.

Young, John D. 1983. *Confucianism and Christianity, the First Encounter.* Hong Kong: Hong Kong University Press.

4

Protest, Reaction, and Renewal: Vernacular Roots in the Niger Delta

THE CONCEPT

A powerful movement of protest and reaction, in response to the consequences of the policy of the Church Missionary Society (CMS) in the Niger
Mission, existed from about 1880 to 1892. The mission had been successfully launched in 1841, and had done gallant work in the Niger Delta as well
as at Lokoja and adjacent areas in the Upper Niger. The principal agents in
the mission were African, including a high proportion of Sierra Leoneans
with Nigerian connection. The aim of the mission was eventually to produce
a self-reliant, self-supporting African pastorate, which would preside over
autonomous Anglican churches in communion with Canterbury. Its sponsors hoped that such a scheme would extend to Nigeria what was already a
full-fledged experiment elsewhere. The idea of a "Native Pastorate" was
Henry Venn's, the secretary of the CMS between 1841 and 1872, and it had
been tried in Sierra Leone where on All Saints' Day in 1861 the CMS handed
over nine parishes to the "Native Church Pastorate," as it was called. By
1878 more churches, including the senior church of the colony, Holy
Trinity, were transferred to the Native Church Pastorate (see Fyfe, 1962,
pp. 300–301, 326–7, and passim).

GRIEVANCES

The basis for such autonomy in the Niger Delta was laid with the
appointment of Bishop Crowther and his African assistants. However, in
the 1870s allegations began to be made about the conduct of the agents
under Crowther's authority, in particular about their moral reputation. One
agent who embodied the ill-starred fate of the mission was William
Fortunatus John, recruited from Fourah Bay College in 1874 and first

Nigeria: Scripture Language Count, 1984

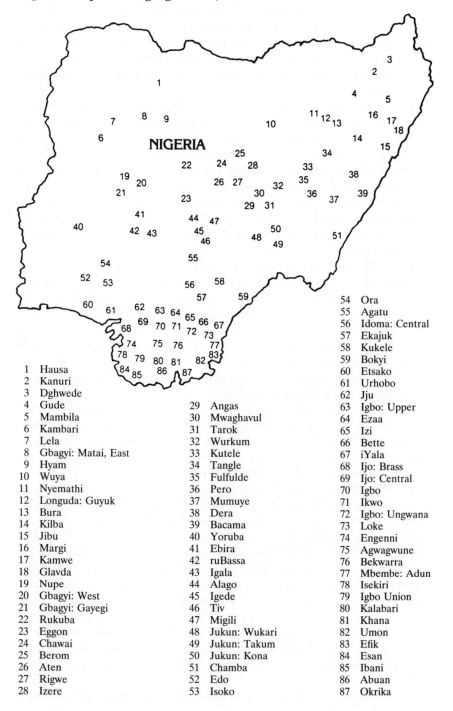

#		#		#	
1	Hausa	29	Angas	54	Ora
2	Kanuri	30	Mwaghavul	55	Agatu
3	Dghwede	31	Tarok	56	Idoma: Central
4	Gude	32	Wurkum	57	Ekajuk
5	Mambila	33	Kutele	58	Kukele
6	Kambari	34	Tangle	59	Bokyi
7	Lela	35	Fulfulde	60	Etsako
8	Gbagyi: Matai, East	36	Pero	61	Urhobo
9	Hyam	37	Mumuye	62	Jju
10	Wuya	38	Dera	63	Igbo: Upper
11	Nyemathi	39	Bacama	64	Ezaa
12	Longuda: Guyuk	40	Yoruba	65	Izi
13	Bura	41	Ebira	66	Bette
14	Kilba	42	ruBassa	67	iYala
15	Jibu	43	Igala	68	Ijo: Brass
16	Margi	44	Alago	69	Ijo: Central
17	Kamwe	45	Igede	70	Igbo
18	Glavda	46	Tiv	71	Ikwo
19	Nupe	47	Migili	72	Igbo: Ungwana
20	Gbagyi: West	48	Jukun: Wukari	73	Loke
21	Gbagyi: Gayegi	49	Jukun: Takum	74	Engenni
22	Rukuba	50	Jukun: Kona	75	Agwagwune
23	Eggon	51	Chamba	76	Bekwarra
24	Chawai	52	Edo	77	Mbembe: Adun
25	Berom	53	Isoko	78	Isekiri
26	Aten			79	Igbo Union
27	Rigwe			80	Kalabari
28	Izere			81	Khana
				82	Umon
				83	Efik
				84	Esan
				85	Ibani
				86	Abuan
				87	Okrika

stationed at Brass. He was accused of immorality in October 1875. First disciplined, he was subsequently reinstated as a secretary to Bishop Crowther. He moved to Onitsha where he was assistant schoolmaster. While there he and his wife were charged with causing the death by physical maltreatment of a teenage slave girl they had themselves redeemed. John, whose career with the mission was by now over, was tried for manslaughter in July 1882.[1]

The charges and allegations had a serious impact on CMS morale at home, and doubts were expressed about the wisdom of continuing to allow Africans to direct the missionary cause in Nigeria. A decision was taken to mount an investigation in situ and to gather evidence that might be relevant in any final steps to be taken. Bishop Crowther cooperated with the notion of an investigative machinery to handle the affair, but, as he admitted later, he had not imagined that his own episcopal authority would be impugned by having young English missionaries set above him in a sphere for which he had ultimate responsibility. It embittered the last days of a great and generous spirit.

The CMS decided to respond to the series of damaging revelations about the Niger Mission by vesting its control in a Finance Committee based in Lagos. This was done in 1879. It was an eight-member committee of five Europeans, including a lay official, J. A. Ashcroft, and three Africans, who were Bishop Crowther as chairman, his youngest son, Archdeacon Dandeson Crowther (1844–1938), then based at Bonny, and Archdeacon Henry Johnson, who was destined for Lokoja in the Upper Niger River area. The Rev. J. B. Wood was secretary of the committee, and in effect prime mover in the strategy to unravel the African strand in the mission. The report he subsequently submitted to the parent committee of the CMS in London, remitted under confidential cover, contained serious aspersions on the competence of the Niger Mission African agents, and worse about their moral conduct. Bishop Crowther was not shown a copy of the report until it had been printed and circulated in London.

The Niger Mission incident has come down in history as a classic instance of missionary imperialism. It is not difficult, taking the evidence at face value, to prove lack of missionary sympathy for African aspirations, and at that level of interpetation it is equally right to object, as critics at the time did, that the failings of Africans and others in the mission should be used as the occasion for passing judgment on Africans as a race, rather than allowing individual characters to be judged on their merit, or in this case their lack of merit. As it was, CMS permitted the view to harden that Africans were as a race unfit to govern in the church, their lack of moral discipline being something of a natural blemish. In fact, African Christian leaders in the Niger Mission were among the strictest of disciplinarians, among them leaders such as Archdeacon Henry Johnson and James "Holy" Johnson.

Nevertheless, the question of missionary high-handedness has continued to haunt the Niger Mission, and it is necessary, therefore, to try to place that question in some sort of perspective. When we ask whether the African reaction to the harsh review of the mission was predictable, we come upon a fundamental plank in the original conception of the mission as such. This has to do with the status of the Niger Mission as an essential element in the creation of an indigenous leadership and the bringing into reality of autonomous churches. The *West African Reporter,* a weekly newspaper owned and operated by Africans in Freetown, Sierra Leone, in its issue of January 4, 1876, contained the following account of the importance for Africans of the Niger Mission:

> The Niger Mission and the native pastorate — which latter has received the encomiums of friends and foes — are standing monuments of the [Church Missionary] Society's labours, and proofs of the permanence of results thus far achieved. Bishop Crowther, the first Negro Bishop, the Rev. James Johnson of Lagos, Dr. Africanus Horton, the distinguished physician and author, and numerous others, less widely known but not less useful, sat under the instructions which have been imparted in the Church Missionary College at Fourah Bay, Sierra Leone. [Cited in Blyden, 1967, p. 49.]

Even Venn, although he at first envisaged the mission as a genuine partnership between Europeans and Africans, looked upon Crowther as "bishop of the 'Native Church' in Yoruba, and [worked] to bolster this up by regarding the Niger Mission as the 'self-propagating' phase of the 'full development of the Native African Church' " (Ajayi, 1965, p. 208).

Venn had expressed himself eloquently on the ultimate object of mission with regard to the "native" question. His statement should not be taken to mean that he envisaged the closing down of missionary societies but, rather, that their role had to be defined in terms of the indigenous reality. He framed his observations in extremely cautious language, but, as the history of mission has shown, the vernacular ambition proved impossible to restrain. In vivid language he spoke about the "euthanasia" of mission. Writing in 1851, he said:

> Regarding the ultimate object of a Mission, viewed under its ecclesiastical result, to be the settlement of a Native Church under Native Pastors upon a self-supporting system, it should be borne in mind that the progress of a Mission depends upon the training up and location of Native Pastors; and that, as it has been happily expressed the *"euthanasia* of a Mission" takes place when a missionary, surrounded by well-trained Native congregations under Native Pastors, is able to resign all pastoral work into their hands, and gradually relax his superintendance over the pastors themselves, till it insensibly ceases; and so the Mission passes into a settled Christian community. Then

the Missionary and all Missionary agencies should be transferred to the "regions beyond." [Cited in Warren, 1971, p. 28, cf. p. 63.]

This idea was expanded by Venn's observation that although churches might be united in devotion and obedience to Christ, it was impossible that "distinctions and defects will vanish. . . . But it may be doubted whether, to the last, the Church of Christ will not exhibit marked national characteristics which, in the overruling grace of God, will tend to its perfection and glory" (Knight, 1880, p. 284; cf. Walls, 1981, p. 48, and Warren, 1971, p. 77).

HOPES

The path to the "Native African Church" lay through the development of the vernacular, a matter that occupied the Niger Mission from start to finish. Bishop Crowther's own contribution to this subject is immense and merits fuller study than has hitherto been done. It is equally true to say that many of his African agents were devoted to the development of the vernacular. One was the Rev. John Garrick of Freetown. He took up the study of the Kalabari language, as well as Brass Ijo into which he translated John's Gospel. Another was the Rev. Henry Johnson, an able, highly educated African who included in his academic career a period of study at the Arabic College in Palestine. He devoted attention to the Mende language in Sierra Leone and the Nupe and Igbira languages in Nigeria, helping to translate the Scriptures into these languages. For his achievements he was awarded an honorary Master's degree in 1885 by Cambridge University. Finally, mention should be made of Archdeacon Dandeson Crowther, whose long life was devoted, among other things, to the vernacular cause, including the translation of the Book of Common Prayer into the Ibo language and parts of the book of Jeremiah into Yoruba. We shall return presently to the Book of Common Prayer, and to Dandeson Crowther himself.

All these individuals helped to strengthen the vernacular cause and to make it a necessary basis for Christian expansion. It would be idle to pretend that all their vernacular work was of an even quality, or that they themselves were more consistent in the tension between vernacular and Western forms. On the contrary, there were some weaknesses. But those weaknesses stand out prominently because of the intense light that the vernacular cause has cast upon the entire landscape. That vernacular factor, more than any other single issue, helps to illuminate several otherwise dim pockets of contradiction and misunderstanding, including the sometimes hostile reception that autochthones on the Niger displayed toward expatriate Creoles and other exogenous elements.

Henry Venn thought that Crowther and his agents should apply this vernacular principle to Nigeria, where the church must find in indigenous sources the potential and wherewithal to become self-propagating, self-supporting, and self-governing—something that would radically undercut any notions of Western hegemony. It would, if carried through, be consistent with the nature of the gospel in showing the lengths to which the principle of the translatability of Christianity could be carried. It would also implicitly reject the wish to import European Christianity, with Africans merely adapting it to African circumstances, the kind of inculturation that leaves intact the forms and suppositions of a different culture. It was not simply that the African soil should assimilate a transplant religion, but that it should come into the abundant harvest that the precious seed of the word yields as it merges with the new environment.

THE PARALLEL OF THE ENGLISH REFORMATION

Venn must have been aware of the painful and tortuous path by which Christianity was assimilated into English culture, a process that stretches back to the Venerable Bede, a man who at the time of his death in A.D. 735 had been translating the Gospel of John, and who in his *History of the English Church and People* chronicles achievements in the English language (1984, pp. 250f., especially). Along that same path trod John Wyclif (ca. 1320–84) and his Lollards in the fourteenth century. Although he did little of the actual translation himself, Wyclif was undoubtedly the major influence on the people who accomplished the task of translation of the whole Bible. John Purvey, Wyclif's secretary, produced about 1395 a revised version of the hitherto stiff and literal translation, with the limitation for distribution, we must bear in mind, that existed in the days prior to printing. Nevertheless, Wyclif's Bible was in great demand, encouraging people to do some barter trade to obtain it.

Then, beginning in 1524, William Tyndale took up the cause at considerable personal cost. In 1525 his translation of the New Testament was ready for printing. Perhaps the greatest innovation of Tyndale's was to approach English as a sufficient linguistic medium in its own right rather than as merely playing second fiddle to the languages of the Bible. In this respect also his translation avoided being shackled by the Latin of the Vulgate, which he consulted. The result was a lively and fresh translation that established an independent standard for English as a vernacular medium. Thus, although Tyndale sought weighty scholarly counsel, and traveled extensively for that purpose, and although he knew several European vernaculars, his use of English was remarkable for its provincial confidence and specificity. "In fact," one source claims, "the largest proportion of his vocabulary is Old English. An exiled scholar, he wrote the language of the *people* of England" (*A Concise History of the English Bible,* 1983, p. 11).

Tyndale's translation had an enormous impact on the development of English national consciousness, his legacy being inherited and enlarged by the King James (Authorized) Version of the Bible. Bishop Westcott testified:

> Not only did Tindale contribute to it directly the substantial basis of half of the Old Testament (in all probability) and of the whole of the New Testament, but he established a standard of Biblical translation which others followed. It is even of less moment that by far the greater part of his translation remains intact in our present Bibles, than that his spirit animates the whole. . . . His influence decided that our Bible should be popular and not literary, speaking in a simple dialect. [Westcott, 1927, p. 158.]

Hilaire Belloc, the English literary figure and a formidable critic of the Reformation, admitted that Tyndale had commenced an immense revolution with his translation. Tyndale, he affirmed, "had created the glories of English prose." He went on:

> The rhythms of that work run through all successive recensions and adaptations of it. Tyndale did not know what he was doing nor did those of his time understand; but a long life-time after, when the men who were then little children were very old or dead, Tyndale's rhythms had begun to vibrate in the minds of a younger generation, and when at last the final version of the English Bible appeared—it was after an interval of nearly eighty years—the spirit of Tyndale still moved through its majestic cadences . . . that mighty thing, the power of prose, was at work, and Tyndale's rhythms were to come across the sea [from Antwerp where Tyndale had taken refuge and from where, in October 1536, by trickery, he was lured and murdered, his body burned as a heretic]. The book existed, though the man was dead . . . . [Belloc, 1931, pp. 193–94.]

In spite of a singular of lack of sympathy for Tyndale, whom he described as "ugly, quarrelsome, zealous to the very limits of zeal," Belloc recognized Tyndale's pivotal importance for the English national spirit. Tyndale, in Belloc's words, "was to prove of singular effect upon the English mind, not in his own life-time nor for a life-time after, but at very long range as it were" (Belloc, 1931, p. 191).

A similar sentiment is expressed by another writer, who claimed that "great consequences have flowed from the fact that the first truly popular literature in England—the first which stirred the hearts of all classes of people, and filled their minds with ideal pictures and their everyday speech with apt and telling phrases—was the literature comprised within the Bible" (Fiske, 1889, p. 54). The impact of the English Bible marked a historical turning point.

No greater moral change ever passed over a nation than passed over England during the years which parted the middle of the reign of Elizabeth from the meeting of the Long Parliament. England became the people of a book, and that book was the Bible. . . . But far greater than its effect on literature or social phrase was the effect of the Bible on the character of the people at large. . . . The whole temper of the nation was changed. [Green, 1882, chap. 7, sec. 1.][2]

Historians have tended to devote more attention to the radical political roots of religion in sixteenth- and seventeenth-century England and far too little to the spiraling effects of translation on the broader culture, although even this line of interpretation acknowledges the importance of the new linguistic medium, as the works of Christopher Hill and others show.[3] Whatever the case, whether we are talking of the Puritan radicals on the left or High-Church stalwarts on the right, the national spirit was deeply molded by the bold affirmation of English in Scripture, liturgy, and the "lectureship," as preaching was called.

The great liturgical triumph of the sixteenth century arrived on the back of this translation movement. Thomas Cranmer, appointed archbishop of Canterbury in 1533 by Henry VIII, was deeply committed to the cause of English as a medium of the church. He drew heavily on Tyndale's translation in an English Bible he published, requiring its installation in every parish church. However, it was his liturgical work culminating in the first English Book of Common Prayer in 1549, subsequently revised in 1552, that established Cranmer's reputation. Charting a middle course between Protestant extremism and Catholic conservatism (G. K. Chesterton, the English Catholic man of letters, dubbed it "the last Catholic book in English Protestantism"), the Book of Common Prayer drew lavishly on Tyndale's translation and carried the whole enterprise to fresh heights. Even today we are struck by the timeless appeal of the Book of Common Prayer: its artless, dignified prose, the poetic intervals of its measured pace, its sonorous cadence, its genial but majestic diction, and the resonant piety and devotion that echo in its unhurried sweep. It is precisely this possibility of stamping upon the national spirit the indelible marks of cultural self-awareness that has marked the course of the translatability of Christianity through the centuries. It implies a continuing need for the gospel, in Scripture and tradition, to engage faithfully the terms of its cultural milieu, and Henry Venn was consistent with this principle when he adopted it for the Niger Mission (see Shenk, 1983, pp. 76, 108f.).

TRANSFORMATION IN THE NIGER DELTA

Although the stakes were equally high, yet the enterprise of vernacular translation in Africa was a mild affair compared to the turbulence that attended its European counterpart. In the first burst of energy that launched the Niger Mission in 1841, Crowther and his African agents naturally expected the flowering of the African cause. In their eyes, everything about the Niger Mission pointed to that future, for the original aims of the mission made African leadership a necessary condition for undertaking it in the first place. This set the context for the conflict between such expectation and the policy of overt missionary control. Rather than concentrate on taking sides in that conflict, we should instead explore it in the context of the sentiments that Christianity had excited by identifying itself with the cause of translatability. (The Sierra Leonean prelate T. S. Johnson, who was consecrated as assistant bishop in 1937, declared in fulfillment of Venn's prophecy: " 'The euthanasia of a mission,' writes the Rev. Henry Venn, C.M.S. Secretary, 'takes place when a missionary is surrounded by well-trained congregations under native pastors.' I think that in Sierra Leone this state has been reached. To-day the spirit of nationalism and racial self-respect is spreading, with the result that the younger Churches áre growing rather restive under what they consider to be foreign domination — a kind of spiritual imperialism which is contrary to the due respect for humanity which is inherent in the Christian faith." [Johnson, 1953, 120]).

It is important, therefore, not to reject the missionary dimension simply on the grounds of a historical conflict between the vernacular and colonial overrule. On the contrary, when we look at the situation we are confronted with the paradox of missionary agency in promoting the vernacular and thus inspiring indigenous confidence at a time when colonialism was demanding paternal overlordship. Africans reacted to this contradiction by appealing to the advantage that the vernacular principle gave them, setting it against the recently developed missionary policy of trying to control the Niger Mission.

The vernacular advantage was not just a moribund native cause. Missionary policy had invoked it as the basis for the entire enterprise, and by so doing made its abandonment inconsistent with the successful expansion of the church. We might say with justice that the drive for statistical superiórity was made a consequence, not the cause, of translation. In an illuminating passage, Venn dwelt upon the follies of using statistical criteria to measure the purpose and effectiveness of Christian mission. He warned:

> There is a danger of regarding all heathendom as a field to be evangelized by European and American missionaries. It is a common calculation, "One clergyman to two or three thousand at home; one to two or three millions abroad: Manchester has so many; Benares not a twentieth part." Now all such calculations — though to a certain extent they may be useful as showing how very little we are doing — are apt to mislead the mind. . . . What, then, is the duty of the Christian church under the present dispensation, but to establish in each district, and especially where there are separate languages, a self-supporting,

self-governing, self-extending native Church. [In Warren, 1971, p. 118.]

Having defined the living context of Christian mission, Venn went on to characterize its modus operandi as, on the negative side, the suppression of its Western form, and, on the positive, the encouragement of indigenous aspirations. From that point of view, he suggested, missionaries, already "reeds shaken by the wind" of scarcity, had a duty to foster vernacular self-confidence. It was their job, he argued, "not to supply an European pastorate, but to prepare native pastors, and to endeavour, by divine help, *to fix the spiritual standard in such Churches by securing for them a supply of Vernacular Scriptures,* and a sound theological literature, which, in this country, and in the English language, so happily abounds" (in Warren, 1971, p. 119; italics added).

By making the translatability of Christianity a common cause with the missionaries, African Christian leaders grasped the political significance of its vernacular premise, insisting that the future of the Niger Mission pointed unmistakably toward local ascendancy in an African pastorate for Nigeria rather than the refined elaborations of a missionary strategy. In the end, in fact, a Niger African pastorate was established, with missionaries being challenged either to consecrate the fruits of their own translation work or to conform to the contradictory strategy of colonial suppression.

The main outlines of the dismantling of the Niger Mission are clear enough. Following the transfer of its authority in 1879 to the Finance Committee in Lagos, a committee of inquiry was set up in August 1890 in Bonny, Nigeria, to investigate charges of corruption and immorality. The commission was in fact presiding over the future of the mission. The secretary was the Rev. F. N. Eden, a young Cambridge graduate in his early thirties. Bishop Crowther, then over eighty, was chairman, in which capacity he was overruled by Eden. It troubled Crowther that in a sphere where ecclesiastical order had given him jurisdiction, the Church Missionary Society (CMS) should allow a subordinate cleric successfully to challenge his authority. But that anomaly can be explained by the fact that there was a growing demand in CMS circles to remove Bishop Crowther and transfer responsibility to Europeans.

Nevertheless, Bishop Crowther was never himself accused of any wrong-doing. Instead, it was his African agents who were charged with grave offenses. Eventually twelve of the original fifteen were dismissed by the commission, with Bishop Crowther finding it impossible to let go unchallenged the repudiation of agents he had himself appointed and installed. He asked the secretary of the commission to say whether he "alone is empowered to dismiss and suspend and do everything else in the Mission. . . . Will you write down, say, please, Bishop Crowther expresses surprise at the statement of the Secretary that he has power as the representative of the C.M.S. to suspend any clergyman from his duty. . . ."

(Ajayi, 1965, p. 253n.). The response of the secretary was to reprimand Crowther for defending the censured pastors, charging him with conduct unworthy of his sacred office. Crowther was dismissed from the committee.

Crowther died on December 31, 1891, broken if still defiant. The ideal of an African pastorate that he had worked for gained in appeal, and, in 1892, in spite of demonstrable missionary opposition, the Niger Delta Pastorate was created. It was staffed by Africans and supported entirely from local contributions. Five of those dismissed from the Niger Mission joined it.

It must be stressed that the Niger Delta Pastorate was not a schismatic movement and never wished to cut loose from its ties with the Anglican church. On the contrary, it wished to maintain those ties, but do so by making Africans leaders in the church. For those Africans who wanted to adopt a more radical approach in the face of European opposition, the Delta Pastorate was viewed as a diversion from the main battle. We shall return to this issue shortly.

Whatever the cautiousness of the men who led the Delta Pastorate movement, in the current atmosphere events moved rapidly toward a showdown. Local Baptists had watched with keen interest the unfolding drama of the Niger Mission and concluded that missionary ties, including their own, were a hindrance. The path was cleared for them by the temporary withdrawal of Southern Baptist missionaries during the American Civil War, and by the time these missionaries returned in the 1870s, local Baptists had learned to get on without them (Webster, 1964, p. 50). Thus when the CMS decided to turn the clock back and repudiate Bishop Crowther's legacy in the Niger Mission, these Baptists experienced a reawakened sense of mistrust of missionary direction. In March 1888, a group splintered off to form the Native Baptist Church, taking with them all the great African pioneers of Baptist work in Nigeria (Webster, 1964, p. 56). The Baptist secession "ushered in a new era of Christianity among the Yoruba. A spell had been broken . . ." (Webster, 1964, p. 61).

Then there rapidly followed a series of separatist moves. In December 1890, Dr. Edward Blyden, the great Pan-black nationalist, arrived in Lagos from Freetown, Sierra Leone, where he was based, calling for the establishment of a quasi-political religious organization, which he called the West African Church, set up in March 1891 (Webster, 1964, pp. 65ff.). The West African Church was seriously hampered by hints of doctrinal schism in its aims. Consequently, African Christian leaders who were attracted by the prospects of independence from mission felt nevertheless alienated by the more extreme prospects of a schism against orthodox Christianity. As a consequence, the West African Church was stifled at birth, with most of the leading local Christians shunning it. That left the way clear for a genuinely religious response to the new missionary policy.

The first subsequent response was the convening of a meeting in Lagos in August 1891 to consider carefully the attitude to be adopted following the displacement of Bishop Crowther. The upshot was a resolution adopted as the foundation statement of the United Native African Church (UNAC). The statement affirmed

> that Africa is to be evangelized and that foreign agencies at work at the present moment taking into consideration climatic and other influences cannot grasp the situation; resolved that a purely Native African Church be founded for the evangelization and amelioration of our race, to be governed by Africans. [Cited in Webster, 1964, p. 68.]

In making a conjunction between Christian success and indigenous ascendancy, the UNAC had invoked a powerful theme in an environment primed to exploit it. In fact, its own response was judged by others to have been too tame, if not timid. It was fighting the narrow issue of administrative autonomy in response to grievances with the Niger Mission, rather than the larger question of the appropriation of Christianity by indigenous criteria. The UNAC was accordingly eclipsed by other forms of African response, forms that took up the bold question of indigenous adaptation.

The fate of Blyden's proposal for a West African church shows that African Christian opinion was deeply conservative on matters of doctrine and polity, a circumstance that requires us to distinguish, however tenuously, between the religious factor and the quasi-political status of late nineteenth-century mission. It was Bishop Crowther's youngest son, Archdeacon Dandeson Crowther, who helped to bring to the fore the religious grounds — and limits — of opposition to the CMS, and to him we now turn.

THE ROLE OF DANDESON CROWTHER

Dandeson Crowther had been specially set aside by his father for the religious vocation. The son became a close and constant companion of his father, who placed him in service in the Niger Mission. Dandeson became a faithful extension of his father's religious designs in the Niger. As part of the eight-member Finance Committee of 1879, Dandeson Crowther was very close to the events that broke down his father and inflamed opinion in both Nigeria and Sierra Leone from where most of the African agents were recruited. As an archdeacon based on the Niger, Dandeson's career was materially affected by the dissolution of the Niger Mission, although he steadfastly refused to see himself as an episcopal successor to his father. In spite of that, his filial obligation, his official position with the mission, his duties as a committee member, and his status as an educated African all combined to thrust upon him a mandate for action.

Spurred on by the goading eloquence of R. N. Cust, a retired member of the Indian Civil Service who found temporary outlet for his energies first as a patron and then as persistent critic of the CMS, Dandeson chose restraint and conciliation. Cust had written to him saying that he had resigned from the committee of the CMS on the issue of what he said was CMS insensitivity to the African question. In a letter, in June 1893, he urged Dandeson to seize the opportunity to make a clean break with the CMS. "Remember," he wrote, "that now or never is your chance of resisting as a church the tyranny of another and alien church. . . . The Committee professes a readiness to appoint an African Bishop at some future time: but five years hence, ten years hence, the same thing will be said, 'The African is not fit for the post of Bishop' " (Hair, 1963, p. 21). In fact it was not till the 1950s that an African bishop was appointed again.

As if to fight fire with paraffin, the CMS had sent out J. S. Hill, a man not renowned for his tact, to review the matter of the vacant bishopric. In his capacity as commissary for the CMS, Hill dropped enough hints to torment Dandeson and others that he himself would fill the vacancy, which he eventually did. But Hill went further. He charged Dandeson with acting *ultra vires* in setting up the Niger Delta Pastorate, and in attempting to reinstate African clergy dismissed from the Niger Mission. In fact it was Bishop Crowther, in his capacity as legatee of the Niger Mission, who had left instructions in 1891 for the creation of a Native Pastorate in the Delta. And as for reinstating those who had suffered dismissal from the mission, the case concerned one Rev. Charles Paul, a Yoruba, who had been dismissed by F. N. Eden over Bishop Crowther's head, and, who, in any case, had died in 1892. So it was a moot question.

Dandeson's task of reconciliation could not have been made any easier when, at the instigation of a vote by the churches of the Delta, a recommendation was sent down to appoint the Rev. James Johnson as bishop to succeed the late Bishop Crowther. Although clearly in support of the recommendation, Dandeson knew it would not be well received by the CMS and would thus harden attitudes in the Delta. In the event Hill, who received the recommendation, ignored it and, instead, made two appointments of his own. Dandeson was distressed but, to show that he was committed to appeasement, he failed to be moved by Hill's action. Instead, in a letter to the archbishop of Canterbury in February 1894, Dandeson offered his surrender, saying he hoped the policy of the missionary society was only a "present temporary arrangement" (Hair, 1963, p. 23). He was obviously trying to find a loophole in the constricting wall of an adamant missionary society.

Cust, who was now Dandeson's self-appointed guardian angel, sensed that his charge would withdraw from confrontation. Accordingly, in spite of his earlier incitements, Cust adopted a more conciliatory tone, either because his own views had changed or, which is equally likely, because he wished to keep in step with Dandeson Crowther. At any rate he put into words a position that reflected Dandeson's own attitude toward the CMS. "You must take care," Cust affirmed to Dandeson, appealing to the American experience, "to keep your Church principles: *you are members of the Episcopal Church: keep to it:* but you are not bound to remain in the

National English Church, any more than the American colonists were bound to . . ." (Hair, 1963, p. 23). Loopholes, as the final comment of Cust shows, were becoming familiar.

If across the gulf of his own militancy Cust could bring himself to appreciate the force of Dandeson's conciliatory mind, then it suggests that Dandeson would leave his mark there rather than in outright confrontation. In fact, the issue of institutional integrity in the church was a stronger matter with Dandeson than the wish to avenge a sense of wrong. He put the case succinctly when he wrote to Cust about this in June 1893: ". . . If the Archbishop of Canterbury be pleased to excommunicate us to please the C.M.S., what should the Pastorate do then? . . . If we insist on having the Rev. James Johnson as our *own* bishop, and if he be willing to cast his lot with us, where can he get consecration apart from England?" (Hair, 1963, p. 22). Respect for ecclesiastical authority, rather than sensitivity with the just exercise of that authority, became Dandeson's consuming concern.

When he thought about the appropriate African response to events on the Niger, Dandeson was influenced, others might say distracted, by his unquestioning high regard for ecclesiastical authority, and this led him to view CMS action as only a challenge whereby Africans might prove themselves worthy of approval. In the process, Dandeson assumed the correctness of pressing forward with the Niger Mission. The alternative, he felt, was to pull out and allow Europeans to run the show entirely. That, he said, would prove "a great want of faith" and "a reproach to the African character." He said there was a lot of commotion about "separation from C.M.S.," but he would not hear of it. The clearest statement he made about the role of Africans on the Niger was in a letter, in June 1892, to J. N. Grant, a Creole leader of Freetown. "If we educated sons and daughters of West Africa," he argued, "with all our intelligence and advantages cannot, or rather shrink now from facing difficulties for the extension of the Gospel of Christ *in our own country* and wait to have it done by others . . . it will be a cause for great humiliation and shame to us—especially in a place like the Delta where we have, since quarter of a century, been in the thick of the fight . . ." (Hair, 1963, p. 20).

In essence, Dandeson saw no future in a cause directed solely by Africans and, instead, counseled loyalty to the CMS as the only sensible choice for him and his African colleagues. We may be inclined to criticize Dandeson's attitude as that of an Uncle Tom, but it might be truer to say that with loyal and dedicated servants like him, the CMS policy of distrust was a cruel recompense, and it did nothing to hold back the movement for indigenous autonomy. The logic of the translatability of Christianity had seen to that.

THE FELL CLUTCH OF CIRCUMSTANCE:
CONFLICT AND RENEWAL

Thus far we have seen how Dandeson Crowther showed not just the grounds but the limits of moderate religious opposition to the CMS on the

Niger. The next stage was to appeal to a stronger principle for the African cause. The man on whose shoulders responsibility now devolved was the Rev. James Johnson, popularly known in Lagos as "Holy Johnson," a sobriquet that has been adopted as the title of a major study by the Nigerian historian, E. A. Ayandele *(Holy Johnson: Pioneer of African Nationalism, 1836–1917).*

Consecrated as assistant bishop of Western Equatorial Africa (and not of the Niger Delta Church as Johnson desired) by the much revered Archbishop William Temple, in January 1900, James Johnson was something of an enigmatic figure, embodying the contradictions of the time. He accepted missionary partnership but encouraged the Delta churches to strive for self-reliance. He was opposed to colonialism, and in this regard was applauded by national figures in Nigeria and elsewhere, yet he ranged himself on the side of the colonial authorities against the emerging prophet movements in the Niger Delta. Missionaries noted his opposition to European manners, customs, and dress with regard to the church in Africa, yet he accepted for himself the vestments of the Western church. His African colleagues resented his attacks on their culture and standards but admired his defense of Africa against European criticism. In order to make sense of all this, it would be consistent to view Johnson as a transitional figure who helped to catalyze the ferment for change in the Niger. From one statement he made, we can see how many would identify with him as one who embodies the African religious initiative. He argued to the effect that

Christianity is a Religion intended for and is suitable for every Race and Tribe of people on the face of the Globe. Acceptance of it was never intended by its Founder to *denationalise any people and it is indeed its glory that every race of people may profess and practise it and imprint upon it its own native characteristics,* giving it a peculiar type among themselves without its losing anything of its virtue. And why should not there be an African Christianity as there has been a European and an Asiatic Christianity? [Cited in Ayandele, 1970, p. 304; italics added.][4]

Shortly after he returned to Nigeria from his consecration, Johnson came into conflict with the church. He was sacked from his parish and his belongings were dumped in the street in Lagos (Webster, 1964, p. 76). This incident exacerbated the festering grievances over the Niger-Mission question, and introduces our theme of the radical religious response. In protest at Johnson's treatment, a group of disaffected churchmen broke away to form the Bethel Chruch. They came accordingly to be called "Bethelites." On the inauguration day of Bethel Church the following statement was issued: "This day [December 22, 1901] we lay the foundation of the church for the black race . . ." (Webster, 1964, p. 78). Its leaders became the founders of the African Church Organization, a strong indigenous movement resolved to overtake the CMS in Yoruba country and create an alternative to Anglicanism (see Webster, 1964, p. 69).

The leaders of the African Church movement were determined to secure it on a sound economic basis. One of the founders was Mojola Agbebi, a local Baptist leader. He regarded himself as a follower of Henry Venn. He came forward to preach what he called "the gospel of coffee, cocoa, cotton and work as well as the Scripture" (Webster, 1963, p. 426), an order that, if it was unintentional, could not have been more significant. Agbebi was also a disciple of Edward Blyden. Agbebi developed a farm near Ijebu-Ode, which prospered until 1908 when its West Indian manager, J. E. Ricketts, died.

Another prominent figure in the African Church movement was J. K. Coker. He was, like Agbebi, especially active in agricultural projects. Coker became a pioneer of cocoa farming in Nigeria. He created a plantation at Ifako where he is claimed to have planted some 30,000 cocoa seedlings. The plantation went through a boom period, and at the height of its prosperity during World War I it had an annual income of £20,000, with 2,000 acres under cultivation and 10,000 laborers in employment.

The entrepreneurship of this emerging new middle class was deeply informed by religion, much in the manner of the Quaker industrialists who were active in the Industrial Revolution in Britain (see M. W. Flinn, 1967). For example, many of the 10,000 laborers employed on the plantation were taught to be literate "in the Yoruba language and were armed with the Yoruba Bible which many of them took with them throughout the length and breadth of the country. The farmers had turned missionary under African direction. . . . Coker himself spent generous portions of his enormous wealth on furthering the cause, travelling extensively to preach, exhort and advise on cocoa production" (Sanneh, 1983, p. 161).

Coker had created a symbiotic relationship between agriculture and Christianty: the growth of the African Church movement was fueled by earnings from cocoa, while increase in church membership helped provide a much needed source of labor for the cocoa plantations. Furthermore, the plantation superintendents, while on preaching duty, recruited church members as laborers. Thus conversion provided the African Church movement with valuable stock for farm and church.

Other members of the African Church movement were active in public life and in circles of budding nationalism. One was J. W. Cole, a wealthy Lagos entrepreneur. He was for two years (1895–97) a member of the Legislative Council in Lagos. Another was H. A. Caulcrick, who was decorated by the colonial government for distinguished service in the Treasury, and a third, E. H. Oke, had been active in the Judiciary Department and after his retirement a member of the Legislative Council (1924–30). Oke was active in cultural circles in Ibadan where he was based. He was president of the Ibadan Branch of the Pan-African nationalist organization, the National Congress of British West Africa, a body that could boast of figures like George Padmore and Kwame Nkrumah, two prominent blooms of the nationalist era. Finally, mention should be made of G. A. Williams, who had been an African agent in the Niger Mission. He resigned from that office after the dismissal of Bishop Crowther and came to Lagos. Subsequently he became active in popular journalism, eventually owning and editing the *Lagos Standard,* which he turned into a mouthpiece of the African cause. He and the others constituted the elite ranks of the African church, occupying the status of elders.

In fact the institutional organization of the African Church movement was a microcosm of the larger traditional Yoruba social system. In that system, the elders wielded power: politically they constituted the council that saw to the installation of the ruler, and, in an advisership capacity, kept a watch on the conduct of affairs; socially they were the custodians of the social code, the providers of largesse to the people, and the depository of traditional mores; religiously they acted as the mediatory agency between the ancestors and the living — a tripartite order that together comprised the community. The community of the living thus took its orders from the elders or their designated representative, who was the ruler. Below the elders in the African church were the junior leaders, who disseminated information and carried out instructions of their superiors. The clergy were recruited from humble sections of the society, as the farmer missionaries of Coker's plantation illustrate. Like the diviner-priests *(babalawo)* of traditional Yoruba society, the clergy could not become principals in the intricate web of local politics, a device that, without denying the relevance of religion to politics, helped to disperse the concentration of both in the same hands. The clergy's greatest weapon was their piety and spiritual devotion, and with that a clergyman might rise in popular esteem and gain trust and respect as a broker. At the bottom of the scale was the congregation with which the clergy shared a common social origin. The congregation was the arena in which deals were formally ratified after they had been previously sponsored by the elders. The congregations, then, like the clergy, were in the pockets of the elders. This completed the process by which Christianity was effectively *translated* into the Yoruba social idiom, a shift no less momentous than its linguistic counterpart. It marked the beginnings of the emergence of the Yoruba national church, an idea that even the CMS had not rejected completely.

Thus, whether we are speaking of the conciliatory Crowthers, the meek and mild UNAC, the enigmatic James Johnson, the revolutionary African Church movement, or even the short-lived and slightly outlandish West African Church of Dr. Blyden, we are dealing essentially with people who were all galvanized by the prospects induced by the notion of translatability.

THE RECOILING EFFECTS OF THE VERNACULAR SPIRAL

It is now time to turn our attention to a different aspect of the effects of vernacularization. This has to do with indigenous tension among Africans themselves, sometimes arising out of missionary measures, but more typically from attempts to apply the vernacular principle to the ethnic cause, with ethnicity becoming a factor in the appropriation of Christianity.

It is obvious that the sentiment for a Yoruba national church would be emulated by other ethnic groups. In fact the Yoruba national sentiment would require the emergence within Yoruba society itself of numerous separate churches, which would not recognize the authority of a central structure. In the second place, the use of African agents from one part of the continent in another part might arouse local ethnic sensibility and lead to a xenophobic reaction. Third, vernacular translation by nonlocal experts might not succeed, with the resulting deficiencies exciting local criticism. All these factors are united by the unwavering commitment of mission to the translation process, with the added consideration that the vernacular issue fostered a highly volatile indigenous environment making for competition and rivalry. It is, therefore, right to say that success in translatability need not imply success on other levels. One might even say that a bad translation can justify the cause of translatability just as well as a good one, for a bad translation would play into the hands of indigenous critics while a good one would vindicate their cause. In either case translation appeals to indigeneous claims. It says something for historical consistency that even when Christian mission was making little or no headway with it, as in Japan, China, India, and the Arab world, or where it undermined missionary suzerainty, the translation enterprise continued to be the centerpiece in the machinery of mission.

In his acute observations on the missionary methods of Francis Xavier, Venn turned, most importantly, to the failure of Xavier to follow consistently enough the logic of translatability and allow principles and agents of indigenous appropriation to determine the transmission of Christianity. Instead, Venn alleged, Xavier made uniformity of practice the goal of his missionary endeavor, thus coming into profound conflict with the "peculiar duties" laid upon him by translatability. Although he carried entirely in his hands the bow of authority, stretching it till it broke, Xavier was nevertheless a model worth imitating, "more especially in respect of the native races [where] he acted the part of a true Missionary, maintaining their rights against the oppression and injustice of his own countrymen, treating them as possessing the same feelings and capacities as their more civilized fellow-men" (Warren, 1971, p. 179).

A similar logic had worked itself out in the Niger Mission, and at its grand development around 1915 it had brought into prominence a powerful prophet movement led by a local convert, Garrick Braide. Braide was deeply molded by the vernacular issue. Without a proper education, he learned to understand his newly adopted faith in the vernacular. However, the use of the Ibo vernacular was not itself straightforward, for it was adopted for peoples who spoke different dialects, sufficiently different to arouse feelings of ethnicity. Braide was borne on that tide.

Baptized in 1910 and confirmed in 1912 by Bishop Johnson, Braide found himself at the head of a mass spontaneous movement, which he infused with his fervent message of faith in one God, adherence to the religious code, the heady appeal to indigenous leadership in the church, and denunciation of the trade and consumption of alcohol (then the scourge of the Delta). Eventually the church authorities decided to curb Braide's activities, fearful of the consequences of Braide's influence outside the church. Even Bishop Johnson was constrained to move against Braide. At a meeting of the Niger Delta Pastorate Board in February 1916, Johnson charged Braide's movement with idolatry, blasphemy, superstition, heresy, and schism, drawing particular attention to Braide's practice of faith-healing which, Johnson insisted, was contrary to church teaching (Tasie, 1978, p. 186). Measures were taken to suppress Braide's movement, but they only succeeded in investing it with the virtue of suffering for one's faith. Some accounts, perhaps embellishing the virtue of resistance with fantasy, speak of Braide having one million followers at one stage (Tasie, 1978, p. 191 and note). In 1916 Braide was arrested, charged with various offenses of a criminal nature, and sentenced to imprisonment. He died on November 15, 1918, shortly after his release from prison. Meanwhile his followers had constituted themselves into Christ Army Church. Between 1918 and 1921, Braide's followers were estimated to number 43,000.

Braide's movement added a particular twist to the vernacular spiral by, at one end, pressing the need for the recognition of dialects in translation and preaching work and, at the other, by raising objections to employing non-Ibo Africans in the Delta churches. To take up the translation issue first, the German missionary and companion of Bishop Crowther, Schön, had done a study of the Ibo language in 1843, complemented by what is claimed to be the first study of the Hausa language. In 1856 Crowther was writing to Henry Venn, urging the development of Ibo (see Ogharaerumi, 1987, pp. 608, 183). John Christopher Taylor, born of Ibo parents in Sierra Leone, was also a pioneer of the study of Ibo, in which work he was engaged in the late 1850s and early 1860s. Described as a careful and methodical linguist, Taylor helped to uncover the rich layers of Ibo in its many dialects. After an interrupted stint, he was able to finish a translation of the New Testament in 1866. He wrote of his experience: "During the course of translation, the harmony [i.e., synopsis] of the Gospel appears to me with greatest clearness and perspicuity. God would not leave his people at an uncertainty concerning his kind intentions towards them" (cited in Ogharaerumi, 1987, p. 204).

Nevertheless, the gathering pace of work in the various Ibo dialects posed a real challenge in the atmosphere of the new missionary policy of the 1890s, and a decision was taken to embark on a project to produce a uniform translation, in other words, to concoct a master dialect that would supersede local variants and, with them, the African agents committed to those variants. To this end in 1905, the Owerri dialect was chosen, a decision that would rankle with other regions in the Delta. As one writer put it, "The result was 'Union Ibo,' a combination of various Ibo dialects. . . . From about 1909 this complex new version of 'nobody's Ibo,' already rejected at Onitsha, was again to be imposed in the Delta districts . . ." (Tasie, 1978, p. 170). This increased the pressure to claim recognition for local dialects, particularly after the colonial administration, utilizing the missionary agency, decided to adopt vernacular teaching in schools (Ogharaerumi, 1987, pp. 301–2; Omenka, 1986). Before then the government policy on the vernacular was that no official support was "required for its encouragement," and should instead be left to "the stimulus of self-interest" (Omenka, 1986, p. 122). In this way the missionary promotion of the vernacular unwittingly fomented sentiments for the ethnic cause. Braide exploited these sentiments.

Braide was equally challenging in the matter of indigenous agents, whom missionary policy had relegated to the periphery. There was mounting dissatisfaction about the use of non-Ibo agents in the territory in which Braide became active. By the time he came on the scene, this dissatisfaction was an open contention, with the Delta peoples feeling that it was unacceptable "for the Niger Delta church to depend entirely . . . on missionary agents recruited from Lagos and Sierra Leone. Strictly, those agents were not natives" (Tasie, 1978, p. 172). As early as 1905 complaints on these lines were being filed with Bishop Johnson. Clearly the Lagos and Sierra Leone connections were viewed with disfavor in the Delta, and even Bishop Crowther's own Yoruba origin was held to be a disadvantage (Tasie, 1978, p. 93). Braide capitalized on this rumbling discontent by commissioning and appointing agents as evangelists, preachers, and healers. "Many of them were simple and ignorant folk, with bare knowledge of the rudiments of Christianity. Some of them were people who had visited Braide at Bakana for one ailment or another; and after cure whom he had exhorted to return to their homes, destroy [their] fetishes and preach Christianity" (Tasie, 1978, p. 179). Nothing better brings out the mass character of Braide's movement than his method of recruitment and commissioning.

Braide came under fire for peddling religious charlatanry, an issue that relates intimately to the question of translatability. Hilaire Belloc complained that Tyndale had taken unwarranted liberties with Scripture by rendering the Greek term *ekklesia* into English as "congregation," and by that step had poisoned the springs of religious orthodoxy (Belloc, 1931, p. 192).[5] In a sense Braide had similarly taken wide liberties in founding a movement whose strength was in its lay rather than its clerical character. Yet the question of abuse is neither helpful nor instructive in distinguishing between religious groups or in appreciating the power of religious symbols. Braide himself clearly drew a line between tolerable and intolerable acts, although his line did not coincide with that of the CMS or its colonial allies. It is equally clear many of his followers showed excess in their veneration of their leader. Braide could argue, from his own vantage point, that the missionary toleration of the alcohol trade, for example, and the detrimental effects of that on his people, was a greater evil than the dispatch of unarmed religious stalwarts to do battle against the devil and his works. It is all a question of perspective. What is important, however, is that the motives of right conduct and serious devotion existed at all in a movement like Braide's, with the refining work of time still to do its work. The translatability of the gospel makes the Tyndales and the Braides inevitable though by no means the final word.

Like Bishop Johnson, Braide also came to have an enormous impact on nationalist feeling in Nigeria. The *Lagos Weekly Record,* in its first issue in 1916, took up the cause of Braide in an editorial comment: Braide was acclaimed as a hero of national identity, a vehicle of God's design for the peoples of Africa. S. A. Coker, a leader of the African Church movement and a contributor to the *Lagos Weekly Record,* defended Braide against missionary attacks, appealing to the Bible to support Braide's religious claims. He pointed out the self-contradiction of the missionary church in acknowledging Braide's good works and attributing them to Beelzebub (Tasie, 1978, p. 195). Otomba Payne, the editor of the *Lagos Weekly Record,* also joined forces with Braide. In an editorial believed to have been composed by him, Payne invoked the Social Darwinist principle and asserted that "Christian churches organized and manned by African natives and following the law and adaptation to environment are more likely to be endowed with 'the promise of potency of life' in the process of natural selection than the offshoots of foreign and exotic organization" (in Tasie, 1978, pp. 195–96).

All of this added to indigenous tension in the reaction to attempts at missionary control. In that respect, both Braide and Johnson were common elements in a common cause, whatever the specific nature of the conflict in their mutual relationship.

CHARISMATIC REVIVAL AND INDEPENDENCY

When we turn to the question of the multiplicity of local churches we come upon another aspect of the widening consequences of the vernacular spiral. Several forces combined to shape and give vent to the vernacular urge of local Christianity. One was the worldwide influenza epidemic of 1918 ("the Great Pandemic"), during which a series of revivalist meetings were held across Yoruba country and beyond. The meetings were in part a response to the urgent need of people for healing, for the epidemic reached its height in Yoruba country in October 1918 (Peel, 1968, p. 62). Many of the central figures in the revival movement had also had CMS connections and were determined to set up independently. Then there was the global economic slump of the 1920s, which drove local people into hardship, causing the government to adopt measures deemed highly unpopular. Almost contemporary with that, the city of Lagos was ravaged by bubonic plague between 1924 and 1926, increasing the need for applied Christianity, which the new religious leaders supplied through charismatic gifts: prayer, dreams, visions, healing, and a sense of community. In addition, there was a severe famine in 1932.

The revival meetings were carefully coordinated, with individuals traveling between meeting points and maintaining an informed network. The formative period was from 1918 to 1930 when "many implicit views of Christianity by leading Christians turned into something explicit" (Peel, 1968, p. 91). In July 1930, at a vast public gathering at Ilesha, the charismatic figure, Joseph Babalola,

> clad in white shorts and shirt, with Bible and handbell, preached to the people to renounce evil practices and witchcraft, and to bring out for burning all their idols and juju, for God was powerful enough to answer all their needs, and to cure them. Furthermore, what became a standard practice, he sanctified the near-by stream by prayer, as *omi iye,* the water of life, as had been revealed to him. A District Officer who attended a meeting noted its purely religious and inoffensive character; it was not dramatic or exciting, and was most impressive when people raised the water-vessels on their heads for Babalola to bless them. He took no money and the crowds were orderly; the worst confusion was on the roads leading to Ilesha from Ife and Ijebu. [Peel, 1968, pp. 91–92.]

Babalola was born in Ilorin Province, now Kwara State, in Nigeria in 1904. He had had a few years of primary school education, quitting at a mature age in 1928. He was subsequently employed as a steamroller driver with the colonial Public Works Department. While engaged in this work he claimed to have heard a voice calling him to devote himself to preaching the gospel. Like his counterparts in Scripture, such as Amos and Isaiah, Babalola was given a parable of his mission. There were three palm leaves attached to the steamroller: one was dead and dry, the other was wilting, and the third was fresh and green with life, which represented those who responded to his message. He was commanded to take a bell as the symbol of his commissioning and was given the promise that prayer and the *omi iye* would cure all manner of illness.

When Babalola burst upon the unsuspecting townspeople they were startled by his wild, dramatic appearance: he was naked and covered in ashes, carrying a bell and calling on people to repent. Finally, after predictable opposition in several places, Babalola arrived at Ebute Metta near Lagos where he was baptized in December 1929 by a fellow charismatic, Odubanjo (Peel, 1968, p. 70).

Babalola's reputation came to rest on his ability to deliver powerful prayers. For example, when he was at the Yoruba town of Ilesha he prayed in the name of *Ọluwa Ọlọrun Alayé*, "Lord God of Life," and when news of this reached the town of Efon, it is reported to have impressed the reigning chief, the Alayé of Efon, because of the apparent pun with his own title (Peel, 1968, p. 92). So when Babalola subsequently arrived at Efon, he was assured of a warm welcome.

The Ilesha revival that inaugurated Babalola's dramatic career was followed by a stirring outpouring of the spirit in Ibadan at the hands of a man who had attended the Ilesha meeting and was on his way back to Lagos. Then a string of other places joined the revival movement: Abeokuta, Ijesha, Ekiti, Ondo, and most impressive of all, Efon where Babalola, the prince of prayer, established a center. His movement became known as the *Aladura,* a Yoruba word that means "prayer." It derived from the Arabic, *al-du'a,* supplicatory prayer. Before long charismatic envoys, prophets, and prophetesses were touring the country, preaching, prophesying, organizing, and healing, reaching places as far apart as Onitsha and Port Harcourt in the Delta and Kano and Sokoto in the Muslim north (Peel, 1968, p. 101). Sitting loosely to denominational considerations, the revival leaders actually helped the missionary churches to increase in membership and to experience a quickening of religious interest.

Nevertheless, from a combination of circumstances, both external and internal, the religious ferment of the revival movement subsequently sought more organized channels, and charismatic churches were established. These churches combined the element of administrative independence from missionary churches with that of internal liturgical adaptation, stressing the importance of prayer, prophecy, and healing, and organizing a community of committed followers on that foundation. Numerous splits occurred within their ranks and along many lines: social and educational, age and status. Yet, surprisingly enough, divisions seldom followed ethnic or tribal lines, suggesting that the splits had more a denominational than a tribal character. These churches became better known as African Independent Churches, with the phenomenon itself characterized as "Independency." They ran the entire gamut of theological orientation, from ecstatic, spirit-filled congregations to sober, respectable hierarchical communities. Some spread across national and international boundaries, with contacts in such places as London, Glasgow, Philadelphia, and Atlanta. They adopted a variety of names: Faith Tabernacle, Cherubim and Seraphim Church, the Church of the Lord *(Aladura),* Savior Apostolic Church (which became Christ Apostolic Church) and a variation (and deviation) of that in Christ Gospel Apostolic Chruch, the Precious Stone Church, and so on. The matter of names, so important in African society, was enthusiastically exploited in the new religious movements of Nigeria.

The phenomenon became familiar in numerous parts of Africa, too, from Swaziland, South Africa, Malawi, Zimbabwe, Kenya, and Uganda to the Ivory Coast, Ghana, and Zaire. In spite of the extent and diversity of these groups, they are all united by the vernacular bond and the reaction to foreign control, which the vernacular inspired. Hence the overlap between movements of renewal and revival, on the one hand, and, on the other, the development of indigenous languages and their use in translation. In recoiling from the effects of the bewildering multiplicity of revival movements and their colorful charismatic figures, missionaries were hoist with their own petard, for it was they who raised the vernacular standard and demanded it as the form of Christian identity. It is scarcely consistent to throw the charge of Beelzebub at the *Aladura* leaders and their unformed followers because the native accent had gone to their heads — and feet.

Missionary critics of the *Aladura* phenomenon considered it a weakness and a blemish that the new prophets encouraged displays of extreme emotion and wild, raving shouts, things that, in the view of the critics, harked back to an unredeemed African past. Citing a remark in the *Methodist Quarterly Review* of New York, dated January 1876, Blyden tried to answer the criticism. One missionary observer had asserted that "An African's religion finds vent at his heels. Songs and dances form no inconsiderable part of the worship at a Southern coloured camp-meeting. If we were constructing a ritual for the race we should certainly include this Shaker element" (cited in Blyden, 1967, p. 275).

Blyden gently took up the theme himself and made a point of it: "In the music of the universe, each shall give a different sound, but necessary to the grand symphony." He continues: "When the African shall come forward with his peculiar gifts, he will fill a place never before occupied" (Blyden, 1967, p. 278). Blyden might almost have been speaking of the prophet movements that would appear on the scene.

Clearly, many missionaries, in embarking on translation, had different motives from their African converts and colleagues, but in this matter, as in so much else, translation is no respecter of motives. Africans were merely following a path laid out for them.

SUMMARY AND CONCLUSION

In this chapter we have explored the historical consequences of vernacular translation in the Niger Delta. First, we examined the Niger Mission in terms of the central role that Bishop Crowther played in it, analyzing the African response to missionary policies by looking at the forces on the ground. Second, we considered the decision of the CMS to end the policy of African leadership for the Niger Mission by dismissing Bishop Crowther as its head, relating the volatile reactions of Africans to forces on the ground. Some parallels were drawn with the English Reformation. Third, the role of Dandeson Crowther, a son of Bishop Crowther, in trying to mollify passions was investigated as a theme in the moderate African response. Fourth, the stiffening of this moderate African response, in the figure of the Rev. (later Bishop) James Johnson, was reviewed. Two stages were thus identified in this response stage: one was the question of institutional challenge, with Johnson as a sponsored candidate for the episcopacy in defiance of missionary intentions, and the other was the popular outburst of feeling under the aegis of the charismatic prophet Garrick Braide. These two stages later coalesced with the *Aladura* revival of 1928–30. The impact of vernacular translation on indigenous attitudes toward missions and on the forces of ferment and renewal internally concluded this survey.

NOTES

1. For details on this and other incidents, see Godwin Tasie, *Christian Missionary Enterprise in the Niger Delta, 1864–1918* (Leiden: E. J. Brill, 1978), p. 252 and passim.

2. See also the series of pamphlets published by the American Bible Society: *A Concise History of the English Bible; The Influence of the English Bible upon the English Language and upon English and American Literature; The Bible and the Life and Ideals of the English-speaking People;* and *The English Bible and British and American Art*. These materials provide abundant evidence, meticulously documented, of the impact of the Bible and the translation process on the poetry, prose, literature, journalism, arts, manners, speech, government, and history of the English-speaking world. It would divert us in a major way from the subject of this chapter to develop many of the great themes treated in these documents, but the interested reader is urged to pursue the general topic there.

3. See Christopher Hill's two important books in this area: *Society and Puritanism in Pre-Revolutionary England* (London: Mercury Books, 1966), and *The World Turned Upside Down: Radical Ideas during the English Revolution* (Harmondsworth, England: Penguin Books, 1975). It is germane to my point to say that although he analyzes the role of Tyndale in radical religious circles, Hill does not, as far as I can see, pay much attention to Tyndale as translator.

4. This is a topic dear also to the heart of Blyden, and the similarity of view may be due to more than coincidence. See E. W. Blyden, *Christianity, Islam and the Negro Race* (Edinburgh: Edinburgh University Press, 1967), pp. 164–68; and the same author's *African Life and Customs* (New York: 1908), pp. 62–64, 66.

5. Barclay argues for translating *ekklesia* as "congregation" (1958).

SELECT BIBLIOGRAPHY

Ajayi, Jacob A. F. 1965. *Christian Missions in Nigeria: 1841–1891: The Making of a Modern Elite*. Evanston, Ill.: Northwestern University Press; repr. 1969.

Ayandele, Emmanuel A. 1963. "An Assessment of James Johnson and His Place in Nigerian History, 1874–1890." *Journal of the Historical Society of Nigeria* 2, no. 1.

_____ . 1967. "Background to the 'Duel' between Crowther and Goldie on the Lower Niger, 1857–1885." *Journal of the Historical Society of Nigeria* 4, no. 1.

_____ . 1970. *Holy Johnson: A Pioneer of African Nationalism, 1836–1917*. New York: Humanities Press.

Ballhatchet, K. A. 1957. "Asian Nationalism and Christian Missions." *International Review of Missions* 46.

Barclay, William. 1958. *The Mind of St. Paul*. New York: Harper and Brothers.

Bede, the Venerable. 1984. *A History of the English Church and People*. Harmondsworth, England: Penguin Books.

Belloc, Hilaire. 1931. *Cranmer, Archbishop of Canterbury, 1533–1556*. Philadelphia: J. P. Lippincott and Co.

The Bible and the Life and Ideals of the English-Speaking People. n.d. New York: American Bible Society.

Blyden, Edward W. 1908. *African Life and Customs*. New York.

———. 1967. *Christianity, Islam and the Negro Race*. Edinburgh: Edinburgh University Press; first published 1887.

Buckingham, Leicester Silk. 1853. *The Bible in the Middle Ages*. London: T. C. Newby.

Concise History of the English Bible. 1983. New York: American Bible Society; rev. ed.

Ekechi, Felix K. 1972. *Missionary Enterprise and Rivalry in Igboland 1857–1914*. London: Frank Cass.

The English Bible and British and American Art. 1935. New York: American Bible Society.

Fiske, John. 1889. *The Beginnings of New England: Or the Puritan Theocracy in Its Relation to Civil and Religious Liberty*. Boston: Houghton Mifflin Co.; repr. 1898.

Flinn, Michael W. 1967. *The Origins of the Industrial Revolution*. London: Longmans.

Fox, John. 1911. "The Influence of the Bible on English Literature." *Princeton Theological Review* (July).

Fyfe, Christopher. 1962. *A History of Sierra Leone*. London: Oxford University Press.

Green, J. R. 1882. *A Short History of the English People*. New York: Harper and Brothers.

Hair, Paul E. H. 1962. "CMS 'Native' Clergy in West Africa to 1900." *Sierra Leone Bulletin of Religion* 4.

———. 1963. "Archdeacon Crowther and the Delta Pastorate; 1892–99." *Sierra Leone Bulletin of Religion* 5, no. 1 (June).

Hill, Christopher. 1966. *Society and Puritanism in Pre-Revolutionary England*. London: Mercury Books.

———. 1975. *The World Turned Upside Down: Radical Ideas during the English Revolution*. Harmondsworth, England: Penguin Books.

Ifemesia, C. C. 1962. "The 'Civilizing' Mission of 1841: Aspects of an Episode in Anglo-Nigerian Relations." *Journal of the Historical Society of Nigeria* 2.

The Influence of the English Bible upon the English Language and upon English and American Literature. 1947. New York: American Bible Society.

Johnson, T. S. 1953. *The Story of a Mission: The Sierra Leone Church, First Daughter of C.M.S.* London: SPCK.

Knight, W. 1880. *Memoir of the Rev. H. Venn: The Missionary Secretariat of Henry Venn*. London: Longman, Green, and Co.

Methodist Quarterly Review. 1876 (January).

Moffatt, James. 1924. *The Bible in Scots Literature*. London: Hodder and Stoughton.

Ogharaerumi, Mark Onesosan. 1987. "The Translation of the Bible into Yoruba, Igbo and Isekiri Languages of Nigeria, with Special Reference to the Contribution of Mother Tongue Speakers." Unpublished Ph.D. dissertation, University of Aberdeen, Scotland.

Omenka, Nicholas. 1986. "The Role of the Catholic Mission in the Development of Vernacular Literature in Eastern Nigeria." *Journal of Religion in Africa* 16, no. 2.

Peel, John D. Y. 1968. *Aladura: A Religious Movement among the Yoruba.* London: Oxford University Press for the International African Institute.

Sanneh, Lamin. 1983. *West African Christianity.* Maryknoll, N.Y.: Orbis Books.

Sawyerr, Harry. 1965. "Christian Evangelistic Strategy in West Africa: Reflections on the Centenary of the Consecration of Bishop Samuel Adjayi Crowther on St. Peter's Day, 1864." *International Review of Missions* 54.

Shenk, Wilbert R. 1983. *Henry Venn: Missionary Statesman.* Maryknoll, N.Y.: Orbis Books.

Tasie, Godwin. 1974. "The Story of Samuel Ajayi Crowther and the C.M.S. Niger Mission." *Ghana Bulletin of Theology* 4, no. 7 (December).

_____ . 1978. *Christian Missionary Enterprise in the Niger Delta: 1864–1918.* Leiden: E. J. Brill.

Tiplady, Thomas. 1924. *The Influence of the Bible on History, Literature and Oratory.* New York: Fleming H. Revell Co.

Walls, Andrew F. 1981. "The Gospel as the Prisoner and Liberator of Culture." *Faith and Thought* 108, nos. 1–2.

Warren, Max, ed. 1971. *To Apply the Gospel: Selections from the Writings of Henry Venn.* Grand Rapids, Mich.: Wm. B. Eerdmans Publishing Co.

Webster, James Bertin. 1963. "The Bible and the Plough." *Journal of the Historical Society of Nigeria* 2, no. 4 (December).

_____ . 1964. *The African Churches among the Yoruba: 1888–1922.* Oxford: Clarendon Press.

West African Reporter. 1876 (January 4).

Westcott, B. F. 1927. *A General View of the History of the English Bible.* New York: Macmillan.

5

Missionary Translation in African Perspective: Religious and Theological Themes

On the frontier between Jerusalem and Athens, that is to say, in the transition between the synagogue and the Temple, Paul announced to one particular group of his hearers that the "unknown God" of the Athenian Greeks at whose altar the devout crowded was none other than the God of the risen Christ (Acts 17:23, 31). The apostle had used the studied modesty of Greek thought to proclaim the gospel. It was a perceptive rejoinder. He had exploited the passion of Greek religious devotion on its downward turn to lift up the resurrected Lord.

The Greeks cannot affirm both that God is and that God is unknown, that adoration is our duty but that ignorance is our fate. Paul is right in his contention. The passion for worship is a cruel affliction unless it can bring us into the light of the knowledge of God — and that was the message Paul had for his Greek audience. The missionary proclamation turns on this double sense of the fact of the "unknown God" and the mood of expectancy generated from worship of that God. By the gospel, Paul was almost saying, we know now how to decode the message of your religious instincts.

Nowhere else were missionaries more anticipated than in the field of scriptural translation. All over that vast field we find evidence of deep and long preparation, in the tools of language as in the habits of worship and conduct, and in the venerable customs of the forebears. God is the ground of existence, the one in whom "we live, and move, and have our being" (Acts 17:28). Great missionary spirits have contended through the centuries that to acknowledge this truth is the urgent imperative of the moral life, a truth whose sparks are entrusted to all living cultures and which the light of the gospel will rekindle into a living flame. And without that truth preceding the person, the missionary is in an acutely contradictory position, for without a previous sense of obligation it is impossible to induce in people the due act of acknowledgment toward their Creator, and that would nullify the whole purpose of mission.

The philosophical society of Athens was thus roused from a dim, shadowy world and its occasional flashes of genuine insight to stare askance at the steady approach of the Christian dawn. Paul was convinced that the gospel contained the fulfillment of the Greeks' yearning, and we ourselves know from Augustine how that world was poised to receive the word of life. But we also know that the fair city of the philosopher increased the bounty of the Prince of Light, and from that inheritance the Eternal Logos was born. The apostle's debt to his hosts was incalculable. "I am greatly indebted," Paul writes, "both to the Greeks, and to the Barbarians" (Rom. 1:14). The missionary obligation, it turns out, grows out of the context of the proclamation, and mission must proceed by arriving on the ground thus laid for it.

Paul on Mars Hill is the symbol of the meeting of God's providential design and the particularity of cultural self-understanding. It is this meeting that mission has come to represent through the centuries, and the history of mission must therefore come to grips with the specific and unique manner in which the gospel is concretized.

THEOLOGICAL REPERCUSSIONS

The central premise of missionary preaching is the reality of God: Creator, Sustainer, Judge, and Redeemer. The specific Christian understanding of this is expressed in the understanding of Jesus Christ as the historical and personal manifestation of God's power. When they came to Africa, missionaries began with a methodical inquiry into the nature and character of God among Africans, and before long it was obvious Africans had a deep sense of the reality of God.

That resolved a fundamental dilemma for mission, for there would be no need to lay the groundwork of the concept of God. But it also presented an unprecedented difficulty, for the multiplicity of languages in Africa meant a corresponding multiplicity in the terms by which God was addressed. And since each language carried widely differing connotations in the concept of God, missionaries could not be sure what precise implications might come to attach to usage. It thus came about that in the religious and theological sphere, missionaries became ultimately helpless in the face of the overwhelming contextual repercussions of translation.

The central premise of missionary preaching is also a most acute source of irony. Many missionaries assumed that Africans had not heard of God and that it was the task of mission to remedy this defect. In practical terms, however, missionaries started by inquiring among the people what names and concepts for God existed, and having established such fundamental points of contact, they proceeded to adopt local vocabulary to preach the gospel. This field method of adopting the vernacular came to diverge sharply from the ideology of mission. After all, it turns out, Africans had heard of God, described God most eloquently, and maintained toward God proper attitudes of reverence, worship, and sacrifice. As Livingstone testified from his own experience, "there is no necessity for beginning to tell even the most degraded of these people of the existence of a God, or of a future state, the facts being universally admitted." He continued:

> On questioning the intelligent men among the Bakwains as to their former knowledge of good and evil, of God, and the future state, they have scouted the idea of any of them ever having been without a tolerably clear conception on all these subjects. Respecting their sense of right and wrong, they profess that nothing we indicate as sin ever appeared to them as otherwise, except the statement that it was wrong to have more wives than one; and they declare that they spoke in the same way of the direct influence exercised by God in giving rain in answer to prayers of rain-makers, and in granting deliverance in times of danger, as they do now, before they ever heard of white men. [Livingstone, 1857, p. 158.]

The problem of Africa might be too much religion, not too little. In that case, it might be asked, what was the task and justification for mission?

Historically, mission arrived in Africa out of the general expansion of Europe abroad, motivated at first by a desire to circumvent Islam and compensate for Muslim resistance, and also by a desire for economic markets, which the maritime discoveries of the fifteenth century had made accessible. The sixteenth- and seventeenth-century missions in Africa were thus for the most part led by the seafaring powers of Portugal, Spain, France, the Netherlands, and Italy. Missions also arrived in Africa from the need to spread the gospel, a need that now found new justifications and fresh means.

Yet, however much mission may have been conceived as the arm of European political expansion, missionaries still had to rely on indigenous languages to preach their message, and this created a distinction between European culture and the indigenous traditions. Consequently, however much mission tried to suppress local populations, the issue of the vernacular helped to undermine its foreign character. By the same token, the new interest in creating vernacular Scriptures for societies that had no Scriptures of their own ushered in a fundamental religious revolution, with new religious structures coming into being to preside over the changes.

One of the most dramatic changes was undoubtedly the popular, mass participation of Africans in this process. It began to dawn on African populations that the missionary adoption of vernacular categories for the Scriptures was in effect a written sanction for the indigenous religious vocation. The God of the ancestors was accordingly assimilated into the Yahweh of ancient Israel and "the God and Father of our Lord Jesus

Christ." But there was a profound difference. The "God" of missionary preaching was a jealous God who forbade worship of other gods, a jealousy that in the religious history of the West often manifested itself in wars and other forms of intolerance. In Africa, however, God was a hospitable deity who was approached through the mediation of lesser deities. The exclusive notion of Western Christianity was replaced with the inclusive rule of African religions, an inclusiveness that helped deepen the pluralist ethos of the gospel. By embarking on translation, missionaries stimulated this ethos, thus helping to lay the foundation for a remarkable stage in the religious evolution of African communities.

In 1737 George Schmidt, a Moravian missionary, arrived among the Khoi-Khoi tribe of South Africa, anxious, he said, to bring the Savior to the people who, in his view, were in ignorance of the subject. He found, however, that he had to communicate with the people in their own language and in the existing categories of their religious life. The people received him deferentially, responding to his mission with an alert spirit. When he told them why he had come among them, a stranger from across the seas, they replied:

> "That is good, *baas* [master]."
> I asked them, Schmidt says, if they knew that there was a great Baas, who had given them their cattle and all they possessed.
> "Yes," replied [the tribesmen].
> "What do you call him?"
> "We call him Tui-qua," was the reply. [Plessis, 1911, p. 2.]

So Schmidt entered the world of the Khoi-Khoi with the newly acquired name of their Supreme Being on his tongue. He was immediately conscious of a craving that the contact with the Khoi-Khoi had induced, and he strove eagerly to learn more. He observed the customs of the people to try and understand what place "Tui-qua" occupied in their lives. He attended their ceremonies and described one such religious ceremony thus:

> At the return of the Pleiades these natives celebrate an anniversary; as soon as these stars appear above the eastern horizon mothers will lift their little ones on their arms, and running up to elevated spots, will show them to these friendly stars, and teach them to stretch their little hands towards them. The people of a kraal will assemble to dance and to sing according to the old custom of their ancestors. The chorus always sings: O Tiqua, our Father above our heads, give rain to us, that the fruits (bulbs, etc.), *uientjes,* may ripen, and that we may have plenty of food, send us a good year. [Cited in Smith, 1950, p. 95.]

His willingness to adopt the Khoi-Khoi word for God had led Schmidt to explore the diverse ways in which the term was employed, and that brought him deeper into the traditions of the people. His role was accordingly reversed. He had come to teach the people, who recognized that by calling him "boss," but in fact he was learning from them. Starting from the most elementary level, he had to determine from them what name he could call God in his new circumstances, an irony that was hardly lost on the Africans, for Schmidt stepped back to announce to the people that he was coming to tell them all about "Tui-qua" as if the people had not heard about him. Sometimes this "stepping back" can assume a complicated, elaborate form, as when missionaries retreated into their enclaves anxious to avoid contaminating contact with indigenous customs. Yet having unbound the beast of the tribe through translation, it is scarcely an effective strategy to put up defenses against its shadow. The quarantine of the missionary enclave eventually yielded to indigenous necessity, and from that contact the vernacular reform impulse was ignited.

The dilemma of the missionary is sometimes easy to dramatize, and Africans, for all their standard reputation for hospitality and deference, could not always avoid playing the leading part in the drama. Some examples now will suggest how Africans became conscious of their position vis-à-vis the missionary.

One example of the "stepping-back" attitude of missionaries may be given. When the first missionary, probably Van der Kemp, arrived among the Xhosa people, he set about trying to determine how the people thought of and addressed the Supreme Being. In the event, he could not communicate with the people. He returned subsequently with a Dutchman and a Hottentot informant, and they translated for him. The Africans then understood what he was trying to tell them.

> He made enquiries among us, asking, "What do you say about the creation of all things?" We replied, "We call him who made all things uTikxo." And he inquired, "Where is he?" We replied, "Usezulwini; he is in heaven." [The missionary] said, "Very well. I bring that very one—i.e., all that relates to or concerns him—to you of this country." [Smith, 1950, p. 101.]

The missionary, having learned from the people the true name for God, then turned around to announce that he was bringing them something new. In fact Van der Kemp's *vade mecum* was a Hottentot elephant hunter who became his preceptor in his linguistic and religious investigations, a relationship highly significant for the climate of mutual interaction normally hidden by the forceful thrust of missionary self-representation. At the hands of his informant the missionary discovered a great deal more than the teasing nuances of the language, so that the dynamics of translation reversed the status of the missionary in relation to the African.

Vernacular agency became the preponderant medium for the assimilation of Christianity, and although missionaries did not consciously intend to occupy a secondary position, their commitment to translation made that necessary and inevitable. The preexisting vernacular came to exert a preemptive power over the proprietary claims of mission over the gospel, and when missionaries assumed that mission must occur by scriptural translation, they invoked that preemptive power without knowing that it would at the same time minimize their role as external agents. Some of them came upon this discovery in a dramatic fashion.

The example of Theophilus Hahn, himself the son of a missionary, makes this clear. He was traveling once by ox-cart through the desert, accompanied by an African guide whom Hahn described as "a raw heathen." He began scolding the guide after the traveling party lost its way and was in danger of perishing in the wilds. The guide reassured him:

> "Tsui//goab will help us," and insisted when Dr. Hahn expressed disbelief: "Truly, master, he will help." They reached water the next day and when they had quenched their thirst and were talking over their troubles, the guide said: "My dear master, yesterday you could almost have killed me but Tsui//goab refused to allow you to do so, and have you now convinced yourself that the Lord has helped?" [Smith, 1950, p. 97.]

Suitably chastened, Hahn tried to rise to the challenge of matching the faith of his "raw heathen" whose polite demeanor contrasted rather unfavorably with his own high-handedness. In answering his guide, Hahn would also be conceding that the God who preserved the party from danger was the same who interceded for the guide against his own threats. Outwardly, however, the missionary remained unrepentant. "We require [Hahn comments] no further evidence to see what the rawest Namaqua, with all his heathendom, means by Tsui//goab" (Smith, 1950, p. 97).

Let us try to characterize the irony in the following terms. Missionaries should have been pleased when they came upon evidence that God had preceded them, and that Africans possessed profound faith in the divine providence. More than that, the willingness of Africans to receive the gospel as confirmation of what they always knew should have delighted missionaries and given them heart that Scripture was being confirmed when it spoke of God not being without witness even when all nations walked in their own ways (Acts 14:16–17), or that God shows no favoritism in dealings with people (Acts 10:34). Instead, the missionaries appear to have been surprised, even antagonized, by examples of faithfulness, hospitality, and forgiveness, standards by which they were purporting to justify the whole enterprise of mission itself.

Faced with this bewildering situation, Africans began earnestly to inquire into the Christian Scriptures, which missionaries had placed in their hands, to see where they had misunderstood the gospel. What they learned convinced them that mission as European cultural hegemony was a catastrophic departure from the Bible. They met the original irony with one of their own: they went on to claim the gospel, as the missionaries wished them to, but in turn insisted that missionary attitudes should continue to be scrutinized in its revealing light.

Missionaries themselves were sometimes to the fore in examining their own attitudes in the light of field exposure, and here Livingstone's experience may again be called into evidence. Having learned to appreciate the linguistic insights of Africans, Livingstone was appropriately conditioned, if not to keep an open mind in general then at least to assume an equal intelligence in the African. The medical missionary once encountered a traditional rainmaker whom he proceeded to challenge. The rain-doctor, Livingstone said, was really a charlatan who exploited the element of chance in the weather to promote a career of deception. The response of the rain-doctor raised a profound question about what room was left for chance in a worldview based on faith in God.

> "So you really believe," [Livingstone challenged,] "that you can command the clouds? I think that can be done by God alone." [The rain-doctor replied:] "We both believe the very same thing. It is God that makes the rain, but I pray to him by means of these medicines, and, the rain coming, of course it is then mine. It was I who made it for the Bakwains for many years, when they were at Shokuane; through my wisdom, too, their women became fat and shining. Ask them; they will tell you the same as I do. . . ." "I quite agree with you," [Livingstone assured him,] "as to the value of the rain; but you cannot charm the clouds by medicines. You wait till you see the clouds come, then you use your medicine, and take the credit which belongs to God only." "I use my medicines," [the rain-doctor retorted,] "and you employ yours; we are both doctors, and doctors are not deceivers. You give a patient medicine. Sometimes God is pleased to heal him by means of your medicine: sometimes not — he dies. When he is cured, you take credit of what God does. I do the same. Sometimes God grants us rain, sometimes not. When he does, we take the credit of the charm. When a patient dies, you don't give up trust in your medicine, neither do I when rain fails. If you wish me to leave off my medicines, why continue your own?" [Livingstone, 1857, pp. 23–25.]

Livingstone left the field of controversy with still a flea in his ear, but he had been challenged in the deepest recesses of faith and trust. Why should he, a man of faith, repose so much trust in modern medicine, of which he was a practitioner, and come to regard traditional healing systems as a contradiction of genuine faith? Either the empirical scientific account of the person was complete and sufficient or faith in God demanded commitment that went beyond empirical demonstrability. In other words, God as the subject of faith cannot also equally be the object of demonstrable proof, and believers by definition cannot to the same extent be empirical determinists. Consequently Livingstone, or any true believer for that matter, cannot have it both ways.

The rain-doctor may therefore be said to have a sensible point. He implied that Livingstone's professional interests were no more and no less in conflict with faith in God than his own. It follows that they must both acknowledge a common religious bond in pursuing their respective professions.

It would, of course, be hazardous to treat that encounter as being a comprehensive statement of the conflict between faith and reason, but we may nevertheless take it as a measure of the critical power of the indigenous idiom.[1] Livingstone tried to explore that idiom with great sensitivity and clarity, being also careful not to conceal his general skepticism. Indeed, the strength of that skepticism shows itself as an alternative faith, which his field labors then placed in sustained dialogue (and tension) with the African religious outlook (see, e.g., Livingstone, 1857, pp. 187, 219, 255, 257, 471–72, 686–87, etc.). One significant contrast is that Livingstone was anxious to exclude the mystical element from what he regarded as true faith, whereas the rain-doctor was intent on showing the more inclusive boundary of the community of faith, being quite willing to extend to the medical missionary the recognition of a fellow professional. Even if Livingstone had regarded that as his natural entitlement, it shows a deep consistency within the indigenous idiom. In spite of the caricatures and stereotypes, it is the pioneer exploration of that indigenous idiom by missionaries that helped to secure the foundations for the present-day scientific study of African languages and religions.

INDIGENOUS AGENCY

Many other missionaries found themselves involved with indigenous African customs as a direct result of their linguistic investigations, and even those who came out with prejudged ideas of Christianity felt the impact of the vernacular. One such was the American missionary T. J. Bowen, whom we met in the previous chapter. Bowen wrote forcefully about mission as "civilization": it is not enough to bring Africans the knowledge of Christ; they must be instructed in the arts of modernity. Yet Bowen acquired a high degree of proficiency in the Yoruba language and, like Livingstone in another regard, wrote admiringly of the beauty and richness of the language. More than that, he confessed a deep appreciation for the invocatory prayers of traditional Yoruba worship, including the cult of Ifa, the Yoruba divinatory system. He wrote a *Grammar and Dictionary of the Yoruba Language* which was published, rather inaccessibly, in the *Smithsonian Contributions to Knowledge,* in 1862. The Nigerian historian J. F. A. Ajayi, a Yoruba, commenting on the role of missionaries in the scientific development of the Yoruba language, says: "The orthography of

Yoruba is today substantially that laid down by the missionaries. Their rules of grammar have been frequently criticized, but their translations are still recommended as works of high literary value" (Ajayi, 1969, p. 128).

The process, then, of acquiring knowledge of the indigenous languages brought missionaries into the sphere of religious customs. One representative Christian figure who reflected in a self-conscious way on this process was Bishop Samuel Ajayi Crowther (ca. 1807–91), the foremost African churchman of the nineteenth century. A native of the Yoruba town of Oshogun, Crowther was taken captive by Fulani Muslim forces of north Nigeria and sold as a slave to a Portuguese slave ship in Lagos. He was eventually rescued, in April 1822, by the British Naval Squadron and taken to the West African city of Freetown, Sierra Leone, where he came under missionary instruction. He was ordained in England in 1843 before being subsequently consecrated bishop at Canterbury Cathedral in June 1864. He played a formative role in developing the missionary outreach to Nigeria, a role in which he was able to use his considerable linguistic gifts.

Crowther recognized that translation was more than a mechanical exercise, and that something of the genius of the people was involved. Language was not merely a tool fashioned to achieve limited and temporary goals. It was also a dynamic cultural resource, reflecting the spirit of the people and illuminating their sense of values. As such it demanded to be imaginatively approached, with the investigator skillful enough in the sort of cultural archaeology by which one may discover the stored paradigms whereby society represented and promoted itself. The translator should be prepared to dig underneath the layers of half-conscious notions and dim familiarities to reclaim the accumulated treasure. Consequently Crowther made a point of befriending ordinary people without regard to their religious affiliation, going on to pay close attention to the speech of the elders in order to get behind new inventions of the language and the colloquialisms that break the line of continuity with the original. He plunged after the widening consequences of the initial missionary contact, finding his way to the vital material, which he was ready to surrender to the double claim of missionary interest and the surviving memory of the past.

> For this reason he befriended pagans and Muslims alike, "watched the mouth" of the elders and, while discussing theology and other serious matters with them, noted down "suitable and significant words." When he tried such words in common speech, he found that, like "thrown away words," they sounded stale, but "to the rising generation, they will sound sweet and agreeable." He went everywhere with pencil and paper. [Ajayi, 1969, p. 128.]

Crowther was perceptive enough to realize that translation led naturally into developing a deeper appreciation for the entire culture, and he pursued this line to its logical conclusion. He wrote in 1844 that his linguistic investigation forced him to delve into other aspects of traditional African life.

Crowther was an infinitely patient man, with a natural flair for languages. He therefore found the missionary enterprise ideally suited to his gifts and temperament, and in that fact we find a clue to the inner nature of Christian mission (even though Crowther was eventually crushed by the machinery of missionary hegemony). Thus, in response to the reverberations of scriptural translation, Crowther was stimulated to follow through to other aspects of the culture, suggesting that literal translation in itself was insufficient to take the full measure of the enterprise. "In tracing out words and their various uses," he admits, "I am now and then led to search at length into some traditions and customs of the Yorubas" (Ajayi, 1969, p. 128n.). As a direct result Crowther began a systematic inquiry into the Egungun secret society and the cult of Ifa divination, and contributed immensely to the strengthening of a sense of Yoruba national identity.

In the example of Crowther, then, we see how mission as translation operates by coming into alliance with dormant or dimly apprehended symbols of the culture and constituting these into coefficients of living experience. Crowther was not afraid to allow what Livingstone called "the eloquence of the native assembly" to give force and shape to the Christian proclamation. The sense of responsibility this created toward preserving the authentic forms of indigenous life and custom constitutes an enduring tribute to Christian mission, even if at the same time it challenges, or induces us to challenge, missionary attitudes.

BRIEF RÉSUMÉ

1. Let me recap the main stages of the argument so far in this chapter. The Apostle Paul recognized that the negative philosophical attitude of the Greeks concerning their "unknown God" did not sit easily with their earnest spirit of worship, and he consequently felt called upon to proclaim the gospel in an attempt to resolve the contradiction.

2. That may act as a paradigm for mission in Africa. The preponderant religious climate in Africa afforded a point of natural contact for missionary preaching, and the enterprise of translation capitalized on this fact.

3. Scriptural translation rested on the assumption that the vernacular has a primary affinity with the gospel, the point being conceded by the adoption of indigenous terms and concepts for the central categories of the Bible. As long as missionaries were committed to translation, so long would vernacular concepts and usage continue to determine the assimilation of Christianity, including the understanding of God by more inclusive criteria.

4. Thoughtful missionaries understood that God had preceded them in Africa, as Dr. Livingstone was at pains to point out, that translation involved esteem for the vernacular culture, if not surrender to it, that the authentic forms of the culture, consecrated by the elders, constituted the

most promising signs for the Christian cause, and that, finally, linguistic investigations and the systematic inventory of indigenous resources were likely to touch off wider and longer-lasting repercussions in the culture. Even from the sternest view of the role of missionaries in Africa, we have to recognize the immense contribution to the revitalization of Africa that this represents.

INTERETHNIC ENCOUNTER AND MUTUAL EXCHANGE

When we consider the wider picture of scriptural translation, we are challenged to notice something that has easily escaped attention, namely, the peaceful and orderly context in which all this linguistic enterprise took place. This is not to say that there were no wars or strife at the time—for there were—but the inquiry that was launched to amass material encouraged habits of patience, reflection, comparison, and critical reflection, all of which went beyond intertribal strife. As a consequence neighboring languages and cultures were exposed to each other in an atmosphere of genuine encounter outside the pressures of war and interethnic strife. In this atmosphere an attempt was made to establish etymologies and the history of developments in the languages and people concerned. Through a staggering wealth of detail, missionaries, aided and guided by local experts, proceeded to investigate and document the various aspects of the language in grammars, dictionaries, vocabularies, primers, commentaries, collections of proverbs, idioms, myths, and folklore. For the first time we have a meticulous inventory of local cultures produced by the most exacting standards of scientific inquiry.

In his critical survey of the history of Zulu literature, Professor C. L. S. Nyembezi of the University of Natal makes the valid point that a general awakening of the Zulu coincided with a new interest in the Zulu language, and that the great pioneers of Zulu language and literature were missionaries and the Zulu agents they trained. It was not simply that "missionaries concerned themselves primarily with grammars, dictionaries and the translation of the Scriptures, some of them recorded folk-lore, proverbs and valuable historical material" (Nyembezi, 1961, p. 3).

It would be naïve to pretend that everywhere the enterprise was prosecuted with the same detached brilliance, for there were some awful specimens of incompetence and invention, but wherever that brilliance was evident it is difficult to exclude missionary agency. Thus the attitude we have learned to deplore in missionaries when they showed a lack of spontaneous appreciation for indigenous customs turns out to be an advantage when they patiently examined the vernacular, stripping it down to its constituent parts in order to increase understanding of its integrated vitality. The religious motive for embarking on translation did not really affect the point at issue, but merely strengthened the case for bringing the best resources available to bear on the translation so that the result would be worthy of the exalted end.

In tracking down correspondences, similarities, "false cousins," and other combinations and permutations in the language, missionaries were helping to establish important links between members of the wider African family, and thus contributing to the reducing of ancient antagonisms and suspicions. Denominational rivalries did, of course, introduce a factor of alienation in many communities, which would have led to catastrophic consequences without the mitigating influence of the vernacular Scriptures. All the major Protestant denominations were forced to set aside their differences and pool resources in helping to make the Bible available in authentic translations. As Tom Beetham observed, "The process of translation helped to heal the divisions of the Church. . . . What has brought Protestant missions together more than anything else has been the fellowship in the work of translation of the Bible" (Beetham, 1967, p. 55). One evidence of this fact has been increasing cooperation between Catholics and Protestants. "Protestant versions in a number of languages have been used through the years by Catholic missions" (Beetham, 1967, p. 56). A new and active sense of ecumenical solidarity has grown between Catholics and Protestants in translation projects, with joint work now in progress in 170 areas (Hogg, 1985, p. 13). And what helped to overcome denominational resistance also worked to enlarge the scope of mutual understanding in Africa. Anyone surveying the scene today will be impressed by the extent of interethnic encounter in church and society alike.

A few examples must suffice on what is a rich subject. The spectacular rise and expansion of the Harrist movement illustrates very well the cross-ethnic dimensions of Christian renewal in Africa. William Wade Harris, the founder of the movement, was a charismatic figure active in the Ivory Coast and southwestern Ghana between 1913 and 1915. He was born in Liberia. His converts, estimated by some sources at well over 100,000, were spread across the colonial boundaries and included numerous ethnic groups of the area (Walker, 1983). The Harrist Church has responded to this ethnic diversity by attempting to create "a comprehensive territorial organization of dioceses and archdioceses with a metropolitan see at Abia-Niambo, complete with cardinals, a sacred college and even a pope" (Barrett, 1968, p. 176). The effort, predictably, failed, for the vernacular ferment was too powerful to reduce to such a uniform mold. Eventually a complex structure was evolved to reflect the pluralist ethos of the movement.

Another example comes from Kenya, on the other side of the continent, and concerns the Church of Christ in Africa (CCA), founded by a Luo, Matthew Ajuoga. Unlike Harris, Ajuoga traced his call to conflict with the Anglican Mission, but in his case, too, the vernacular and ethnic factor was of considerable importance. In 1953 the Luo Old Testament was published, and Ajuoga was struck by the word the missionaries translated as *hera,* namely, the Greek *philadelphia* and the English "love." He claimed that *hera,* "brotherly love," was absent in missionary treatment of African converts, and he concluded that such treatment represented a scandalous failure of love. After some years of protest and discussion aimed at major reforms in the church, Ajuoga and his followers established the CCA in 1957, when it was a purely Luo church. But its outreach soon extended beyond the ethnic divide, being able to appeal to several ethnic groups at once. "By 1965 the CCA claimed members among fifty-six of the tribes and sub-tribes of Kenya, Uganda and northern Tanzania; by 1967 eight dioceses had been formed in the three nations. Among its seventy clergy then there were two Teita, two Kikuyu, six Luyia (including one archdeacon) and one Gusii—all from Bantu tribes traditionally somewhat hostile to the Luo" (Barrett, 1968, pp. 260–61). Yet another example, to return to West Africa, is the Church of the Lord *(Aladura),* founded by Josiah Olunowo Oshitelu of Nigeria. The Church of the Lord *(Aladura)* established branches in different parts of Nigeria, and founded an active missionary movement in Ghana, Liberia, and Sierra Leone (Turner, 1967).

All this is evidence of a widespread feeling in much of black Africa for social harmony and mutual tolerance, and that feeling has burst into the open with these Independent Churches and the entire phenomenon of the Charismatic Revival, called *Aladura* in West Africa and "Zionism" in Southern Africa. Many of these new religious movements have spread beyond so-called tribal communities and now embrace an impressive mosaic of peoples, languages, and cultures. These movements have extended the idea of mutual exposure far beyond the original notion of fledgling communities under the ever watchful eye of the missionary. And thanks to literacy in the vernacular, much of the religious heritage of the old Africa has been made available in parallel and other translations, to be shared with the world community. Thus Africans have made their own unique contribution to the spiritual heritage of all humanity, an occurrence that has vindicated the truth of the principle that you do not have to sacrifice your roots to branch out to others.

We must also take note of the concentrated discussion that ensued in missionary and local communities about how, precisely, the task of translation should be carried out. This intense discussion, insofar as it affected the ultimate destination of the message, took place on the spot, not around a missionary table in London, Rome, New York, Paris, Berlin, Stockholm, or Copenhagen. In the light of such field inquiries, the debates, such as there were, in the metropolitan countries appear rather abstract and fractious. Long before the statistical center of gravity shifted from European Christianity to Africa, there was this momentous shift of translation—a shift that ran like a deep fault in the hard crust of perceptions of European mastery of what they saw as the Dark Continent. Missionaries involved in translation work groped after rules and procedures that would guide them in the more deeply shaded layers of encounter with the Dark Continent.

They had to proceed by field experience, and the more enlightened ones among them understood that they were as good as having lost their footing if they had to have recourse to Western criteria.

A lively debate thus ensued in the field, with missionaries helping to draw attention to details of the culture in new and creative ways. In many significant cases, the rivalry among missionaries was about who could produce the most authentic vernacular translation, and not about statistical success or denominational advantage. Competence in the vernacular, as Francis Xavier or Valignano discovered for Japan, was the test of missionary effectiveness, and in time came to be regarded as a factor of genuine, credible conversion, as Livingstone testified from his experience.

Several consequences follow from this, but let us here pinpoint two for comment. The first is that missionaries accepted, or at any rate conceded implicitly, that mission was not the instrument for sifting the world into an identity of cultural likeness, with our diversities being pressed into a single mold in preparation for some millennial reckoning. So obedience to the gospel was distinguished from loyalty to a universal cultural paradigm. It seems to this writer that everyone concerned with the religious motive of mission agreed that each people must be afforded the opportunity of discovering Christ in its own idiom, and against this view the advocates of universal Westernization were in necessary conflict.

The second consequence relates to the increased self-awareness of Africans in the light of explicit missionary interest in their language and culture. In the first ardor of their enthusiasm, Africans no doubt rushed to conclusions about the demands of the new religion. Yet even at that stage there was recognition of the need to reflect among themselves and share in the general exchange of ideas that missionaries had initiated.

Some examples will now illustrate these points. To begin with the last, Xhosa converts used to argue among themselves about the meaning of the indigenous term for God, *uTikxo,* one saying that uTikxo was above (a *deus absconditus*) and the other that *uTikxo* was below. " 'At length,' [said one of the disputants], 'the word *uTikxo* was universally accepted on the arrival of the missionaries. For we used to speak of the whole heaven, saying, "*uTikxo* dwells in the whole heaven"; but did not clearly understand what we meant' " (Smith, 1950, pp. 101–2). And then in a remarkable piece of religious adaptation, Xhosa Christians grafted the new religious material onto the older tradition, claiming both as authentically theirs. What the Xhosa Christians did was to attach a concluding Christian section to an ancient hymn.

Thou art the great God—He who is in heaven.
It is Thou, Thou shield of Truth.
It is Thou, Thou Tower of Truth.
It is Thou, Thou Bush of Truth.
It is Thou, Thou who sittest in the highest.

Thou art the Creator of life, Thou madest the regions above.
The Creator who madest the heavens also.
The Maker of the stars and the Pleiades.
The shooting stars declare it unto us.
The Maker of the blind, of thine own will didst thou make them.
The trumpet speaks — for us it calls.
Thou art the Hunter who hunts souls.
Thou art the Leader who goes before us.
Thou art the great Mantle which covers us.
Thou art He whose hands are with wounds.
Thou art He whose blood is a trickling stream — and why?
Thou art He whose blood was spilled for us.
For this great price we call,
For thine own place we call. [Callaway, 1870, pp. 63ff., 105.]

We should not be misled by the notion of anthropological purity into expunging the Christian material in that hymn and think by that to be preserving the original, an editorial intervention that repeats the principle of theological exclusion. It is clear that the Xhosa regarded God as infinitely superior to the creature that the human being is, and when they came upon the gospel they saw it as confirmation of that. However, the idea of redemptive suffering supplied a fresh symbol by which the creature's infinite moral distance from the Creator was encapsulated. The Christian material did not, therefore, so much infringe the earlier sense of religious propriety as deepen it. New converts would now possess a richer repertoire of religious feeling.

Missionaries were deeply exercised about the direction in which they ought to proceed, and in the initial stages some ungainly maneuvers were made to avoid confronting the issues squarely. In the end, of course, all had to fall into line with the force of the vernacular. For example, the Methodists were unpersuaded of the wisdom of embracing the Zulu term for God, *uNkulunkulu,* fearing that they would be conceding more than they wanted to. So they coined the unwieldy term *uJehova.* The Anglican bishop of Natal in the mid-nineteenth century, Bishop Colenso, for his part tried a more cultured modification of the Latin *Deus* to *uDio.* Both experiments were submitted to field verification where the verdict was scarcely in doubt. African informants, advancing upon the accumulating evidence of field investigations, swept away such artificial contrivances and the assumptions on which they were based. In the end the Zulu term for God was triumphantly adopted. Bishop Colenso produced a Zulu dictionary, which reported on the evidence collected on the subject. The missionary of the American Board of Commissioners for Foreign Mission, J. L. Döhne, at first put up a strong resistance with a dictionary he produced in 1857, wherein he depreciated the Zulu term for God as only the name of a proto-ancestor of the race. But he, too, yielded to field pressure.

Eventually all the major missions accepted the Zulu word *uNkulunkulu* as the name for God. Bishop John W. Colenso produced a New Testament translation in 1897 with the standard Zulu term; the first complete Zulu Bible, done in 1883 by the American Board, kept the Xhosa word *uTikxo,* as did the new edition in 1893. But the revised Zulu New Testament of 1917 reverted to *uNkulunkulu,* as did the revised version of the whole Bible in 1924. In 1922 the Lutherans followed suit, retaining *uNkulunkulu* as the vernacular term for God.

The background of this religious translation work is the detailed linguistic investigations that have become standard in missionary translation. In 1850 Hans Schreuder published a grammar of the Zulu, and John W. Colenso in 1855 published another grammar of the Zulu. In 1859 Lewis Grout of the American Board in Natal published his grammar of the Zulu. Similar attention was devoted to the production of dictionaries. In 1855 Perrin's dictionary of Zulu was published. In 1857 J. L. Döhne published his Zulu dictionary. Bishop Colenso's own *Zulu-English Dictionary* was published in 1861, and in 1880 Charles Roberts produced a similar work.

In parallel to these developments, work was progressing in other types of linguistic activity. In his important book, *The Religious System of the AmaZulu,* for example, Canon Callaway made meticulous use of Zulu concepts and terminology. In 1859 Bishop Colenso visited the Zulu king, Mpande, and took with him two Zulu schoolboys, Magema and Ndiyane, and a teacher, William. The result was a landmark in the history of Zulu literature, for the party published a book containing accounts in Zulu of the meeting with King Mpande. The three Zulu texts, written by Magema, Ndiyane, and William, were the earliest published contribution by a Zulu (Nyembezi, 1961, pp. 3-4).

All this translation activity concentrated attention on the vernacular, leading missionaries to a critical comparative perspective on the West while thrusting Africans into the world of literacy and the wider opportunities that represents. Missionaries, for example, dreamed of realizing in Africa the perfect replica of the primitive church as the answer, as they saw it, to the declining fortunes of the Western church. Africans, on the other hand, saw vernacular literacy as the door to increased opportunities in society and the world.

RECIPROCITY

We may characterize the new interrelationship between missionaries and Africans as reciprocity. Missionaries paid huge "vernacular" compliments to Africans, enabling many peoples to acquire pride and dignity about themselves in the modern world, and thus opening up the whole social system to equal access. For their part Africans returned the compliment by coupling a faith forged in the Scriptures with a commitment to social and political issues. Missionaries as vernacular agents thus helped Africans to become modernizing agents. The old categories of antagonism and alienation by which we have assessed the missionary impact are insufficient to take account of this factor of reciprocity, and therefore the need to go beyond them now is demonstrably clear.

However, reciprocity does not deny the tension that existed between mission and Africa. For one thing, the complex discussion about what terms to employ in describing God suggests that competing forces were at work. For another, the scientific outlook of the missionary, which for many of them remained unassimilated to the outlook of the world of the Bible, often conflicted with the assumptions of African religiosity. The rational spirit of Western Christianity had shifted the burden of faith to the method, process, and ways of knowing rather than to the subject and substance of religious conviction. Thus belief, like the passive construct of thought, came to predominate over faith, the active subject of life. Africans could not meet this massive force in Western Christianity without being jolted. So tension there certainly was, and aplenty.

We may observe in this connection that missionaries and Africans played complementary roles in the establishment of the religion. Consequently, a certain double entendre came to characterize the history of Christianity in Africa: indigenous aspirations were promoted by the vernacular prospects of scriptural translation, while missionaries were committed to translation from motives of numerical success. This difference in perception, arising from a common source in translation, allowed two apparently divergent tendencies to develop. In the first place, missionaries continued to be committed to the development of the vernacular as a foil to the establishment of the Christianity they knew and trusted. In the second place, Africans acquired from vernacular resources a strengthened determination to reject foreign interpretations of the religion. It is the common nature of this tension that the concept of reciprocity tries to elucidate.

Looked at simply, we may say this: if people are trying to learn your language, then they can hardly avoid striking up a relationship with you however much they might wish to dominate you. And assuming that they do wish to control you, your best defense is the weapon they have as yet learned to grasp only imperfectly, namely, your language and all that goes with it. However, if it turns out that the pillars upon which your language has been established have been put in place by missionaries, as in many instances they were, then your achievements owe a great deal to those missionary pioneers. It therefore follows that your success should include not only how you use the instruments of mission to good effect but how you also understand the place missionaries gave to your language and its concomitants. Reciprocity is one way of dealing with this reality.

In much of the relevant ethnographic literature, Africans have been portrayed as the victims of missionary oppression, either because they were forcibly converted or because missionary contact proved fatal to indigenous originality. In the one case, Africans, being under duress as spiritual slaves of the West, could not lay legitimate claim to the heritage of the "freeborn" missionary, and in the second case, being charged with guilt by association, they were denied any power to speak out of the fullness of their experience. A curious catch-22 situation then arose: if Africans embraced Christianity they were confirming their victimization; if they resisted it they were disqualified by the challenge.

The concept of reciprocity tries to move us beyond this impasse without, of course, overlooking areas of tension and critical challenge. In undertaking translation, missionaries demonstrated the limited usefulness of European languages, while indigenous Africans, confronted with the stimulus of missionary interest, received the Scriptures as written warranty for the vernacular.

THE FUNCTION OF TRANSLATION

It is in this light that we must seek to understand the cultural changes that missionaries pressed upon Africans as a condition for adopting Christianity. Henceforth, any Western cultural innovations introduced by missionaries would be subject ultimately to vernacular vetting. In time Africans could complain about the unacceptable degree of Westernization in the church, believing, with justice, that they have support for their position in the highest quarters of scriptural Christianity itself. And everyone concerned would accept that Westernization is not a necessary or sufficient basis for Christian orthodoxy. This kind of debate grows naturally out of the vernacular nature of Christianity and occurs with consistency from the time of the apostles down to our own age. This is different from saying that everywhere in Africa Christianity succeeded in striking vernacular roots — for that is not the case, but merely that one can demand or even require a vernacular direction for the faith in the interests of orthodoxy.

Needless to say, Christian mission did not adhere consistently to the rule of translation, but translation in itself implies far-reaching implications that are worth considering, whatever may be the position of particular missions toward it. The tension that arises in Christianity from resistance to or encouragement for translation is profoundly related to the original conception of the gospel: God, who has no linguistic favorites, has determined that we should all hear the Good News "in our own native tongue." Mission as cultural diffusion conflicts with the gospel in this regard, and historically we can document the problems, challenges, and prospects that have attended Christian expansion across cultures under the consistent rule of translation. Where mission has resisted translation, there it has also sought to suppress the vernacular. In such instances mission has proceeded as "cultural diffusion," imposing a uniform pattern on local populations in the interests of "normative Christianity." However, mission as cultural diffusion tends toward self-contradiction when the uniform pattern is unmasked as itself a translation of the gospel, a discovery that places a legitimizing seal upon translation as a continuous process. In the final analysis there is no satisfactory alternative to Christianity as a dynamic translation movement.

Indeed, where mission failed to achieve a vernacular credibility it has called forth and deserved every criticism it received, then or in retrospect. Ethnographers and other scholars who have criticized mission for its foreign nature have in a backhanded way conceded the principle that Christianity and vernacular credibility are related. In this regard, their unsuspecting allies are the missionaries themselves who pointed the way with vernacular translation and who, often in self-contradiction, have not played to the script and followed the consequences of their own action. The historian of religion may, therefore, attempt to retrieve the subject of translation from its isolation in colonial studies and bring it forward as a central category in the revitalization of indigenous societies, a step that does not bypass deserved criticism of mission. What it does do, however, is to review the ideological opposition to mission, for such opposition is an obstacle to open-minded inquiry and to the advancement of the subject in its own right. If we proceed in this manner and overlook the ideological rhetoric in much of the literature, we should be able to restore a corrective perspective to the place of translation in both mission and the renewal of African societies.

One eminent anthropologist, Monica Wilson, considers the factor of translation in Christian mission, but hastily sets it aside to pursue what she herself describes as "peripheral" matters, which have to do with the imposition of Western culture on Africans. The following passage indicates she is grappling with issues that appear to elude her confident grasp.

Acceptance of Christian teaching implied a radical change in the manner of life of converts; the Christian gospel has been a yeast fermenting change in societies for two thousand years. The writing of the vernacular, the translation of the Bible, and teaching converts to read it (which for Protestant missionaries was fundamental to their mission) was in itself revolutionary. Family relationships and the political structure were radically changed by the condemnation of polygyny, and the insistence that death was not caused by witches. It could not have been otherwise. But the missionaries were also mostly from Britain, and they were Victorians imbued with a conviction of the value of their whole manner of life . . . and they pressed all sorts of peripheral changes which later generations have questioned. Not only did they preach the Protestant gospel of work, but they expected their converts to wear a Western style of clothing; to build square houses rather than round ones; to settle in a village round the church and school rather than in scattered homesteads; to change the division of labour between men and women, and to abandon ancient festivals, such as the traditional initiation dances, which were judged by whites to be lewd, and became illegal west of the Kei. [Wilson, 1969, p. 266.]

We know from more recent evidence enough to realize that the ideology of mission—for example, the insistence that death was not caused by witches—is no guide to missionary effectiveness. Rituals of initiation continue to play a predominant role in the new churches of Africa, as do dancing and the drama of healing, with churches prescribing from the Psalms remedies for witchcraft. And as for polygamy, attitudes toward this question vary enormously, with some Independent Churches sanctioning the practice and others prohibiting it entirely. But it is relevant to Monica Wilson's assertion to say that many missionaries, after learning enough of the indigenous society, swung around to defending the system. For example, Bishop Colenso, who had espoused the custom, startled everyone at Lambeth Conference in the 1860s by coming out in favor of African polygamy. Colenso had written in 1855 that to require a polygamous catechumen to put aside all but one of his wives as a condition for baptism is theologically inconsistent, for it is asking him to commit the sin of divorce to remedy the offense of polygamy. Few missionaries were willing to grasp that nettle (Colenso, 1855).

In the sphere of vernacular translation and literacy, however, missionaries were a great deal more effective, even if their effectiveness stemmed from unintended consequences. With the help of vernacular Scriptures, for example, Zulu Christians found sanction for their habit of dressing in skins (Gen. 3:21), and began to criticize missionaries for not being properly dressed according to the Scriptures. The same criticism was voiced with regard to church services, with Africans insisting that missionary churches were unfaithful to the Scriptures, which call for dancing and music in worship and praise (Judg. 11:35; 1 Sam. 18:6; 2 Sam. 6:14; Ps. 149:3; 1 Chron. 15:16; Lk. 7:32, 15:25; Matt. 11:17). As for the custom of singing, Africans found in the Scriptures a stream in full spate. No amount of missionary resistance could stand in their way.

Another eminent anthropologist, Sir Edward Evans-Pritchard, gave some thought to the issue of missionary translation, and although he is more straightforward in his account, he fails to press the right conclusions from his own premises. He writes:

I have read . . . of the predicament of missionaries to the Eskimos in trying to render into their language the word "lamb," as in the sentence "Feed my lambs." You can, of course, render it by reference to some animal with which Eskimos are acquainted, by saying, for instance, "Feed my seals," but clearly if you do so you replace the representation of what a lamb was for a Hebrew shepherd by that of what a seal may be to an Eskimo. . . . How do you translate into Hottentot "Though I speak with the tongues of men and of angels and have not charity . . ."? In the first place, you have to determine what the passage meant to St. Paul's hearers; and, apart from the "tongues of men and of angels," what exegetical learning has gone into the elucidation of eros, agape, and caritas! Then you have to find equivalents in Hottentot, and, since there are none, you do the best you can. [Evans-Pritchard, 1965, pp. 13–14.]

A fundamental difference between lambs and seals in the two respective cultures, as Sir Edward hints, is that lambs belong to a farming culture whereas seals are part of the Eskimos' hunting way of life. In the words "you do the best you can," Sir Edward hints at the indigenous necessity of translation, with corresponding implications for the role of foreign expertise. In another passage, he suggests that profound changes are implied in translation, with the missionary at a disadvantage if he or she worked only with Western notions. In the final analysis the missionary is at the mercy of indigenous presuppositions. Citing a passage from A. M. Hocart, who had Fiji in mind, Sir Edward invites us to reflect as follows:

When the missionary speaks of God as *ndina,* he means that all other gods are non-existent. The native understands that He is the only effective, reliable god; the others may be effective at times, but are not to be depended upon. This is but one example of how the teacher may mean one thing and his pupil understand another. Generally the two parties continue blissfully ignorant of the misunderstanding. There is no remedy for it, except in the missionary acquiring a thorough knowledge of native customs and beliefs. [Evans-Pritchard, 1965, pp. 7–8.]

The words "a thorough knowledge of native customs and habits" may stand for indigenous necessity, a step that brings the missionary to accepting the primacy of the vernacular. This is why, in the successful assimilation of Christianity in Africa and elsewhere, God as an exclusive, jealous being was made to yield to considerations of inclusiveness in both the social and the religious dimensions. The reason is obvious. When *ndina* or other indigenous equivalent is adopted as the God of the Scriptures, then those worshiping in God's name have necessarily brought within range all the familiar associations of the term. As such, when new converts prayed to the God of Jesus Christ as *ndina,* for example, they created an overlap to preserve and perpetuate the earlier notions in the environment of the new dispensation. This does not deny the possibility of change. On the contrary, it helps to legitimize change and resolve, without bypassing, potential difficulties. The point of convergence remains the familiar medium of the vernacular and its often hidden presuppositions. From the heightened awareness occasioned by the availability of the written Scriptures in the vernacular, local converts appropriated the gospel without running it through Western filters first. The changes that followed arose from the internal critical ferment of written sanctions in the language of the people acting upon traditional customs.

This situation could not have been avoided by mission as translation. The concession that missionaries made that local populations may legitimately call upon the God of the Bible in their own language turned out to be a major step in bringing forward the indigenous framework as the basis for assimilation. The subsequent attempts to qualify this assimilation by attaching Western cultural conditions were a cosmetic resort. The larger procedure had struck at the heart of any normative claims for Western culture so far as effective mission is concerned.

This might explain why those missionaries who viewed mission as the "white man's burden" came to hold an envious esteem for Islam, a religion that gives short shrift to vernacular pretensions. From its lofty position of a universal, untranslatable sacred Scripture and a militant monotheist creed, Islam is engaged with the question of indigenization only as a handicap. The great and resounding *takbīr,* the *allāh-u-akbar* of the muezzin, reminds all Muslims, irrespective of place or time, of the counterfeit that its vernacular equivalent most assuredly is. A Christian, on the other hand, may be under equal obligation to witness to God, but if so only as a mirror-image of the Islamic case. There is scriptural sanction for, though there might be political prejudice against, calling upon *ndina* or *uNkulunkulu* or *Gott* or *Dieu* as "the Yahweh of ancient Israel" and "the God and Father of our Lord Jesus Christ." So to proclaim the gospel anywhere is in fact to invoke local paradigms. Sir Edward spotted this, but misidentified it as an impediment instead of as the natural strength of the religion.

Some missionaries recognized that the vernacular logic of Christianity was against the perpetuation of Western forms of the religion, and tried to buy time for themselves. J. Sandström, the first Swedish missionary at Ceza in northern Zululand, arriving there in 1905, was extremely wary of the future for people like him. He later (1926) wrote:

> Our aim is of course an African Christian National Church with which eventually the Lutheran National Church must merge, with the peculiar gifts and blessings that have been bestowed upon her. But will we get the time to reach our first goal, a strong, self-supporting and self-propagating Lutheran Zulu Church, before the development overtakes us and the Natives' own National Church builds its walls higher and higher, attracting the masses perchance by concessions with regard to polygamy, church discipline etc.? [Sundkler, 1976, p. 250.]

Sandström's fears about Africans offering easy compromises were unfounded, for the Zionist churches of Southern Africa have gone on to impose some of the most uncompromising rules of discipline on their followers, from fasting and other feats of self-denial to the most robust forms of muscular religion. Many converts to these new religious movements testify to their being attracted by the much stricter code enforced there in contrast to what they considered the comparatively lax attitude in missionary churches.

Other missionaries accepted gracefully that the missionary enterprise taught them things that they did not know before they arrived and for which they were grateful. For such people the exposure of the field-setting was an immensely useful cross-cultural experience. One such was the English Benedictine priest, Dom Bernard Clements, who served in Ghana. He testified:

> I think God sent me to Africa five years ago so that I might learn from you some lessons of humility and love and service which my rough heart didn't learn in Europe and you Africans whom God has used as tutors to teach me these things I thank very much, because even when I have been very foolish and said sometimes hateful and stupid things to you, you have still gone on in great patience. . . . And so perhaps in the end I have learned some of the things which God set you to teach me. [Laing, 1944, p. 31; cited in Debrunner, 1967, p. 269.]

One contemporary missionary described with humor how he was outperformed by the prophet-leader of a new religious movement who challenged him to preach a sermon in Zulu on the scriptural text John 7:37–38. The missionary confessed: "My little homiletical effort in Zulu was followed by a long exposition by William Chiliza on the same text. He was immediately at home with all these images and what is more, he could bring them to life" (Sundkler, 1976, p. 91).

This issue of the logic of mission as translation leading to the establishment of indigenous churches may be reinforced by developments in the intellectual climate of the culture of the missionary. Even if it were so reinforced, that has to be distinguished from the primary nature of the vernacular reaction. William R. Hutchison, the American religious historian, for example, has explored this ideological background of Western missions, and even from his own perspective he confirms the shift toward the primacy of indigenization: "Historicism and cultural relativism about one's religious forms suggested some degree of syncretism in dealing with religious forms evolved by non-Christian peoples; and they further implied a determination that Christian churches, once established abroad, might be left to themselves" (Hutchison, 1974, p. 119).

The religious motive often encouraged missionaries to try to produce translations of excellence. The Rev. J. G. Christaller, a German linguist, served with the Basel Mission in Ghana. He became a foremost promoter of Akan language and culture, in particular the Twi language, doing more than anybody else to establish the study of Akan on secure foundations. Between 1871 and 1881 he became absorbed in mammoth tasks of translation and interpretation, carrying off the entire enterprise with rare distinction. He completed a translation of the Bible in 1871, then wrote a widely acclaimed dictionary and grammar of the Twi language in 1875, and crowned it in 1879 with a methodical compilation of 3,600 Twi proverbs and idioms. He developed a deep and abiding love for the Akan. In the preface to his collection of proverbs he wrote:

> May this Collection give a new stimulus to the diligent gathering of folk-lore and to the increasing cultivation of native literature. May those Africans who are enjoying the benefit of a Christian education, make the best of the privilege; but let them not despise the sparks of truth entrusted to and preserved by their own people, and let them not forget that by entering into their way of thinking and by acknowledging what is good and expounding what is wrong they will gain the more access to the hearts and minds of their less favoured countrymen. [Cited in Danquah, 1944, p. 186.]

Christaller thus repeats the plea of many other missionaries, namely that educated Africans fit themselves for the special task of indigenization to which the success of the Christian cause was directly related. His *Twi Dictionary,* published in 1881, has been hailed as an "Encyclopaedia of Akan Civilization" (*West Africa,* 1986, p. 1472). Christaller also helped found the *Christian Messenger* in Basel in 1883, a paper devoted to the promotion of Akan life and culture. From 1905 to 1917, when it was transferred to Ghana, it published articles in Twi, Ga, and English, and covered local events as well as international news such as the Russo-Japanese War of 1904, Halley's Comet in 1910, and the sinking of the *Titanic* in 1911. The use of the vernacular to report on world news and instruct its readers in local affairs was a major contribution of the paper, for it suggests that its audience could keep abreast of happenings without literacy in the European languages. As a piece of indigenous journalism it deserves more serious interest than the near-total silence with which it is treated in accounts of African journalism.

The greatest tribute to Christaller was that paid by J. B. Danquah, the founding spirit of modern Ghanaian nationalism. Danquah's was the inspiration that set the stage for Kwame Nkrumah, the founder of modern Ghana. An ethical philosopher, and still enamored of the idea of the Akan as having originated in the Near East, Danquah wrote *The Akan Doctrine of God,* which was published in London in 1944. It is a dense, Kantian treatise that attempts to expound the Akan worldview in terms of its social system and religious psychology. In that work, Danquah acknowledged Christaller as the source and antecedent of his book. He said Christaller's work was "the Old Testament," the foundational Scripture of the Akan, and that his own book was "the New Testament," which depended on the earlier enterprise.

Others also paid equally sincere tributes to Christaller. One was a contemporary, the Rev. David Asante of Akropong. He was trained at

Basel from 1857 to 1862, and subsequently ordained in 1864. As a protégé of Christaller, Asante had imbibed the latter's enthusiasm for the vernacular, translating works from German and English into Akan, including John Bunyan's *Pilgrim's Progress.* He was clearly a major national figure. "But such is the preoccupation of Ghanaian biographers with 'merchant princes' and nationalist firebrands that, outside the small circle of the Presbyterian Church and an entry in the *Encyclopaedia Africana,* not much is known of such pioneers as Asante. Yet in the translation of the Bible and in his other books he helped to introduce new concepts, new words and phrases into Ghanaian literature" (Amegatcher, 1986, p. 1472). As one who should know, Asante wrote to Christaller in 1866 paying his respects to the missionary for his achievement.

> The Psalms are translated perfectly and brilliantly. Nobody can read this translation without deep feelings of awe. They resemble in many ways the songs of mourning *(Kwadwom)* in our Twi language; the Twi people will be glad to read them. May the Lord give His blessing to your labours. I want to congratulate you personally and in the name of Africa. May the Lord give you strength for more such work. [Cited in Debrunner, 1967, p. 144.]

It is not necessary to repeat here in detail how scriptural translation helped Africans to preserve their name for God and the religious and social worlds that depended on that. One provocative question is the extent to which Christianized Akan have a much better-preserved pre-Christian heritage than their Muslim counterparts, say, in north Nigeria. The Akan today feel much closer to sources of indigenous life than the Hausa or Fulani of Muslim Africa. For example, Hausa or Fulani Muslims have, to all intents and purposes, allowed *Allāh* to displace the god or gods of pre-Islamic times, for the *takbīr* of the five daily prayers institutes the Arabic formula as the exclusive standard of devotion. This is an issue best developed in a separate work on Islamic mission. For the moment, however, the provocative question this begins to suggest is how Christian progress in Africa seems to be tied to indigenous necessity whereas the corresponding Islamic case appears to depend on the marginalization of the vernacular. The great prophet movements of Africa have coincided with a recrudescence of interest in ancestor figures, deceased and living elders, traditional healing, mortuary rites, and vernacular literature, whereas the Reform Tradition of nineteenth-century Islamic Africa depended for its legitimacy on the repudiation of the vernacular.

SUMMARY

It might again be useful to attempt a brief summary before moving to the concluding stages of the discussion. The peaceful exposure of neighboring cultures was a concomitant of the efforts at scriptural translation, and this led to greater interethnic encounter. The new religious movements which have arisen in modern Africa have promoted this spirit of interethnic solidarity. Similarly, a lively discussion took place among missionaries and between them and local Africans about the procedures and principles of translation. Two direct consequences of such activity were (1) the implicit acceptance of pluralism in terms of all languages having an equal part to play in the expression of the gospel, and (2) an increasing awareness of Africans of the significance of their own vernacular culture in the universal design of God for all peoples. David Asante in the nineteenth century and J. B. Danquah of the twentieth century both gave voice to this perception.

The preceding pages have suggested that all these considerations should lead us to ask a fundamental question about the apparent connection between the Christian enterprise and the depth of indigenization, with a possible reversal of that situation in the African Islamic example. Our aim now will be to explore further this connection between Christian religious activity and indigenous renewal.

RELIGIOUS RENEWAL AND INDIGENOUS REVITALIZATION

A casual glance at a religious map of Africa will appear to confirm the impression that the areas of greatest Christian influence overlap almost exactly with those of the primal religions and cultures. This overlap is for reasons other than mere historical coincidence.

One of the first and most detailed accounts of the connection between African culture and the success of Christian religious activity is the work of John Peel, a British sociologist. In his book *Aladura: A Religious Movement among the Yoruba,* Peel provides an articulate and lucid account of the Yoruba appropriation of Christianity, showing the continuity of indigenous Yoruba themes in the new Christian setting. Peel sets the stage with a description of Yoruba society before going on to consider in detail the rise of African churches and the role of certain religious subjects such as prayer and visions, medicine, and holiness. Next he explores the activities of the new churches and the role of praying bands and other charismatic aspects. Against this rich religious background, the author delves into the sociological basis of the new churches.

In the patient and open-minded way in which Peel analyzes the phenomenon of prophet movements, we learn a great deal about the necessary backup of indigenous culture whose insights and values have persisted into the new religion, with a mutual transformation of numerous common elements. Peel is rare among social scientists in conceding the primary importance of indigenous Yoruba religion in the Yoruba social system, and, instead of seeking to emasculate it into a sociological abstraction, he infers from it details of social behavior and political organization. As a result he is able to present a coherent account of the interrelationship between the various parts of the Yoruba social and religious world, and thus he does not commit what an earlier British anthropologist, Rattray, called the error of "construing the customs in terms of our own psychology" (Rattray, 1927, pp. viif.), or what Evans-Pritchard called "If I were a horse fallacy" (Evans-Pritchard, 1965, p. 43).

Those responsible for the enterprise of scriptural translation had adopted the name of the Supreme Being of the Yoruba, *Ọlọrun* or *Ọlọdumare,* as the *deus revelatus* of the Bible. Yet the entire edifice of Yoruba popular piety rests not so much on an exclusive preoccupation with *Ọlọdumare* as in the regular and constant negotiation with intermediary powers, called *ọrịṣas.* The cult of Ifa divination is for this reason the most prominent feature of religious practice among the Yoruba: it is related to prayers of many sorts, sacrifice, and hierarchical notions of social, political, and religious power (see, e.g. Bascom, 1941). Ifa is a technical divinatory art in which the diviner, called the *babalawo* ("master of mysteries"), consults the relevant *ọrịṣa,* or intermediary spirit, for the specific needs of the client. The *ọrịṣas* themselves are innumerable (some accounts speak of up to 401), but are ranked in order of importance, thus adding to the systematic complexity of the Yoruba religious world.

It is clear that in invoking *Ọlọrun,* the translators of the Bible had rung a bell at the lower reaches of the Yoruba worldview where the *ọrịṣas* as intermediary powers and personal deities predominated. We have early signs of this fact in much of the historical evidence. When Samuel Ajayi Crowther confronted a *babalawo* then practicing in Freetown, the diviner answered his Christian critic with the defense that he could not give up his art, that before giving his medicine to anyone he consulted his *ọrịṣa* whether or not he should give it, and that he acted strictly in accordance with the wishes of Ifa (Sanneh, 1983, p. 84). Another Ifa diviner in the same town assured Christians that he had incorporated Jesus Christ into the Ifa system. Before making any sacrifice to the *ọrịṣa,* he asked his clients first to call upon the name of Jesus Christ. Both *babalawos* were convinced that since the cult of Ifa existed for the good and benefit of persons, to devote attention to the cult must necessarily be in harmony with the worship of the God of Christianity. This may be one reason why new churches among the Yoruba, initially at least, looked upon Jesus as the supreme *ọrịṣa,* the infallible guide and intermediary who guaranteed access to the mind and will of God (Peel, 1968, pp. 135, 141, 147). Peel correctly notes that "Christ, having been man as well as God, is much the more appropriate vehicle for prayers, sometimes seen, perhaps, as lower than God the Father, the all-powerful *Ọba* ('ruler')" (1968, p. 147).

In another aspect of the system of Ifa divination, the concordance of a prospective encounter with Christianity is supplied. Bishop James Johnson, Crowther's compatriot and successor in what remained of the Niger Mission, had come into contact with the Ifa divinatory system in Freetown and elsewhere. Like Crowther he was critical of the practice although in his case, too, controversy had its many uses. He testified in 1876 that the names of Ifa could justifiably be adopted as attributes of the God of the Bible: "great, Almighty one," "the Child of God," the "One who is mightiest among the gods and prevailed to do on a certain occasion what they could not," and, most remarkably, the "One who came whom we have put to death with cudgels causelessly" (Ajayi, 1969, p. 235n.). Johnson felt, after hearing the Ifa priest speak in such terms, that the Christian proclamation had to take account of such material.

Thus when preaching to Yoruba populations in Yoruba, such an overlap, if it was not made by missionaries, would undoubtedly be made by ordinary people reared on popular piety. The success of the Christian cause came in this way to evoke a profound recollection of indigenous materials. We have evidence that even when an indigenous cult is in some decline from internal factors, the Christian presence can act as a stimulating second wind (Sanneh, 1983, p. 237).

It is therefore no mere accident that at the root of prophet movements in African Christianity we have an explicit appeal to indigenous categories of the religious life. An early convert of the British missionary at Ibadan, Nigeria, the Rev. David Hinderer, was Shadrach Mogun. At the turn of this century, Mogun was reported to be living in self-imposed seclusion in the Yoruba village of Emure-Ekiti. One account describes how "he lives alone with Jesus Christ — to use his own expression. . . . He preaches to the farmers, and now and again visits the town to preach. He looks like an old prophet, and is a veritable John the Baptist preparing the way for Christ's second advent" (cited in Peel, 1968, p. 58).

It was by such a natural congruence with the vernacular that the Christian impact sent sound waves reverberating throughout the land, and there were numerous communities of people for whom the message of the new prophets came as confirmation of old dreams. Conversion for these people meant sharing in the redeemed fellowship of God's people, something that the sense of kinship implied in the phrase *Omo Oduduwa,* "children of the ancestor/ancestress," had already prepared them for. The difference now is that *Oduduwa* was itself kin to the cosmic Christ. Conversion did not mean a psychological "migration" out of the African world, since it was a consequence of encountering the gospel in the vernacular. Thus in the colorful tones of the Yoruba tongue, the *Aladura* revival amplified the message of the Bible. A new level of religious understanding was initiated as people experienced forgiveness and a sense of personal acceptance in the fellowship of believers, a fellowship often inadequately grasping after "the mind of Christ," but still identified with Christ's name.

It must be stressed that, for most converts, the Bible that they came to know was the vernacular Scripture, so that in the new vessel of a written sacred text converts heard God addressing them in the old, familiar idiom. One modern missionary statesman commented on this phenomenon, saying:

The urge to translate the Bible into every language may have helped to prolong the life of a dialect where reason suggested it ought to lose itself in a regional *lingua franca*. . . .What is important [in this regard] is that men and women, not least women, without any schooling on the Western pattern, learned to read in their own language because the Bible was there. In the days before special adult literacy programmes inspired by Dr. Laubach's methods, an old grandmother would come to Sunday School week after week painfully learning the alphabet, then short words, then sentences. Then came the day when, with a friend finding the place for her in the Bible bought at the market that week with her saved-up shillings, her face shone with the joy of recognising, as she read, treasured words learned by heart long ago—a sentence from the 14th chapter of John's Gospel or the story of the woman sweeping her room for a lost coin [Lk. 15:8].

The Bible strengthened the Church among the people. It was a family business, the reading of the Word, as anyone knows who has been privileged to come out of the guestroom into the hall of a compound house as the sounds of dawn strengthen and the light of an oil lamp share [*sic*] in the Bible-reading and the family prayer. [Beetham, 1967, p. 55.]

The missionaries had provided written, if critical, authority for the force of oral tradition.

This matter of the overlap between the Christian revival and the revitalization of indigenous culture remains one of the most undervalued themes in the study of Christian expansion, although in Africa and elsewhere it stares us in the face at almost every turn of the road. As early as 1954 Absalom Vilakazi, himself a Zulu, wrote an M.A. thesis, entitled "The Church of the Nazarites," at the Hartford Seminary Foundation. In it Vilakazi propounded the view that the charismatic revival was the agent for "the regeneration of Zulu society." He proved this by calling attention to certain Zulu notions of illness, medicine, and healing, suggesting in addition how the idea of "covenant" became the stimulus for the creation of new forms of community among the Nazarites.

Vilakazi, then, appears to be suggesting that we stand the established theological and historical methodology on its head by viewing new forms of Christian religious life as some of the best examples of authentic forms of indigenous custom. Normally we tend to assume that Christian contact of any kind is tantamount to a denial of authenticity, an assumption that has hardened with the adding of the colonial theme. But it may be that Vilakazi's point needs more general recognition. For if his tacit contention is correct, then our defense of "anthropological purity" would take us to the new churches of Africa with a corresponding downgrading of the village as the repository of ancient custom. Indeed, not to put too fine a point on it, it may well be that these new churches provide us with a unique opportunity to observe how Africans, presented with a new challenge, adopt and direct it in time-tested channels, a process of assimilation that might help to shed new light on the question of origins in history, society, and ideas.

In a short but acute essay, the historian Terence Ranger tries to come to grips with the specific grounds of Christian renewal in Africa (in Barrett, 1971, pp. 109–45). Ranger takes as his case study the example of Tanzania, where he tries to account for the relative sparsity of the phenomenon that he characterizes as "Christian independency." In a series of closely argued steps, he discounts many of the factors we tend to take for granted. He takes up the colonial theme but says it is hard to make much of it in the context.

The issue confronting us is why Tanzania seems relatively unreceptive to African Christian Independency. Ranger believes the answer lies in the special environment of Tanzania. The variety of missions in Tanzania, he argues, cannot be used to say that they met needs otherwise fulfilled by Independency (in Barrett, 1971, pp. 130–31). Nor can we credit the High Church and liturgical traditions of the major missions in Tanzania for not representing the kind of Calvinistic threat that might inflame passions for Independency. The real reason, Ranger feels, for the surprising weakness of the Independency impulse in Tanzania is what he calls the prestige of Swahili society, with its strong Muslim population. For, in his view, Independency gained ground mostly in places profoundly influenced by Christianity (in Barrett, 1971, p. 133).

Ranger has amplified a critical question. Yet in his attempt to find the answer in the success of Christian penetration of African societies, he has only repeated the question in a different way, of which the negative side is, as he says, the dominance of an Islamized Swahili society. The real question is why Christianity should succeed everywhere except in strongly Islamized areas or, another form of the same question, why Islamized communities should constitute such an impenetrable barrier to Christian renewal. After all, religion has prestige in most African communities, and the influence of Islam depends a great deal on its religious appeal. It therefore remains a pertinent question why, in the identical African setting, Christianity should exert comparatively little appeal in spite of its obvious religious profile. When Ranger talks about "the prestige of Swahili society" he also seems to mean the continuing prestige of religion, and it would therefore be reasonable to expect Christianity, with its religious and theological tradition, to exert a similar appeal. Yet it seemingly does not, and Islamic influence continues to be an obstacle. Why should this be?

All the examples of Christian renewal in Africa that Ranger cites are from areas of profound indigenous religious influence and areas, also, where missionaries were able to furnish the Scriptures in the vernacular. Missionaries also mastered Swahili and produced scriptural translations in that trade language. In spite of that, Christian success was limited.

Obviously, then, it takes more than translation to penetrate society with the gospel, and that is a clue to the problem.

In light of the available evidence, it would be reasonable to proceed as follows. When missionaries translated the Christian Scriptures into Swahili, they were tacitly measuring the Bible against the Holy Book of Islam. There the advantage lay with the Muslims, who could claim that translation conceded the inferior status of the message whose original is to be encountered in the pristine, untranslatable Arabic of the Qur'ān. Thus there was a widespread psychological predisposition in Swahili society against translation, with a corresponding denigration (interesting etymology) of the vernacular, or at any rate a widely held esteem for the canonical devotions of Islam, which, for all Muslims, must be performed in Arabic. The scholars who peruse the sources of law and religion in the sacred language of Arabic constitute the visible social prestige of the religion.

Thus the popular and elite perception of Muslims acted as the *cordon sanitaire* to insulate society against esteem for the vernacular. Everywhere that such an attitude toward the vernacular exists, we can predict that Christian renewal will have minimal impact, whether in Swahili East Africa, in north Nigeria, Mali, Sene-Gambia, or Muslim North Africa, and this in spite of long Christian contact. It may sometimes happen that Christian renewal fails to take place without the Islamic factor or any other forces that might suppress the vernacular, but in that case we have to ask about the status of the vernacular in religious work. Dahomey is a good example where there was no evidence of Christian renewal although the British Methodists had a mission there. The reason in that case was the absence of any significant translation work into the Fon language, a situation that persisted until the late 1960s. Whatever the historical reasons for that, whether it be found in the prejudice of French-language proponents or in the unimaginativeness of the particular missionary situation, it represents a major weakness, for Christian renewal of the revivalist type depends largely on the cultivation of the vernacular.

By contrast, Islamic strength is almost proportionate to the weakening of the vernacular, as Rex O'Fahey has shown in his pioneering study of Dār Fūr in the Sudan (O'Fahey, 1980). It is instructive to observe that "revivalism" as a technical term by which we may seek the signs of the Spirit in the believer does not occur in mainline Islam, though the Sufis, considered peripheral, practice a version of it in *ma'rifah,* Islamic gnosis. Thus we may say that conversion in Islam necessitates "migration" to Mecca out of Africa. Although no legal obligation falls on those who are genuinely unable to make the pilgrimage to Mecca, every Muslim is required to consider it as a duty, and most would regard it as a deficiency not to have undertaken it. Religious psychology, not juridical sanction, brings ordinary Muslims to this perception. And attachment to the pilgrimage ideal correspondingly loosens the hold of local habits. It completes the downgrading of the vernacular. (The present writer has been involved with successful plans to send an aunt on pilgrimage to Mecca. She is typical of many pilgrims: she had never traveled out of her town, does not read, write, or speak Arabic of any kind, and has no idea of city life let alone of the map of the world. She traveled by air for the first and probably the last time in her life. Yet her feeling that she ought to make the *hajj* was so strong that she was prepared, with help and encouragement, to plan carefully and commit uncommon resources, to say nothing of braving unprecedented difficulties, in order to accomplish her objective. She would return with the proud headband of the pilgrim, carrying the name *Hajja,* which would precede and overshadow her given name. Her elevated social distinction would be in spite of her strong native roots, and henceforth those roots would be consciously—and unconsciously—recast to reinforce a Muslim identity. Over the course of generations Islam has acted in such ways to displace the old standards of affiliation, with Mecca as the uncompromising point of orientation in religious devotion and feeling, and ultimately in pilgrimage as the religious ideal.)

In his seminal work on Christian renewal in Africa, David Barrett identifies this vernacular factor with great consistency. He writes:

> Vernacular scriptures have far greater power to communicate and create religious dynamic than versions in *linguae francae* such as Swahili, Hausa, Arabic, French or English, which have been in circulation in many areas long before the onset of independency without fomenting disaffection. The vernacular translation enables the ethnic group concerned to grasp the inner meanings of . . . profound and intricate biblical doctrines. . . . Further, it is clear that these vernacular translations—with all the attendant expenditure of effort on orthography, grammars, dictionaries, and studies of tribal cultures—have contributed markedly to the recovery by Africans of the cultural identity of their tribe, later expressed in such bodies as tribal political parties, welfare societies, and particularly in tribal independent churches. [Barrett, 1968, p. 133.]

The irruption of Christian forces in contemporary Africa is without parallel in the history of the church. A few examples make this clear. In late 1893 there began in Buganda country (now part of Uganda) a mass movement in Christianity, "one of the most remarkable and spontaneous movements for literacy and new knowledge which the world has ever seen" (Oliver, 1952, p. 184). This followed the efforts of scriptural translation led by the lay missionary George Pilkington. Then African evangelists, both men and women, came foward to carry the vernacular Scriptures into the chief districts of the country. In 1896 there were 200 of these evangelists in regular employment, with 500 others in auxiliary positions. In 1902 the numbers had increased to 2,000 men and 400 women operating as far as the periphery of the forests of the Congo. Pilkington's translated Bible sold

1,100 copies in the year of publication, with an additional 4,000 New Testaments, 13,500 single Gospels, and 40,000 Bible-story readers. After visiting Uganda in 1910, Theodore Roosevelt witnessed for himself the staggering results of this work, which he characterized as nothing short of "astounding" (North, 1938, p. 14). Similarly, the Roman Catholic missionaries, inclined to skepticism, admitted that "in truth a violent wind of Pentecost has stirred over these people" ("En verité le vent violent de la Pentecôte a soufflé sur ce peuple") (Oliver, 1952, p. 187). When a census was taken in 1911, of 660,000 Bagandans, 282,000 claimed to be Christian, the figure being nearly evenly divided between 155,000 Catholics and 127,000 Anglicans (Oliver, 1952, pp. 193–94).

Let us now consider this African theme within the broader picture of the vernacular Scriptures. As we saw in chapter 2, above, with reference to Africa both Coptic and Punic were used in the early church, although the Scriptures were translated only into Coptic. Then followed the translation of the Bible into Ethiopic around 650. Outside Africa itself the Goths, Armenians, and, later, the Slavs had the Scriptures and other religious literature available in their languages. The next major step came in the wake of the sixteenth-century Reformation. By 1550 portions of the Bible were available in thirty-three different languages of the world, including Ethiopic and Arabic, both used in parts of Africa. However, there was a dramatic increase in numbers as of December 1984. At that date translations of the Scriptures were available in 1,808 of the world's 2,800 languages, with Africa alone claiming nearly one-third of these, with 522 different vernacular translations (*Scriptures of the World,* 1984, p. 7). As of the present writing, continuing efforts are being made to provide translations into an additional 238 African languages, so great is the demand.[2] The scale of the phenomenon places Africa in a separate category altogether.

This pattern of the correlation between indigenous cultural revitalization and Christian renewal is a consistent one in Africa, and as a theme it goes back to the very beginnings of the primitive church. In Africa, too, Christ died and descended into the African Hades, to emerge in the exalted company of the ancestors. Africans have encountered this risen Christ in the glorious company of apostles and the goodly fellowship of prophets, and with the indefatigable voices of the white-robed "Cherubim and Seraphim," the name of one of the prophet movements in Nigeria, they went on to publish abroad "the wonders of His name." As they pored over the vernacular Bible, Africans found scriptural sanction for relating the creative concept of the Old and New Testaments to the old and new dispensation of their immediate situation. The message of the Bible that God's work *(missio Dei)* is not done but continues in the new age brought an invigorating tone to African societies confronted with new challenges.

With the written assurance thus provided, local Christians threw themselves enthusiastically into projects of renewal, unburdened by the requirement that they deny the old dispensation in order to claim the promise of

Abraham. The challenge of the Bible was to integrate the old and the new, not to overthrow the old assurance for the new vision. The effect was to set up a critical evaluation of the demands of Western missions. That was as much the point of departure for the successful transplanting of the church in Africa as it was also the logical conclusion of the process of vernacularization begun by mission.

NOTES

1. Those interested in the subject of faith and reason may wish to consult, among others, John Hick, *Faith and Knowledge,* 2nd ed. (Glasgow: Fontana Books, 1974).

2. See the *Christian Science Monitor,* Sept. 3, 1985. For an up-to-date linguistic account of the African continent, see David Dalby, *The Language Map of Africa* (London: International African Institute, 1976).

SELECT BIBLIOGRAPHY

Ajayi, Jacob F. A. 1969. *Christian Missions in Nigeria: 1841–1891: The Making of an Elite.* Evanston, Ill.: Northwestern University Press, repr. of 1965 ed.

Amegatcher, Andrew W. 1986. "Akropong: 150 Years Old." *West Africa* (July 14).

Barrett, David B., 1968. *Schism and Renewal in Africa: An Analysis of Six Thousand Contemporary Religious Movements.* Nairobi: Oxford University Press.

Barrett, David B., ed. 1971. *African Initiatives in Religion.* Nairobi: East African Publishing House.

Bascom, William R. 1941. "The Sanctions of Ifa Divination." *Journal of the Royal Anthropological Institute* 71.

Beetham, T. A. 1960. *A New Order in Africa.* Beckley Pamphlets, fifth series, no. 2. London: Epworth Press.

_____ . 1967. *Christianity and the New Africa.* New York: Frederick A. Praeger.

Bloch-Hoell, Nils E. 1984. "Norwegian Mission to South Africa 1880–1920: Colonialistic Confrontation or Apostolic Approach?" In Torben Christensen and William R. Hutchison, eds., *Missionary Ideologies in the Imperialist Era: 1880–1920,* 2nd ed. Aarhus, Denmark: Forlaget Aros. Distributed in North America by *Harvard Theological Review.*

Bowen, T. J. 1862. *Grammar and Dictionary of the Yoruba Language.* Smithsonian Contributions to Knowledge, vol. 9, pt. 4.

Callaway, H. 1870. *The Religious System of the Amazulu.* London: Trübner.

The Christian Messenger. Missionary Archives, Basel.

Christian Science Monitor. 1985. (September 3).

Colenso, John W. 1855. *Remarks on the Proper Treatment of Polygamy.* Pietermaritzburg, South Africa.

Dalby, David. 1976. *The Language Map of Africa.* London: International African Institute.

Danquah, J. B. 1944. *The Akan Doctrine of God.* London: Lutterworth Press.

Debrunner, Hans W. 1967. *A History of Christianity in Ghana.* Accra: Waterville Publishing House.

Evans-Pritchard, E. E. 1965. *Theories of Primitive Religion.* London: Oxford University Press.

———. 1981. *A History of Anthropological Thought,* ed. André Singer. New York: Basic Books.

Hick, John. 1974. *Faith and Knowledge,* 2nd ed. London: Fontana Books.

Hocart, A. M. 1914. "Mana." *Man: Journal of the Royal Anthropological Institute.*

Hogg, William Richey. 1985. "God's Mission — Our Ministry." *Perkin's Journal* (summer).

Hutchison, William R. 1974. "Modern Missions: The Liberal Search for an Exportable Christianity: 1875–1935." In John K. Fairbank, ed., *The Missionary Enterprise in China and America.* Cambridge, Mass.: Harvard University Press.

Laing, G. E. F. 1944. *Dom Bernard Clements in Africa.* London.

Livingstone, David. 1857. *Missionary Travels and Researches in Central Africa.* London: John Murray.

North, Eric M. 1938. *The Book of a Thousand Tongues.* New York: Harper and Brothers.

Nyembezi, C. L. S. 1961. *A Review of Zulu Literature.* Pietermaritzburg: University of Natal Press.

O'Fahey, Rex. 1980. *State and Society in Dār Fūr.* London: Christopher Hurst Publishers.

Oliver, Roland. 1952. *The Missionary Factor in East Africa.* London: Longman; repr. 1970.

Peel, John D. Y. 1968. *Aladura: A Religious Movement among the Yoruba.* London: Oxford University Press for the International African Institute.

Plessis, J. du. 1911. *A History of Christian Mission in South Africa.* London: Longman, Green and Co.

Rattray, R. S. 1927. *Religion and Art among the Ashanti.* London: Oxford University Press; repr. 1969.

Sanneh, Lamin. 1983. *West African Christianity.* Maryknoll, N.Y.: Orbis.

Scriptures of the World: A Compilation of the 1808 Languages. 1984. London, New York and Stuttgart: United Bible Societies.

Smith, Edwin. 1950. *African Ideas of God.* London: Edinburgh House Press.

Sundkler, Bengt. 1976. *Zulu Zion and Some Swazi Zionists.* Oxford: Clarendon Press.

Turner, Harold W. 1967. *History of an African Independent Church: The Church of the Lord (Aladura),* 2 vols. London: Oxford University Press.

Vilakazi, Absalom. 1954. "The Church of the Nazarites." Unpublished M.A. thesis, Hartford: Hartford Seminary Foundation.

Walker, Sheila. 1983. *The Religious Revolution in the Ivory Coast.* Chapel Hill: University of North Carolina Press.

West Africa. 1986. (July 14).

Wilson, Monica. 1969. "Co-operation and Conflict: The Eastern Cape Frontier." In Monica Wilson and Leonard Thompson, eds., *South Africa to 1870,* vol. 1 of The Oxford History of South Africa series. Oxford: Clarendon Press.

6

"Familiarity Breeds Faith": First and Last Resorts in Vernacular Translation

Putting eternal truths into the speech of everyday life reflects exactly
the style of the Greek New Testament. The New Testament books
were not written in the high-flown Asian style of the schoolmasters of
the first and second centuries A.D.; they were couched in the words of
the common people, who were seeking the truth about the living, risen
Christ. For those who sought life, the dead forms of outmoded
grammatical styles were useless. So today, the missionary translator
carries on that same tradition, giving people the Word of God in their
own language, though the idioms may seem strange to us. [Nida,
1952, p. 23.]

The distinguishing mark of scriptural translation has been the effort to
come as close as possible to the speech of the common people. Translators
have consequently first devoted much time, effort, and resources to
building the basis, with investigations into the culture, history, language,
religion, economy, anthropology, and physical environment of the people
concerned, before tackling their concrete task. This background work was
often indispensable to the task of authentic translation.

In an important way, such activity demonstrates commitment to the
context of the translation rather than to the text as a self-contained
normative system. In another important way, the adoption of local idiom
suggests a radical shift from the literalness of the text to a fresh discourse.
Confronted with an unfamiliar audience, the translator had no recourse
except to try to break through on the terms of his or her audience, which in
effect becomes the first and last resort. In this chapter we shall draw on
examples from a variety of contexts to elucidate the issue. As will be
evident, many of the examples come from the work of Eugene Nida, one of
the foremost linguists in the field. His material is supplemented from other
sources, including personal experience of the present writer.

THE FIELD DIMENSION IN TRANSLATION

Long before anthropology made field work an indispensable part of scientific inquiry, the agents of scriptural translation had blazed trails in that world, making connections that often illuminated hitherto inaccessible worlds of thought and life. Sometimes — perhaps often — the price paid was the committing of gratuitous errors or a blind persistence that elicited completely different responses from what the Bible translator expected. Whatever the case, translators had no way to acquit themselves other than through canons of the local idiom

The story is told of how Bible translators among the Chols of southern Mexico were recounting the sad story of John the Baptist — his arrest and imprisonment by Herod, who eventually had the preacher decapitated and his gory head delivered on a plate. The people broke out in riotous laughter. "They laughed because they felt so sorry for John. At funerals the people do not cry — rather, they express their deep sympathy by laughing heartily so that they will not cry. At times, however, they cry for joy. The translation helper who finally finished the translation of the Gospel of Matthew began to cry as the last verse was completed" (Nida, 1952, p. 39). The present writer can remember from his early childhood hearing a missionary tell the story of John the Baptist in Bakau, the Gambia, where John was referred to as "John the Swimmer," which, considering that the Atlantic Ocean was virtually on the doorstep of people, added a comic impression to the ordinary. In the same context, the missionary in question translated the Prologue of the Gospel of John to mean something like "In the beginning there was palaver, and the palaver was with God, and the palaver was God." When children reported this to their Muslim parents, the reaction was "May God be far removed from such contention," scarcely the intended aim of the missionary.

In some situations the error is committed before the translator has discovered the cultural gap. One translator in Latin America rendered Revelation 13:15, "gave breath to the image," in a way that rendered it as "He made the image stink" (Nida, 1952, p. 43). One missionary in Latin America translated 1 Corinthians 9:5 ("Do we not have the right to be accompanied by a wife?") as "leading around like some unruly animal," "leading a wife around like an ox." Some missionaries in the Sudan, struggling gallantly to translate "Holy Spirit," found themselves speaking of "clean breath," which introduces the incongruous idea of washing, for the people associated cleanliness not with godliness but with washing away dirt. The literal rendering of the Greek *pneuma* stirred a hornet's nest. To the Zanaki people living along the shores of Lake Victoria, translating the sentence "Behold I stand at the door and knock" (Rev. 3:20) implied that Christ was declaring himself to be a thief, for in their culture only thieves make a practice of knocking on doors (to be certain no one is in). "An honest man will come to a house and call the name of the person inside, and in this way identify himself by voice" (Nida, 1952, p. 47). The appropriate translation would, therefore, be, "Behold I stand at the door and call."

A further example of this phenomenon is the experience of one missionary in Central Africa, who thought he was telling the people, "Enter the kingdom of heaven" when in actual fact he was saying, "Go sit on a stick" (Nida, 1952, p. 16). Missionaries in East Africa had been saying, or thought they had been saying, for more than fifty years, "The Lord be with thy spirit," without realizing that they implied "Yes, the Lord be with *your* spirit, for we don't want him." When they discovered this fact, the missionaries protested that they had not been properly guided by their African informants, who replied that Africans had grown used to hearing missionaries say a lot of odd things and had reckoned that this was one more strange utterance of theirs in which all missionaries seemed to concur! In West Africa, missionaries had translated the story of Mary "sitting at the feet of Jesus" into the unwitting sense of Mary sitting "on Jesus' lap." In Liberia, missionary translators had rendered the words "Lead us not into temptation" as "Do not catch us when we sin," a sentiment already appreciated by the Liberians, but now with the added force of scriptural authority.

The Mossi of Burkina Faso (formerly Upper Volta) have no idea of ships or anchor, living as they do on the fringes of the Sahara in the Sahel. To translate literally Hebrews 6:19 to say that God is "a sure and steadfast anchor of the soul" would confound more than it would enlighten. As pastoralists the Mossi are instead more at home in the world of herds and fields. Consequently, it would make more sense to speak of "a strong and steadfast picketing-peg for the soul." The Mossi themselves employ "picketing-peg" as a metaphor in the proverb "A Man does not tie a good horse to a bad picketing-peg" (Nida, 1952, p. 46).

Quite often the translator will find no analogous expressions in the culture. For example, as already noted in a previous chapter, the Eskimos have no lambs, so that in translating for them "Feed my lambs" the translator has a particularly onerous task of representing the sense to an Eskimo. Although seals might be a natural equivalent, in fact seals do not play the same role in Eskimo culture as sheep did among the ancient Hebrews, for seals are hunted whereas sheep are farmed. A similar example occurs among the Shipibos of the Peruvian Amazon, for whom there are no games of chance. Therefore, in translating Mark 15:24, where the soldiers "cast lots" for the garments of Jesus, a thick wall of difficulty intervenes, forcing the translator to resort to allusive devices (Nida, 1952, p. 47).

In one example, a profound cultural reaction was unintentionally provoked by missionaries and they themselves became the focus of its immediate consequences. In a part of West Africa the word for "save" literally meant to "free," and "freeing" had the sense of relief from physical labor. The children who attended missionary schools decided that their being "saved" meant the right not to do any work on the roads or pay government taxes. "Hence, for most people, becoming a Christian and being 'freed' had no spiritual significance. They thought only of political and economic freedom. . . . For years the earnest preaching of consecrated missionaries had fallen on materialistic ears" (Nida, 1952, pp. 47–48). Whatever the soundness of the view that true Christianity is spiritual, it is obvious that translation involves interpretation, and who is to say that a political and economic understanding of the gospel is off the mark?

The cultural factor again comes into play when the Shilluk say "good bad" to mean "very good," something that sounds like a specimen of double-talk until we remember that in American-schoolyard dialect "wicked cool" or "mean" may stand for, according to eleven-year-old Kelefa Sanneh, "very good" or "superb," or how in England "awfully nice" means "extremely nice." On the other hand, a felicitous translation may make an undistinguished part of the Bible shine forth. For the Chols the verse "The way of peace have they not known" (Rom. 3:17) becomes "They have not known the road of the quiet heart" (Nida, 1952, p. 40).

In one Indian language in Mexico, missionaries wanted to translate the idea of the Word being "full of grace and truth" (Jn. 1:14). The word rendered as "grace" was taken to mean "gift of life" or, more literally, "a living gift." However, since the only "living gifts" people exchanged in the culture were chickens, the people understood the phrase to say the Word was "full of chicken and truth" (Nida, 1952, p. 48).

Among the Uduk people living on the Ethiopian border their expression for "worry" and "being troubled" is "shivering in one's liver." For them translating John 14:1 would come out as "Do not shiver in your livers; you believe in God, believe also in me" (Nida, 1952, p. 23). Whereas, for the Navajo Indians, "worry" is expressed by the form "My mind is killing me." To consider another example, for the Cuicatec Indians of Mexico, the word for "worship" comes from the same root as that for a dog wagging its tail, leading to the idea of worship as "wagging the tail before God." It is not the sort of idea we normally associate with "worship" in European usage, suggesting the kind of criticism Karl Marx leveled at Asian religion. However, for the Cuicatec Indians the phrase indicates unwavering loyalty and intimate devotion, which is what "worship" is supposed to be in its highest form.

Such vivid expressions abound in many languages. The Kikwango people speak of "alms" as "gifts of love," while the Barow Eskimos describe a "hymn" as a "song of prayer." The Mazatec people of Mexico speak of miracles as "long-necked things," that is, things that so amaze and arouse people's curiosity that they stretch their necks to see what has happened. The figure of metonymy helps to represent that fact. Among the Shilluk of the Nilotic Sudan, the expression "having a big heart" is used of miserly persons, while its opposite is used for those regarded as generous. It is a cultural paradigm in which it is understood that miserly persons are those who aggrandize things for themselves, storing them away in their hearts.

Consequently, their heart is large. Generous persons, by contrast, acquire a small heart by giving away all that they have. Sometimes indigenous usage may challenge in more sophisticated ways. The Piro Indians, neighbors of the Shipibos, insist that the word for "to believe" is interchangeable with that for "to obey," because to them faith carries the understanding of obedience in action (Nida, 1952, p. 121). A similar idea is contained in the Aztec dialect, which defines "faith" as "following close after." The Valiente Indians speak of "faith" as "catching God in the mind," an expression derived from hunting, where an animal is tracked, located, and "caught," that is, becomes one's possession (Nida, 1952, p. 120).

A central category for translation is the concept "God," and it may happen that both the notion and the name are readily accessible. But where this is not the case, the translator is at a serious disadvantage. For the Valiente Indians of Panama the name for God is a great mystery. When the missionary Efrain Alphonse tried to discover the name, he was taken to see an old medicine woman in the tropical forest of Bocas del Toro. The woman then engaged in a séance, and, in a trancelike state, she pronounced the sacred name of God. "These men," she declared, "are talking about *Ngobo*, the God of heaven and earth. Listen to them!" (Nida, 1952, p. 38). *Ngobo*, falling from the lips of the old diviner, became equally the hallowed name for the God of the Scriptures of the Christians. There is no need to dwell on symbolic significance of Alphonse following the trails of the initiated in order to find and claim *Ngobo* as his God.

To stay awhile with the theme of "God," the Ila of Zambia tell the story of an old woman who went in search of God. She had been afflicted from her youth by God and was determined to succeed in her search. "God" is called *Shikakunamo* ("the Besetting One") by the Ila. The woman built a series of towers to reach God in the sky; however, the timbers rotted before she could reach the heavens, frustrating her efforts. She then set out on a long journey, which proved futile too. In the course of her journey she met people who said to her, "In what do you differ from others? The Besetting One sits on the back of every one of us, and we cannot shake him off!" The women died, heartbroken, and her problem, according to the Ila, remains unsolved to this day (Smith and Dale, 1920, I: 197–198; cf. Mbiti, 1982, p. 13).

That Ila story makes three crucial points: God eludes firm human grasp; the religious will is undeterred by natural obstacles; and ultimately God is One with whom we have always to do, for "he sits on the back of every one of us, and we cannot shake him off." It suggests that the finishing point of the quest is also the starting point, so that genuine faith rests on religious coherence.

Another variation on the concept of God is the reference by an Xhosa poet to God as an *ingubo,* a sheepskin mantle in which one wraps oneself on a chilly evening. The idea is echoed by the psalmist's cry, "Thou, O Lord, are a shield about me" (Ps. 3:3; cf. 28:7; 33:20; 115:9; Prov. 3:5). A Sotho poet employs a term that blends endearment with intimacy by talking of

"God of the dewy nose," a reference to the value that the culture attaches to cattle.

Such cultural presuppositions lie behind the work of translation. For example, the Valiente Indians speak of people in authority as "those on the handle," a concept they use in translating Mark 11:28: "By what authority do you do these things?" as "What people on the handle told you to do these things?" (Nida, 1952, p. 19). The Valientes think of their ruler as one who holds the handle of the hunting knife in his hand, while others, in comparison, could only grasp the "blade" of disadvantage. Thus by the device of transferred epithet, the ruler is one who is "on the handle." To take a different example, the idea of "hope in God" is expressed by the phrase "resting the mind in God."

For the Gbeapo people of Liberia the word for a prophet of the Bible is "God's town-crier," who is the official mouthpiece of the chief. As such he is more readily acceptable as God's spokesman, whereas words like "diviner" and "soothsayer" carry such odors of sorcery as to distort the biblical intention.

For the Karre people of Equatorial Africa the Paraclete, or Comforter, of John's Gospel is understood as "one who falls down beside you," that is, the one who accompanies, protects, and sustains people on their journey, just as in Karre country a helper accompanies the traveler through hard and dangerous bush (Nida, 1952, p. 21).

There is no end to such a catalogue but, to taste the sea, one draught is enough. The principle of the translatability of Christianity has brought missionaries into some very rough waters indeed. Dr. Livingstone had warned his Western colleagues that the languages of so-called primitive peoples are full of unsuspecting subtleties, and no amount of prior training can prepare them for what will confront them in the field. The point is clear. Any Western missionary would be unprepared for a language such as Zulu, which has 120 different words to describe distinct kinds of walking, or for the Malagasy language where native speakers distinguish more than 200 different kinds of noises or differentiate over 100 different colors (Nida, 1952, p. 16). To pile an even more complex layer on the scale of difficulty, in the "Quechua language of Bolivia it is possible to take almost any verb root and add more than 50,000 combinations of at least twenty sets of suffixes and particles which combine to make up these complicated forms" (Nida, 1952, p. 16).

PHILOSOPHICAL ASSUMPTIONS OF TRANSLATION

In his masterly account of the scientific basis of translation, Eugene Nida has articulated the philosophical premise upon which translation proceeds, but one about which practicing translators may not, and need not, always be conscious. We have in numerous parts of this book called attention to the fact that translatability assumes, and often proves, that culture is only an instrumental means at our disposal rather than an end within a self-reinforcing normative scheme. Linguistic philosophy, especially in the hands of writers like Willard V. Quine, Ernst Cassirer, and Ludwig Wittgenstein, has sought to establish the symbolic value of language (Nida, 1964, pp. 5–7). Bible translating may be considered the applied dimension of this view. Language is a verbal symbol of instrumental power, rather than the locus of things and classes (Nida, 1964, pp. 47–56). As such, no one linguistic maneuver is inherently superior to another, and all language use is conditioned by its special context. For example, to take one principle of Wittgenstein's: if we recognize that knowing something rests intimately on "seeing as," with some sort of appeal to familiarity, then clearly language use is freed from fixed, immutable criteria of meaning. Nevertheless, Wittgenstein may be making too much of a good idea when he asserts that "historical proof is irrelevant to belief," if he implies that faith is necessarily impermeable by historical veracity. This is not the same as saying that religious zeal may owe nothing to the true facts of history (Wittgenstein, 1980, p. 32).

Such an idea may have been present to the mind of the Catholic bishop of Enugu, Nigeria, the Most Rev. Dr. Godfrey Okoye, when he addressed the Society for the Promotion of Igbo Language and Culture in 1973.[1] He called into question the desirability of literalism in translation, saying it is not helpful to lift words from the Greek or Latin and implant them into Igbo. Instead, he appealed for flexibility and freedom to represent ideas and things, and in the special case of Igbo and its many dialects, he counseled action on the lines of the controversial Union Ibo language project, saying a good Igbo translation should help to unite the different dialects and thus lay the basis for a sense of Igbo national unity (Ogharaerumi, 1987, pp. 380–81).

This writer can remember from his youth how, when an airplane first appeared in the hinterland of Gambia, an excited lad gave it the name "up boat," which, in the native language, also carries the descriptive name "flying boat"; or how even today in the Mandinka language a bicycle is called "a rubber horse," suggesting the freedom with which people adapt and assign symbols. In a different instance, the word for "song" means, literally, "the egg of a dance," with the assumption that rhythmic bodily movement is incubated in vocal music until dance appropriately "hatches" from it. In practical terms, missionaries became the agents of such cultural incubation of Christianity by exposing the message to new climates, believing that cultural differences, however deep and ancient, could not constitute an impenetrable barrier against cross-cultural exchange. On the contrary, translatability makes of cultural differences its best argument.

THE FACTOR OF RECIPIENCY

A necessary precondition for effective translation is the surrender to the terms of the receptor culture, whatever exalted notions the translator may have about faithfulness to the original forms. As Nida put it, a "translation must conform to the grammatical tradition of the language (whether this is formulated in textbooks or passed on by the oral tradition of usage), but in any case a translation in order to be effective must represent the way people speak" (Nida, 1952, p. 34). This commitment to the fresh linguistic context may work itself out in terms of greater involvement in the culture so as to establish old connections and correspondences and retrieve lost or hidden meanings. "The translator's objective is to discover with the aid of his collaborators those intimate resources of spiritual experience which are revealed in meaningful language. In his search for these rich lexical treasures he experiences some of the most thrilling aspects of his work" (Nida, 1952, pp. 39–40).

It is hard to exaggerate the importance of "recipiency" in determining what is or what is not a successful translation. One example makes this clear. When the Gospels and the book of Acts were translated into Aymara, the language of Indians in the highlands of Peru and Bolivia, some native experts pointed out the wooden quality of the translation, suggesting major and extensive revisions to bring it more into line with the language of the villages. Against some opposition, these experts pressed for a more natural translation, and apart from their resolve, there was the additional evidence that "the awkward literalism was the reason why people . . . in the congregation used to go off to sleep during the reading of the Scripture . . ." (Nida, 1952, p. 112). Thus the recipients of the message established by their active and passive response that the rules of success were founded on local principles. In the end, the committee responsible for the translation yielded to the criticism and allowed native experts to do the job. The operative criterion in translating was that the thoughts were to be the thoughts as expressed in Spanish, "but the language was to be in every way their own mother tongue" (Nida, 1952, p. 112). That "mother tongue" was to be the language of everyday speech. The result was predictable, expressed by the testimony that because of the successful translation, "it is as though Jesus Christ were living in our villages" (Nida, 1952, p. 114).

This identification of message and setting was brought about by a true translation. Where it was achieved it led to intriguing examples of reversal (or interchange) of cultural values. One Swedish missionary in South Africa was told, as a farewell appreciation, that though his skin was white, "his heart is as black as any of us" (Nida, 1952, p. 117). Such a remark is the unfamiliar lefthand of what we are more familiar with as the quibble of missionaries that, if educated converts assimilate too much to Western culture, then their "black" skins cease to be an indication for their indigenous effectiveness, a quibble that we see as tending to racism. Without denying that racist charge entirely, we should nevertheless examine the view in terms of the "recipiency" and, more to the point, "reciprocity" model. In this matter, too, race, like language, becomes an arbitrary, interchangeable cultural value, which readily shifts with our experience.

NOTION AND RELATIVE VALUE OF CULTURE AND
LANGUAGE

Translation is primarily a matter of language, but it is not only that, for language itself is a living expression of culture. Lexical resources must be deepened with the force of usage, custom, and tradition in order to become meaningful, particularly if we want to represent the dynamic quality of life. Language is not just the "soul" of a people, as if it belongs to some sort of elite gnostic circle. Language is also the garment that gives shape, decorum, and vitality to conscious life, enabling us to appreciate the visible texture of life in its subtle, intricate variety and possibility.

The effort of scriptural translators to come as close as possible to the speech of ordinary, everyday life is a remarkable example of their confidence that the profoundest spiritual truths are compatible with commonplace words, ideas, and concepts. In this regard, when the missionary Efrain Alphonse plunged into the Panamanian forest to discover at the secret shrine of an old diviner the true name for God, he was at the same time lifting God to the level of everyday usage. He had consummated a genuine religious development. At the time of his arrival, the shrine cult had moved out of daily life to the margins of settled living. The number of people competent to speak authoritatively about it had dwindled, leaving only a frail diviner to guard its fragile memory in a shadowy grove. The missionary entered the scene to rescue a suppressed religion, not, of course, in its entirety but in its positive tendencies. It is as if he had picked up the dying torch in a relay race and ignited it with common applause. Those who henceforth want to discover the real power of the true name for God, including its underlying idea of accessible human community, must seek it in the open arena of the Christian setting.

Thus, providing written, documentary resources for cultures that previously lacked these or taking those resources and recasting them from an esoteric system into a popular medium represents the kind of "divulging of secrets" (Mk. 4:22) necessary in successful translation. There are, of course, some intractable problems with such translation, for it may happen that a given culture has at its heart a closed esoteric system with which its survival is bound. This would predispose it against the values of openness and cross-cultural exchange, thus posing a massive barrier against inquiry with other traditions on an equal footing. On the other hand, such innovative translation may set the stage for a trickle-down effect on the rest of society, producing a new level of consciousness, sometimes without a corresponding predisposition toward the church, as happened in Japan and China.

It may be this idea that Nida picks up in his impatience with elitist survivals in culture. He writes in one place:

What is one to do in a language where the religious vocabulary is borrowed entirely from Pali, a derivative of ancient Sanskrit and the language of the Buddhist priesthood? Such words are sanctioned through time and usage by those regarded as the religious leaders, but these words are often almost as meaningless to the common people as the Latin mass is to many English-speaking people. The words may "smell of holiness," but they do not instruct men in holiness. So strong has been the hold of literary tongues and religious vocabularies upon the people of the Orient that only very slowly has this chain of tradition been broken here and there. [Nida, 1952, p. 23.]

At the center of the issue is the contention that if we define culture as all learned behavior, which is socially acquired and passed from one generation to the next, then "there are no cultures which are so isolated and restricted by their environment that the people could not do something different from what they are doing" (Nida, 1954, p. 39).

Culture as an organic whole is greater than the sum total of its parts, those parts being material, social, and religious, with language as the "system of symbolization for its explicit parts" (Nida, 1954, p. 40). Culture is transmissible and accumulative, and religious culture, especially, depends on critical appropriation for its continuing integrity. The religious ferment works within culture to create a moral transparency: using ordinary language to signify the things of the spirit, and conversely, seeing eternal truths as destined for human adoption. The scholars of the Enlightenment had defended translation on the grounds that all languages obeyed the same laws of reason, so that the diversity of idioms merely concealed a uniformity of meanings, which translation perpetuated. For this reason a universal grammar was possible, a grammar that would unite and explicate the bewildering plurality of languages. In religious translation, however, the operative assumption was a theological notion that a universal God had seen fit to apportion the human family in the diversity of nations (Acts 17:26) in preparation for the establishment of the true kingdom (Dan. 7:14). Our very differences, now safeguarded by religious sanction, demand translation. The twentieth-century heirs to the Enlightenment for their part may argue the opposite, namely, that our differences vitiate the translation enterprise, with language in their view being inextricably bound up with cultural particularity. This is cultural absolutism rather than cultural relativism.

For this reason we might say that humanistic culture, in both its traditional and modern secular forms, tends to resist change, with communities inclined to venerate national monuments such as war memorials, national holidays, national constitutions, and military hardware as sacred symbols charged with fixed, unvarying meanings. They become the locus of power and have available to them appropriate systems of ritual. In such an atmosphere uniformity is the preponderant instrument, conformity and submission the chief virtues, and translation a betrayal. By contrast, Christian translation work rests on the inclusive principle of the religion of Jesus. The religious spirit, which begins with discerning the things of God in the human spirit, develops into the plurality of views about the earthly arrangements proper and necessary for human fulfillment. The religious community helps to telescope the due proportions of the larger community. The minority thus concentrates the tendencies that in the majority find vent in the diffuse criss-cross of individual pursuit. The ordinariness of religious language and the common purpose around which believers gather are significant for what promotes and defines the worthwhileness and wholesomeness of human solidarity. That we understand what Scripture says, and in a language common to all, is a principle also for authentic human community. Religious participation belongs with social and political participation.

Essentially culture is a human enterprise, and whether we are dealing with so-called high culture in architecture, the arts, literature, music, painting, poetry, and technology or with class, clothing, food, gender, language, and nationality or race, it is the human factor that all these have in common. It is even tempting to say that without us none of these things would be, although even that speculative sentiment is a function of being human.

This creates a pluralist environment of incredible variety and possibility, and invests it from the Christian perspective with an ethical, qualitative purpose. That purpose may be defined as the capacity to participate in intercultural and interpersonal exchange, as the recognition that whatever and however we are doing now, we can do differently and, under certain circumstances, we must do differently in order to live ethically.

The missionary application of this principle in non-Western societies was of enormous significance for the coming into being of a world community in which the parts, in living tension with the aggregate whole, contextualize the universal truth of our equal, not to say mutual, proximity to one another and to God. This kind of pluralism is founded on a radical principle, what Nida has called "relative relativism" (Nida, 1954, p. 50) in which the human, the religious, and the cultural are held in dynamic tension rather than in absolutized fragments. Such radicalism rejects what was once fashionable in anthropological circles as "cultural relativism" where cultural practices among "primitives," such as rules for disposing of noneconomic members of the community or for dispensing with sexual restrictions, were deemed adoptable elsewhere in' the West. Such facile transpositions are flawed by the logic of pluralism, which conceives practices, and the norms for changing them, as explicable by the terms of the cultures within which these things originated. To assume a universal applicability for particular cultural practices is to sunder them from the roots that gave them life; and those roots, of course, were what translation sought to preserve and perpetuate. Similarly, to confine particular cultures to the societies in which they are found without the possibility of a wider community of sharing is to encourage absolutizing tendencies in those cultures.

The contention by critics that mission is an unwarranted interference in other cultures is a sensitive charge and deserves careful consideration. Nevertheless, it seems to be rooted in an absolute principle, which imposes a view on the cultures affected. It denies the possibility of genuine cultural exchange and, beyond that, it seals culture from the possibility of change. It is too extreme a position to adopt, recognizing neither the principle of religious autonomy nor that of cultural development stemming from internal and external stimuli. Enough has been said to suggest that even when it was blatant cultural interference, mission excited sufficient vernacular initiative to commence a critical appropriation process. In any case, critics should also be sensitive to the nuances of the vernacular appropriation of Christianity, recognizing, for example, that missionaries were often active agents of that process.

The sort of radical pluralism represented by translatability promotes cultural particularity while affirming in God its relativizing universal. To take the matter at its most extreme, that strand of the missionary enterprise that adhered to the *sola-scriptura* principle of the sixteenth-century reformers saw the Bible as the primary rule of faith. That in turn led to making the Bible in its translated form the chief object of missionary endeavor. Two important consequences followed: first, the vernacular acquired the significance of a revelatory medium, becoming more than an autonomous linguistic device (though that was important), but also carrying the implication that God was at work in that medium. Second, the *sola-scriptura* principle resulted in uncoupling the Bible from the tradition of Western commentaries, and thus from an important source of Western cultural and intellectual values. We could say, therefore, that the biblicism of Protestant missions helped to suppress the transmission of Western cultural presuppositions to indigenous societies. The objection of some Western missionaries that such biblicism encouraged blockheaded fundamentalism is in part a recognition of the power of the vernacular Scriptures to force a serious reckoning on the whole matter of gospel and culture, and to do this without the controls of the Western church. Obviously excesses will be committed, but they will be indigenous excesses rather than Western ones.

It follows from this that radical pluralism is radical in the boldness with which the word of God is assumed to have a vernacular form, and pluralist in denying to any one language an exclusive claim in the "plan of salvation." It is one of the interesting ironies of the Western missionary enterprise that the evangelical motive actually helped to shield indigenous populations from the unmitigated assault of the West and that, through the elevation of the vernacular in translation, missions furnished the critical language for evaluating the West in its secular and religious impact. In attempting to understand the full implications of this historical irony it would be necessary to turn to theology and explore the subject in terms of the *missio Dei*, God's mission, as a movement in which missionaries certainly played a part, but one also in which vernacular factors, including indigenous agents, participated fully. When that theological analysis has been done, it will be found that mission is more than the story of particular Western missionaries and their immensely complex motives. It is also the story, as missionaries understood it, of the forward thrust of God's kingdom, a tripartite endeavor in which the Western motif is a minority and often fragile strand within the extraordinary tapestry of vernacular languages and cultures upon which God's favor rests. From across the barriers of cultural blindness or intransigence, we can hear in the historical record of mission an echo of the psalmist's song, "Surely, the wrath of men shall praise thee; the residue of wrath thou wilt gird upon thee" (Ps. 76:10).

To return to matters of language, we noted above that in the Mandinka language the name for bicycle is "rubber horse," pointing out how linguistic symbols are freely and interchangeably assigned. That same imaginativeness led an African, riding on a dirt road, to dismount from his bicycle with a flat tire, remove the inner tube, and stuff the tire with straw gathered from the surounding bush. He was thus able to continue his journey after a piece of ingenious "translation" into the context of his environment.

Mobility is in this respect a good metaphor for translatability. Cultural symbols are regenerated from usage and new applications. Among a group of Africans it is considered bad luck for a crawling child to step on the tracks of a crawling creature, such as a snake. The belief is that by the contagious force of that contact, the child would be reduced to a "crawl" long after it was supposed to walk. Now to show that "creatures that move along the ground" is a concept whose "message" may be readily transferred, the same people operate a law of opposites, which says that if a crawling child is placed in the hot tracks of a motor vehicle, which the colonial administration had introduced in the area, then the child's development will correspondingly be "speeded up" — with the result that enterprising mothers rushed with their children to meet passing vehicles, to the alarm of unsuspecting drivers. Thus in both cases contagious contact is believed to carry potency by a sympathetic force.

This writer can recall crowded scenes at Kotoka International Airport in Accra where pilgrims bound for Mecca surrounded a jetliner with ablution kettles in hand, dousing the airplane with ritual water to purify it for the sacred journey. It may sound quaint, but it is in fact the mirror image of Dr. Livingstone's determination to demonstrate to the rainmaker how the latter's exploiting of coincidence to maintain his practice was fraudulent (see p. 163 above), which led some zealous missionaries to scurry around with steaming kettles and pieces of glass to show how condensation causes rain. As far as the traveling pilgrims were concerned, anyone familiar with the religious potency of the *qiblah*, the direction of Mecca for the mandatory five daily prayers of Islam, will appreciate the significance of the symbolic transformation taking place on the tarmac. A strange, unfamiliar technological invention was reduced to the familiar terms of religious devotion and practice, and in that form used like a canal that discharges only what it receives. Whether it is the bicycle with a flat tire, crawling snakes, speeding motor vehicles, or chartered jetliners, there is a fluid exchange of symbolic values going on, of the sort that enabled translators to move with confidence, if sometimes with not much competence, in both familiar and unfamiliar fields. Such religious entrepreneurs believed that no cultural frontier was distant or alien enough in principle to remain inaccessible, an article of faith, it turns out, which is of a piece with the intrinsic value of culture as symbolic. It was this radical faith that brought such a bewildering variety of cultures within the massive arc of the modern Christian movement.

The translators in the Christian tradition, then, assumed that God's universal truth was the reasonable guarantee and safeguard for responsible pluralism. Bible translators believed that in Jesus Christ was to be found the message of salvation, a message that was expected to cohere in the vernacular. Thus they expected the vernacular to be the congenial locus for the word of God, the eternal *logos* who finds familiar shelter across all cultures, but one also by which and in which all cultures find their authentic, true destiny. Jesus Christ was assumed to be universally accessible through the medium of particular vernacular cultures, so that universality might propagate the spirit of unity without demanding cultural conformity for its real efficacy. We must separate this from a popular misconception that translation is possible only because there is something intrinsic about the nature of language as divine. Rather, translation, particularly in its Christian form, stripped language of its inert, fixed power and invested it with a potential for mutuality. Linguistic variety was not, for missionaries, a religious problem but, rather, a vocational challenge that often resulted in cultural self-criticism. When missionaries could not adequately translate a Western cultural notion, they encountered in that difficulty the issue of radical pluralism, of how dispensable in the Christian scheme Western culture was to indigenous appropriation.

In a perceptive essay, the Mexican writer Octavio Paz puts his finger on the cross-cultural implications of translation. After observing that translation is ultimately an impossible task, he moderates that view with an acknowledgment that "the change demanded of us by the passage from one civilization to another is tantamount to a genuine conversion" (Paz, 1987). The theological issue that Octavio Paz says persists through all translation appears at its sharpest in Christianity, where linguistic translation necessarily overflows into religious practice and custom, and that in turn pits the indigenous custodians against the new Christian functionaries. It would bring consistency into the discussion to acknowledge that not only local populations but also missionaries are caught in the tide of change and conversion. When Octavio Paz, in his essay, describes how the Pygmies overcame their natural shyness and gathered round a wireless set without understanding the news about the first Soviet journey into outer space, and how eventually, alarmed at the voice of Edith Piaf from the phonograph, they took to their heels, he is describing a context that Bible translators took special care to avoid. It holds little hope for achieving a durable Christian presence. It is a context defined by curiosity and the tenuous gestures of strangers, not by familiarity and the assurance of long residence.[2]

In fact the missionary endeavor among the Pygmies and adjacent peoples has helped to affirm their particularity by uncovering linguistic and cultural details for transposition into Christian terms. From 1737, when George Schmidt, the Moravian missionary, set to work among the Bushmen, to 1857, when Dr. Livingstone tried to educate Africans out of superstition, missionaries have been notable for their ethnographic and similar achievements, whatever their cultural ideals and religious motives. Local converts appreciated at once the significance of indigenous languages and cultures for the new Christian enterprise. Their perception of what was good in the changes happening around them was rooted in an appreciation for their own languages and cultures, something that Christian translation assured them.

Whatever the attitudes of Bible translators, they began something that changed the world. Once they introduced vernacular literacy, translators could not turn back the clock or pretend that things would remain the same. The genie was out of the bottle. The disputes and controversies that have followed Bible translation, while often regrettable, nevertheless show that translators were themselves often at the mercy of the forces they unwittingly unleashed. Yet we may find that fact doubly assuring, for it proves, for one thing, that translatability acquired a life of its own, which translators could not control; and, in any case, had they been able to control it, we would still have accused them of political domination. For the other, vernacular translation might have excited local activism bordering on excess, although here the prophetic impulse might in response be stirred. In either case, both translators and the recipient cultures would be denied that absolute triumph, which, if it were possible, would instigate cultural absolutization. We have seen that such an outcome conflicts with what we understand by translatability.

Historians of religion have the opportunity to observe in translatability something both unique and general, and in doing so to resist defining or judging it by motives alone, or by the rules of church history, where doctrinal development is seen as the expression of ideas in the mind of God. Translatability ushered in a revolution in both the religious and the cultural spheres, and perhaps because translation touched on so many areas of life at once, its very wide-ranging effects have left it without a specific domain of its own. In spite of that, translation is a catalyst of major proportions.

Translation touches on the vitality of language and much of what hinges on language. To take full account of the role of Christian missions in the process of language use, we need to go beyond the narrow sphere of vernacular Bible use. We need also to look at the ancillary linguistic and cultural projects of compiling grammars, dictionaries, vocabularies, primers, and comparative lexicons, and of instituting orthographies and vernacular alphabets. Missionaries were directly involved in all these areas, both as pioneers and as users. Such linguistic work often set the standard for rigorous investigations in anthropology, historical research, linguistics, customary law, primal religions, musicology, and other fields. Consequently, the narrow scope of religion is inadequate to define the range of issues with which missions concerned themselves.

The history of missions, therefore, is more than the account of organizing the missionary effort in Europe and North America, important as that may be. It is also about actual reception and operation in the field where the richness of detail makes the question of the missionaries' alleged cultural motives somewhat peripheral. If we accept this shift of focus and follow the missionary story to the receiving societies, then it makes sense that scholars who propose to expound the missionary theme should pay attention to the indigenous factor. Looked at in this light, we may say that today a vexing discrepancy exists between the concrete practice of mission and the weighty books that purport to descirbe the history of mission.

The whole question of motives has set on edge the teeth of historians, and scholars in general have found irresistible the prickly stigma that has attached to mission. The subject is hard to digest, but easy fare to put down. An apocryphal story makes the point well. A visiting party had arrived in a bush village to learn of the sad fate of a missionary who had died of cannibalism. His enemies had contracted dysentery as a consequence, and this suggestion of retributive justice did not escape the attention of the visiting party. The leader confronted the village chief, rebuking him with the observation that the villagers' plight was proof that no one could keep down a good man. The chief retorted with a double entendre, saying that he and his people also served their fellow man. In many instances, missionary motives came to similar grief, with local populations responding from vernacular stimulus.

Scholars may thus further the cause if they reject the victim view of mission as too simplistic, and instead come to grips with the subject in its field dimension. That missionaries victimized and were in turn victimized might be sensational news, but it does not finally tell us much of historical significance, unless we set that in context. As soon as we take that step and get past the lightheadedness of cross-cultural misunderstanding, a different world meets our view, with much in it to amuse us, naturally, but much also to instruct and inspire.

A rich and challenging field is now open to us with translatability as a theme in the history of religion and culture. As we saw in the preceding chapter, altogether scriptural translation has been undertaken in 1,808 of the world's languages, with Africa accounting for 522 of these languages. It is instructive that cultural creativity in much of Africa and elsewhere coincides almost exactly with developed interest in the vernacular and with a willingness to do things differently from the way they have been done. As a force, translatability endows persons and societies with the reason for change and the language with which to effect it.

SUMMARY AND CONCLUSION

The main arguments of this chapter may be set out as follows. First, vernacular translation begins with the effort to equip the gospel with terms of familiarity, and that process brings the missionary enterprise into the context of field experience. Second, certain pitfalls are unavoidable in trying to master the vernacular, including the adoption of terms and concepts that may be strange to the translator. This shows the important need for an intimate grasp of vernacular usage and concepts. Third, in endeavoring to accomplish this vernacular task, translation may make commonplace passages of Scripture come alive, while also stimulating indigenous religious and cultural renewal. Fourth, for the purposes of scriptural translation, language may therefore be regarded as instrumental in function and contextual in character, with Christian mission helping thus to strengthen vernacular languages in their diverse particularity and enormous multiplicity. Such confidence in the value of the vernacular has encouraged the role of recipient cultures as decisive for the final appropriation of the message. Fifth, the internal developments that generally follow from the promotion of the vernacular have included the anti-elitist popular impulse of ordinary usage, the consequences for society of the open and public nature of religious faith and organization, the premium that missionary translation places on pluralism in language and culture, and the political ramifications of the importance Christians attach to free and equal access to the things of God.

This way of underding the matter implies a reappraisal of the issue of missionary interference in other cultures, which may partly be resolved by taking into account vernacular primacy in translation. It can be argued that mission is fundamentally consistent with indigenous cultural integrity, especially when we view mission as the *missio Dei*. There is a radical pluralism implied in vernacular translation wherein all languages and cultures are, in principle, equal in expressing the word of God. In this regard, the biblicism of extreme Protestantism, inherited from the reformers of *sola scriptura*, relegated Western theological commentaries to a peripheral place in translation, thus suppressing in the mission field an important source of the diffusion of Western cultural and intellectual values. By that procedure, such missionaries acted to shield indigenous cultures from Western religious and intellectual dominance. Equally important, such stress on the Bible as alone sufficient to effect God's purpose conferred on the vernacular an autonomous, consecrated status as the medium of God's word, a consecration often more in tune with indigenous attitudes toward language than the attitudes of missionaries toward their own culture.

Two general ideas stem from this analysis. First is the inclusive principle whereby no culture is excluded from the Christian dispensation or even judged solely or ultimately by Western cultural criteria. Second is the ethical principle of change as a check to cultural self-absolutization. Both of these ideas are rooted in what missionaries understood by God's universal truth as this was revealed in Jesus Christ, with the need and duty to work out this fact in the vernacular medium rather than in the uniform framework of cultural homogeneity. This introduces in mission the *logos* concept wherein any and all languages may confidently be adopted for God's word, a step that allows missionaries and local agents to collaborate, if sometimes unevenly, in the *missio Dei*. Doing the history of mission is enunciating the concrete facts of the inner workings of this theological dynamic. Consequently, translatability, still an insufficiently studied theme, is of immense fruitful potential for the historian of religion.

NOTES

1. On the whole question of the attitude of the Catholic Mission to the vernacular, the reader should consult Nicholas Omenka, 1986, pp. 121–37.

2. It is interesting to reflect that because of Christian interest in the culture of the Pygmies we have knowledge of a Pygmy hymn about God, *Kmvoum*, as a "word which comes out of your mouth. . . . It is past, and still it lives! So is God" (Young, 1940, p. 146).

SELECT BIBLIOGRAPHY

Belloc, Hilaire. 1932. *On Translating.* Oxford: Clarendon Press.

Donovan, Vincent A. 1978. *Christianity Rediscovered.* Maryknoll, N.Y.: Orbis Books.

Livingstone, David. 1857. *Missionary Travels and Researches in Central Africa.* London: John Murray.

Mbiti, John S. 1982. *Concepts of God in Africa.* London: SPCK.

Needham, Rodney. 1979. *Belief, Language and Culture.* Oxford: Basil Blackwell.

Nida, Eugene A. 1952. *God's Word in Man's Language.* New York: Harper and Brothers.

———. 1954. *Customs and Cultures: Anthropology for Christian Missions.* New York: Harper and Brothers.

———. 1960. *Message and Mission.* New York: Harper and Brothers.

———. 1964. *Towards a Science of Translating: With Special Reference to Principles and Procedures Involved in Bible Translating.* Leiden: E. J. Brill.

Nida, Eugene A., and William D. Reyburn. 1981. *Meaning Across Cultures.* Maryknoll, N.Y.: Orbis Books.

Ogharaerumi, Mark Onesosan. 1987. "The Translation of the Bible into Yoruba, Igbo and Isekiri Languages of Nigeria, with Special Reference to the Contribution of Mother Tongue Speakers." Unpublished Ph.D. dissertation, University of Aberdeen, Scotland.

Omenka, Nicholas. 1986. "The Role of the Catholic Mission in the Development of

Vernacular Literature in Eastern Nigeria." *Journal of Religion in Africa* 16, no. 2.

Paz, Octavio. 1987. "Edith Piaf among the Pygmies." *New York Times Book Review* (September 6).

Rieu, E. V. 1952. *The Four Gospels.* Harmondsworth, England: Penguin Books.

Smith, Edwin W., and A. M. Dale. 1920. *The Ila Speaking Peoples of Northern Rhodesia*, 2 vols. London: Macmillan.

Smith, Wilfred Cantwell. "On Mistranslated Book Titles," *Religious Studies,* vol. 20, 27–42.

Wittgenstein, Ludwig. 1980. *Culture and Value.* Ed. G. E. von Wright, trans. P. Winch. London: Oxford University Press.

Young, T. A. 1940. *Contemporary Ancestors.* London.

7

Translatability in Islam and Christianity, with Special Reference to Africa: Recapitulating the Theme

Christianity had had the fortune of later architects of genius; and in its passage through time and clime had suffered sea-changes incomparably greater than the unchanging Jewry, from the abstraction of Alexandrian bookishness into Latin prose, for the mainland of Europe: and last most terrible passing of all, when it became Teuton, with a formal synthesis to suit our chilly disputatious north. . . .

Islam, too, had inevitably changed from continent to continent. It had avoided metaphysics, except in the introspective mysticism of Iranian devotees. . . . In Arabia, however, it had kept a Semitic character, or rather the Semitic character had endured through the phase of Islam . . . expressing the monotheism of open spaces, the pass-through-infinity of pantheism and its everyday usefulness of an all-pervading, household God. [Lawrence, 1962, p. 365.]

There are striking differences between Islam and Christianity in spite of their common missionary ambition, yet nothing is more fundamental than their contrasting attitudes to the translatability of their respective Scriptures. Scriptural translation, we have said, is the vintage mark of Christianity, whereas for Islam universal adherence to a nontranslatable Arabic Qur'ān remains its characteristic feature. This has major implications for how we view mission and pluralism in the two traditions, as well as for the nature and purpose of conversion. It is in this context that we should clarify "reform," "renewal," and "revival."

THE ISLAMIC PARADIGM

In several parts of this book passing references have been made to Islam as a contrasting case to Christianity, with the argument that the Islamic paradigm operates upon culture in a different way from the Christian instance, and that cultural diversity belongs with Christian affirmation in a way that it does not with Islam. For the sake of coherence, let us now formulate this Islamic paradigm in a sketchy way before we consider local contexts where the principle of translatability, or, in this instance, nontranslatability, was applied. The subject is too vast and complicated to treat satisfactorily in a concluding chapter, but it impinges so closely on the theme of the book that even a cursory exposition may be justified.

Muslims ascribe to Arabic the status of a revealed language, for it is the medium in which the Qur'ān, the sacred Scripture of Islam, was revealed. In several passages the Qur'ān bears testimony to its own Arabic uniqueness, what the authorities call its *i'jāz*, or "inimitable eloquence" (see Qur'ān 10:38–39; 11:1–2, 16; 16:104–5; 28:49; 39:24, 29; 41:41–42; 43: 1–3). The author of the Qur'ān, who is God, thus came to be associated with its speech, so that the very sounds of the language are believed to originate in heaven (see Guillaume, 1956, p. 74; Gibb, 1963, pp. 36–37). Consequently, Muslims have instituted the sacred Arabic for the canonical devotions. Given the lay character of Islam, these canonical devotions have brought the sacred Arabic to the level of the ordinary believer, although normally it is religious specialists who understand the language in any satisfactory fashion (Grunebaum, 1962, pp. 37–59).

The active participation of lay Muslims in the ritual acts of worship (*ṣalāt*), fasting (*ṣawm*) and, less frequently, the pilgrimage(*hajj*) to Mecca means that Arabic phrases, however imperfectly understood, remain on the lips of believers wherever and whoever they happen to be. In thinly or unevenly Islamized areas, the natural imperfections arising from the obligation to employ the sacred Arabic provide the motivation for reforming local practice, rather than yielding to indigenous forms.

An intriguing situation arises in which the prestigious and revered status of Arabic acts to disfranchise the vernacular. Mother-tongue speakers find themselves in the anomalous position of conceding that their languages are "profane" or "mundane" (*'ajamī*) for the decisive acts of the religious code, a concession that bears little relationship to one's fluency in Arabic. In fact, both the expert Arabist and the illiterate convert share a common veneration for the sacred language, with the knowledge of the expert being the standard toward which the convert aspires or, at any rate, the rule to which he or she concedes prescriptive authority.

One example may suffice for what is a rich topic. There was once a public controversy at the Great Mosque, Madras, where the issue of Arabic as indispensable for the established rites came to the fore. A Muslim scholar had decided that for those Muslims for whom Arabic was an obstacle, it was necessary to substitute Hindi rather than have them perform the rites in an unfamiliar language. Accordingly, he instituted Hindi for prayers in the mosque, translating portions of the Qur'ān to this end. This provoked a strong response from the *'ulamā*, leading to the promulgation of a *fatwa*, authoritative legal opinion, condemning the practice in the strongest possible terms. The scholar in question was described as "an infidel, an atheist, and a wanderer from the truth. He also causes others to wander." (Sell, 1907, p. 349). In its defense, the *fatwa* cites the opinions of the Four Orthodox Imāms—Shāfi'ī,—Mālik, Hanbal and Ḥanafī—all of whom place a ban on the use of vernacular in *ṣalāt*. The legal opinions cited refer specifically to Persian as "unlawful" for translation, the Madrasi *'ulamā* extending this by analogy (*qiyās*) to the vernacular question in general. Such an inflexible position on the indispensability of the Arabic Qur'ān excited the following comment. Islam may be considered a lenient, even lax, religion on many matters, yet for the advocate of the vernacular "to approach God in prayer through the medium of his mother tongue was an offence so great that he could only be regarded as an outcast" (Sell, 1907, p. 352).

The success of Islam as a missionary religion is founded upon the perpetuation of the sacred Arabic. As the religion arrived among what has become preponderantly non-Arab populations, its appeal was closely bound up with the authority of its sacred Scriptures in Arabic, and often non-Muslim populations may appropriate Qur'ānic phrases long before they convert to Islam. There is in fact an old tradition of venerating the sacred script by non-Muslims. For example, there is the "Veil of St. Anne," which is kept in a fifteenth-century Venetian bottle in the church of Apt, Vaucluse, France. In fact the "holy" relic is an Arabic inscription containing the Shahādah, the Muslim creed, as well as the names of the Fāṭimid caliph, al-Musta'lī (reigned 1094–1101) and his prime minister, Afḍal, with an indication that the textile was woven in Egypt in 1096–97 (Schacht and Bosworth,1974, p.298). The characteristic missionary institution of Islam is the Qur'ān school where little boys and girls memorize passages of the sacred book in Arabic. That, rather than scriptural translation, has been the mode of Islam's expansion through sub-Saharan Africa and elsewhere.

It is important to separate this matter from the question of adopting Arabic as the language of administration, business, and education, for that has happened in only one black African country, namely, the Sudan, where one could say that" "Islamization" was accompanied by "Arabization." However, in the rest of the continent one may speak as confidently of "Islamization" being accompanied by the enthronement of the sacred Arabic as the uncompromising standard of religious orthodoxy, even though in those instances Muslims have continued to employ the vernacular in everyday life, sometimes with significant developments in vernacular religious literature. This is undoubtedly the case with Ṣūfī mystical literature (see Schimmel, 1975) as well as in the biographical literary genre (*sīrah*) of the Prophet (see Schimmel, 1985). The example of Urdu stands out strongly, although the fact that the first Urdu speakers were already Muslim places it in a special category. It may, furthermore, happen that Islamic vernacular activity generates and guides local nationalism, which would strengthen the argument for vernacular translation being linked to cultural nationalism. Nevertheless, the point at issue is whether translatability may be claimed by its proponents to undergird the orthodox profession in Islam or whether it conflicts with that. In the case with which this writer is familiar, including his own mother tongue, Muslim vernaculars retain an inferiority complex toward Arabic as the revealed language. It is this phenomenon that we should investigate in a preliminary way as a counterpoint to the Christian case.

It is possible to develop the argument that one effect of the preeminent, exclusive role of the sacred Arabic has been to discourage general Muslim interest in the languages of non-Muslims. This is not the same as saying that Muslims did not learn other languages, for they did, but that such languages, apart from their practical value, had no status in the Muslim dispensation. In this connection Bernard Lewis writes:

> Of intellectual interest in Western languages and the literatures enshrined in them, there is not the slightest sign. We know of no Muslim scholar or man of letters before the eighteenth century who sought to learn a Western language, still less of any attempt to produce grammars, dictionaries, or other language tools. Translations are few and far between. Those that are known are works chosen for practical purposes and the translations are made by converts or non-Muslims. [Lewis, 1982, p. 81.]

It is in fact the case that African Muslims who have only a nodding acquaintance with the Arabic of the mosque feel deeply proprietary about it, unwilling to allow non-Muslims to take responsibility for it. For example, ordinary Muslims have in certain countries organized to oppose in secondary schools the teaching of Arabic by non-Muslim Arabic speakers. In their eyes the religion of Islam has a right to exercise proprietary control over Arabic, whether it is the Arabic of the Qur'ān or that of the market place. Conversely, non-Muslims might also resist the introduction of Arabic in schools for fear that Islamic conversion might be demanded as a price. In both cases we have a synthesis of language and religion, and it is surely one of the deeply interesting facts about Islam that in its remarkable missionary expansion it has preserved this synthesis, defying the forces of vernacular usage to carve a prestigious place for the sacred language.

THE CHRISTIAN COUNTERPOINT

The contrast with Christian mission is obvious. As we have shown in this book, translatability became the characteristic mode of Christian expansion through history. Christianity has no single revealed language, and historical experience traces this fact to the Pentecost event when the believers testified of God in their native tongues (Acts 2:6, 8, 11). Consequently, in what was tantamount to a revolutionary move, the disciples were prepared to relinquish Jerusalem as the exclusive geographical center of the new religion. They struggled against this idea at first, for they believed that true religion, as Islam was to exemplify, must make geographical rootage its indispensable prerequisite. In the end, however, translatability won out over uniformity. Nevertheless, this capacity to translate encouraged the early Christians to adopt as normative the central paradigms of Hellenistic culture, thus turning their backs on the principle that justified "the Gentile breakthrough." So profound was this acculturation, what W. H. C. Frend, in his monumental study *The Rise of Christianity*, calls the process of "acute Hellenisation," that the historical character of the Gospels was exchanged for the philosophical categories of the Greeks. Thus, for example, the timeless *logos* of the Greeks was substituted for the historical Jesus, a piece of intellectual transposition that at the same time signaled a retreat. As one authority remarks, "The human qualities and human sufferings of Jesus play singularly little part in the propaganda of this period; they were felt as an embarrassment in the face of pagan criticism" (Dodds, 1970; p. 119).

We also saw how in the ninth century a dispute erupted about the issue of translatability in the context of the mission to the Slavs. The brothers Constantine-Cyril and Methodius took the mission to the Slavs at the invitation of the ruler, Ratislav. The two brothers, previously based in Byzantium, were knowledgeable in the south Slavonic dialect then preponderant in the Balkans. Constantine-Cyril was the more scholarly of the two, and he invented an alphabet, known after him as the Cyrillic alphabet, with which he launched a vigorous translation movement. He came under challenge from the Carolingian bishops of Germany, and in his defense Constantine was able to draw on the experience of Pentecost as well as other sources in Scripture. He adopted the principle that in translating from Greek texts he would make the vernacular the final criterion. The effect of such work among the Slavs was to transpose Christianity into the terms of Slavic culture. The religion became synonymous with the project of Slavic self-identity. Constantine himself made "a passionate appeal to the Slavs to cherish books written in their own language" (Dvornik, 1970, pp. 117–18).

Even in earlier centuries, writers were able to point to successful examples of the translatability of Christianity. We saw how Tertullian, in his characteristically flamboyant style, called attention to the enormous social diversity of the church, implying that the rule of homogeneity, if not of uniformity, had been gladly abandoned (Harnack, 1908, II:175–76). Similarly, Christianity had made a breakthrough among the Armenians by at least the beginning of the fourth century. It was a lineal descendant of Gregory the Illuminator, the first Catholicus of Armenia, who, with the help of an educated monk, devised a fresh alphabet for the Armenian language. As Latourette observed, Christianity and Armenian nationalism became identical (1937, I:106). Eusebius in his *History of the Church*, recounts the strong conversion movement that took place in upper Egypt under fierce persecution (1965, pp. 337f.). The Coptic Church dates its founding to the period coinciding with that persecution, for Coptic villages in the upper Nile, long resistant to conversion, now embraced the new religion for which they were prepared to suffer martyrdom. This occurred in about the middle of the third century. There soon followed, in the late fourth and early fifth centuries, the commencement of a vast and vigorous Coptic literature, which enabled the Copts to maintain a strong, if at times inhibiting, sense of identity, especially under Muslim Egypt (Harnack, 1908, II: 304-23; Butler, 1884). Yet Coptic translation work marked a genuine advance on the earlier cumbersome system, which excluded ordinary people. Latourette agrees that

> In Egypt it was the successful effort to provide the masses of the population with a literature in the speech of everyday life which halted the exclusive use of the alien Greek for the written page and which stimulated the development of an alphabet which could be quickly and easily learned by the multitude in place of the ancient hieroglyphics which could be the property only of the few. Through this medium Coptic Christian literature came into being, largely the work of monks. [Latourette, 1975, I:250–51; cf. Frend, 1984, p. 577.]

Similarly, with the introduction of Christianity into Ethiopia, schools were established and by the middle of the seventh century most of the translation work into Amharic had been completed, with the Ethiopian Orthodox Church becoming the nerve center of Ethiopian nationalism (Tamrat, 1972; Davis, 1967, pp. 62–69; Haile, 1985, pp. 86–95).

These and other materials begin to suggest that scriptural translation and similar linguistic activity is a force in the development of the national sentiment, and this would certainly appear to be the case in many places in Asia, Latin America, and modern Africa (as we showed in chap. 3 and subsequently). If so, it leaves us with a pressing question about the implications of this for indigenous renewal in a pluralist Africa, and indeed about the missionary role in instituting the whole translation enterprise and thus helping to undermine the logic of continued foreign domination.

By contrast, we are confronted with a reverse picture for Islamic gains in Africa and elsewhere, with Muslim orthodoxy holding to the principle of nontranslatability with which vernacular self-understanding is rendered incompatible, and this notwithstanding the fact that Africans were themselves the preponderant agents in the dissemination of the faith, and thus presumably free from external pressure to adhere to prescriptive Islam.

It is within this symmetrical framework that we have to ask about the status of linguistic and cultural pluralism under the decisive rubrics of faith and practice in Islam and in Christianity. An unconventional conclusion awaits our evaluation of the evidence.

THE ISLAMIC ASSESSMENT OF "HELLENIZATION"
IN CHRISTIANITY

In A.D. 995 the Muslim scholar 'Abd al-Jabbār, chief *qāḍī* of the city that preceded Tehran, wrote a book that set out to prove the truth of Islam against Christianity. In his vigorous polemic, 'Abd al-Jabbār shows an acute insight into some of the major issues that divide the two religions, and here he considered the language factor to be paramount. He was particularly scathing in his comments on what he termed the Hellenic "falsification" of Christianity, scandalized by the willingness of Christians to surrender so wholeheartedly to Greece and Rome. He felt "translation" to be not only a mistake but corruption indistinguishable from unbelief. His uncompromising views state cogently the distinctive grounds on which the two religions approach their missionary vocation.

The sticking point for 'Abd al-Jabbār is that Christianity came into the empire not in *discontinuity* with it but as an elaborate improvisation, thus compromising the teachings of Christ. The empire itself became the instrument for transforming Christianity, first by giving it its own Sabbath—Sunday—and by instituting the Roman festival of the Birthday of Time as the birthday of Christ, and thus as Christmas. Even the signal incident of the "conversion" of the emperor Constantine could in fact be interpreted as the insinuation of extraneous pagan values into the religion. Thus, for example, was the use of images in worship, a practice adopted from Roman ideas, according to 'Abd al-Jabbār.

> If they argue that these things are innovations introduced into Christianity, just as there are similar innovations in Islam, the answer is as follows: The Romans have eaten pork, practised mutilation, raided other nations, have taken captives, killed some and reduced others to slavery, held the views about fornication which we have mentioned, and in general followed the practices described above, before the Christian epoch. When they were converted to Christianity they just went on in the same way and did not give up their old habits. So when did that moment of "innovation" occur? Someone who claims that such an innovation took place, might as well claim that originally the Romans had different customs and these customs were only adopted by them when they became Christians. Anyone who did put forth such an argument would clearly be branded as an obstinate man who denies the obvious, and with whom there is no point in arguing.[Stern, 1968, pp. 149–50.]

It is the scope of this continuity with its pagan environment that makes 'Abd al-Jabbār impatient with Christianity. The upshot of all this is that Christians abandoned the religion brought by Jesus, which had at its heart observance of the Mosaic code, including details of ritual purification, the dietary code, holy days, and the direction of prayer. In its place Christians introduced their own canon of Scripture, hermeneutics (*tafsīr*), and adopted the pagan almanac as their own religious calendar. The resulting confusion about the standard of authority, in 'Abd al-Jabbār's view, left Christianity completely unrecognizable as the religion preached by Jesus. He makes the point that if the learned doctors of the church seem so confused as to leave little hope for agreement among them about what the "gospel" is, then Islam was right to ascribe to the "illiterate" (Arab *ummī*) prophet Muḥammad the seal of truth for giving such a clear, exact account of the "Evangel" of Jesus, who preceded Islam by several centuries (Stern, 1967, p. 35). In 'Abd al-Jabbār's opinion Christians are guilty of the major offense of *taḥrīf*, falsification of the divine message.

Many issues rankled with 'Abd al-Jabbār, including the special role of Saint Paul in providing the intellectual justification for what 'Abd al-Jabbār called "the paganization" of Christianity, but nothing succeeds better at showing the scale of Christian mischief than the language issue. His own words attest to this. After describing how through a process of recension the church arrived at its canon of four Gospels, each written by a different author to augment the deficiencies of earlier "gospels," 'Abd al-Jabbār went on:

> None of these gospels is, however, in the language spoken by Christ and his disciples, i.e., Hebrew, the language of Abraham, God's Friend, and the other prophets, in which they spoke and in which God's books were revealed to them and to the rest of the children of Israel, and in which God addressed them. The [Muslim] scholars said to them: "That you Christians abandon the Hebrew language used by Christ and the prophets before him, for other languages, is surely a trick and a ruse and a way of avoiding being caught out; that is why no Christian in any religious act ever recites the gospels in the Hebrew language." The people said to them: "The Hebrew language was abandoned in order to enable your early authorities to introduce false doctrines and to cover up their lies and disguise the imposture committed by them to gain power, since those who spoke the Hebrew language were the People of the Book and the scholars of that time. So these persons changed the language or rather totally abandoned it, so that the scholars should not readily understand their doctrines and intentions and so be able to confuse them before their doctrine was firmly established and thus frustrate their aim. Thus they turned to other languages not spoken by Christ and his disciples . . . such as the Romans, Syrians, Persians, Indians, Armenians and other barbarian-speaking nations." [Stern, 1968, pp. 135–36.]

And so it was that what Stern calls "the greatest authority of the theological school of the Mu'tazila at its later phase" should inveigh against

Christianity for dropping Hebrew and embracing the languages of the empire as its own. But 'Abd al-Jabbār is remarkable not so much for his general strictures against Christianity, a position he shares with his co-religionists, as for his specifying so accurately the pluralist ethos of the church and the intrinsic incompatibility of that ethos with any one normative linguistic standard. He surely put his finger on it when he declared that the empire had captured Christianity for itself and that the Pauline rule, enunciated in 1 Corinthians 9:20–21, about the apostle as "the man for all seasons," ended any hope of securing an original identity for the faith (Stern, 1968, pp. 133–34).

With the linguistic issue is bound the cultural foundations of religion. 'Abd al-Jabbār denounces Christians for repudiating the rules of ritual purification, even to the extent of allowing menstruating women to participate in ritual activities. All the major innovations in the religion, he argues, were made against the intention and example of Christ himself: the abandoning of circumcision and obligatory fast, the observance of feast days and holy days, including Sunday, the license to eat pork and meat obtained from animals not slaughtered by the People of the Book, intermarriage with those who have no scriptural tradition — all these are sins of omission and commission in direct contravention of the teaching of Jesus. For 'Abd al-Jabbār translation had brought Christianity to the point of antireligion, causing it to abandon all that belongs properly with sound religion.

Here is a summary of 'Abd al-Jabbār's main criticisms: (1) that Christians abandoned the rules of purification established by Moses and the prophets; 2) that Christians pay no regard to the code establishing religious ritual; 3) that Christians flouted the directives on worship given to them by Christ; 4) that Christians suppressed the mission of Christ to revive the Mosaic code; 5) that Paul was the main culprit in the Christian perfidy toward Judaism; 6) that the inconsistencies in the gospel accounts prove the fabricated nature of the Christian scriptures; 7) that the conversion so-called of Constantine was insincere and an act of political expedience; 8) that the adoption by Christians of the Roman calendar proves that Christianity represented no decisive change in the Hellenic world; and, finally, 9) that all these faults and inadequacies in Christianity stem from the abandonment of the sacred Hebrew and its replacement with Greek, the language of Roman paganism.

There is no need to identify ourselves with 'Abd al-Jabbār's polemical premise to accept his descriptive procedure, which shows a fundamental grasp of the Christian attitude toward linguistic pluralism. His basic contention reveals a perceptive grasp of the issues. We can, for example, appreciate the fact that whereas the Muslim *hijrah* bequeathed a legacy of geographical and linguistic centrality, the Christian Pentecost created the reverse. The *hijrah* was not merely the *flight* to safety of the Prophet and his community (though as a strategy it did accomplish that) but the event which marks the historic birth of Islam. The intensity of the event helps dissolve all autonomous claims for mother tongues. The *hijrah* is thus the reversal of Pentecost. The Muslim confides in Arabic, the Christian in what lies to hand. Muslims celebrate the *mawlid*, the Prophet's birthday, in a lunar cycle that spins on the *hijrah*. Christians, by contrast, scarcely know the Bethlehem of the Christ child, turning instead to places and events thrust up by time's hallowed hand. Muslims are revived from the innocence of their first century youth, whereas Christians find strength in the centuries-long expansion of Christianity. Muḥammad had no need of Paul or Constantine. Christ has need of both.

Such ideas recognize what is both distinctive and common in the two traditions, and even if Muslims and Christians had not needed each other on the road they have traveled together, their divergent approaches would still have been mutually instructive. Even if they could only agree about their differences, that would be in fact more valuable than if they were to get no further than disagreeing about their common ground where similarities have in the past led to charges and counter-charges of imitation and incompleteness. It is by such distinctive paths that Christianity and Islam have penetrated the African continent where their remarkable growth and development have concentrated the attention of African converts on the unique claims of the two religions. It is, therefore, a matter of deep interest that in its spread in Africa, Islam should be able to promote a remarkably uniform adherence to the rule of nontranslatability even though it was encountering mostly illiterate populations. It would be important, therefore, to pursue the theme in Africa and see how Islamic agents set about cultivating an authoritative regard for the sacred Arabic.

REFORM, RENEWAL, AND REVIVAL

When we consider the nature and outcome of renewal movements in Islam and Christianity in Africa, we find a situation that conforms to the pattern dictated by the translation question. In the Islamic tradition the springs of reform and renewal are fed by the perennial premillennial figure who appears at the head of every Islamic century to set right the affairs of the people. In African Islam the earliest occurrence of such messianic ideas was in the correspondence between the king of Songhay, Askiya al-Ḥājj Muḥammad Ture, and the itinerant North African scholar, 'Abd al-Karīm al-Maghīlī (d. 1505/6). The askiya had inquired of al-Maghīlī, who was visiting Songhay in 1502, about the conditions under which religious reform might be necessary, a momentous question whose consequences extended into the nineteenth-century reform movements in other parts of West Africa. It is worth quoting this tradition in full. Al-Maghīlī acquainted the askiya with the following authoritative opinion regarding reform.

Thus it is related that at the beginning of every century God sends [people] a scholar who regenerates their religion for them. There is no doubt that the conduct of this scholar in every century in enjoining what is right and forbidding what is wrong, and setting aright [the] people's affairs, establishing justice among them and supporting truth against falsehood and the oppressed against the oppressor, will be in contrast to the conduct of the scholars of his age. For this reason he will be an odd man out among them on account of his being the only man of such pure conduct and on account of the small number of men like him. Then will it be plain and clear that he is one of the reformers (*al-muṣliḥūn*) and that who so opposes him and acts hostilely towards him so as to turn people away from him is but one of the miscreants, because of the saying of the Prophet, may God bless him and grant him peace: "Islam started as an odd man out (*gharīb*) and thus will it end up, so God bless the odd men out." Someone said, "And who are they, O Messenger of God?" He said, "Those who set matters aright in evil times." That is one of the clearest signs of the people of the Reminder (*ahl al-dhikr*) through whom God regenerates for people their religion. [Hunwick, 1985, pp. 66–67; see also Hiskett, 1962, p. 584.]

In al-Maghīlī's hands, reform and renewal are complementary. Reform may be more narrowly understood as undoing the harm resulting from neglect of the religious code, while renewal may be taken to mean the level at which prescriptive standards are applied after the removal of impediments. The two parts are conjoined in the standard scriptural injunction: *amal bi-maʿrūf wa nahy ʿan al-munkar*—"to enjoin good works and restrain from what is disapproved of" (Qurʾān 13:21–22). "Revival" in the technical sense of religious enthusiasm is discouraged by Muslim religious authorities, for the issue as they see it is alignment of conduct to make it conform to established prescriptions, not that of seeking the signs of the Spirit.

Consequently al-Maghīlī's opinions on mixing Islam with African religion carry the mark of a rigorist. He is not satisfied with less than the explicit application of the code; it is not just sufficient to imply in conduct acknowledgment of its authority. Thus he spells out what is to be done with those Muslims who also participate in non-Islamic rites. These, he says, "are polytheists (*mushrikūn*) without doubt, because anathematizing (*takfīr*), according to the manifest meaning of the Law, is for less than that, and there is no doubt that Holy War against them is better and more meritorious (*afḍal*) than Holy War against unbelievers who do not declare the witness of faith: 'there is no god except God; Muḥammad is His Apostle' " (Hiskett, 1962, p. 584, translation amended by L. S.). Al-Maghīlī is thus particularly severe toward those Muslims who continued to imbibe from a pluralist religious world, and their offense in his eyes is more serious than that of nonbelievers. Halfheartedness is more objectionable than nonmembership.

In a similar way, the learned men who are implicated in religious compromise are the more reprehensible, for they ought to know better. Al-Maghīlī castigates them as "venal scholars"(*'ulamāl-sū'i*). They make a career of frequenting the corridors of power, titillating the fancies of ignorant rulers and bolstering their unjust authority. They add to the mischief of the land by doing the round of obscure villages and carrying, as a show of piety and learning, satchels that contain only cockroaches. Their charlatanry deserves no mercy and a suitable example ought to be made of them. The askiya put the following provocatory question to his mentor:

And in spite of that (i.e., their lack of true understanding) they have books which they study, and tales which they utter concerning God's religion, and they maintain that they are the inheritors of the prophets and that it is incumbent upon us to imitate them. I seek from God Most High that He will help me to carry this burden which the heavens and the earth have refused to carry, and I seek from you that you will give me a decision, by what God has taught you, concerning these Qur'ān readers — is it lawful that we should act according to what they say concerning God's religon? [Hiskett, 1962, p. 581.]

"This burden which the heavens and the earth have refused to carry" refers to the passage in the Qur'ān where human beings are entrusted with the stewardship of the world, whence the idea of *khalīfah* (33:72). Al-Maghīlī wrote back tersely: "It is said by the Scriptures and the *Sunnah* and the consensus of the learned that many of these Qur'ān readers of this community are only venal scholars, and they are more harmful to the Muslims than all the mischief-makers" (Hiskett, 1962, p. 581).

If the branches are in contention, then the root cannot be sound, and al-Maghīlī 's diagnosis of the Songhay state is an attempt to identify the root cause of the problem as he saw it, which was the failure of political authority to uphold the religious code. He justified the coup d'état of 1492, an ideological revolution in which Askiya Muḥammad, a general of the imperial army and at that time at the head of the Muslim agitators, seized power from a ruler, Sonni 'Alī (d. 1492), who stopped short of applying the full rigor of the Islamic code. Such rulers are the scourge of rightminded Muslims, al-Maghīlī contends.

There is no doubt that they are the greatest of tyrants and wrongdoers who sever what God has commanded shall be united, and make mischief in the land. The Holy War of the *amīr* Askia against them and his taking of the *sultanate* from their hands is the most meritorious Holy War, and the most important; and as for the people of the *Qibla*, are they infidels or not? No one from among the people of the *Qibla* should be anathematized because of sin . . . and that which you have mentioned concerning the condition of Sonni 'Alī indicates unbelief without doubt, and if the matter is as you have described it, then he is an unbeliever. [Hiskett, 1962, p. 585.]

Several factors galvanized the reform impulse in African Islam: the concern with safeguarding the monotheist ideal against the sin of "association" (*shirk*), grievances over the unjust treatment of foreign Muslims in the state, the burdensome nature of levies and imposts, compromises in Muslim behavior and conduct, the threat of the organized state becoming the instrument of a well coordinated traditional religious life, and the scandal of the nimble-tongued scholars pandering to the esteem of capricious rulers—all this increased the tension. By throwing in the idea of a messianic dispensation almost at hand, al-Maghīlī set to it an incendiary charge.

Yet the fundamental question has still to be asked as to why such materials should continue to appeal to African Muslims long and far removed from the Islamic heartlands, or why, given this distance in time and space, the Islamic legacy should be able to preserve its affinity with the Islam of first-century Arabia. The capacity of Muslims to invoke the ideal past as a model for their own time and place remains one of the most remarkably consistent features of the religion, and that without a "Vatican" or similar universal bureaucratic structure. By what principle, then, do African Muslims act to rescind the authority of indigenous tradition and practice and replace it with the prescriptive force of Islam?

A few provisional ideas are necessary on what is a large and complicated issue. We should dismiss outright the idea that Muslim opposition is forced by the nature of the inherent corruption and contradiction in indigenous traditions, for that accepts the verdict of a protagonist. Nor should we be content with looking for justifications in structural factors, such as the limitations of traditional political institutions when faced with the demands of a supra-tribal world of Muslims, foreigners, a cosmopolitan trading community, a literate elite, and the wider orbit of international diplomacy. All those factors are important, but they do not add up to the intense single-mindedness of Muslims cast in vastly different circumstances and time.

We have a clue in the impatient outburst of al-Maghīlī regarding what he considered an incriminating defect in the scholars. "One of their characteristics," he charges, "is that they are not Arabic-speaking (*'ajam*); they understand no Arabic except a little of the speech of the Arabs of their towns, in an incorrect and corrupted fashion, and a great deal of non-Arabic, so that they do not understand the intentions of the scholars" (Hiskett, 1962, p. 581). Writers make relatively little of this complaint even though it recurs in much of the standard literature. Its force stems from the nontranslatability of the Muslim Scriptures, and it is therefore able to sweep before it the obstacle of local resistance and overcome at the same time the handicap of its foreign identity. Those African Muslims who begin their life with the obvious disadvantage of worshiping in a strange and foreign language will sooner or later reach, or be made to reach, the stage where practice, however imperfect, creates proximity—and culpability. Our appreciation of this point should help to illuminate other areas of Muslim objection.

One writer who was quick to appreciate the value of nontranslatability in Islam was Dr. Edward Blyden. In an illuminating passage he set about trying to define the special quality that the words, poetry, and music of the Qur'ān holds for Muslim devotees, many of whom might be frankly ignorant of the sense of the words they are saying. Writing in 1875, Blyden affirms that for Africans

> the Koran is, in its measure, an important educator. It exerts among a primitive people a wonderful influence. It has furnished to the adherents of its teaching in Africa a ground of union which has contributed vastly to their progress. Hausas, Foulahs, Mandingoes, Soosoos, Akus, can all read the same books and mingle in worship together, and there is to all one common authority and one ultimate umpirage. They are united by a common religious sentiment, by a common antagonism to Paganism. Not only the sentiments, but the language, the words of the sacred book are held in the greatest reverence and esteem. And even where the ideas are not fully understood the words seem to possess for them a nameless beauty and music, a subtle and indefinable charm, incomprehensible to those not acquainted with the language in which the Koran was written, and, therefore, judging altogether as outsiders, to indulge in depreciating its merits. Such critics lose sight of the fact that the Koran is a poetical composition, and a poetical composition of the earliest and most primitive kind, and that therefore its ideas and the language in which they are conveyed cannot well be separated. The genuine poet not only creates the conception, but the word which is its vehicle. The word becomes the inseparable drapery of the idea. . . . Among Mohammedans, written or printed translations of the Koran are discouraged. The Chinese, Hindoos, Persians, Turks, Mandingoes, Foulahs, etc., who have embraced Islam, speak in their "own tongues wherein they were born," but read the Koran in Arabic. [Blyden, 1967, pp. 6–7.]

In the sphere of its monotheist tradition, therefore, Islam is able to act with effective authority because its judgment is enshrined in the material of a nontranslatable Qur'ān, which itself fosters a devotion and veneration bordering on the magical. In the area of worship, the reformers had the advantage of trying only to reorient and restrict a wide habit, which took in worship at many shrines at once, rather than having to invent the habit at all. The instrument of restriction was the mosque and its responsibility for the prescribed acts of worship. Not even the high ground of kingly prerogative could allow Sonni 'Alī to escape that restriction, though he judged it, correctly, to be antithetical to his power. As for the other factors of limited literacy of the Muslim educational elite, the pressures of a foreign community, the impact of trading contacts and of the larger world of dealing with other nations and their nationals—these build on the united front of pressing hard on indigenous traditions, precisely the point at which the sacred Arabic is stridently different. Al-Maghīlī and Askiya Muḥammad, two individuals separated by what would ordinarily be a huge cultural gap, had nevertheless found an enduring common ground, not just in a common religious attitude of pietism, but in how specifically such an attitude should properly be signified, namely, in the primacy of Arabic in Scripture, law, and devotion. The central task of the reformers was to achieve in black Africa the sacralization of the Arabic cultural milieu with which Islamic mission is properly identified. They could argue that their case was made in heaven, with Africa as its footstool. The very strangeness of Qur'ānic Arabic adds to its religious authority and to its appeal as the blueprint for a righteous social order, the more attractive for embodying the religious ideals.

The dilemma of Sonni 'Alī under such circumstances is a classic one: he had adopted the religion, observed its tenets in a haphazard fashion, and encouraged its propagation under official direction. Yet he perceived that Islam in its irreducible Arabic scaffolding raised the specter of being a state within a state. By the time he decided to check this incipient political force, it was too late. The foundations of indigenous institutions felt a violent shock with the charge of *'ajamī* ("foreign," "barbarous") leveled at them. In Sonni 'Alī's case, even his pedigree was divested of legitimacy by a claim that his mother came from an outlandish country (Hiskett, 1962, p. 579).[1] In spite of the violent turn of events in his relations with Islam, it was Sonni 'Alī's achievement in setting up the Songhay state that made it attractive enough for Muslims to want to control it, suggesting that coexistence was deemed only as a necessary means to the Islamic religio-political order. That scarcely warrants our elevating such a view of coexistence into a principle of genuine pluralism.

The reference to Sonni 'Alī 's foreign origin, supposedly made by 'Uthmān dan Fodio (1754–1817), indicates that what happened in Songhay came to exert a powerful influence on Muslims elsewhere and in different times. Dan Fodio was the creator of the nineteenth-century Fulani caliphate in north Nigeria. He was familiar with al-Maghīlī writings, invoking him as an authority for his own project of reform (Hiskett, 1962, pp. 580, 591; see also Hiskett, 1973).

The religio-political triumph of the Fulani *mujāhidīn* gave them a rare opportunity to articulate in the new conditions of Africa the significance of the Prophet's heritage. An ethnic minority themselves, the Fulani became the sponsors of an aggressive Islamization process, which sought completely to overhaul African customs and institutions, replacing the *sarauta* chieftaincy system of the Hausa with state organs decreed by the Islamic religious code. In this process the employment of Arabic was a paramount duty. Here is a succinct account by Dan Fodio on the methodical regime that reform calls for:

> Most of the people are ignorant of the Sharī'a, and it is obligatory that there should be, in every mosque and quarter in the town, a *faqīh* teaching the people their religion. So also is it, in every village, obligatory on every *faqīh* who has completed his *fard'ain* [collective duty binding on Muslims] and has devoted himself to the *fard kifāya* [individual obligation without collective implication], that he should go out to the people neighbouring on his town in order to teach them their religion and the obligatory parts of their Shar' [religious code]. If one person does this, sin falls off the remaining people: otherwise all of them will carry the sin together.
>
>   As for the learned person, the sin will be because of his neglecting to go out (and preach). But as for the ignorant, it will be because of his shortcomings in avoiding knowledge. Every layman who knows the conditions governing prayer is obliged to teach it to others . . . . (T)he sin of the *fuqahā* is greater because their ability to propagate knowledge is more obvious and it is a duty more appropriate to them. [Balogun, 1975, pp. 74–75.]

The Shehu ('Uthmān dan Fodio) then goes on to set out the missionary obligations of the ordinary Muslim: in teaching and propagating the faith, he said, the Muslim must begin with himself, than go to his family and relations, then to his neighbors, the people of his ward, the inhabitants of his town, the adjacent suburbs of his city, "and so on to the furthest part of the world" (Balogun, 1975, p. 75). In all the vicissitudes of worldly events and circumstances, Muslims must, in the Shehu's view, strive to realize the goals of an Islam informed by its inseparable Arabic milieu. It is by this standard that his own brother and the intellectual chronicler of the Fulani jihād, 'Abdallāhi dan Fodio, assessed the Shehu's legacy, as the following passage makes clear:

> And many an error quenched while it was a live
> coal blazing fiercely
> And you rose up in a land whose customs
> became excessive,
> And which conflicted with the *sunna*
> of the joyous Prophet . . . .
>
> You ['Uthmān] overcame them as a strong man
> overcomes, as a stallion.

And you broke them with the bright swords
of His Qur'ānic verses,
With spears of the *sunnas* of the
dark-eyed Prophet,
May God bless him as long as the
east wind shakes
The tips of the branches
in pleasant meadows. [Fodio, 1963, pp. 91–93.]²

'Abdallāhi himself, an adept of the Arabic medium, nevertheless felt he had a permanent disability as a non-Arab. In words that Sonni 'Alī could sympathize with, though from one he would not envy, he confessed:

A poor slave, ignorant, drowning in a sea of sin,
Confused in a sea of fantasy.
Humble, speaking Arabic incorectly, non-Arab in tribe,
His mother and his father are from the family of 'Al.
[Fodio, 1963, p. 97.]

The Sokoto caliphate, which lasted from about 1807 to 1902, was a spectacular example of the success of prescriptive Islam without direct intervention from Mecca. Indeed, though he pined for the privilege of visiting the *Ḥaramayn* of Mecca and Medina, the Shehu and his principal lieutenants never knew Arabia from personal contact (Hiskett, 1973, p. 33). Yet that failure achieved its antidote in the resolve to replicate in black Africa the conditions of the Prophet's Mecca. The Shehu said in a poem:

I wept and tears poured down like heavy rain
in longing for this Prophet, Muḥammad.
I am as one afflicted with longing for him. . . .
Were I to visit Ṭayba, I would achieve
the height of my ambition,
sprinkling myself with the dust of
Muḥammad's sandal.
[Hiskett, 1973, p. 33.]

Although they wrote in the vernacular, the men of the Fulani Muslim caliphate looked upon Arabic as the preeminent standard of the religious and political life. Hiskett pinpoints this element in the Muslim reform heritage, saying it was the universal principle that guided the reform movement and inspired the leaders.

These forces of Islamic ideology served to create in these men a sense of Islamic universalism. That is to say, they had a vision of a single, world-wide Islam, in which the way of life, the way of government and the morality and social behaviour of all individuals were regulated according to the *Sharī'a* and *Sunnah*, the Law and Tradition of the

Prophet. They were determined that they would tolerate nothing less than this in their own countries. The *jihāds* were the practical expression of this determination . . . [Hiskett, 1984, pp. 170-71.]

The large stock of vernacular Islamic literature that exists serves only as embellishment on the Arabic motif.[3] It must be stressed that accommodating religious functionaries, whom we class under the generic title "clerics," have continued to preside over a vigorous tradition of Islamic practice. Patrick Ryan, for example, has shown how Muslim Yoruba have ingeniously blended Yoruba tradition with their understanding of Islam (Ryan, 1978). Certainly at that level there is a form of translation going on, and no one who is familiar with Muslim Africa can question that. Ioan Lewis has argued forcefully for a formulation that includes within mainstream Islam elements previously consigned to the periphery and outside the core as marginal or syncretic (Lewis, 1983, pp. 55-67). Yet what remains fascinating in so many of the accounts of Muslim conversion is how people began their journey by embarking on the familiar path of, say, divination, only to arrive at the point where, eventually, the unfamiliar and for them modest medium of the sacred Arabic operates as normative divine standard. For example, among the Mossi, barrenness in non-Muslim women may be treated through divination by the idea that it is a sign that children refuse to be born save as Muslims. The obvious remedy is conversion. Among the Giriama of Kenya, to take a second example given by Lewis, people falling ill are diagnosed as having been possessed by Muslim spirits for which the cure is conversion to Islam. In both cases, however, the destination is clear, or soon to be clear, even if the route is arcane. No community of Muslim converts, however distantly placed, can avoid encountering Islam through the sacred Arabic, for it is inconceivable to claim the Muslim name without sooner or later performing at least some of the mandatory five daily prayers, and to do that worshipers are obliged without exception to employ the Arabic of the Qur'ān.

The present writer has examined in detail one outstanding historical example of an African Muslim clerical tradition centered in the Jakhanke (or Jahanke) people who achieved a major transposition of Islam by repudiating for themselves—but not for others—*jihād* and other forms of armed militancy, and by cultivating a reputation for political neutrality. This pacific clerical tradition has a long history behind it, the accounts speaking of its roots going back to the thirteenth century (Sanneh, forthcoming). Such peaceful dissemination of Islam inevitably implies a high degree of tolerance for mixing, and Jakhanke Islam is no exception. Yet both in the traditions concerning the founder of that clerical tradition as well as in the detailed work of the clerical center—the Jakhanke themselves refer to that center as the *majlis*—Mecca remains the unwavering point of religious orientation, reinforced by observance of the *ṣalāt*, the standing reminder of the *ḥājj* obligation, and the use of Arabic in study, teaching, and counseling (Sanneh, 1976).[4]

THE COMPARATIVE AFRICAN CHRISTIAN EXAMPLE

The picture of mission and renewal in Christian Africa has some interesting parallels with Muslim Africa. To find a good example we have to turn to African Christian Independency and the Prophet Movements it spawned. We see, for instance, an identical religious commitment expressing itself in the call to repentance and to change in lifestyle, the same resolve to make Scripture the rule of religious activity in personal and public life, and the same wish to recapture for Africa the original promises of God. In both cases we find close attention to details of ritual purity, to matters of sartorial propriety. There is the same regard for the public character of religion, for the display in public places of appropriate religious symbolism and imagery. Reform Islam sought to rivet the code on the lukewarm and fainthearted, while Prophet Movements aspired to a similar commitment among their followers. In each case the "Word of God" was understood to carry great power, and therefore those religious leaders who had access to it were believed to possess commensurate authority. Consequently, religious style became extremely important in defining or buttressing religious claims.

It is important to understand how Africans pursued Islam and Christianity in their distinctive forms, appropriating their messages in light of African experience without reducing them to parodies. Few can miss the distinctive flavor of each religious tradition in Africa, the pattern and rhythm that distinguish Muslim and Christian Africa from each other in spite of impressive coexistence. Africa's pluralist heritage has been deepened and extended from the impact of the two religions.

In developing their version of Islamic and Christian particularity, Africans have helped clarify some of the implicit tendencies of the two traditions, bringing out important themes of difference. In the Christian example the stress on the vernacular brought the religion into profound continuity with mother-tongue aspirations. By contrast reform Islam pressed for a choice between the old and the new, and although there were gaps, the pressure was toward the "orient" in terms of orientation toward Mecca and Medina. The "reform" tradition in Christian Africa moved in the opposite direction and espoused greater identification with the African setting. It did this not because Christianity had assumed too great a foreign character, though Western breast-beating might support that view, but because the new prophets saw a connection between the vernacular Scriptures and vernacular self-understanding. It was the vernacular Scriptures that shaped the antiforeign accent of Prophet Movements, and inspired fresh possibilities within existing local forms. As "renewal" and "revival" movements spread, old loyalties and allegiances were reformulated, with whole communities repositioning themselves to take command of new economic and political forces. Such internal readjustments involved a modernist tendency of the importance of individual experience as well as a "conservative" cultural impulse of indigenous authenticity. "Renewal" and "revival" in this sense became a two-sided phenomenon of indigenous change. "Renewal" reappropriated the new teachings and ideas of Christianity within vernacular self-understanding, while "revival" spurred converts with the promptings of the Spirit, making the life of the believers the subject of intense spiritual concentration, with the reward of charismatic gifts. Ordinary men and women, who were otherwise denied a role in religious and social life, found in "revival" a vocation and an affirmation. As Christianity consecrated mother tongues so did their speakers assume corresponding historical significance.

The language issue was absolutely pivotal to the rise of reform, renewal, and revivalism in the Niger Delta. From the 1850s, when Bishop Crowther was writing to Henry Venn urging the development of Ibo, to 1909 when "Union Ibo" was concocted as a new amalgam of dialects, the language question worked like a time fuse at the strategy to impose missionary tutelage. From the perspective of our thesis, a good translation aided the cause as well as a bad one abetted it, for a good, successful translation vindicates indigenous claims, while a bad, unsuccessful one justifies the charge of foreign incompetence. In either case translatability had made the vernacular framework the indispensable coefficient of the range and scope of Christian expansion, with a corresponding marginalization of foreign agents and their cultural norms. The operative standards for success and effectiveness were vernacular ones, not those of Home Committees and Mission Boards.[5]

To deploy the final stage of our summary, the vernacular principle, as we saw in chapter 4 above, was the pulse of the "revival" movements which swept across the Niger Delta and Yorubaland in the first decades of the twentieth century. The *Aladura* revival, occurring between 1928 and 1930, was the bearer of this revival legacy, and a representative figure was the charismatic Joseph Babalola. The manner of his preparation and call, his appearance when he first emerged as a prophet, and the stress he placed on the spiritual gifts of prayer, healing, and prophecy, what may be considered the golden charismatic triad, made "revival" a tangible, popular force in local Christianity.

A little before the dramatic experience of Babalola, another charismatic figure with Creole roots, Abiodun Akinsowon, in 1925 an eighteen-year-old girl, experienced a trance on Corpus Christi Day (June 18, 1925). Her father, a clergyman of the African Church Movement at Porto Novo, Dahomey (now Benin), summoned the help of one Moses Orimolade, a charismatic leader who enjoined prayer, asking people in the house to clap and call on the Spirit of God to heal Abiodun. People rushed to the place where Abiodun was, and after the spiritual ministrations, she recovered, and subsequently joined Orimolade to found a spiritual society, called then the Seraphim Society, with Holy Michael the Archangel adopted by special vision as Patron or Captain of the society. In 1927 the name of the society was expanded to Cherubim and Seraphim, indicating that the revival leaders were keeping very high company indeed. "All the major doctrinal and ritual developments were sanctioned by vision. Meetings were held in numerous private houses and parlours, as a widening circle of members became adept in the spiritual activities which Orimolade and Abiodun had initiated" (Peel, 1968, p. 73). One active member confessed, "Prayer was the object. In our [previous mission-founded] churches with their set services there was not sufficient time for us to develop spiritually. When you do a thing you must reap the benefits; what we were taught in church we do not experience in practice. We Africans are so low in everything, but by prayer we may win everlasting power in God's Kingdom. In a word, practical Christianity" (cited in Peel, 1968, p. 73). Peel writes:

> What brought the Seraphim to people's notice more than anything else were the huge anniversary processions, involving thousands of people arrayed in white robes with special uniforms and adornments for different ranks and sections. A contemporary report describes how Moses Orimolade and "energetic assistant Captain Abiodun" sat together in a go-cart under a canopy very similar to that used at Corpus Christi and inscribed with a motto celebrating the power of the Trinity. Twenty-four elders with stars as ornaments on their clothes and long staffs accompanied them, followed by 3,000 members. They made their way to Balogun Square and as the moon appeared the leader "delivered the usual message of Christ and his love." [Peel, 1968, p. 75.]

As the membership grew by leaps and bounds, the prayer sessions and processions were backed by a support network of Bible study groups, each under a leader. Orimolade acquired the sobriquet Baba Aladura, the "prince of prayer," while the spiritual elite who formed the backbone of the revivalist intercessory meetings was called the Praying Band, *Ẹgbẹ Aladura*, so important was that exercise in the entire revival atmosphere. *Aladura* itself is of Arabic derivation, *al-du'a*, invocatory or supplicatory prayer.

The numerous unconnected centers experienced an "outbreak" of revival showers, with spontaneous outpourings of charismatic powers and gifts and dramatic instances of personal conversion. The entire religious landscape in Yorubaland and beyond began to stir with the *"sturm und drang"* of the *Aladura* cavalcade. In this spiritual upheaval St. Michael the Archangel "became an appropriate 'Balogun,' or war-chief, leader of the Seraphim in their fight for victory over the forces of Satan" (Peel, 1968, p. 149). According to a popular teaching of the Christ Apostolic Church, considered an elite among the charismatic churches, prayer, which is the activating force of revival, *isoji* in Yoruba, is likened to gunpowder, and the Holy Spirit, that terror of the invisible enemy, is regarded as the gun, with the Bible as the ramrod. This is perhaps the closest Christian revival came to the theme of the "sword" of the Muslim reformers, though even here the revival theme made the believer both subject and object, agent and target, of the message. One leading convert, for example, spoke of participating in a "tarrying meeting," waiting for the manifestation of the Holy Spirit, when "there was something like a storm and I see that my tongue is changed; since then, ah! (he laughed)—there is a happiness in my life!" (Peel, 1968, p. 146). The "sword of truth," the Muslim *sayf al-ḥāqq*, had for Christian revivalists the effect of making them the primary and principal targets, just as, less directly, translatability had brought missionaries to the point of critical self-scrutiny, both in the sense of having their Western notions challenged and in facing indigenous demands for autonomy. Thus "renewal" and "revival" advanced mother-tongue aspirations and strengthened the indigenous cause.

SUMMARY AND CONCLUSION

It is important to identify areas of mutual distinctiveness in the historical interaction between Islam and Christianity. In considering matters over which Islam and Christianity appear to differ, we may increase appreciation for each other's heritage. One such matter is the question of the translatability of the respective Scriptures of the two traditions. Clarification of this point should help understanding of the contrasting attitudes of the two faiths to mission and conversion. Several issues emerge from this approach. First, in the Christian tradition there was an early move to relinquish Jerusalem as the geographical center of the faith. This led, on the one hand, to the coming into being of centers of Christian activity in various parts of the empire and beyond, and to the employment of a multiplicity of languages in the propagation of the faith, on the other. Second, it allowed the new religion to assimilate into the Hellenic cultural milieu and to adopt Greek philosophical categories as natural extensions of its life, with the upshot of transposing certain scriptural categories concerning the historical Jesus into Greek philosophical terms. That process of "acute Hellenization" resulted in the controversial "normatization" of Hellenism as the Christian paradigm, although the notion of contextual adaptation intrinsic in that process continued to be a live option.

Islam, for its part, stands in radical contrast to this mode of mission, for it requires the establishment of the sacred Arabic in worship, law, and devotion. The Islamic *hijrah*, with its absolute consecration of Mecca and Medina as holy sites, is the counterpart to the Christian instance. It is from this point of view that one early Islamic scholar offered a radical critique of Hellenized Christianity, focusing in particular on the language issue. That issue surfaces in the reform tradition in African Islam, for in that context the nontranslatable Qur'ān is the rallying standard for the troops. The tradition of militancy on this point goes back at least to the Islamic revolution of Askiya Muḥammad of Songhay. He and his principal adviser, al-Maghīlī, advanced arguments to justify armed opposition to religious pluralism on the part of professing Muslims, to the scholars who led those Muslims, and to the rulers who presided over affairs. This set the stage for another and much more major revolutionary outburst with the Fulani revolution of the nineteenth century, where similar issues were thrashed out in much more detail and volume. Clearly the Muslim reformers wished to achieve in black Africa the ideals of an Arabic and Arab-inspired Islam, with the commanding figure of the Prophet as their model and inspiration. Reform Islam aspires to the establishment of social and political institutions responsive to Middle Eastern authorities. The reformers are generally hostile to autonomous local forms of Islam, and are not loathe to invoke the sword in the struggle.

When set against that background, the Christian comparison is with the vernacular translations and their dramatic impact on populations in the Niger Delta. Both in the perception of leading Christian figures and in the conduct of congregations, the promise of vernacular ascendancy galvanized the national resolve and encouraged movements for local autonomy.

Still working on the basis of what is distinctive about the two traditions, it is necessary for us to clarify the concepts of "reform," "renewal," and "revival." Of these, "revival" is the most problematic for Islam, with its suggestion of subjective authority displacing the prescriptive standards of the faith. Furthermore, the quietist, pacifist connotations of "revival" undermine the role that reform counsels assign to armed militancy. By contrast, the new prophet movements have made "revival" the hallmark of commitment and renewal, throwing off by that means the inhibitions of institutional constraint. A further point is that prophet movements draw no distinction between the agents and targets of revival. Indeed, in the forefront of revival are the advocates themselves, who are thus the line of least resistance in the Spirit's path. Such charismatic prophets are in fact spoils as well as victors in their version of religious reform.

At this stage it is worth making explicit the comparative assumptions of this book as a whole. Implied in all that we have said is the idea that pluralism is a prerequisite for authentic Christian living, since translation assumes cross-cultural encounter where the notion of multiple living cultures makes it necessary to exchange one form of communication for another. In both its Protestant and its Catholic forms, Christianity has affirmed with the Gentile breakthrough the shibboleth of God's faithfulness toward all peoples. This idea persists as a major theme in the counsels of the Catholic Church, with a fresh prominence given in conciliar statements to the vernacular question. In these statements indigenous materials are given priority over imported arrangements.

A similar emphasis occurs in Protestant missions. Even those missionaries who held a rather narrow view of the Bible as *sola scriptura* were no less significant in facilitating cross-cultural participation in the Christian movement. They did this by promoting vernacular languages as autonomous instruments, rather than judging them by the standard of Western commentaries and the intellectual and cultural values enshrined in those commentaries. Thus even what may be regarded as the weak link in missionary extremism turns out to add to the cumulative weight of the indigenous factor in mission as a cross-cultural enterprise.

The Christian missionary impact has created a worldwide pluralist movement distinguished by the forces of *radical pluralism* and social destigmatization, spread out on a massive arc at the center of which mission placed "the true and living God" of the disciples. On this way of understanding it, Islam, with its nontranslatable Scriptures, would appear to be at a considerable distance from the point at which Christianity engages culture. All this implies that the strength of Islam in generating a spontaneous devotion to its universal teachings is the weakness of Christianity in its multiple local manifestations, and that, conversely, the strength of Christianity in recognizing the vernacular as a worthy medium for the transmission of the message is the weakness of Islam which excludes the vernacular from the decisive acts of faith and devotion.

Of the same order is the question of religious bureaucracy and organization, for Christianity is prominent for its hierarchical structures, whereas Islam is striking for its lack of central organization, in the light of which it is challenging to reflect on how Muslims from across cultural and national boundaries exhibit far greater unity of faith and practice than Christians. For example, Muslims would have little difficulty in proceeding to perform the canonical *ṣalāt*, whatever their national, cultural, and denominational differences, whereas Christians have enough trouble with ecumenical acts of simple devotion, let alone having to unite in central rites such as marriage, baptism, and Holy Communion. Disputes, of course, have erupted among certain Muslims concerning the position of the hands during *ṣalāt*, whether they should be placed folded on the chest or dropped by the side. Yet such disputes do not weaken commitment to the *ṣalāt* as an obligatory rite with a fixed, invariable order. Whatever the case, in their contrasting strengths and weaknesses, Islam and Christianity are perfect mirrors, rather than parodies, of each other, and their wholehearted adoption by Africans affords a unique opportunity to observe their authentic character on common ground. Such a rounding up of the themes which both bind and set us apart is designed to encourage careful reflection and mutual appreciation for the whys and wherefores of our common missionary obligation.

NOTES

1. Hiskett cites for this statement a nineteenth-century work, *Sirāj al-Ikhwān*, believed to have been composed by 'Uthmān dan Fodio (see folio 11).

2. For a comprehensive list of 'Abdallāhi's works, see John O. Hunwick, "The Works of 'Abd Allāh b. Fūdi," *Arabic Literature in Africa*, Bulletin of biographical

and bibliographical information, ed. J. O. Hunwick and R. S. O'Fahey, no. 2, Sept. 1986, pp. 17–39.

3. This has been amply demonstrated in some recent works—see J. Haafkens, *Les Chants Musulmans en Peul*, (Leiden: E. J. Brill, 1983). Haafkens was writing mainly of Adamawa in the present Republic of Cameroun. It is intriguing to reflect on how the Fulani Muslim leaders came to lose most of their own language as the reform impulse strengthened under the caliphate. Hausa became the preponderant language of the Fulani reformers, a shift which the thoroughly Islamized status of Hausa warranted. It is most certainly the case that the Muslim Fulani had no wish to make the Fulfulde language the basis of religious reform, and champions of the language elsewhere were accounted a trace too heretical, or at any rate outlandish. Thus it was that the headquarters of the reform order was constituted to reflect the ethos of a Middle Eastern Arabic-speaking environment—see Hiskett, *A History of Hausa Islamic Verse* (London: School of Oriental and African Studies, 1975), p. 136.

4. For a continuation of that theme into the modern era, see L. Sanneh, 1981, "The Jakhanke Clerical Tradition in Futa Jallon," *Journal of Religion in Africa* 12, nos. 1 and 2.

5. There is a fascinating discussion between Henry Venn and John Christopher Taylor, an Ibo who devoted himself to translation work. In his correspondence with Venn, Taylor challenged the position of Rev. J. F Schön, the German missionary partner of Bishop Crowther, asking whether Schön was better qualified to lead the Ibo translation enterprise than himself. "Let me as a subordinate," he challenged, "propound a question to you. . . . Can I teach Mr. Schön German?" Venn did not answer that question directly, but in references to the issue he accepted the necessity for indigenous leadership in the enterprise (Ogharaerumi, 1987, p. 212).

SELECT BIBLIOGRAPHY

Balogun, Isma'il A. B. 1975. *The Life and Works of 'Uthmān dan Fodio,* Lagos: Islamic Publications Bureau.
Bello, Muhammad. 1957. *Infāq al-Maisūr.* Arabic text ed. C. E. J. Whitting. London: Luzac Co.
Blyden, Edward W. 1967. *Christianity, Islam and the Negro Race.* Edinburgh: Edinburgh University Press; first published 1887.
Brenner, Louis. 1984. *A West African Sufi.* Berkeley: University of California Press.
Butler, A. J. 1884. *The Ancient Coptic Churches of Egypt.* London: Oxford University Press.
Chun, Ibrahim Ma Zhao. 1986. "Islam in China: The Internal Dimension." *Journal* (of the Institute of Muslim Minority Affairs) 7, no. 2 (July).
Coulson, N. J. 1964. *A History of Islamic Law.* Edinburgh: Edinburgh University Press.
Davis, Asa J. 1967. "The Orthodoxy of the Ethiopian Church." *Tarikh* 2, no. 1.
Dodds, Eric R. 1970. *Pagan and Christian in an Age of Anxiety.* New York: W. W. Norton.
Dvornik, Francis. 1970. *Byzantine Missions among the Slavs: SS. Constantine-Cyril and Methodius.* New Brunswick, N.J.: Rutgers University Press.

Earthy, E. D. 1955. "The Impact of Mohammedanism on Paganism in the Liberian Hinterland." *Numen* 2.

Eusebius. 1965. *The History of the Church*. Harmondsworth, England: Penguin Books.

Fisher, Humphrey J. 1969. "Islamic Education and Religious Reform in West Africa." In Richard Jolly, ed., *Education in Africa*. Nairobi: East African Publishing House.

Fodio, 'Abdallāhi dan. 1963. *Tazyīn al-Waraqāt*. Ed. and trans. Mervyn Hiskett. Ibadan: Ibadan University Press.

Frend, W. H. C. 1984. *The Rise of Christianity*. Philadelphia: Fortress Press.

Gibb, Hamilton A. R. 1963. *Mohammedanism*. London: Oxford University Press.

_____ . 1963. *Arabic Literature: An Introduction*, 2nd ed.; repr. 1974.

Goldziher, Ignaz. 1967–71. *Muslim Studies*. Trans. and ed. C. R. Barber and S. M. Stern, 2 vols. London: George Allen and Unwin.

Griffith, Sidney H. 1988. "The Monks of Palestine and the Growth of Christian Literature in Arabic." *The Muslim World* 78, no. 1 (January).

Grunebaum, Gustav E. von. 1953. *Medieval Islam*, 2nd ed. Chicago: University of Chicago Press; repr. 1966.

_____ . 1962. "Pluralism in the Islamic World." *Islamic Studies* 1, no. 2 (June).

_____ . 1970. *Classical Islam, A History 600–1258*. London: George Allen and Unwin.

Guillaume, Alfred. 1956. *Islam*. Harmondsworth, England: Penguin Books; repr. 1962.

Haafkens, J. 1983. *Les Chants Musulmans en Peul*. Leiden: E. J. Brill.

Haile, Getatchew. 1985. "A Christ for the Gentiles: The case of the za-Krestos of Ethiopia." *Journal of Religion in Africa* 15, no. 2.

Harnack, Adolf von. 1908. *The Mission and Expansion of Christianity*, 2 vols. New York.

Hiskett, Mervyn. 1957. "Material Relating to the State of Learning Among the Fulani." *Bulletin of the School of Oriental and African Studies* 19, no. 3.

_____ . 1960. "Problems of Religious Education in Muslim Communities in Africa." *Overseas Education* (London: Her Majesty's Stationary Office).

_____ . 1962. "An Islamic Tradition of Reform in the Western Sudan from the 16th to the 18th Centuries." *Bulletin of the School of Oriental and African Studies* 25, no. 3.

_____ . 1971. "The Song of the Shehu's Miracles: a Hausa Hagiography from Sokoto." *African Language Studies* 12.

_____ . 1973. *The Sword of Truth: The Life and Times of Shehu Usuman dan Fodio*. New York: Oxford University Press.

_____ . 1975. *A History of Hausa Islamic Verse*. London: School of Oriental and African Studies.

_____ . 1984. *The Development of Islam in West Africa*. London: Longman.

Hiskett, Mervyn, and A. D. Bivar. 1962. "The Arabic Literature of Nigeria to 1804." *Bulletin of the School of Oriental and African Studies* 25, no. 1.

Hodgkin, Thomas. 1962. "Islam and National Movements in West Africa." *Journal of African History* 3, no. 2.

Hunwick, John O. 1966. "Religion and State in the Songhay Empire 1464–1591." In I. M. Lewis, ed., *Islam in Tropical Africa*. London: Oxford University Press for the International African Institute.

_____ . 1972. "The Word Made Book." (Review article of Jack Goody, ed.,

Literacy in Traditional Societies [London: Cambridge University Press].)
Transactions of the Historical Society of Ghana 13, no. 2.

———. 1985. *Shari'a in Songhay: The Replies of al-Maghīlī to the Questions of Askia al-Ḥājj Muḥammad*. London: Oxford University Press of the British Academy.

———. 1986. "The Works of 'Abd Allāh b. Fūdī." *Arabic Literature in Africa* (Bulletin of Biographical and Bibliographical Information, eds. John O. Hunwick and Rex O'Fahey), no. 2 (September).

Johnston, H. A. S. 1967. *The Fulani Empire of Sokoto*. London: Oxford University Press.

Khalidi, Omar. 1986. "Urdu Language and the Future of Muslim Identity in India." *Journal* (Institute of Muslim Minority Affairs) 7, no. 2 (July).

Knight, W. 1880. *Memoir of the Rev. H. Venn: The Missionary Secretariat of Henry Venn*. London: Longman, Green, and Co.

Last, Murray. 1967. *The Sokoto Caliphate*. London: Longman.

Latourette, Kenneth Scott. 1937–45. *A History of the Expansion of Christianity*, 7 vols. New York: Harper and Row.

———. 1975. *A History of Christianity*, 2 vols.; rev. ed. New York: Harper and Row.

Lawrence, T. E. 1962. *Seven Pillars of Wisdom*. Penguin.

Lewis, Bernard. 1982. *The Muslim Discovery of Europe*. New York: W. W. Norton.

Lewis, I. M., ed. 1966. *Islam in Tropical Africa*. London: Oxford University Press for the International African Institute.

———. 1983. "The Past and Present in Islam: The Case of African 'Survivals'." *Temenos* 19.

Nida, Eugene A. 1952. *God's Word in Man's Language*. New York: Harper and Brothers.

North, Eric M. 1938. *The Book of a Thousand Tongues*. New York: Harper and Brothers.

Ogharaerumi, Mark Onesosan. 1987. "The Translation of the Bible into Yoruba, Igbo and Isekiri Languages of Nigeria." Unpublished Ph.D. dissertation, University of Aberdeen, Scotland.

Paden, John. 1973. *Religion and Political Culture in Kano*. Berkeley: University of California Press.

———. 1986. *Ahmadu Bello: Sardauna of Sokoto*. London: Hodder and Stoughton.

Peel, John D. Y. 1968. *Aladura: A Religious Movement among the Yoruba*. London: Oxford University Press for the International African Institute.

Ryan, Patrick J. 1978. *Imale: Yoruba Participation in the Muslim Tradition*. Mont.: Scholars Press.

Sanneh, Lamin. 1976. "The Origins of Clericalism in West African Islam." *Journal of African History* 17, no. 1.

———. 1977. "Christian-Muslim Encounter in Freetown in the 19th Century." *Bulletin of the Secretariat for Non-Christian Religions* (Rome) 12, nos. 1–2.

———. 1978. "Modern Education among Freetown Muslims and the Christian Stimulus." Edward Fasholé-Luke, Richard Gray, Adrian Hastings, and Godwin Taise, eds. in *Christianity in Independent Africa*. Bloomington: Indiana University Press.

———. 1979. "Muslims in Non-Muslim Societies of Africa." In *Christian and Islamic Contributions towards Establishing States in Africa South of the*

Sahara. Stuttgart: Council for Foreign Relations, Federal Republic of Germany.

_____. 1980. "The Domestication of Islam and Christianity in Africa." *Journal of Religion in Africa* 11, no. 1.

_____. 1981. "The Jakhanke Clerical Tradition in Futa Jallon." *Journal of Religion in Africa* 12, nos. 1–2.

_____. 1986. "Critical Reflections on the Life of Malcolm X." *Journal* (Institute of Muslim Minority Affairs) 7, no. 2 (July).

_____. 1986. "Source and Influence: A Comparative Approach to African Religion and Culture." In Merry I. White and Susan Pollak, eds., *The Cultural Transition.* London: Routledge and Kegan Paul.

_____. 1987. "Tcherno Aliou, the *walī* of Goumba: Islam, Colonialism and the Rural Factor in Futa Jallon, 1867–1912." In Nehemia Levtzion and Humphrey J. Fisher, eds., *Rural and Urban Islam in West Africa.* Boulder, Colo.: Lynne Rienner Publications.

_____. 1987. "Saints and Virtue in African Islam: An Historical Approach." In John Stratton Hawley, ed., *Saints and Virtue.* Berkeley: University of California Press.

_____. Forthcoming. *The Jakhanke Muslim Clerics: A Religious and Historical Study of Islam in Senegambia.* Lanham, Md.: University Press of America.

Schacht, Joseph, and C. E. Bosworth, eds. 1974. *The Legacy of Islam,* 2nd ed. Oxford: Clarendon Press.

Schimmel, Annemarie. 1975. *Mystical Dimensions of Islam.* Chapel Hill: University of North Carolina Press.

_____. 1985. *And Muḥammad Is His Messenger.* Chapel Hill: University of North Carolina Press.

Sell, Edward. 1907. *The Faith of Islam,* 3rd. ed. London and Madras: SPCK.

Stern, S. M. 1967. "Quotations from the Apocryphal Gospels in 'Abd al-Jabbār." *Journal of Theological Studies* 18, pt. 1 (April).

_____. 1968. " 'Abd al-Jabbār's Account of How Christ's Religion Was Falsified by the Adoption of Roman Customs." *Journal of Theological Studies* 19, pt. 1 (April).

Tamrat, Taddesse. 1972. *Church and State in Ethiopia: 1270–1527.* Oxford: Clarendon Press.

Trimingham, J. Spencer. 1949. *Islam in the Sudan.* London: Oxford University Press.

_____. 1952. *Islam in Ethiopia.* London: Oxford University Press.

_____. 1959. *Islam in West Africa.* Oxford: Clarendon Press.

_____. 1964. *Islam in East Africa.* Oxford: Clarendon Press.

_____. 1968. *The Influence of Islam Upon Africa.* London: Longman.

Ullendorf, E. 1988.*Ethiopia and the Bible.* London: Oxford University Press.

Appendices

A. THE VERNACULAR PRINCIPLE IN CATHOLIC TEACHING: VATICAN COUNCIL II, 1963–1965

The issue of the vernacular loomed large at Vatican Council II, but by that stage numerous reforms and experiments in the liturgical life had virtually sealed the undeniable importance of the vernacular in the Roman Catholic Church. The pronouncements of Vatican II, therefore, gave formal recognition to a subject of increasing significance among Catholics. It would be useful to examine how Vatican II treated the subject.

In the Constitution on the Sacred Liturgy (*Sacrosanctum Concilium*) the following general principle is enunciated:

Liturgical services are not private functions, but are celebrations of the Church. . . . The rites should be distinguished by a noble simplicity; they should be short, clear and unencumbered by any useless repetitions; *they should be within the people's powers of comprehension*, and normally should not require much explanation. [Nos. 26, 34; italics added.]

The emphasis on the public nature of faith and the need for understanding and for simplicity laid the foundations for innovations in language use. Consequently mother tongues featured prominently, even though Latin was "to be preserved in the Latin rites" (Sacred Liturgy, no. 36.1). The upshot of the pronouncement on the liturgy was to extend the role of the faithful in the observance of the Mass, and once this fact was conceded, it was natural to adopt the vernacular as the most convenient means to that end. Therefore, following the brief paragraph on the Latin rites, comes this statement:

But since the use of the mother tongue . . . is frequently of great advantage to the people in the Mass, the administration of sacraments and other parts of the liturgy, the limits of its employment may be extended. This will apply in the first place to the readings and directives, and to some of the prayers and chants . . . . [Sacred Liturgy, no. 36.2.]

Responsibility for use of the vernacular was vested in the local bishop acting within the general collegial framework laid down by Vatican II. This included the bishop having direction over translations from the Latin rite. These permutations and combinations had the obvious consequence of downgrading Latin as the language of popular devotion and promoting in its place the vernacular. Yet the vernacular principle, as we have pointed out in this book, conflicts with the demand for uniformity, though not necessarily with that for unity, for it promotes pluralism of the indigenous variety. Vatican II recognized this, and regarded it as a positive force in the life of the church. It is necessary to cite the document on this point at some length:

> Even in the liturgy, the Church has no wish to impose a rigid uniformity in matters which do not implicate the faith or good of the whole community; rather does she respect and foster the genius and talents of the various races and nations. Anything in these people's way of life which is not indissolubly bound up with superstition and error she studies with sympathy and, if possible, preserves intact. Sometimes she even admits such things into the liturgy itself, so long as they harmonize with its true and authentic spirit.
>
> Provision is to be made, when revising the liturgical books, for the legitimate variations and adaptations to different groups, regions and peoples, especially in the missions, provided always that the substantial unity of the Roman rite is preserved; and this should be borne in mind when drawing up the rites and devising rubrics for them. . . .
>
> In some places and circumstances, however, an ever more radical adaptation of the liturgy is needed, and this entails even greater difficulties.
>
> Wherefore:
>
> The competent local ecclesiastical authority . . . must, in this matter, carefully and prudently consider which elements from the traditions and culture of each of these peoples might appropriately be admitted into the liturgy. Adaptations which seem useful or necessary should then be submitted to the Holy See, by whose consent they may be introduced. [Sacred Liturgy, nos. 37–38, 40.1.]

Such a view of the role of mother tongues places tremendous initiative in the hands of local bishops and their congregations, "the communities of the faithful" in official parlance. The implications of such a shift are major. First, innovations and adaptations in the liturgy were recognized as coming from local use and custom. Second, the rule of strict uniformity was relaxed, and the Vatican Council decided that unity need not be equated with inflexible conformity. This enshrines flexibility into the very heart of Christian practice, showing that the Catholic church was prepared to follow through with the implications of translatability on a scale comparable to Protestant translations of the Scriptures. Third, the ecclesiastical machinery would maintain its integrity within the context of devolution of power, thus encouraging the variety of gifts, talents, and resources prevalent at the local level in the building of the church. Finally, pluralism is given a positive value in the calculations of renewal, with a significant revision of the place of central authority in the development and progress of local congregations. It represents a reordering of priorities, with hierarchy more cognizant of vernacular factors than heretofore and given the mandate to build on those factors in formulating policy. The old order is thus radically recast, with the church coming to where the people are and not the other way around, as had been the case. As a Catholic commentator observed: "No theological commentary is necessary to convince the reader that the teaching contained in these documents is really new, i.e., represents an extraordinary doctrinal development and thus transcends the official ecclesiastical teaching of the past" (Baum, 1966, p. viii).

Mission was an obvious area where the vernacular factor was encountered at its sharpest and most enduring, and here Vatican Council II applied the principle with new urgency. Missionaries, the council affirmed through the Decree on the Church's Missionary Activity (*Ad Gentes Divinitus*), were to be fortified with a daunting array of virtues to the point where they must be ready to spend and be spent for others (2 Cor. 12:15). The counterpart to such spiritual preparation, including knowledge of the theological counsels of the church, was adequate training in the sciences of the societies to which they go,

> so that they may have a more extensive knowledge of the history, social structures and customs of the peoples involved and a better grasp of their moral system, their religious tenets and the concepts they have formed of God, man and the world from the background of their own traditions. They shall learn the languages to an extent that will enable them to speak with fluency and without offence, and thus have an easier approach to the minds and hearts of the people. [Missionary Activity, no. 26.]

The establishment of specialized centers to provide high-level training for missionaries has been a characteristic of the church in mission, particularly from the notable example set by the Dominicans in their language institutes in the Arab world and beyond. Vatican II sanctioned this, and gave it added importance under curial responsibility of the Sacred Congregation for the Propagation of the Faith (Propaganda Fide) which was first set up in the early seventeenth century. Even in the first decades of its existence, the Propaganda Fide was confronted with the vernacular question in the Capuchin missionaries who went to West Africa (Sanneh, 1983, pp. 44ff.), although at that stage the Propaganda Fide did not see the full indigenous implications of the vernacular factor, with enormous negative consequences for the church. The action of Vatican II would ensure that what was a costly episode in the history of the church was not repeated by the suppression of mother tongues and mother-tongue speakers in the life and witness of the church. Only a tenuous line separates this view of translatability from the Protestant position even though the canon of authority is different in each instance. What each tradition regards as its authoritative standard is what it is prepared to submit to the demands of translatability.

Pope Paul VI was alert to the whole spirit of Vatican Council II, and in *Evangelii Nuntiandi* (On Evangelization in the Modern World), he spoke with particular eloquence about the place of the local church in the history of Christian expansion. After calling attention to the church's universal character, he pointed out the specific cultural environment of individual churches and how the concrete cultural details of those individual churches enrich Christian expression and practice, thus helping to give solidity to Christian identity. He affirmed in this sense that the

> universal Church in practice incarnate in the individual Churches made up of such [and] such an actual part of mankind, speaking such and such a language, heirs of a cultural patrimony, of a vision of the world, of an

historical past, of a particular human substratum. Receptivity to the wealth of the individual Church corresponds to a special sensitivity of modern man.

Let us be very careful not to conceive of the universal Church as the sum, or, if one can say so, the more or less anomalous federation of essentially different individual Churches. In the mind of the Lord the Church is universal by vocation and mission, but when she puts down her roots in a variety of cultural, social and human terrains, she takes on different external expressions and appearances in each part of the world.

Thus each individual Church that would voluntarily cut itself off from the universal Church would lose its relationship to God's plan and would be impoverished in its ecclesial dimension. But, at the same time, a Church *toto orbe diffusa* would become an abstraction if she did not take body and life precisely through the individual Churches.

The individual Churches, intimately built up not only of people but also of aspirations, of riches and limitations, of ways of praying, of loving, of looking at life and the world which distinguish this or that human gathering, have the task of assimilating the essence of the Gospel message and of transposing it, without the slightest betrayal of its essential truth, into the language that these particular people understand, then of proclaiming it in this language. . . .

Legitimate attention to individual Churches cannot fail to enrich the Church. Such attention is indispensable and urgent. It responds to the very deep aspirations of peoples and human communities to find their own identity ever more clearly. [Paul VI, 1975, nos. 62–63.]

In a formal address he gave shortly after ascending the throne of Saint Peter, Pope Paul VI spoke movingly of the elevated place Africa occupies in the counsels of the church. He spoke of Africa's pervasive spiritual sense and its reckoning with humankind's ultimate religious significance. The idea of God, he said, was deep-rooted in Africa (cf. Homer's comments in the *Iliad* on the Greeks repairing to Africa for the honor of attending the solemn feasts of sacrifice). Pope Paul said:

This concept, perceived rather than analyzed, lived rather than reflected on, is expressed in very different ways from culture to culture, but the fact remains that the presence of God permeates African life, as the presence of a higher being, personal and mysterious. People have recourse to Him at solemn and more critical moments of life, when they consider the intercession of every other intermediary unavailing. Nearly always fear of God's omnipotence is set aside and He is invoked as Father. Prayers made to Him, whether by individuals or groups, are spontaneous, at times moving, while among the forms of sacrifice the sacrifice of first fruits stands out because of what it plainly signifies. [Paul VI, n.d., p. 16.]

Then follows this positive evaluation of Africa's heritage:

The Church views with great respect the moral and religious values of the African tradition, not only because of their meaning, but also because she sees them as providential, as the basis for spreading the Gospel message and beginning the establishment of the new society in Christ. This We Ourselves pointed out at the canonization of the Martyrs of Uganda, who were the first flowering of Christian holiness in the new Africa, sprung from the most vigorous stock of ancient tradition.

The teaching of Jesus Christ and his redemption are, in fact, the complement, the renewal, and the bringing to perfection, of all that is good in human tradition. And that is why the African who becomes a Christian does not disown himself, but takes up the age-old values of tradition "in spirit and in truth" (Jn. 14:24). [Paul VI, n.d., p. 19.]

Expanding on these sentiments, the Secretariat for Non-Christian Religions, under Paul Cardinal Marella, affirmed that

African religions have been and still are *necessary*, because without them there would be no interlocutor for the Christian. . . . In the same way that the religion of Babylon was "pedagogic" for Abraham, while it taught him to be the servant of God, though it was finally bypassed in order to allow him to accomplish his providential destiny, the African religions have been and still are "pedagogic" to prepare the way for Christ. These religions were not merely pedagogic, by a preparation willed by God and ripened through thousands of years. They were and still could be *an exceptional way to salvation* for a section of humanity of which we only catch a glimpse, if one [reckons] from the obscurity of pre-history to the Day of the return of the Lord and of the assembly of all the Nations around His holy mountain. This great mystery of the salvation of Nations, on whose horizons the Secretariat for Non-Christians opens in an ever-increasing light, is the mystery of the salvific love of the Father who, in the words of St. Thomas, is not bound by the visible sacrament. Even if the normal way to be linked with Christ is by faith and baptism, there could still exist, outside of explicit faith, an implicit faith which would take a believer of good will who corresponds to the benevolent and supernatural grace of God, and justify him by Christ, who is the only "Way, Truth and Life." The traditional African religions can help with their sense of the majesty of God, their cults, their offerings and their moral rules, in this justification by God which depends on the human dispositions. On the level of these dispositions, these religions are certainly useful. . . .

As St. Justin said, speaking of Plato and of certain philosophers of antiquity whose search for wisdom was in fact a search for God: "Everything good that they have said has benefitted us Christians, because the ancient authors had insight into reality thanks to the innate action of the Logos." [Secretariat for Non-Christian Religions, 1969, pp. 127ff.]

REFERENCES

For quotations from Vatican Council II documents, see the relevant document in *The Teachings of the Second Vatican Council: Complete Texts of the Constitutions, Decrees, and Declarations* (Westminster, Md.: Newman Press, 1966).

Baum, Gregory. 1966. Introduction, in *The Teachings of the Second Vatican Council.*

Mbiti, John. 1976. *The Prayers of African Religion*. Maryknoll, N.Y.: Orbis Books.
Paul VI. n.d. *Message to All the Peoples of Africa*. Vatican Publication.
Sanneh, Lamin. 1983. *West African Christianity*. Maryknoll, N.Y.: Orbis Books.
Secretariat for Non-Christian Religions. 1969. *Meeting the African Religions*.
    Rome: Libreria Editrice Ancora.

B. CHRISTIAN SCRIPTURE LANGUAGE COUNT

A statistical summary of Christian Scripture publication in world languages according to geographical distribution by continent or major area.

	Portions	Testaments	Complete Bibles	Total
Africa	238	175	109	**522**
Asia	220	139	90	**449**
Australia/New Zealand/Pacific Islands	154	96	24	**274**
Europe	106	21	55	**182**
North America	42	17	6	**65**
Caribbean Islands/Central America/ Mexico/South America	166	146	1	**313**
Constructed Languages	2	0	1	**3**
Total	**928**	**594**	**286**	**1808**

C. FIRST COMPLETE PRINTED BIBLES IN LANGUAGES

Although Christian Scripture publication has occurred in 1,808 languages and dialects, the complete Bible has appeared in only 286 of these (and in 3 of the "union" languages). The table below lists the 289 languages, in alphabetical order, in which complete Bibles exist.

Date	Language	Date	Language
1933	Afrikaans	1478	Catalan
1936	Alur	1917	Cebuano
1840	Amharic	1956	chiBemba
1879	Aneityum	1922	chiChewa (Nyanja Union)
1671	Arabic	1962	chiGogo
1963	Arabic:North African	1963	chiLuchazi
1666	Armenian:Ancient	1962	chiLunda:chiNdembu
1883	Armenian:Modern, Eastern	1955	chiLuvale
1853	Armenian:Modern, Western	1957	chiNdau
1833	Assamese	1894	Chinese:Cantonese
1961	aTeso	1884	Chinese:Foochow
1891	Azerbaijani	1916	Chinese:Hakka
1961	Bambara	1912	Chinese:Hinghua
1953	baNgala	1874	Chinese:Kuoyu
1979	Bari	1901	Chinese:Ningpo
1958	Basque:Guipuzcoan	1908	Chinese:Shanghai
1865	Basque:Labourdin	1908	Chinese:Soochow
1969	Bassa:Cameroon	1922	Chinese:Swatow
1976	Batak:Simalungun	1914	Chinese:Taichow
1894	Batak:Toba	1902	Chinese:Wenli, Easy
1809	Bengali	1822	Chinese:Wenli, High
1970	Beti	1905	chiNyanja:Eastern
1914	Bikol	1949	chiShona Union
1981	Boro	1963	chiTonga Union
1866	Breton:Leon	1957	chiTumbuka
1866	Breton:Treguier	1920	chiYao
1900	Bugis	1970	Chokwe
1864	Bulgarian	1977	Chol:Tumbala
1940	Bulu	1861	Cree:Plains
1835	Burmese	1488	Czech
1973	Byelorussian	1879	Dakota

Date	Language	Date	Language
1550	Danish	1913	Igbo Union
1858	Dayak:Ngaju	1906	Igbo:Upper
1890	Dehu	1956	Ijo:Brass
1953	Dholuo	1909	Ilokano
1926	Dobu	1974	Indonesian
1872	Duala	1685	Irish
1522	Dutch	1978	isiNdebele
1868	Efik	1859	isiXhosa
1535	English	1883	isiZulu
1871	Eskimo:Labrador	1977	Isoko
1926	Esperanto	1471	Italian
1739	Estonian:Tallinn	1883	Japanese
1918	Ethiopic	1854	Javanese
1913	Ewe	1927	Kachin:Jinghpaw
1951	Fang:Ogowe	1983	Kakwa
1948	Fante	1969	Kalenjin [Kipsigis-Nandi
1948	Faroe		Union]
1964	Fijian	1831	Kannada
1642	Finnish	1883	Karen:Pwo
1530	French	1950	Kashgar
1943	Frisian	1899	Kashmiri
1983	Fulfulde	1978	Kate
1866	Ga	1968	Khana
1801	Gaelic	1891	Khasi
1924	Garo:Achik	1954	Khmer
1743	Georgian	1908	kiGiryama
1466	German	1956	kiKamba
1478	German:Low	1975	kiKaonde
1951	giGikuyu	1905	kiKongo
1893	Gilbertese	1916	kiKongo:San Salvador
1979	Gouro	1951	kiLuba
1518	Greek:Ancient	1982	kiMakhua:Emeto
1840	Greek:Modern	1980	kiMbundu:Luanda
1900	Greenlandic	1964	kiMeru
1823	Gujarati	1980	kiNandi
1923	Gun-Alada	1954	kinyaRwanda
1932	Hausa	1967	kiRundi
1838	Hawaiian	1928	kiSanga
1599	Hebrew	1960	kiSukuma
1912	Hiligaynon	1914	kiSwahili:Central
1835	Hindi	1891	kiSwahili:Southern
1968	Hmar	1960	kiSwahili:Zaire [Ngwana
1590	Hungarian		Union]
1901	Iai [2]	1911	Korean
1584	Icelandic	1927	Kuba:Inkongo
1959	ichiLamba	1971	Kuki
1982	ichiNawanga	1928	Kusaien
1970	Igala	1898	Kutchin:Eastern

Date	Language	Date	Language
1979	Lango	1914	Nepali
1932	Lao	1972	Ngunese
1895	Lapp:Norwegian	1911	Nias
1811	Lapp:Swedish	1969	Nicobarese:Car
1456	Latin	1904	Niuean
1689	Latvian	1834	Norwegian
1970	liNgala	1921	Norwegian:Nynorsk
1968	Lisu:Central	1953	Nupe
1735	Lithuanian	1975	oluLuyia Union
1930	Lithuanian:Samogit	1927	Omyene Union
1930	loMongo Union	1815	Oriya
1896	luGanda	1899	Oromo:Western
1966	Lugbara	1974	oshiKwanyama
1951	luLogooli	1954	oshiNdonga
1982	Lun Bawang	1966	oTetela
1900	Macassar	1853	Paganyaw
1835	Malagasy	1971	Paite
1733	Malay	1917	Pampango
1841	Malayalam	1915	Pangasinan
1932	Maltese	1959	Panjabi
1773	Manx	1895	Pashto
1851	Maori:Cook Island	1978	paZande
1858	Maori:New Zealand	1838	Persian
1956	Mara	1561	Polish
1821	Marathi	1751	Portuguese
1903	Mare	1688	Romanian
1956	Marovo	1679	Romansch:Ladin Sut
1982	Marshallese	1718	Romansch:Sursilvan
1663	Massachusetts	1964	runyaNkore-ruKiga Union
1980	Mbai:Moissala	1912	ruNyoro-ruTooro
1959	Mende	1865	Russian
1952	Mikir	1937	Samarenyo
1959	Mizo	1855	Samoan
1978	Mofa	1966	Sango
1928	Mon	1822	Sanskrit
1840	Mongolian:Literary	1914	Santali
1983	Moore	1804	Serbo-Croatian
1912	Mota	1904	seSotho:Northern
1973	Motu	1878	seSotho:Southern
1925	Mukawa	1970	seTswana:Central
1910	Mundari	1857	seTswana:seTlhaping
1961	Mungaka	1892	Shan
1970	Naga:Angami	1923	shiRonga
1964	Naga:Ao	1951	siLozi
1967	Naga:Kyong	1954	Sindhi
1966	Nama	1823	Sinhala
1939	Nandi	1581	Slavonic
1918	Nauru	1832	Slovak

Date	Language	Date	Language
1584	Slovenian	1964	Tiv
1979	Somali	1862	Tongan
1796	Sorbian:Lower	1960	Toraja
1728	Sorbian:Upper	1927	tshiLuba
1553	Spanish	1936	tshiVenda
1829	Spanish:Judaeo	1827	Turkish
1891	Sundanese	1871	Twi:Akuapem
1541	Swedish	1964	Twi:Asante
1645	Syriac:Ancient	1903	Ukrainian
1852	Syriac:Modern	1963	uMbundu
1905	Tagalog	1843	Urdu
1838	Tahitian	1977	Urhobo
1884	Taiwanese	1916	Vietnamese
1727	Tamil	1588	Welsh
1854	Telugu	1910	xiTshwa
1883	Thai	1907	xiTsonga
1948	Tibetan	1821	Yiddish
1956	Tigrinya	1884	Yoruba
1983	Tinata-Tuna		

Index